Damien Simonis

Florence

The Top Five

1 Palazzo Vecchio
Immerse yourself in the turbulent history of Florence (p86)
2 Galleria dell'Accademia
See Michelangelo's David (p95)
3 Duomo
Climb the Duomo's dome for breathtaking views over the city (p75)
4 Galleria degli Uffizi
Indulge in an intense assembly of fine Florentine painting (p81)
5 Fiesole
Visit the 1st-century BC Roman amphitheatre (p113)

Contents

Published by Lonely Planet Publications Pty Ltd
ABN 36 005 607 983

Australia Head Office, Locked Bag 1, Footscray,
Victoria 3011, ☎ 03 8379 8000, fax 03 8379 8111,
talk2us@lonelyplanet.com.au

USA 150 Linden St, Oakland, CA 94607,
☎ 510 893 8555, toll free 800 275 8555,
fax 510 893 8572, info@lonelyplanet.com

UK 72–82 Rosebery Ave, Clerkenwell, London,
EC1R 4RW, ☎ 020 7841 9000, fax 020 7841 9001,
go@lonelyplanet.co.uk

France 1 rue du Dahomey, 75011 Paris,
☎ 01 55 25 33 00, fax 01 55 25 33 01,
bip@lonelyplanet.fr, www.lonelyplanet.fr

© Lonely Planet 2004
Photographs © Juliet Coombe and as listed (p228), 2004

Printed through The Bookmaker International Ltd
Printed in China

The Author

DAMIEN SIMONIS

Years ago in a snowy winter, Damien wound up in Siena, the medieval archrival of Florence and an extraordinary Tuscan enclave itself. Although he had already travelled to various parts of the country, on and off assignment, this was his first foray 'under the Tuscan sun'. And so he learned about Florence through impressions coloured by the centuries-old antipathy of the Sienese towards their splendid competitor to the north. Indeed, his first contact with Florence came on a bus trip from Siena, and he found it a magnificent way to be introduced to the riverside capital of the Italian Renaissance!

Florence began to leave its indelible mark on Damien with further visits over the years and, while on assignment, Damien moved to a centuries-old garret on Via di San Niccolò in Florence. He remained longer than intended, and explored the unending nooks and crannies of this extraordinary city, soon discovering why this place is on just about everyone's list of must-visit cities in Italy. The only thing Damien doesn't understand is why it took him so long to fully discover it in the first place.

PHOTOGRAPHER
JULIET COOMBE

As a full-time freelance travel photojournalist, Juliet has taken pictures which have appeared in more than 200 Lonely Planet guidebooks. She has won the prestigious British Guild of Travel Writers award for Travel Photographer of the Year. Her images have also been published in the *New York Times* and *Geographical* magazine. Juliet has had her fair share of challenges in taking the ultimate photograph, including being put in prison after being mistaken for a spy and walking with man-eating tigers in the jungles of Northern Thailand. She finds that, in Florence, everything is art, even the way they make their ice cream.

Julia is represented by Lonely Planet Images. Many of the images in this guide are available for licensing: www.lonelyplanet images.com.

Introducing Florence

Deeply tanned, immaculately dressed and good-looking Florentines hang about the town's bars sipping deep red Tuscan wines while chatting over the day's events. Surrounding them is the densely packed old city. Knowing looks and a little chatting up accompany occasionally heated banter. Getting ahead in this town is not always a straightforward business. You have to know people and find ways around a labyrinth of rules. Little has changed since the days of the Medici.

Of course much has changed. Florence's short-lived selection as capital of the newly united Kingdom of Italy in 1865 was like a shot of adrenaline. In the last decades of that century the city bulldozed, constructed, rearranged avenues, wiped out whole quarters, tore down the medieval walls. And so the scene was set for the modern regional capital of Tuscany. Along the broad *viali* (avenues) that encircle old Florence a confusion of endless traffic tears around in chaotic style. Horns honk and brakes squeal as Florentines dart in and out of lanes in search of a break in the traffic. Ignorant of fear, *motorini* (mopeds) dash in and around larger vehicles, as if protected by some divine force.

The once glorious jewel of Renaissance Italy remains what it essentially always was – a busy business centre. Even before the Renaissance was over, the wily Florentines had to concede that their town was on the wane, increasingly ignored on the European stage. But they never forgot their proud heritage and it was rediscovered in earnest by the rest of Europe in the late 18th and early 19th centuries. By then the Grand Tour was in full swing, and Florence joined Rome and Venice at the head of the list for curious and admiring travellers, particularly the English. Locals knew how to cash in, and still do, with utter aplomb.

The fortunate few get their first glimpse of Florence from the south. The road from rival Siena leads you to the heights backing the south bank of the Arno. Suddenly, through the trees, the glories of Florence burst into view – Giotto's Campanile (bell tower), Brunelleschi's dome, the Basilica di Santa Croce. Only the hardest of hearts can remain unaffected.

The memory of the Medici, who for centuries commanded the city's fortunes and were, as generous patrons, at least partly instrumental in unleashing the Renaissance, lives on. To this day the family crest of six balls adorns many public buildings, although the city's official emblem (the medieval Guelph faction's red lily on a white background) is older still. The city's artists and sculptors, supported by the Medici and other powerful families, regaled the city with the finest of their creations. Michelangelo, Leonardo, Donatello, Giotto, the Lippis, Masaccio, Botticelli, Pontormo and a host of others left their mark, and formidable galleries such as the Uffizi, Pitti and Accademia house many of their works. The central square, Piazza della Signoria, is itself an outdoor sculpture gallery and has been for centuries!

Medieval and Renaissance Florence was a financial powerhouse but it was never a romantic place. Its great families built fine mansions and lavished money on churches and public buildings and certainly some had a genuine passion for the arts. But there was an element of hard-headed showiness in it all. To *display* greatness was to be great. Florence, even long after it had been eclipsed, remained stubbornly determined to excel in appearance. In its great buildings, from the Romanesque Baptistry to the Gothic Duomo and Renaissance basilicas and palaces, Florence is a showplace of architectural prowess.

To this day other Italians will tell you that Florentines are a vain lot, heaping money on fine clothes and flash cars. Perhaps there is a touch of envy in such observations, for the Florentines have retained something of their banking forebears' financial nous too. When it comes to money matters, they are to Italy what the Scots are to Britain.

Home to the likes of Gucci and Ferragamo, Florence for some means only one thing – style. Aside from art and architecture, there are plenty of shopping opportunities.

When the shops close it's time to eat. You can sit down to a simple Tuscan meal of tomato stew followed by prime steak in a family-run trattoria or splurge on one of the city's growing number of stylish designer restaurants. Florence is known for its top-grade Chiantis, but you should make the acquaintance of other exquisite tipples too – Montalcino's Brunello, the Vino Nobile di Montepulciano and the more daring Super Tuscans.

Using Florence as a base you can easily explore Tuscany: enjoy the medieval splendours of Siena, Pisa, Lucca and San Gimignano, and wander the undulating Chianti countryside.

DAMIEN'S TOP FLORENCE DAY

A leisurely coffee and read of the paper at Gilli on Piazza della Repubblica is the perfect way to start the day. I can't resist a stroll up Via Roma, stopping to window shop along the way, into Piazza di San Giovanni and the adjacent Piazza del Duomo. The physical beauty of the city seems concentrated here, from the Baptistry to the Campanile. I just need an occasional reminder that it's real. From there, I like to meander through the busy pedestrian streets at the heart of old Florence to Piazza della Signoria, where the Uffizi and Palazzo Vecchio beckon – I can only tackle one of these a day! Sightseeing always induces hunger, so a quick eastward wander leads me to good food at Osteria de' Benci. The Oltrarno works a special magic, so I can't help wandering across the Ponte alle Grazie and then on to Porta San Miniato to follow the bucolic lane along the city walls towards the Forte di Belvedere, where the views over Florence are wonderful. Then it's time to get across to Piazza Santo Spirito for an evening tipple on the square, before repairing to Ristorante Becco-fino for a late evening culinary splurge.

My Essential Florence

- Wine-tasting and snacking in a Florentine enoteca (p131)
- Galleria dell'Accademia (p95)
- Galleria degli Uffizi (p81)
- Palazzo Vecchio (p86)
- Piazza del Duomo (p65)

City Life

City Life

Parachute into central Florence and you get the feeling time has stood still from the end of the Renaissance. It was a flourishing centre of banking, commerce and industry and, for a time, the epicentre of Renaissance art. But Florence had always been a troubled place. Wars, palace coups and general unrest marked much of its history until the Medici dynasty, after more comebacks than Lazarus, brought stability. But by then the city was already sliding towards provincial powerlessness. Today it is a bustling regional capital. The entrepreneurial spirit of the Florentines' forefathers lives on in the small businesses, and that special Italian version of modern urban madness that fully dominates the city today. It is a self-consciously stylish place and something of a fashion centre, even if it lost first place to Milan some time ago. Florentines and visitors alike cannot help glorying in the city's past. It is largely for the wonders left behind from those centuries between medieval and modern times that most people flock here. And the locals themselves take immense pride in their town's beauty, as if they themselves had somehow had a direct hand in the effort.

FLORENCE TODAY

Florentines would agree that the city has its rightful place as capital of Tuscany, Italy's best-known region; one it came to dominate during the period of the Grand Duchy after centuries of harassing and occupying surrounding cities and towns. Some might even suggest it should have been made capital of Italy, as it was for a few years from 1865 before Rome was finally incorporated into the nascent Kingdom of Italy.

Florence owes a good deal of its modern prosperity to tourism and Florentines' unfailing business nous. Although there is little industry, it suffers many of the problems of the modern city. Intense traffic helps keep air pollution high, the urban sprawl west and north continues virtually unchecked as people from elsewhere in Tuscany and beyond converge on the capital in search of work. Students flock to the haughty university (those who make it through their prestigious fine arts courses can be proud of getting through all the hoops!). Illegal immigrants reaching Italy from North Africa and the Balkans choose Florence as one of their preferred destinations. And so street prostitution (brothels are illegal in Italy) has become as big a problem on Florence's dark boulevards as in many other Italian cities.

Florence's fine arts don't just attract tourists and students. Since the disastrous floods of 1966, the city has become a world leader in restoration. Florentines have always squabbled among themselves, and they do so with equal gusto in the restoration business – so much so that they couldn't decide on whether or not Michelangelo's *David* should get a good restorative bath without first having a public spat (see the boxed text, p34).

Florence and its inhabitants have a natural tendency to conservatism. When the new train station was built in Mussolini's day the modern design had locals up in arms. Planning and building a limited tram system to link the centre more efficiently with its distant suburbs and take some commuter strain off the roads has been a Herculean struggle of bureaucracy and competing interests.

And if tramways are controversial, imagine the outcry over an overtly modern addition to the exterior of the Uffizi, planned by a foreigner to boot! Any attempt to change the age-old urban landscape is always likely to raise hackles. Plans to expand the Uffizi have been on Florentine minds for decades. It finally looks like it will happen but opponents to Arata Isozaki's design for an imposing exit on the east side of the Uffizi will continue to enrage opponents for some time to come. Mind you, if Parisians could get used to Beaubourg and the Louvre pyramid, Florentines will probably make their peace with Isozaki's exit.

Hot Conversation Topics

- Does Michelangelo's *David* need a scrubbing down? Well, he's going to get one anyway.
- Is Isozaki's planned hypermodern exit for the Nuovi Uffizi a stunning innovation or horribly out of place? And will the brand-new and much enlarged museum really be open by 2006?
- Now the contract has been signed, Florentines are in for more traffic hassle as the Florence–Scandicci Tramway is built – will it really be finished in three years?
- Cough, splutter…with all the cars and *motorini* (mopeds) polluting the air, we need still more 'ecological' buses!
- AC Fiorentina football club has its old name back, and who cares if a little scandal attaches to its unexpectedly rapid promotion to Serie B?
- Florentines will be able to reach Milan in one to 1½ hours and Bologna in just 30 minutes on new high-speed rail lines, but will be waiting until at least 2007.
- Arresting the occasional illegal female immigrant for street prostitution and even repatriating them to Africa or Albania is not helping either the women, exploited by people traffickers, or the citizens whose streets are increasingly plagued by the degradation and petty crime that accompanies these unfortunate night workers.

CITY CALENDAR

Florence is at its best in spring and, to a lesser extent, autumn. Optimal months are April and May, when the air is crisp and clear, and several unique festivities take place. If you want to see the curious Scoppio del Carro you'll have to be visiting around the busy Easter break. Otherwise, steer clear of Florence that week as the place is full to the brim and accommodation costs are at a premium. Summer, especially July and August, is best avoided as the stifling heat and humidity can be insufferable – which explains why most Florentines leave and half the restaurants are shut (especially during the central fortnight in August). The only advantage of August is that many hotels put on generous deals. If you are around in late summer, ask at the tourist office about *sagre* (festivals devoted to foodstuffs, anything from pizza to penne) held in towns and villages around the city. The quietest period is winter, especially early December and most of January and February. It can be chilly and wet, but at least the number of tourists in town is considerably down. The APT office (p220) publishes a list of annual events, including the many religious festivals staged by almost every church in the city. A selection follows.

JANUARY
ANNO NUOVO (NEW YEAR'S DAY)
A peculiarly Florentine touch to the first day of the year is the *tradizionale uscita del primo dell'anno dei canottieri*, when the Società Canottieri Firenze rowing club organises a parade of boats along the Arno near the Ponte Vecchio.

BEFANA (EPIPHANY)
In Italy this is traditionally the day when children receive the gifts that in Anglo circles are distributed at Christmas. The weight of commercialisation has brought the attention on Christmas to Italy, but the parade of the *Re Magi* (Three Wise Men) on 6 January still captivates hordes of people on the day of the Befana.

MARCH
CAPODANNO FIORENTINO
This is the Florentine New Year. See the boxed text, p11.

APRIL/MAY
SCOPPIO DEL CARRO
The Explosion of the Cart occurs on Easter Sunday. See the boxed text, p11.

FESTA DEL GRILLO
The Cricket Festival happens on Ascension Day (forty days after Easter). See the boxed text, p11.

CELEBRAZIONI PER LA MORTE DI SAVONAROLA
On 23 May the death of the radical theocrat in 1498 is celebrated by a mass in the Palazzo Vecchio and parades in Piazza della Signoria.

MAGGIO MUSICALE FIORENTINO

Starting in late April and spilling over into June, Florence's Musical May was inaugurated in 1933. It is a high point on the musical calendar, with top names performing opera, ballet and classical music at the Teatro Comunale (see p152) and other venues across the city.

MOSTRA INTERNAZIONALE DELL'ARTIGIANATO

This prestigious expo of handmade products, of every possible type and colour, is held in Fortezza da Basso. Unfortunately the exhibits aren't for sale!

JUNE

FESTA DI SAN GIOVANNI

The *fuochi artificiali*, or spectacular fireworks, let off on 24 June in Piazzale Michelangelo on this feast day of Florence's patron saint, St John, is the culmination of the city's festivities. In the four or five preceding days, teams from the city's four historical districts battle it out in the *Gioco del Calcio Storico* (Historical Soccer Game – see the boxed text, p11).

JULY/AUGUST

FLORENCE DANCE FESTIVAL

Since the late 1980s Florence has hosted this annual celebration of dance. The location changes

Cycling in style

from year to year and there is usually something for every taste, from classical ballet to modern. The **Florence Dance Centre** (Map pp248–50; ☎ 055 28 92 76; Borgo della Stella 23/r) has information.

FIRENZESTATE

Throughout the broiling months of summer, the city hosts a rich palette of cultural events, ranging from outdoor cinema cycles to music concerts. Many Florentines flee the city but those who remain behind and the city's many summertime visitors are regaled with activities. See the boxed text, p147.

SEPTEMBER/OCTOBER

FESTA DELLE RIFICOLONE

The Festival of the Paper Lanterns is held on the 7 September. See the boxed text, p11.

CHIANTI WINE HARVEST FESTIVALS

Several Chianti towns have festivals at the time of the wine harvest. You need to ask at the APT office or check the local papers for details.

FRINGE FESTIVAL

The city stages a modest fringe theatre festival as Florentines get back into the swing of things after the summer holidays. Check out the APT office for information.

RASSEGNA INTERNAZIONALE MUSICA DEI POPOLI

Local and international musicians come together to perform traditional and ethnic music from all over the world in this festival, which lasts for a month. Many of the performances are held in the **Auditorium Flog** (see p148).

BIENNALE DELL'ANTIQUARIATO

Every odd-numbered year this prestigious event is held in Palazzo Strozzi. It's an opportunity to search for high-quality antique furniture, paintings, jewellery and a host of other antique objects.

NOVEMBER

FIRENZE MARATHON

If you feel the urge to dash around Florence you can be part of the marathon (www.firenzemarathon.it) towards the end of November. The finish line is in Piazza di Santa Croce, where, the day after the race, prizes are awarded to the winners.

Top Five Quirky Events

- **Capodanno Fiorentino (Florentine New Year)** What Westerners take for granted as the start of the new year (ie 1 January) has only been a widely accepted date since Pope Gregory XIII ushered in the Gregorian calendar in 1582. Most Christian states, many of which had long had their own starting dates for the new year, enthusiastically adopted the new 'universal' system but Florence had to be different. Since early republican days Florentines had considered the coming of spring the start of the new year and celebrated it on 25 March. They continued to do so, only officially adopting the January date in 1749! To this day many Florentines, although they don't really think of it as New Year's Day, flock to the Chiesa di SS Annunziata to celebrate the 25 March. On the same day market stalls set up in the square before the church and since 2001 the town hall has organised colourful historical processions to remind Florentines of the uniqueness of the occasion in their city's history.

- **Scoppio del Carro (Explosion of the Cart)** For centuries, the Florentines have maintained the annual tradition of 'distributing Holy Fire' to the populace in this festival on Easter Saturday. A centuries-old ox-drawn cart, laden with fireworks, is led outside of the Duomo for the ceremony. From the high altar inside the Duomo the archbishop lights the *colombina* (little dove), virtually a small rocket, which he then launches along a wire into the cart outside. The subsequent explosions last for several minutes. They have been using the same cart since the 18th century, but the tradition goes back at least to the 15th century. The origins are unclear. Some say Pazzino de' Pazzi, a hero returned from the First Crusade, started the tradition on the day before Easter by lighting a fire with stone flints from the Holy Sepulchre in Jerusalem given to him for his courage in battle. Others say the original *carro* was a war cart captured in Fiesole, made to explode in victory celebrations.

- **Festa del Grillo (The Cricket Festival)** The crickets that once featured in this fair held in May in the Cascine are no longer put to any pains as a result of environmentalists' protests. Traditionally in this welcome to spring, men placed a cricket at the door of their lovers. Nowadays people buy colourful little cages with crickets inside, which they then (supposedly) release onto the grass.

- **Gioco del Calcio Storico** A somewhat lawless series of centuries old-football-style games held in the context of the June Festa di San Giovanni. This 'game' was first played in 1530 as a display of nonchalance on the part of the Florentines before troops of Emperor Charles V, who had the city under siege. A cross between football (soccer) and rugby, each team of 27(!) aims to launch the ball into the opponents' net. No holds are barred, so it can get pretty nasty on the field. On the first day the game is preceded by a procession of hundreds of people in traditional costume in Piazza di Santa Croce, which becomes the pitch for the matches. Walking and boat races also feature on the programme of festivities. The Società San Giovanni (St John Society) has been organising the festivities and dedicating itself to good works since it was constituted in 1796.

- **Festa delle Rificolone (Festival of the Paper Lanterns)** A procession of drummers, *sbandieratori* (flag-throwers), musicians and others in medieval dress winds its way from Piazza di Santa Croce to Piazza della SS Annunziata to celebrate the eve of Our Lady's supposed birthday on 7 September. Children with paper lanterns accompany them. Smaller processions for kids and their families are organised in other quarters of the city too. On 8 September, for one day only, the walkway around the sides and façade of the Duomo is opened to the public.

CULTURE
IDENTITY

The Florentines have an elusive slant to their character, which can be expected in a provincial capital inundated by a constant stream of foreigners and Italians from the rest of the country. Outsiders are treated affably enough but Florentines take a certain haughty pride in their city, basking in the reflected glory of its splendid past and simply letting the hordes from outside wash by.

The spectacular rise of modern tourism in Florence and throughout Tuscany since the 1960s has helped inject unprecedented wealth into a city that had, since before the final fall of the Medici, sunk into decay and considerable poverty. That wealth has made Florence one of the most expensive cities in Italy (and for that matter Europe) and no one is more aware of that than the Florentines themselves.

Italians from other parts of the country gently rib the Florentines, accusing them of being, above all, slaves to appearance. *Fare bella figura* ('to look good'; a term covering much more than simply dressing well) is of prime importance to many a Florentine. One might observe that all Italians have this preoccupation, but to the Italians themselves the Florentines excel.

In medieval days, sumptuary laws were repeatedly introduced to curb the peoples' excessively dressy habits in the interests of bourgeois decorum, although such laws remained largely unenforced. Savonarola railed at the Florentines' vanity at the end of the 15th century. Mind you, his puritan tastes soon lost their appeal and he (literally) went up in smoke. Centuries before him even Dante took his countrymen to task for their excessive attachment to sartorial splendour. All that said, local tastes tend to be rather classic – there is little room for the wild or outlandish.

Indeed a solid conservatism dominates the average Florentines' horizons. They are strongly attached to the family and most tend to keep largely to themselves, their families and their life-long friends. Convinced that they live in a sort of a paradise on earth, few would consider abandoning their city or the splendid surrounding region for a life elsewhere. That so many outsiders choose to settle in and around Florence only serves to confirm them in their beliefs.

Still, central Florence is becoming less Florentine all the time. Tourism has brought prosperity but it has also helped bring pressures to bear that some locals cannot withstand. Salaries do not keep pace with the cost of living, especially housing. Only a small minority of well-off Florentines can afford to live in or near the centre. The rest are being edged out further into the suburbs and even nearby towns like Prato.

Aside from the tourists, a sizable portion of the Italians who reside in Florence are from other parts of the country. Some are students (but few remain after they have finished their studies), while others are internal migrants. Although the bulk of poorer Italians from the south traditionally made for northern cities like Milan and Turin in the search for work, some chose Florence. Those great waves of internal migration are largely a thing of the past but many families in Florence today trace their roots to other regions.

No-one would claim Florence was a multicultural place. But like many other Italian cities, it has attracted its fair share of illegal migrants since they started arriving in considerable numbers in the 1980s. They come mainly from Africa (Tunisia and Senegal) or the Balkans. For many years now, Rom and Sinti families from Albania and Kosovo have lived in precarious makeshift settlements on the edge of the city.

Although their numbers are relatively small, many less charitable Italians (not overly mindful of their own people's long history of emigration) view the presence of these *clandestini* with a mix of fear and disdain.

LIFESTYLE

Florentines like the good life. Dressed to the nines and zipping about in fast cars, they certainly have a nice city to have fun in. Although the centre of the city is under more or less constant siege, Florentines still have their favourite eateries and watering holes to take refuge in. The young and the beautiful crowd have a special penchant for the bars and restaurants around Piazza Santo Spirito, and many wind up in the Cascine clubs in the west end of the city.

Their leisure activities frequently take them beyond the city. Better off Florentines keep a country house, more often than not to the south of town, where they seek peace and quiet on weekends. Many think nothing of driving out of town to, say, San

These boots aren't made for walking

Gimignano, for dinner. Others are not averse to summer traffic jams to get to (and from) the Tuscan beaches around Viareggio, some 100km away. In winter they switch swimming costumes for ski gear and head for the moderate Abetone slopes north of Pistoia.

But Florence is not just about having fun. Florentines remain as adept at business as their forebears. The city buzzes with countless small enterprises in various sectors and just getting to work can be hell. The broad *viali* (avenues) that encircle the city centre thunder most of the day with constantly streaming traffic.

What local students know simply as *la facoltà* (the faculty) is an important element in Florentine life. The prestigious Università degli Studi di Firenze traces its history back to the Studium Generale established in 1321. Pope Clement VI granted this institution permission to issue full degrees in 1349, after the universities of Bologna and Paris. Italy's first theology faculty was also founded in Florence. In successive centuries the various faculties were split up and spread across the city and Pisa. Today the Florentine facilities are known above all for the their fine arts faculty.

FASHION

It's no wonder Florentines like dressing up and looking good. They've been doing it for centuries! The wool, silk and textile industries were a pillar of the local economy from the early 14th century, and Florence exported finery all over medieval Europe.

Family Feud

By the time Guccio Gucci founded a modest saddlery store in Florence in 1904, he had fallen out with his father, a straw-hat maker. Guccio had five sons whom he brought into the slowly growing business, but he must have been one difficult individual. Having broken with his father, he set about encouraging rivalry between his sons, whom he also pushed to snitch on one another. For their misdeeds he would dish out violent beatings.

Having thus created the ideal harmonious family, he could hardly have been surprised by the thunderous rifts that would come later.

Aldo got the ball rolling in 1938, when he followed the family tradition and thumbed his nose at father, marching off to establish the first Gucci store in Rome. Aldo invented the company's double G logo and, in the wake of Guccio's death in 1953, expanded operations across Europe and eventually into the USA.

Aldo's son Paolo persuaded him and his brothers to broaden business by selling Gucci goods through outlets other than their own. By the early 1980s, the Gucci label had spread to products as diverse as coffee mugs and perfumes. Profits were booming, but Aldo and Rodolfo in particular resented what they saw as a cheapening of their products and name.

Boardroom spats became so venomous that Paolo tipped US authorities off about Aldo's tax evasion schemes, a step that ultimately landed the ageing head of the family empire in jail. Paolo got the sack, set up his own business (which failed) and in 1994 filed for bankruptcy. He died a year later.

Meanwhile the star of Rodolfo's son, Maurizio, was rising. He had defied his father in 1972 by marrying Patrizia, a laundry woman's daughter that Rodolfo described with consummate tact as a 'gold-digger'. In 1983, Maurizio inherited half the Gucci empire when Rodolfo died. He dumped Aldo from the board and bought out Paolo's brother Giorgio. Two years later he left his wife. In 1993 he sold Gucci to Investcorp, a Bahrain-based company.

Patrizia was less than euphoric. To her way of thinking, her divorce settlement of US$1 million had been 'little more than a plate of lentils' and she feared her two daughters might miss out altogether. That she wouldn't have minded seeing Maurizio dead was common knowledge. Wishful thinking became reality when Maurizio was gunned down in 1995. In 1998 Patrizia, who by then was known as the Black Widow, was found guilty of hiring the killer who sent her former husband to Jesus. With that, it would seem that the Gucci family, who would have done any feuding medieval Florentine clan proud, had consumed itself. The only one left in the rag trade is Robert Gucci of House of Florence, on Via de' Tornabuoni.

The fashion label fared rather better than the family that created it. Under the creative guidance of Texas-born Tom Ford, who joined the company in 1990 and was chief creative director by 1994, Investcorp's Gucci Group became a leading luxury goods brand. In 1999 it acquired Yves Saint Laurent and teamed up with Pinault Printemps Redoute, a major distribution company. PPR ended up taking a two-thirds share of Gucci and promised to take up the rest by April 2004. Ford's touch has not proved so magical with YSL and in November 2003 he announced his departure from the entire conglomerate. Having made millions, Ford can probably afford to take a little break.

Blinded as we are by the fashion lights of Milan, it is perhaps not so well known that Italy's postwar challenge to the fashion hegemony of Paris was launched in Florence. Long home to the likes of Gucci and Ferragamo, Florence also became the scene, in 1951, of Italy's first fashion parade in a local patrician's private home. An international band of journalists and buyers was pleasantly surprised by the quality and came back the following year for the second edition, held in the Grand Hotel. Each year thereafter brought increasing success and recognition. In 1954 an Italian fashion centre was established in Florence.

By the 1960s, Italian fashion was becoming big business. Roman interests muscled in and the *haute couture* parades started taking place in the capital in 1967, leaving specialist shows and the emerging *prêt-à-porter* business in Florence. In the late 1970s the cool-headed business world of Milan finally made its move. Women's high fashion and a growing troupe of international names moved to Italy's London, and since then Milan has spearheaded the country's competition with Paris.

Florence has remained a major, if quiet, player, hosting numerous shows and attracting big buyers from around the globe. The Istituto Politecnico Internazionale della Moda, a fashion design school, was founded in 1986 and 10 years later the ambitious Biennale della Moda staged. The latter was a nice idea, bringing art and fashion together, but it didn't really work. It was revamped in 1998, but it has died a quiet death.

Any shopper knows that some of the finest names in Italian fashion come from Florence, including Gucci, Pucci and Salvatore Ferragamo. They and many local artisans keep churning out high-quality garments and accessories today. When it comes to shoes and other leather goods, you can still find modest workshops turning out first-class products.

SPORT

An earthquake shook the Florentine football world in the torrid summer of 2002. The club's owner, cinema impresario and former senator Vittorio Cecchi Gori, finally had to surrender and go into bankruptcy after a financial scandal that broke the previous year, leaving the *viola* (the 'purples') immersed in debt. The club disappeared from the face of Italian football and was reborn under the name of Florentia Viola, obliged to start life in the lowly C2 division. The team was later promoted to C1 (third division) and in May 2003 its new owners purchased rights to the old name, AC Fiorentina. More scandal washed over Italian football when just before the 2003–04 season kicked off AC Fiorentina was unexpectedly promoted to Serie B, the second division, leap-frogging over the C1 division. Extra room had to be made for the Florence side and three other equally unexpected additions causing many well established Serie B teams to boycott the opening matches of the season. Fiorentina's recent history has been, at least off the field, anything but boring. A long haul still awaits the team on the road back to the premier division Serie A from which it so ignominiously fell.

Trying on a hat for size at Mercato Centrale (p171)

Historically Tuscany's only representative in the premier league, AC Fiorentina came to life on 26 August 1926. The team was the result of a fusion between two local clubs, Palestra Libertas and Club Sportivo Firenze. In those early years the team's home ground was in Via Bellini, but in the 1930s it moved to the Fascist-built Stadio Franchi, still in use today.

In 1931 Fiorentina entered Serie A and finished the season a creditable fourth. It had already discovered a fashion that would in following years come to dominate the game all over Europe – the purchase of star foreigners. That Fiorentina made it to fourth spot on the table was in no small measure due to the Uruguayan Pedro Petrone's 25 goals!

By 1938 the club had slipped to Serie B but was back in the top league after the war. They have managed to win only two shields – in 1955–56 and 1968–69. On the other hand, they have taken the Coppa Italia (Italy Cup) six times, lastly in 2001, just before the brown stuff hit the fan.

Although a minority activity, some Florentines like to profit from the Arno by heading out for a good row. Two riverside clubs cater to this activity and one, the Società Canottieri Firenze, has quite a distinguished competition record.

In winter, Florentines who can't afford or can't be bothered heading north for the Alps get in their ski thrills at Abetone, north of Pistoia on the regional frontier with Emilia-Romagna. Some cool young dudes who have seen too many surf movies from Hawaii and Australia take their boards and windsurfing kit in search of wind and waves off parts of the Tuscan coast, such as the nippy Golfo Baratti to the southwest.

See p153 for tips on getting involved in rowing, as well as other sport activities in town.

MEDIA

You can get all the national newspapers and many foreign ones at newsstands all over central Florence. The local media scene is decidedly small town. *La Nazione* is the most venerable of the city's papers. Its only competition comes from the racier tabloid format *Il Corriere di Firenze*. A regional rag, *Il Giornale Toscano*, prints local editions throughout the region, including one for Florence. A couple of fairly dire local TV stations supplement the main national diet.

LANGUAGE

Florence may have sent Dante Alighieri into exile but it still likes to bask in his reflected glory. He is generally credited with breathing life into a serious, literary Italian language at a time when Latin still held sway in learned discourse. And so Florentine, or more generally Tuscan, is enthusiastically held up as the preeminent example of 'good' Italian. Whatever the merits of the claim, a modern standardised language only really started to gain ground in the 19th century. The Milanese novelist Alessandro Manzoni struggled with Tuscan to lend his writing a more broadly national appeal in his seminal work, *I Promessi Sposi* (The Bethrothed). The modern media have, since the close of WWII, really taken a standardised Italian into the hearts and minds of Italians up and down the peninsula. And the Florentine variant? It has a rather husky, full flavour to it and a couple of quirks that set it apart from the standard language and other regional accents and dialects. The most notable is the conversion of the hard 'c' into a heavily aspirated 'h'. *Voglio una Coca Cola con cannuccia* (I want a Coca Cola and a straw) in Florentine becomes: *Voglio una Hoha Hola hon hannuccia*! See the Language chapter, p224.

ECONOMY & COSTS

In 1189 Florence gave the world the silver florin *(fiorino)*, a currency bearing the lily of Florence and the bust of its patron saint, St John the Baptist. By the time the city started to mint the gold version in 1252, the city's banks and currency already had a reputation throughout Europe as being among the most stable in the world of medieval business.

As the inventors of double entry book-keeping and a forerunner to the cheque, Florentines were considered the masters of international commerce. All this may sound terribly boring, but Florence was, and is, largely a middle-class merchant city, the central Italian equivalent of the burgher towns of the Netherlands.

Of course, banking alone does not an economy make. The central pillar of Florence's prosperity was textiles. Experts in the selection and use of dyes, Florentines often imported the raw materials (especially wool) from northern Europe (although their own supplies were not inconsiderable) and then exported the finished products back. Although not a sea power, Florence also did a brisk trade in the export of grain, wines, timber, oil and livestock.

Long eclipsed as a power to be reckoned with, Florence was by the 19th century a provincial backwater. The city rejected industrialisation – as late as 1870 local politicians were still declaring that smoke-stacks were not for Florence, which should instead rely on handmade products and tourism. Not everyone agreed, and indeed a big foundry had been operating in the Pignone district since 1842. The optics specialists of the Officina Galilei came into being in 1860 and, now based in Rifredi, are still going strong today. Manetti & Roberts, long famous in Florence for its talcum powder, is another business that continues to thrive.

Overall, however, Florence has proved either unwilling or unable to make itself an important industrial centre. Nowadays, furniture making, food processing, rubber goods and chemicals dominate industrial production in the western suburbs. Various companies have opted to pursue the development and production of precision instruments for use in the fields of space, military and medical technology.

It will come as no great surprise that tourism plays a key part in Florence's economic life. It is estimated that 3.75 million tourists flocked to the city of the Medici in 2000 (and stayed at least one night), with tourism-related business turnover around US$2 billion. The 11 September 2001 attacks in New York clearly put a brake on things, bringing the number down to 2.6 million, which remained little changed in 2002. Still, even when things are going badly overall, Florence remains perennial flavour of the month. In 2001, according to one survey, three of the top tourist attractions in Italy were in Florence (the Uffizi, Galleria dell'Accademia and Galleria Palatina). And on the back of tourism comes the sale of arts, crafts and high fashion (whether locally produced or not).

How Much?

Pizza – €6-10
Good mid-range meal – €30-45
Entrance to the Uffizi – €6.50
One litre of mineral water – €1-2
Large beer – €4
One day's bicycle hire – €12
Admission to dance clubs – €10-20
Normal priority paid letter (20g) within Europe – €0.62
Cocktail – €6

GOVERNMENT & POLITICS

Florence is the capital of Tuscany (Toscana to the Italians), one of the 20 regions into which the country is divided.

Tuscany is bound to the west by the Tyrrhenian and Ligurian Seas and to the north by the region of Emilia-Romagna, with which it shares a good chunk of the Apennines. To the east and south, Tuscany borders Le Marche, Umbria and Lazio.

The region is further divided into 10 provinces, each named after its respective capital: Florence (Firenze), Prato, Pistoia, Lucca, Massa, Pisa, Livorno, Siena, Grosseto and Arezzo. These are subdivided into local administrative *comuni* (districts).

The *comune* of Florence takes in a relatively small area, falling short of Amerigo Vespucci airport in the west and extending about 4km east of Ponte Vecchio along the Arno. At its southernmost point it reaches only 2km south of the Palazzo Pitti. To the ordinary citizen, such fine distinctions are noticeable only by the signs on roads leading out of the city, which show 'Firenze' with a red line through it. To the northwest, and into the *comune* of Sesto Fiorentino especially, the city sprawl goes on and on. Heading clockwise from Sesto are the districts of Fiesole, Bagno a Ripoli and Scandicci.

From medieval times the city (which until a century ago was largely confined to the area within the last set of city walls) was subdivided in various ways. Up to the end of the 12th century, it had four administrative units, all on the northern side of the river. With expansion beginning to take on more substance on the southern bank, the city was reorganised into six *sestieri*, five on the north side and one on the south bank.

In 1343 the *comune* reverted back to a system of quarters, of which there were three on the north bank (Santa Maria Novella, San Giovanni and Santa Croce) and one on the south (Oltrarno). Each quarter was further subdivided into districts known as *popoli*.

Nowadays the *comune* is made up of five local councils, or *quartieri*. They are: Centro Storico, Campo di Marte, Gavinana-Galluzo, Isolotto-Legnaia and Rifredi-Le Piagge.

The mayor in the driver's seat since July 1999 has been Leonardo Domenici. He fronts a centre-left coalition led by the former communists, the Democratici di Sinistra (DS).

ENVIRONMENT

THE LAND

The Romans founded Florence at a strategic point on the Arno, approximately 85km inland from the Tuscan coast. Even this far from the Mediterranean, the river was still navigable but crossing was not arduous. Since the settlement was also perfectly placed to give access to three passes north across the Apennines, Roman Florentia was very well positioned as a trade centre. Being next to a river later proved crucial to the city, as much of its wealth would eventually come from the textiles industry, for which a decent water source is indispensable.

The Arno rises in the Tuscan Apennines near Monte Falterona, describes an arc south towards Arezzo and then heads northwest to Florence. From there it winds westwards, emptying out into the Mediterranean about 11km west of Pisa. In all it is about 240km long. Several minor mountain streams, the most important of which is the Mugnone, feed into the Arno from north of Florence.

When you look down at the pathetic puddle that the Arno is in high summer, it is hard to imagine it thundering down from the east, crashing into the city, sweeping away bridges and leaving countless dead. And yet that is precisely what it has done repeatedly throughout the city's history. In 1177 and 1333 floods swept away the Ponte Vecchio's predecessors, and some thought the same would happen in the disastrous flood of 1966. Some of the flood control works in place today were designed by Leonardo da Vinci.

Electric minibus around the centre of the city (p205)

The original Roman camp *(castrum)* lay on the north bank of the river, and the bulk of the city has developed there for the simple reason that the valley is relatively wide and flat on that side of the river. The foothills of the Apennines reach down to within 10km of the Arno and closer still on the eastern side of the city. As a consequence, the bulk of the suburban sprawl has been channelled west towards Prato.

South of the Arno, development is more limited. Historically the hills crowding up to the river allowed urban spread only within a rough triangle bounded by Porta Romana (Roman Gate), Ponte Amerigo Vespucci and Ponte alle Grazie.

In the past century the westward march of suburban expansion on the north bank has to some extent been mirrored to the south with the development of areas such as the factory zone of Pignone and Isolotto.

GREEN FLORENCE

Florence's biggest environmental problem is air pollution. Efforts to reduce traffic approaching the centre and the introduction of buses using natural gas (which represent about one-sixth of the total) and others on types of diesel with reduced emissions have helped. Florence is one of the first European cities to run regular electric bus lines, and three such lines traverse the centre of the city. Still, on a hot, smoggy day you realise there is a long way to go.

Noise, especially in the centre, is another problem. The rattling of two-stroke engines on *motorini* (mopeds) is not likely to go away anytime soon! Indeed, it is estimated that the density of vehicles per capita in Florence is one of the highest in Europe. There are 200,000 *motorini* alone on Florence's often clogged roads.

The collection of refuse is improving. All over the town centre are large bins for the separated collection of rubbish (paper, glass, plastic and so on). The average citizen seems to take this reasonably seriously.

Another problem is pesky animals. Although not as serious as Venice's pigeon plague, Florence has a fair-sized problem and the town authorities are forever trying to work out how to clip the pigeon population's wings. Of greater concern is the *norvegicus* rat, a beast the size of a small cat, weighing up to 3kg. These charmers live in the sewerage pipes and along riverbanks and streams. Just how to get rid of them is a question to which no-one has yet come up with a satisfactory answer.

URBAN PLANNING & DEVELOPMENT

The unchecked urban and suburban sprawl, fuelled by land speculation that seemed to leave successive city governments helpless, has greatly depleted any sense of green in Florence. This is particularly so north of the river, although a few parks and patches remain. As if by a miracle, parts of the Oltrarno are still a haven. South of the walls protecting Via di San Niccolò, you can wander almost immediately into what to all intents and purposes is a stretch of countryside, dotted with villas and kept productive with the fruit of the vine.

Arts & Architecture

Arts & Architecture

Say Renaissance and most respond: Florence. Which is not to say Florence was some kind of genteel haven where carefree artists could sweetly indulge their whims. Far from it. Florence was a vipers' nest. Cloak-and-dagger intrigue, assassination, riots and merciless wheeler-dealing were this turbulent town's bread and butter. The riverside city grew rich and bold in a risky environment. Wars and pestilence, revolt and suppression, and dodgy diplomacy with restless neighbours all created a crackling atmosphere for painters, sculptors, architects and writers. Patronage was everything and it so happened that the people who mattered most in Florence were generous and anxious to show themselves at the forefront of rapidly changing tastes. Renaissance Florence was a place of incredible ferment.

The fun lasted until well into the 16th century. But there had been plenty before. As elsewhere in Italy, Florence had known the artistic brilliance of the Romanesque and Gothic periods, which taken together represent a more ponderous artistic evolution in more fearful, circumscribed times when the Church was all and few people dared move beyond their own town quarter. And while the decline of the Renaissance signalled the end of Florence as artistic epicentre, the city still managed to give rise to engaging movements, such as the 19th-century Macchiaioli.

In the Renaissance, a rediscovery of classical writings, especially the Greek philosophers, and imperial Roman art and architecture awakened a curiosity in young thinkers and artists. Instead of attributing everything to God, people began to search for human explanations and to explore the natural world with a more open, 'scientific' rather than superstitious mind. The Church, anxious to maintain control in the Christian world through a monopoly of 'acceptable' knowledge and doctrine, rode uneasily with all of this, although it embraced the artistic flourishes (while viewing warily scientific developments, which were regarded as bordering on heresy).

The birth of the Renaissance in Florence earlier than elsewhere is coincidental. The city was wealthy and anxious to wear new clothes. There was also the matter of intellectual taste. Although far from a perfect democracy, the rowdy republic was not (yet) a one-man dictatorship. While some families (such as the Albizi) viewed dimly the new-fangled learning and rediscovery, others (such as the Medici) lapped it up. Happily for posterity, the Medici would come to hold increasing power and prove generous patrons.

By the time Cosimo de' Medici returned to Florence in 1434, to become its ruler in

Interior of Basilica di San Lorenzo (p92)

deed if not in name, the city had already long been one of Europe's most prosperous trading and banking centres. So the money was also there to invest in art.

Indeed, those with dosh were honour-bound to lavish some of it on the prestige of the city (which in turn reflected well on the benefactors). The mercantile dynasties had in the past subscribed to the building of the great churches – the Duomo, Santa Maria Novella and Santa Croce. They hoped to do their souls some good too – Cosimo de' Medici once said: 'I shall never be able to give God enough to set him down in my books as a debtor.' This habit of patronage continued into the Renaissance.

The city's growing monumental magnificence was good for business. In the way modern cities try to attract attention and investment by staging the Olympics or with ambitious urban redevelopment programmes, so did the great cities of medieval and Renaissance Italy by raising great public and private buildings sumptuously decorated with frescoes, sculptures and paintings.

Architects, painters and sculptors were often masters of more than one medium. Leonardo da Vinci is best known as a scientist and yet was a great painter. Michelangelo is revered as a sculptor, and yet he was just as deft with the brush. Some architects started as goldsmiths.

The definition of a 'Florentine' is equally difficult to settle. Many fine non-Florentine artists left works behind in the city of the red lily. Equally, many Florence-born artists wandered far and wide during their careers. It was in the nature of the business – they went where the work was.

Florence was the heart of Italy's early Renaissance painting and saw the greatest blossoming of sculpture. Although other regions produced capable sculptors, most either came from Tuscany or wound up in Florence at some stage of their careers. The innovations undertaken by Brunelleschi and others helped revolutionise architectural thinking throughout the country.

Geological features benefited Florence's tradition of artistic patronage. Tuscany was abundantly rich in the raw materials for sculpture and building. The white marble of Carrara still draws sculptors today, while the green marble used mainly in the façades of great buildings was quarried in the hills near Prato. Pink marble came from the Maremma district in southwest Tuscany. Various kinds of stone could be found around Florence itself, including the dun-coloured *pietra forte* ('strong stone') that characterises the exterior of so many great Florentine buildings. From the 13th century it became the most commonly used material in civic and private construction, virtually replacing brick. The Boboli quarry was one of its handiest sources. The stone par excellence of the Renaissance was, however, the grey *pietra serena* ('tranquil stone') used mainly for interiors. Brunelleschi propelled the use of this easily worked stone to prominence as a building material. It became common to couple it with plain whitewashed stucco *(intonaco)* elements such as window mouldings.

Circumstances conspired to lift Florence, a city of bankers and traders without even its own university, to the lofty heights of innovative artistic cauldron.

ARCHITECTURE

Until the late Gothic period and early into the Renaissance, little credit was given to the master builders behind the churches and bell towers, the palaces and castles that were raised in Italy and Europe. With little more than the status of skilled tradesmen, the forerunners to modern architects remained in complete anonymity. Even the masters behind the Duomo and its breathtaking *campanile* (bell tower), Arnolfo di Cambio and Giotto, barely get a passing mention in the literature that comes down to us, but from that point they began to leave their signature on their works.

One of the odd things about much Italian church architecture is that façades were often tacked onto the body as if in afterthought (and sometimes subsequently

Top Five Notable Buildings

- Basilica di Santa Croce (p100)
- Duomo (p75)
- Palazzo Medici-Riccardi (p94)
- Palazzo Vecchio (p86)
- Ponte Vecchio (p109)

changed to meet new tastes). The Duomo and the Basilica di Santa Croce only got their façades in the 19th century! Many other churches never received theirs – a peculiarly Florentine quirk. It appears money was frequently hard to come by for this final touch.

ROMANESQUE

As Florence recovered from the centuries of barbarian invasion, wars, devastation and confusion that ensued from the fall of the Roman Empire, its people could devote some energy to public building.

From the northern Lombard plains, a modest building style now known as Romanesque began to spread across much of Europe. Characterised by a beguiling simplicity, in some way it symbolises a reawakening from the Dark Ages.

The standard church ground plan, generally composed of a nave and two aisles, no transept and between one and five apses, topped by a simple bowl-shaped cupola, followed that used in Roman-era basilicas. Initially, churches tended to be bereft of external decoration (inside, the walls and columns were frequently covered in murals, mostly long since disappeared) except for the semicircular arches above doorways and windows. The apses tended to be semicircular too. Such churches were most commonly accompanied by a freestanding square-based bell tower, also adorned with layers of semicircular arched windows.

In Tuscany, the early rediscovery of that favourite of Roman building materials, marble, led to a rather more florid decorative style, the best examples of which can be seen in Pisa and Lucca. The key characteristics of this variant are the use of two-tone marble banding and complex rows of columns and loggias in the façade.

At the heart of old Florence, amid the tight lanes and bustle of a town embarked on rapid growth on the back of the wool trade and, increasingly, banking, emerged what remains one of the loveliest of its buildings – the Baptistry (p65) dedicated to St John (San Giovanni). Although its marble-banded façade dates to the 11th century, the building could have been preceded by others as far back as the 5th century. Some see in it the one clear tenuous link to Roman Florentia, as it is surmised a Roman temple stood here. The finest example of Florentine Romanesque is, however, the Chiesa di San Miniato al Monte (p105) high up on a hillside south across the Arno.

GOTHIC

The slow transition across Europe from Romanesque to soaring Gothic was uniformly spectacular but extraordinarily varied in its results. It brought much destruction, for while Romanesque edifices were left standing in many places, in cities like Florence a go-ahead, knock-'em-down approach led to the disappearance of many monuments, to be replaced by bigger and better ones (so contemporaries felt).

More daring building techniques born of greater skill and a desire to more fully express human devotion to God spurred the development of this new style. The first examples went up in the Île-de-France in the 12th century and slowly spread across northwest Europe.

Complex structures were perfected using pillars, columns, arches and vaulting of various kinds to support soaring ceilings. Rather than relying on the solidity of mass, and thick, heavy walls, priority was given to an almost diaphanous light pouring through tall pointed windows. Such fragile structures could not stand the weight of the roof, so outer walls connected by buttressing took the strain. The whole was topped off by an almost obsessive desire to decorate. Such churches are bedecked with pinnacles, statues, gargoyles and all sorts of baubles. The busier the better.

Examples of that north European style of Gothic are rare in Italy, and nonexistent in Florence. The city's two great Gothic churches are Santa Croce and Santa Maria Novella, built for the dominant mendicant orders of the time, respectively the Franciscans and the Dominicans. They, along with other less publicised orders, were in keen competition and went to enormous lengths to demonstrate their piety and clerical clout by erecting imposing churches in cities across Italy. Construction of both began in the 13th century but was not completed until well into the 14th century.

Consulting a map at the Duomo (p75)

In terms of volume they are as impressive as their northern counterparts. Inside the Basilica di Santa Maria Novella (p89), designed by Dominican friars, you can admire the complex ribbed vaulting of the main ceiling above the nave, but there ends the similarities. Decoration is minimal. The bicolour banding that edges arches and vaults is a Tuscan touch. The width of the nave and lack of clutter make up for this and allow in plenty of light.

The Basilica di Santa Croce (p100) was designed by Siena-born Arnolfo di Cambio (c 1245–1302), the first great master builder in Florentine history. It shares with Santa Maria Novella the broad nave and simplicity of interior decoration. The privileged position given to uncovered stone is reminiscent of the Gothic of northern Europe and, in contrast to the Dominican church, an A-frame timber ceiling (a carena) obscures the roof vaulting.

Florence was not a town of pious church-goers. Just as the Gothic style took hold, the city was emerging as a vibrant republic. The florin, which would rapidly come to be medieval Europe's benchmark currency, was first coined in 1252. The land-holding nobles had ceded ground to increasingly wealthy burghers who came to exercise corporate power in Florence. As much as the Church, such an institution required a suitable home and so Arnolfo received the commission to design the Palazzo Vecchio (p86; known when it was built as Palazzo dei Priori and later as Palazzo della Signoria) in 1299. Built of *pietra forte* with the rusticated surface typical of many grand buildings in Florence, it is one of the most imposing government buildings of the medieval Italian city-states. It appears to have been plonked in the only available space in the then teeming and crowded town. Its odd shape and the off-centre placing of the distinctive tower do, however, lend the structure a brooding but powerful, no-nonsense aspect, no doubt the desired effect in a city continually facing factional strife. The Guelph and Ghibelline factions (see History p52) had already been at each other's throats for 80-odd years by the time the town fathers moved into their as yet unfinished palazzo in 1302. That very year Dante himself was exiled from the city in renewed faction feuding – he would never return.

Arnolfo also designed the Gothic Duomo (p75; aka Santa Maria del Fiore – the flower being the red lily emblem of the city), or cathedral, and it is considered that, when he died, construction of the nave had reached the transept. Giotto (see Visual Arts, p28), although fundamentally a painter, was entrusted with designing the cathedral's bell tower. It is quirkily unique, betraying Giotto's preference for a soft if graceful simplicity in structure and decoration. He only completed the base and was succeeded by Andrea Pisano (c 1290–1348), who unfortunately was one of the many victims of the horrible wave of plague, the Black Death, that swept through the city and decimated its crowded populace, and finally Francesco Talenti (active 1325–69). Clearly Gothic elements are evident in the style of the windows (decidedly French), while the dual colour banding is typical of the Tuscan approach to decoration already evident in Romanesque buildings. Talenti amended Arnolfo's design for the Duomo and added unique polygonal apses, each with five chapels. Circular windows *(oculi)* in lace were another novel element introduced in some Gothic churches. Talenti drew an octagonal dome between the apses, but had no grander ideas on how to build it than did Arnolfo.

BAD BOY BRUNELLESCHI

Enter Filippo Brunelleschi (1377–1446), one of the hotter tempers in the history of Italian architecture. After failing to win the 1401 competition to design a set of bronze doors for the Baptistry (see Visual Arts, p29), Brunelleschi left in a huff for Rome, where he focussed on mathematics and architecture. He and sculptor pal Donatello spent their time measuring up ancient Roman monuments, collecting knowledge that would later come to fruition. The locals thought they were using bizarre divining methods to look for buried treasure!

Brunelleschi would launch the architectural branch of the Renaissance in Florence. It manifested itself in a rediscovery of simplicity and purity in classical building, with great attention paid to perspective and harmonious distribution of space and volume.

His single most remarkable achievement was solving the Duomo dome conundrum. He proposed to raise the octagonal-based dome without the aid of scaffolding, unheard of at the time. Although incredulous, the Signoria agreed to commission him. Brunelleschi's double-skinned dome, raised in sections, was the greatest feat of its kind since ancient times. In later years Michelangelo, when commissioned to create the dome for St Peter's (San Pietro) in Rome, observed with undisguised admiration, 'io farò la sorella, già più gran ma non più bella' (I'll make it the Brunelleschi dome's sister – bigger, yes, but no more beautiful).

That feat alone was tremendous but Brunelleschi's importance goes beyond the splendid dome. He 'created' the role of architect. Rather than act as a foreman, guiding construction as it progressed and to some extent making it up as he went along, Brunelleschi devised formulae of perspective and balance that allowed him to create a completed concept at the drawing board. Inspired by Roman engineering and Tuscan aesthetics, he launched a new era in construction. In essence, the architectural Renaissance, based on the rational tackling of human and mathematical problems, took flight with him. Other examples of Brunelleschi's keen sense of human proportion are: the portico of the **Spedale degli Innocenti** (p99; 1421), considered the earliest work of the Florentine Renaissance; the **Sagrestia Vecchia** (Old Sacristy) in Basilica di San Lorenzo (p92; 1428); and the Cappella de' Pazzi in the **Basilica di Santa Croce** (p100; 1430). If Gothic sought to exalt God with impossibly lofty construction, dwarfing its admirers, Renaissance building aimed as much to exalt human reason, pleasing with its geometrical harmony and more earthly proportions.

Brunelleschi also designed the **Basilica di San Lorenzo** (p92; 1425) and the **Basilica di Santo Spirito** (p105; 1436). San Lorenzo had Medici money behind it, allowing the architect some latitude in design and choice of materials. He died long before either project reached completion and the supervisors who came after him were not completely faithful to his plans, particularly in the case of the latter church.

A mean-tempered fellow, Brunelleschi more than once flounced out of meetings and dropped projects if he did not get his way. But he was good, and most of the time he achieved what he wanted. We owe a considerable debt of thanks to his genius.

BEYOND BRUNELLESCHI

It is generally accepted that Cosimo de' Medici commissioned Michelozzo di Bartolommeo Michelozzi (1396–1472) to build his new residence. Brunelleschi had proposed something altogether too grand for Cosimo's liking, whose policy was to keep his head down while effectively ruling the city. Brunelleschi, predictably, flew into a rage and smashed the model.

Michelozzo's building, now known as **Palazzo Medici-Riccardi** (p94) was nevertheless no dwarf. Three hefty storeys with a fortress air are topped by a solid roof whose eaves jut far out over the streets below – a typical trait of Florentine *palazzi* (mansions) of the period. The lowest storey features rustication (which you can also see on the Palazzo Vecchio). This describes the rough-hewn, protruding blocks of stone used to build it, as opposed to the smoothed stone of the upper storeys. The mansion ushered in an era of grand patrician building and other influential families would soon follow suit.

It is thought that the initial 15th-century core of the **Palazzo Pitti** (p108; begun in 1458) was built for the powerful if rather mouthy Luca Pitti by Settignano-born Luca Fancelli (1430–95) but experts are increasingly convinced that Brunelleschi provided the design.

Benedetto da Maiano (1442–97), meanwhile, was chosen by Filippo Strozzi to build the Strozzi family mansion (p92). In terms of size alone it outstrips any other *palazzo* raised during the Medici era. The courtyard, attributed to Simone del Pollaiuolo (1457–1508), better known as Il Cronaca, is considered one of Florence's finest. To Benedetto's brother, Giuliano da Maiano (1432–90), is generally attributed another mansion, the **Palazzo dei Pazzi** (p116).

The acclaimed theorist of Renaissance architecture and art was Leon Battista Alberti (1404–72). Born in Genoa into an exiled Florentine family, he was a true Renaissance figure, learned and multitalented. To his native city he contributed only the striking façades of the **Palazzo Rucellai** (p92) and Basilica di Santa Maria Novella. His influence on artists, sculptors and architects in Florence and beyond came above all through his theoretical writings.

Statue of Michelangelo, the Uffizi (p81)

MICHELANGELO

Michelangelo Buonarroti (1475–1564) was foremost a sculptor and painter (see Visual Arts, p31) but in later years he also turned his attention to building design. In 1516, after stints in Rome, he was called back to Florence to design a façade for the Basilica di San Lorenzo but the project was dropped and he ended up working on the **Sagrestia Nuova** (New Sacristy; p93) for the same church, intended as part of the funerary chapels for the Medici family. This was as close as Michelangelo got to finishing one of his architectural-sculptural whims in Florence.

Another of Michelangelo's tasks in the same church was the grand staircase and entrance hall for the **Biblioteca Medicea Laurenziana** (Laurentian Library; p93), which Michelangelo never saw completed, as he returned to Rome beforehand. It is a startling late-Renaissance creation, with columns recessed into the walls (and thus deprived of their natural supporting function) and other architectural oddities, precursors of mannerism.

MIND YOUR MANNERISM

Most scholars date the end of the later, or High, Renaissance around 1520. Certainly by 1527, with the sack of Rome (a real bonfire of the vanities) led by Charles de Bourbon, it was all over, if only because war and suffering had snuffed out the funds and desire to continue creating in such quantity.

What followed is generally called mannerism, although this intermediate phase between the Renaissance and baroque is not easily defined. For many, Michelangelo's work in San Lorenzo is clearly mannerist, breaking with the more austere classical lines of the Renaissance. For others, the mannerists were a fairly unimaginative lot, fiddling around the edges of what had been the core of Renaissance thinking.

In Florence little of moment was built in the hangover period after the sack of Rome. The menacing **Fortezza da Basso** (p111), aimed more at controlling disgruntled Florentines under the miserable reign of Alessandro de' Medici than protecting the city, was among the few exceptions.

Giorgio Vasari (1511–74), born in Arezzo and better known to us for his biography of the great artists who preceded him, became a big wheel in Florence and created the **Uffizi** (p81).

DON'T BAROQUE THE BOAT

The 17th century brought little new construction of note in Florence, although many projects to restructure, expand or finish existing sites were underway. This was the baroque era, which often had more impact on decor than architectural design. At its most extreme, moreso in Rome, such decoration was sumptuous to the point of giddiness, all curvaceous statuary, twisting pillars and assorted baubles. In Florence, a long-established tradition of architectural sobriety excluded such excesses, and clear cases of baroque architecture are rare.

A couple of notable examples include the **Chiesa di San Gaetano** (p90) and the façade for the **Chiesa di Ognissanti** (p90). The former, finished by Gherardo Silvani (1579–1675), is considered the finest piece of baroque in Florence and a demonstration of the restraint typical of the city – in stark contrast to the flimflam buoyant baroque of Rome.

URBAN RENEWAL

The trend already set in the 17th century continued into the 18th. Florentines tinkered with their city without troubling themselves over great or worthy additions.

After Napoleon's French rulers retired in 1814, the process of urban renewal continued. The space around the southern flank of the Duomo was cleared and fronted by neoclassical buildings. The architect behind that project was Gaetano Baccani (1792–1867), who also built the singular **Palazzo Borghese** (p116) in distinctive imperial style on Via Ghibellina. It was around this time that the former Stinche prison, also on Via Ghibellina, was converted into a neoclassical theatre (now the **Teatro Verdi**, p103).

Between the 1840s and 1870s (ie from the unstable years prior to the Europe-wide uprisings of 1848 through to Florence's limited days as capital of the newly united Italy), a programme of street-widening gathered pace. It may have improved traffic flow and hygiene, but it meant tearing away centuries of history. Neoclassical façades replaced medieval leftovers. In the 1890s engineers carved out **Piazza della Repubblica** (p79), for the sake of which much of the heart of old Florence and its timeless Mercato Vecchio (Old Market) were mercilessly ripped out.

Between 1865 and 1869 the city walls north of the Arno were pulled down and replaced by the boulevards you see today. The *lungarni*, the roads that follow the course of the river, were also laid out in this period.

The **Mercato Centrale** (p93), finished in 1874, is a rare Florentine example of the late-19th-century passion for iron and glass structures. It was designed by Giuseppe Mengoni (1829–77), the Bologna-born architect responsible for Milan's Galleria Vittorio Emanuele II.

The Train of Modernity Arrives in Florence

In the early 1930s it was decided Florence needed a new train station. The end result may look like an average train station to the modern eye but at the time it caused quite a tempest. The winning project presented in Rome was a revolutionary design (for the times) by a young group of Florentine architecture students under the watchful eye of Giovanni Michelucci (1891–1991). It unleashed a storm of conservative protest in Florence – how could you plant such a modern monstrosity in the midst of this historic city? But young intellectuals, such as the writer Pratolini, were just as vehemently behind the project. Mussolini no doubt liked the clean rational lines, reflecting the Fascist go-ahead self-image, although it lacked the monumental pomposity of other Fascist-era buildings. He probably also saw an opportunity to get the intelligentsia, generally not well disposed to his rule, on side for once. The use of local *pietra forte* and a design approach that was ahead of its time attracted accolades from various quarters, including Frank Lloyd Wright.

THE 20TH CENTURY

One of the few early-20th-century residences to survive is the **Casa Galleria** (p89) by Giovanni Michelazzi (1879–1920). Its Art Nouveau façade contrasts with a city without much whimsical architecture.

Mussolini was not averse to controversy, and gave the go-ahead to the design for the city's main train station, **Stazione di Santa Maria Novella** (see the boxed text above), completed in 1935.

Sport was also important to the Fascists and so the city was graced with the **Stadio Franchi** (p14) in Campo di Marte.

Little of interest has appeared on Florence's skyline since the interwar years and town planning has been haphazard to say the least. The sprawling suburbs to the north and west are a disheartening jumble where the colour green has been submerged beneath a wave of third-rate housing and factories.

VISUAL ARTS

In the chaos of invasions, pillage and general dissolution of the Roman Empire and ushered in the fearful centuries of the early Middle Ages in Italy, the whole classical heritage of Greco-Roman art, exemplified in its sculptures and mosaics, was seemingly lost forever.

As some degree of stability and a slow return to wealth, trade and improved communications helped Europe out of the mire, a whole new artistic environment emerged. As Romanesque architects dared increasingly to raise impressive churches and secular palaces, so artists began to fill them with frescoes, painted altarpieces, timber and stone statuary.

This 'new' Romanesque art, which evolved in tandem with Byzantine iconography and mosaic work in the East (where elements of the Roman Empire had managed to survive), has to modern eyes a naive, two-dimensional feel, especially when compared with the grandeur of classical statuary. And yet it was full of bright and bold colour, shimmering gold, deep reds and daring black. It was almost exclusively religious, and served a didactic purpose in an age when even kings and emperors were often illiterate. The crucifixion, the Virgin and Child, Christ Pantocrator (enthroned Christ), the saints and numerous Old and New Testament scenes jostled alongside deeply symbolic images that conveyed the essence of Christian teaching to the masses.

It was also full of extraordinary detail: images of saints undergoing grisly martyrdoms with almost divine indifference to pain, scenes influenced by medieval Europe rather than any imagined New Testament Israel. Were Romanesque artists incapable of capturing human features in a realistic fashion? To the people of the time, their images had to exude a strangely detached other-worldliness to differentiate them from life on earth. This basic precondition remained at the heart of European Christian art until the Renaissance, and its flouting coincided with the general wave of humanist thinking (see Literature, p35) that opened the way to a new curiosity and appreciation of human qualities. As the joys of reason and learning washed over Europe, the portrayal of holy figures with demonstrable, human feeling became possible. In the process it brought these figures closer to our own earthly experience, precisely what the Church had so long opposed.

We like to divide developments in art history into neat packages, one succeeding the other. Unfortunately it was not quite so neat. Gothic art is marked by an increasing sophistication and more lifelike rendering of figures compared with the stiff Romanesque. But Gothic is subdivided into many types, both geographically and in time.

In Florence, the circumstances described earlier (see Architecture, p21) conspired to provoke a revolution in artistic thinking. But this was hardly uniform either. Giotto made some early steps and by general standards was well ahead of his time. And while later Renaissance artists were sweeping Florence with a new broom, artists in other cities (even as close as Siena) remained self-confidently faithful to Gothic precepts. In Florence itself 'old style' artists still got plenty of commissions.

Top Five Museums

- **Museo Archeologico** (p97)
- **Museo di Storia della Scienza** (p86)
- **Museo dell'Opera del Duomo** (p77)
- **Museo Horne** (p102)
- **Palazzo del Bargello** (p95)

Top Five Galleries

- **Galleria dell'Accademia** (p95)
- **Galleria Palatina (Palazzo Pitti)** (p108)
- **Museo di San Marco** (p97)
- **Museo Marino Marini** (p90)
- **The Uffizi** (p81)

Much of this was down to the tastes or daring of whoever was the patron. It so happened that the trendsetters in Florence were the Medici and they liked this modern stuff! Even through the Renaissance, artists were considered tradesmen, the interior decorators of their day. Until the late 13th century artists remained completely anonymous. Still, the emergence of the artist as protagonist coincides largely with the Florentine Renaissance.

In Florence especially, but also elsewhere in Italy and beyond, wealthy and powerful laypeople began to commission art for public places or their own homes. This promoted a broadening of themes, and so alongside the still dominant religious strain emerged portraits, busts and sculptures of (self-)important people, scenes from battles and classical mythology. Even some of the more religious paintings were filled increasingly with more detail.

Florence as a centre of art began to decline noticeably as the Renaissance was succeeded by mannerist, baroque and subsequent genres. As Florence stagnated, the great revolutions in Western art took place on other stages. That remains the case to this day.

EMERGING FROM THE MIDDLE AGES

Before the 13th century little of artistic note was happening in Florence. In Tuscany, Pisa was on the rise. Master of Sardinia and a busy sea trade, Pisa was more open than Florence to external influences and artistic interchange. This was perhaps no more clear than in building and sculpture. Nicola Pisano (c 1215–78) is best known for his work on Pisa's Baptistry and influenced fellow sculptors all over Tuscany.

Arnolfo di Cambio (see Architecture, p22) was a student of Pisano and not only designed the Duomo and Palazzo Vecchio, but also decorated the former's façade. Some of this sculpture remains in the Museo dell'Opera del Duomo (p77) but most was destroyed in the 16th century.

Andrea Pisano (c 1290–1348) moved from Pisa to Florence for a while and left behind the bronze doors of the south façade of the Baptistry, which he finished in 1336. The realism of the characters combines with the fine linear detail of a Gothic imprint, reveal that already in the 14th century a transition was in process.

Detail in Galleria dell 'Academia (p95)

GIOTTO & CO

If any proof were needed that things were on the boil in 14th-century Florence, one need look no further than the work of Giotto di Bondone (c 1266–1337). Born in the Mugello, northeast of Florence, he is one of the pivotal names in the Italian artistic pantheon. In Giotto the move from the symbolic, other-worldly representations of Italo-Byzantine and Gothic religious art to something more *real*, more directly inspired by observed truth than the desire to teach conceptual truths, is clear. His figures are essentially human and express feeling, something quite alien to earlier phases of art in Christian Europe.

Better known for his work in other towns, in particular Padua (Cappella degli Scrovegni), he left behind several works in Florence. Among the most important are the frescoes in the Peruzzi and Bardi chapels in the Basilica di Santa Croce (p100).

Confirmation of Giotto's influence comes in the work of several other painters active at the same time. Maso di Banco, of whom little is known except that he was at work in the eight or so years prior to the plague of 1348, was a student of Giotto. His *Storie di San Silvestro* (Stories of St Sylvester) series in the Basilica di Santa Croce (p100) reflects in its luminosity and simplicity the hand of his master.

Andrea di Cione Orcagna (active 1343–68), however, is a perfect illustration of the fact that Renaissance artist's thinking did not simply one day replace earlier methods. His most important remaining works are the Gothic tabernacle and statuary inside the Chiesa di Orsanmichele (p80). Indeed, Gothic was anything but dead. Artists delivered what their patrons wanted, and clearly many remained attached to established styles.

THE 15TH CENTURY & THE RENAISSANCE

In 1401, Lorenzo Ghiberti (1378–1455) beat the irascible Brunelleschi in a competition to create a second set of bronze doors on the venerable Baptistry (now on the northern flank). Ghiberti's was an exquisite solution in the International Gothic style, a loose description for the final wave of enthusiasm for Gothic to wash across Europe.

But Ghiberti soon saw which way the wind was blowing. Called on to do another set of doors on the eastern side, he dedicated 17 years to what an admiring Michelangelo (and it was not Michelangelo's wont to admire anything much) would later dub 'Porta del Paradiso' (Gate of Paradise), a remarkable Renaissance masterpiece. All of this serves as a reminder of how complicated it can get identifying what period any given building belongs to. The Baptistry is, as we have seen, one of Florence's oldest surviving monuments and a Romanesque jewel. It is, however, full of Byzantine-style mosaics inside (probably executed by or under the supervision of Venetian masters) and decorated with exquisite Gothic and Renaissance doors!

Ghiberti's workshop was a prestige address; apprenticed there was Donatello (c 1386–1466). As the Renaissance gathered momentum in the 1420s and '30s, Donatello produced very forceful and dynamic sculpture. A stay in Rome between 1432 and 1433 seems to have been decisive. Armed with his classical knowledge he set to work. The results swing from his rather camp bronze *David*, the first nude sculpture since classical times (now in the Bargello; p85) to the racy *Cantoria* (Choir), a marble and mosaic tribune where small choirs could gather, done for the Duomo (now in the Museo dell'Opera del Duomo; p77).

Meanwhile, the young Masaccio (1401–28) can probably be given a good deal of the credit for the definitive break with the Gothic style in Florentine painting. Born in an Arno village at the dawn of the 15th century (what the Italians call the Quattrocento, or the 'Four Hundreds'), his brief but dynamic career (he died in Rome at the age of 27) makes him for painting what his contemporaries, the older Brunelleschi and Donatello, were for architecture and sculpture.

You don't need to look long and hard at his Florentine masterpieces, such as the Cappella Brancacci frescoes (Basilica di Santa Maria del Carmine; p104), to see what sets Masaccio apart. The relatively new game of perspective dominates his pictorial solution. Colours are subtle and characters brought into relief by the use of light and shadow. His best-known image, the *Cacciata dei Progenitori* (Expulsion of Adam and Eve) in the Cappella Brancacci, depicts all the anguish and shame of Adam and, especially, Eve. Never before had such raw and believable human emotion been depicted.

Following in Masaccio's footsteps were two masters who in temperament could not have been more different from one another.

Fra Angelico (c 1395–1455), a Dominican monk later known as Beato (Blessed) Angelico for his piety, for a while dominated the Florentine art world. His work, much of it done for the Museo di San Marco (p97), is suffused with a diaphanous light aimed at emphasising the good in humankind. He takes on board the lessons of perspective, depth and foreshortening imparted by Masaccio, but remains faithful to the aims of a religious painter.

Although also a friar, Fra Filippo Lippi (c 1406–69) had an appetite for sex, drink and general carousing that left him the father of two by a nun. Some of his finest pieces can still be seen in Florence. A *Madonna col Bambino* (Madonna with Child) in the Uffizi (p81) and another in Palazzo Pitti (in the Sala di Prometeo; p108) demonstrate his mastery of light and shadow, a weighty reality about the characters and an eye for detail.

A strange bird was Paolo Uccello (1397–1475). More preoccupied with perspective studies than making a living, Uccello did manage to crank out a few masterpieces. They include the *Diluvio* (Deluge) fresco in the Basilica di Santa Maria Novella (p89) and the *Battaglia di San Romano* (Battle of San Romano) done for the Medici family and now (in part) in the Uffizi (p81).

Although active as a painter, Andrea del Verrocchio (1435–88) is best remembered for his sculpture. His virtuosity can be admired in the tomb monument to Piero and Giovanni de' Medici in the Basilica di San Lorenzo (p92). His masterpiece, however, is the bronze equestrian statue of Colleoni in rival Venice, which is where he died.

Benozzo Gozzoli (c 1421–97) introduced a cheerfully naive touch to paintings, an element notable by its absence in the often more brooding works of some of his confrères. One of the last painters of the International Gothic style, his work confirms that more than one tendency in the arts could happily co-exist. Gozzoli's big break came when the Medici commissioned his sumptuous *Corteo dei Magi* (Procession

The Campanile (p66)

of the Magi) in 1459 for the Palazzo Medici-Riccardi (p94).

Mythologised in the 19th century, Sandro Botticelli (1445–1510) has, as a result, probably been the least understood painter of the period. By most he is remembered for the milky dreaminess of *Nascita di Venere* (Birth of Venus) and *Primavera* (Spring), in the Uffizi (p81). The preaching of Savonarola (see History p55) had a profound effect on the artist who, fired by a new religious fervour, in his later years produced works of greater, almost disturbing intensity. His *Calunnia de Apelle* (Calumny of Apelles), finished in 1498 and now in the Uffizi (p81), is a good example of the transition. Botticelli fell out of step with his time, however, and in his last 10 years he received few commissions – he died an unhappy man.

Filippino Lippi (1457–1504), Fra Filippo's son, worked in Botticelli's workshop but was more directly influenced by Leonardo da Vinci and Flemish artists. Lippi's frescoes of the *Storie di San Giovanni Evangelista e San Filippo* (Stories of St John and St Phillip) in the Cappella Strozzi (Basilica di Santa Maria Novella; p89) reveal a move away from the humanist ideals of Quattrocento painting. In one of the frescoes, depicting St Philip exorcising the devil in the temple of Mars, perspective has been flattened and the subject has a disturbing quality absent from other works of the time. The architectural business and attention to detail in people's faces presage mannerism.

Although he would subsequently be best known for his crowd-pleasing decorative, glazed terracotta, Luca della Robbia (c 1400–82) for a while showed promise as a sculptor, as examination of his exquisite *Cantoria* (Choir), now in the Museo dell'Opera del Duomo (p77), will reveal. His nephew Andrea (1435–1525) and the latter's son Giovanni (1469–1529) continued the successful family ceramics business. The pretty terracotta medallions and other more complex pieces adorning buildings all over Florence and beyond came to be known as *robbiane*. A good collection can be admired up close in the Bargello (p85).

THE GENIUS FROM VINCI

Leonardo da Vinci (1452–1519), born in a small town west of Florence (his name means 'Leonard from Vinci'), stands apart. Painter, sculptor, architect, scientist and engineer,

Leonardo brought to all fields of knowledge and art an original touch, often opening up whole new branches of thought. In the thousands of pages of notes that he left behind, he repeatedly extols the virtue of sight and observation. Paying little heed to received wisdoms, whether Christian or classical, Leonardo barrelled along with unquenchable curiosity. His learning was all-embracing and in Leonardo we have the model of the 'Renaissance man'.

To Leonardo, painting was the noblest art and much of it he did far from home (he spent 20 years in Milan alone). There were probably good reasons for this. These were tormented times for Florence. The rapid decay of Medici power after the death in 1492 of Lorenzo de' Medici brought a fleeting occupation by the French and the short-lived theocracy of the Dominican firebrand Savonarola (see p55). Leonardo did get a commission in quieter times between the demise of Savonarola and the return of the Medici in 1512. He and Michelangelo were each asked to provide battle scenes for the Palazzo Vecchio. What a combination! Events overtook them, however, and the work barely got off the ground.

Still, a few of the grand master's works can be seen in Florence. His *Annunciazione* (Annunciation), in the Uffizi (p81), reveals his concern with light and shadow. His techniques were quite different from those of his contemporaries. His unfinished *Adorazione dei Magi* (Adoration of the Magi), also in the Uffizi, reveals how he first applied a dark wash to the surface, from which he could then extract his figures and shed light upon them. Among his most beguiling portraits are the *Mona Lisa* and *Madonna col Bambino e Sant'Anna* (Madonna with Child and St Anna), both now in the Louvre in Paris.

THE FIERY FLORENTINE

While Leonardo was in Milan, Michelangelo Buonarroti (1475–1564) was asserting himself as a rival painter, albeit of a very different ilk, and first and foremost as a sculptor. It was in this capacity that he left his greatest gifts to the city. As a young lad he got the luckiest break in his life when he came to the attention of Lorenzo de' Medici, who had a keen eye for talent and the patience to deal with artistic temperaments.

Michelangelo was a testy individual and, early on in life, got what was coming to him when he made some acidic remarks about a drawing by the sculptor Pietro Torrigiani one day in the Cappella Brancacci. Torrigiani thumped the smart-alecky Michelangelo, and left him with a *very* broken nose. After a stint in Rome, where he carved the remarkable *Pietà*, Michelangelo returned to Florence in 1501 to carry out one of his most striking commissions ever, the colossal statue of *David* (p95). By now, Michelangelo had long established himself as the champion of full nudity. The body, he argued, was a divine creation and its beauty without peer. Only three years before, under the greatest prude of recent Florentine history, the monk-dictator Savonarola (whose rantings had convinced Fra Bartolommeo (see the next section, From High Renaissance to Mannerism) to destroy all his studies of the nude in a bonfire of the vanities), such a work would have been unthinkable.

In 1516, after another stint in Rome, Michelangelo was back. With a Medici as Pope (Leo X) and the family back in the saddle in Florence, it is easy to imagine the artists of the day toing and froing between the Arno and the Tiber.

Among Michelangelo's last great works, not quite completed, are the statues in the Medicis' Sagrestia Nuova (New Sacristy) of San Lorenzo (p93). That so many of his works were left unfinished is indicative perhaps of the temperament of an artist incapable of satisfaction with his own work. The *Pietà* he began to work on for his own tomb so disappointed him that in a fit of temper he took to it with a hammer. It was later cobbled back together and stands in the Museo dell'Opera del Duomo (p77).

In contrast to Leonardo's smoky, veiled images, Michelangelo demonstrated a searing clarity of line in painting. His greatest project was the ceiling of the Sistine Chapel in Rome. In Florence, the *Tondo Doni* (depicting the Holy Family), in the Uffizi provides stunning insight into his craft.

Always a difficult character in life, this lover of the human (especially male) body was, by all accounts, little fussed by personal hygiene. They say he rarely bothered to wash and that, when he died, his clothes had to be prised from his crud-encrusted corpse.

FROM HIGH RENAISSANCE TO MANNERISM

Lesser artists were at work around the turn of the century in Florence, not to mention outsiders like Raphael who stopped in Florence for a while before heading off to pursue their careers elsewhere.

Among the Florentines, Fra Bartolommeo (1472–1517) stands out for such paintings as the *Apparizione della Vergine a San Bernardo* (called Vision of St Bernard in English), now in the Galleria dell'Accademia (p95). A follower of Savonarola, Fra Bartolommeo's art is clearly devotional, with virtually all incidental detail eliminated in favour of the central subject. Piero di Cosimo (c 1462–1521), on the other hand, was interested in nature and mythology. Several of his works can be seen in the Palazzo Pitti.

Michelangelo's almost tormented search for new, more emotionally satisfying ways of representing beauty led him to play around with the classical rules that in part lay behind the Renaissance. In this he is often said to have been one of the earliest exponents of the post-Renaissance style known as mannerism.

Andrea del Sarto (1486–1530) remained essentially true to the values of High Renaissance painting, turning out works with grace and dignity but none of the tumultuous conflict that would be associated with the likes of Jacopo Pontormo (1494–1556), his student. An initial comparison of frescoes by the two artists in the atrium of the Chiesa di SS Annunziata (p95) is enough to identify the differences. In Pontormo's *Visitazione* (Visitation) his figures seem furtive or preoccupied, as indeed they do in his frescoes in the Chiesa di Santa Felicita. It is this sense of movement that breaks the classical bounds set by the Renaissance.

Il Rosso Fiorentino ('the Florentine Redhead'; 1495–1540) also worked on the SS Annunziata frescoes before heading to Rome. In his works one detects a similarly fretful note, although his style is different from Pontormo's. The flashes of light and dark create an unreal effect in his characters.

A student of Pontormo, Il Bronzino (1503–72) began the move away from mannerism. Employed by the Medici family, his approach lacked the disquiet evident in his tutor's work. Rather he fixes images in a static fashion, reflecting perhaps his patrons' desire to convey the sureness of their sovereignty, however spurious. His greatest achievement was Eleonora de Toledo's chapel in the Palazzo Vecchio (p86).

The works of Giorgio Vasari (1511–74) and his students litter Florence, some better than others. His particular boast seems to have been speed – with an army of helpers he was able to plough through commissions for frescoes and paintings with great alacrity, if not always with equal aplomb. He is most important in the history of Italian art as the author of *Lives of the Artists*, a rich compendium of fact and fiction about Italian artists until his own day. Vasari and company were largely responsible for the decoration of the Palazzo Vecchio (p86). Vasari was a lucky fellow. As much a bureaucrat as an artist, he rose quickly through the ranks under Duke Cosimo de' Medici, who after the fall of yet another short-lived Florentine republic in 1530, brought a hitherto unknown dynastic stability and relative quiet to Florence. And Cosimo saw art and architecture as a key instrument of family propaganda.

Not only Vasari and his minions were at work. Sculptors were increasingly called on to decorate ducal Florence's public places. The master goldsmith, Benvenuto Cellini (1500–71), was also a dab hand at sculpture, turning out the bronze *Perseo e Medusa* (Perseus and Medusa), which stands in the Loggia della Signoria (p84). Bartolommeo Ammannati (1511–92) is best known for the *Fontana del Nettuno* (Neptune Fountain) in Piazza della Signoria, which has met more often than not with disapproval. Michelangelo, for one, thought Ammannati had ruined a perfectly good block of marble. Giambologna (Jean de Boulogne; 1529–1608), a Flemish sculptor who arrived in Florence around 1550 dominated the Florentine scene in the latter half of the 16th century. Some 20 years after the autocratic Cosimo's death, in 1594, his successors had Giambologna raise the grand equestrian statue of Cosimo in Piazza della Signoria (p79), where it still stands triumphant today. His is considered an early herald of the turbulent baroque style, all curves and movement and best expressed in his *Ratto della Sabina* (Rape of the Sabine Woman) in the Loggia della Signoria (p84).

BAROQUE

Cosimo's autocratic dynasty proved a lasting affair and ushered in a long period of relative tranquillity in Florence. With it came artistic mediocrity, at least compared with the previous two centuries. Perhaps mayhem was an essential ingredient for flourishing creativity. As the 17th century wore on, flocks of artists continued to work in Florence, but few of great note. Giovanni da San Giovanni (1592–1636) was the leading light of the first half of the century, and some of his frescoes remain in the Palazzo Pitti.

The arrival of artists from out of town, such as Pietro da Cortona (1596–1669) and the Neapolitan Luca Giordano (1632–1705), brought the winds of baroque taste. Baroque artists used a riot of colour and movement, leaving any semblance of reality behind. Angels and chariots charge at you from the heavens in a whirlwind of exaggerated movement. One of Florence's senior court sculptors, Giovanni Battista Foggini (1652–1725), immersed himself in the baroque circles of Rome, where the style became particularly florid, and when he returned put his new-found knowledge to use in reliefs and other decoration in several churches, notably the Basilica di Santa Maria del Carmine (p104).

THE MACCHIAIOLI

By the middle of the 19th century, Florentine art was stuck in a rut, as the slumbering capital of the Grand Duchy of Tuscany had long ceased to be a centre of any great importance. Painters produced soulless, academic pieces that, after the excitement of the 1848 Europewide revolts, seemed inadequate. Venetian landscape painters began to have an influence, and then in 1855 several Florentines visited Paris for the Universal Exposition. They came back with news of the developments that were taking place in French naturalist painting that proved a precursor to impressionism.

In Florence anti-academic artists congregated in the Caffè Michelangelo and declared that painting real-life scenes was the only way forward. This movement, which lasted until the late 1860s, was known as the Macchiaioli (which could be translated as the 'stainers' or 'blotchers') because of a disparaging newspaper article written in 1862 about their technique of splotching various colours onto the canvas to explore effects of tone before proceeding. They abandoned the religious and historical themes to which painting, no matter how innovative in style, had largely been bound for centuries. Then they dropped chiaroscuro effects in favour of playful use of colour plus light or colour plus shade or both.

As the movement peaked, Florence joined the newly created Italian kingdom and briefly became its capital before it was moved to Rome in 1870. This fleeting moment was in many respects Florence's last brush with political or artistic significance.

Telemaco Signorini (1835–1901), born in Via de' Macci, moved around Europe and dabbled in such things as journalism, poetry and painting. Despite his restlessness, he remained true to his hometown. His work followed two thematic lines, Florentine life and warm Tuscan landscapes, although he painted wherever he travelled.

Although the hub of their activity was Florence, many of the Macchiaioli came from all over Italy. They included Livorno-born Giovanni Fattori (1825–1908), Neapolitan Giuseppe Abbati (1836–68) and the Emilian painter Silvestro Lega (1826–95). Many (including Signorini) fought in the conflicts leading to the unification of Italy. You can see works by various of these artists in the Galleria d'Arte Moderna in Palazzo Pitti (p108).

THE PRESENT DAY

Florence's decline as a centre of artistic ferment seems to have been sealed during the 20th century. Futurism did not have the impact here that it did elsewhere, although that is not to say that the conservative and introspective Florence of the day was inured to the Futurists' battle cry: 'We don't care a fig about the past!' Futurism preached an all-embracing faith in science, technology and the future. At their more extreme they declared that museums, libraries, all repositories of past splendour, should be destroyed to make way for the brave new world. In retrospect, flowering as it did before WWI, the movement was touchingly innocent. Although some of the big names of the movement, like Giacomo Balla exhibited in Florence, Futurism failed to really ignite the Florentine scene. The Novecento (the '20th Century') movement, which preached a return to order in the wake of various avant-garde tendencies, also bore precious little fruit in Florence.

At the turn of the century, painter Primo Conti (1900–88) came into the world. In his long Florentine career (by 1941 he was professor of painting at the Accademia di Firenze), he remained faithful to his hometown, experimenting with all sorts of styles and winding up in a sprawling studio-cum-house in Fiesole. The house is now open as a gallery of his art (p113).

After WWII, the Arte Oggi (Art Today) movement of so-called dissident artists in Florence championed a 'classical abstractism', but by and large the 20th century art scene overlooked Florence. This can be partially explained by the fact that, regardless of its history, Florence is little more than a middle-class provincial capital, and its conservatism becomes all the more prominent by the enormity of its cultural golden age – the Renaissance.

Perhaps even more so than with painting, there hasn't been a substantial modern movement in Florentine sculpture. The awe-inspiring legacy of the great masters has proved too great a burden for sculptors to shake off and experiment with new styles. This is not to say activity ground to a complete halt. The Pescia-born Libero Andreotti (1875–1933) and the tormented Florentine Evaristo Boncinelli (1883–1946) were among the prominent figures in the first half of the century, while Pistoia-born Marino Marini (p90; 1901–80) was doubtless the torchbearer of 20th-century Tuscan sculpture. You can admire his work in the museum dedicated to him in Florence.

Why Fix it if it Ain't Broke?

The tragic events of 4 November 1966 would have been enough to convince an atheist of the existence of a wrathful god. As enormous high tides inundated the extraordinary lagoon city of Venice to the north, torrential rain swelled the banks of the Arno to create the worst flooding Florence had known in centuries. Both cities, two of the world's greatest treasure chests of human creativity, lay covered in grime and mud. The damage to art and buildings was incalculable. Many fine works were destroyed, countless more seriously damaged.

Some good came of the extraordinary twin disaster. As funds and aid poured in from Rome and abroad in the following years, Florence and Venice became world leaders in the business of art restoration. A whole new science was created and methods revolutionised. The fruits of the enormous labour in those two cities have since been applied to countless other works in need of repair elsewhere. Students from around the globe come to Florence to learn the trade, many to the Istituto Specializzato per il Restauro, established in 1975 in the premises of the centuries-old Opificio delle Pietre Dure (p98).

Few deny the value of restoring badly damaged paintings and statuary. In the 19th century in particular fairly rough old jobs were often done to reinject life into fading paintings or grimy statues, often doing more harm than good. All that has changed but has the pendulum swung too far the other way? Controversy over the ethics of restoration will doubtless rage into eternity – some will argue that artworks should be left alone, even if that means allowing their deterioration, rather than artificially perking them up. Some believe, for example, that the cenacolo (the Last Supper) by Leonardo da Vinci in Milan bears little or no resemblance to the original and is therefore a travesty.

In mid-2003 an enormous storm in a teacup erupted. Michelangelo's David, we were told, was in need of a good scrub down. After 10 years of studying in minute detail the makeup and state of the marble, the main restorers could not, however, agree on how to proceed and very publicly fell out. One wanted to wash the dirty marble pores with wet poultices, the other thought this invasive and advocated a light brushing. Artists from around the world signed a petition demanding that nothing be done until further assessment had been carried out! In the end, the liquid bath theory prevailed and work began in September.

The niceties of modern restoration do provoke a chuckle. To think that in the 19th century a good old-fashioned acid bath was considered in order for David (he survived that assault)! Or that for several centuries earlier the statue had cheerfully withstood the elements and the occasional riot in Piazza della Signoria. Few (if any) visitors who behold the statue today are struck by David's dirtiness – they are too mesmerised by his beauty. And let's face it, his creator Michelangelo wasn't too keen on baths either!

LITERATURE

THE MASTER

Long after the fall of Rome, Latin remained the language of learned discourse and writing throughout much of Europe. The elevation of local tongues to literary status was a long and weary process, and the case of Italian was no exception.

In the mid-13th century, Tuscan poets began experimenting with verse and song in the local tongue, inspired by the troubadours of Provence. But all the poetry, song, didactic and religious literature of 13th-century writers couldn't compare to the genius of the Florentine Dante Alighieri (1265–1321). Dante wrote on many subjects and often in Latin, but when he composed *La Divina Commedia* (The Divine Comedy) in the 'vulgar' tongue of his countrymen, he was inspired. The work is split into three parts: Hell, Purgatory and Heaven, and the first part (where the language is most venemous in regards to a man exiled from his hometown) is generally seen as the most gripping. The text is best read in the original language and dense with references to contemporary events and personalities. The modern reader needs a well annotated edition, whether in Italian or English.

The gloomy circles of Dante's hell do not serve merely to remind his readers of the wages of sin. Far more interestingly, they become an uneasy resting place for a parade of characters, many of them his contemporaries, whom he judged worthy of an uncomfortable time in the next life.

Dante's extraordinary capacity to construct and tell stories within stories would have ensured him a place in the pantheon of scribblers regardless of his language of delivery. But Dante's decision to write in his Tuscan dialect was a literary coup. In doing so he catapulted Italian, or at least a version of it, to the literary stage. Scholars have been enthusing ever since that Italian was 'born' with Dante's *La Divina Commedia*.

Dante died in exile in Ravenna. As keen as Florence's rulers had been to see him ago, they have ever since wanted to have his ashes back. The city that took him in has rightly stood fast and refused.

PETRARCH & BOCCACCIO

Dante does not stand alone, and two Tuscan successors form with him the literary triumvirate that laid down the course for the development of a rich Italian literature.

Petrarch (Francesco Petrarca; 1304–74), born in Arezzo to Florentine exiles, wrote more in Latin than in Italian. *Il Canzoniere* (The Canzoniere) is the result of his finest poetry. Although the core subject is the unrequited love for a girl called Laura, the breadth of human grief and joy is treated with a lyric quality. So striking was his clear, passionate verse, filtered through his knowledge of the classics, that a phenomenon emerged known as *petrarchismo* – the desire of writers within and beyond Italy to emulate him.

Contemporary and friend of Petrarch was the Florentine (possibly born in Certaldo) Giovanni Boccaccio (1313–75). His masterpiece was *Il Decameron* (The Decameron), written in the years following the plague of 1348, which he survived in Florence. His 10 lusty characters, seven women and three men who have fled to a country retreat to avoid the plague in Florence, each recount a story in which a various personalities, events and symbolism are explored. It is akin to Chaucer's *The Canterbury Tales*.

THE RENAISSANCE

These three would have made a hard act for anyone to follow, and while the visual arts knew a seemingly boundless creative explosion in the Renaissance, Florence could not continue to produce writers of the same stature. That said, it was writers and thinkers who provided the intellectual roots for the artistic rebirth.

Top Five Books

- *Buio (Darkness)* Dacia Maraini
- *Il Principe (The Prince)* Niccolò Machiavelli
- *La Divina Commedia (The Divine Comedy)* Dante Alighieri
- *L'Avventure di Pinocchio* Carlo Lorenzini
- *Una Storia Italiana* Vasco Pratolini

Machiavelli's Manoeuvres

Born in 1469 into a poor branch of what had been one of Florence's leading families, Niccolò Machiavelli got off to a bad start. His father was a small-time lawyer whose practice had been all but strangled by the city authorities as he was a debtor. Young Niccolò's prospects were not sparkling.

Somehow he managed to swing a post in the city's second chancery at the age of 29, and so embarked on a colourful career as a Florentine public servant. His tasks covered a range of internal dealings in Florence and some aspects of foreign affairs and defence. Our man must have shown early promise, as by 1500 he was in France on his first diplomatic mission.

Impressed by the martial success of Italian-born Cesare Borgia and the centralised state of France, Machiavelli came to the conclusion that Florence needed a standing army. The city, like many others in Italy, had a habit of employing mercenaries to fight its wars. But mercenaries had few reasons to fight and die for anyone. They took their pay and as often as not did their level best to avoid mortal combat.

Machiavelli managed to convince his rulers of the advantages of an army raised to defend hearth and home and so in 1506 formed a conscript militia. In 1509 he got to try it out on the rebellious city of Pisa, whose fall was largely attributed to the troops led by the wily statesman. He was back there two years later to dismantle a French-supported schismatic council (in retaliation to anti-French sentiment by the papacy).

Florence, however, was not Rome's flavour of the month and troops from the Holy See and its allies marched on the city. Machiavelli was now defending not only his hearth but his future – to no avail.

The return of the Medici family to power was a blow for Machiavelli, who was promptly removed from all posts. Suspected of plotting against the Medici, he was even thrown into the dungeon in 1513 and tortured. He maintained his innocence and was freed, but reduced to penury as he retired to his little property outside Florence.

It was in these years that he produced his greatest writing. *Il Principe* (The Prince) is his classic treatise on the nature of power and its administration. In it he developed his theories not only on politics and power but on history and human behaviour (Voltaire later said that the rational telling of history began with Machiavelli).

With time, his views have taken on a negative connotation. All he advocated were realism, common sense and decisiveness. The term Machiavellian has a tone of sneakiness. But the unemployed public servant argued simply that, if honesty and sincerity were likely to endanger a prince and his state, then the prince had an obligation to be street-smart and flexible with the truth. A ruler owes it to himself and his subjects to be firm in war, cunning in diplomacy and just to his people. It is these sorts of qualities he advocates. He exemplifies Cesare Borgia, son of Pope Alexander VI and scourge of central Italy. Machiavelli didn't like Borgia, but he recognised that when a leader had ambitions he had to have the conviction to pursue them. He admired this single-minded focus on the pursuit of power. The aims of any given individual, such as Borgia, were quite another matter.

Published after his death, his little manual came to be read in the halls of power throughout Europe. They say Richelieu, among others, wholly concurred with Machiavelli's conclusions.

Machiavelli regained office but never as solidly as before. After the fall of the Medici he again fell from grace and died in 1527 frustrated and, as in his youth, on the brink of poverty.

Nurtured by such open-minded rulers as Lorenzo de' Medici, the so-called humanists, spurred on by their rediscovery of the classics, thirsted for knowledge and new realms of learning. Their goal was the attainment of *humanitas*, by which they meant knowing to combine knowledge and wisdom with action. The ideal humanist was compassionate and merciful, but also strong, eloquent and honourable. Action without knowledge and wisdom was barbaric, but the sedentary accumulation of knowledge barren.

The best known literary figure to emerge from this environment was Niccolò Machiavelli (1469–1527), celebrated for his treatise on the nature of power and politics, *Il Principe* (The Prince; see the boxed text above). But he was a prolific writer in many fields. His *Mandragola* is a lively piece of comic theatre and a virtuoso example of Italian literature, considered by many the best of the 16th century.

PINOCCHIO

It was not until the 19th century that a local writer would become a household name. Carlo Lorenzini (1826–90), better known to Italians by his pseudonym of Carlo Collodi, created

L'Avventure di Pinocchio (The Adventures of Pinocchio). Outside Italy, Pinocchio is known more in his saccharine Walt Disney guise, but in Italy this bestseller has been a bedrock source of amusement and instruction for children and adults for generations. Get a hold of the bilingual edition translated by Nicholas J. Perella and published by the University of California Press.

THE MUSSOLINI YEARS

In the 1920s and '30s Florence bubbled with activity as a series of literary magazines flourished, at least for a while, in spite of the Fascist regime. Magazines like *Solaria*, which lasted from 1926 to 1934, its successor *Letteratura* (which began circulating in 1937) and *Il Frontespizio* (from 1929 to 1940) gave writers from across Italy a platform from which to launch and discuss their work. Most of the magazines, including Vasco Pratolini's short-lived *Campo di Marte*, fell prey sooner or later to censorship. That some lasted as long as they did is remarkable.

MODERN TIMES

Standing tall among a handful of notable Florentine writers since WWI is Vasco Pratolini (1913–91), son of a manual labourer and self-taught writer who dabbled successfully in theatre and cinema as well as the novel and poetry. Among his most enduring works is the trilogy *Una Storia Italiana* (An Italian Story), whose first part, *Metello*, set off a heated debate in Italian literary circles. Those who liked it saw in the novel a mature departure from neorealism to a more robust realism. Pratolini's detractors regarded him still caught in a rigid ideological trap. The trilogy follows the lives of working- and middle-class Florentines, through whom Pratolini analyses political, social and emotional issues. The narrative is interlaced with stories of people's lives told with verve and colour.

One of the most prolific and respected women writing today is the Rome-based Florentine Dacia Maraini (b 1936), columnist and outstanding feminist novelist, poet and playwright. Author of 10 novels and several collections of stories, she confronts some tough subjects. One of her most striking recent works, *Buio* (Darkness; 1999), is a collection of 12 stories of children neglected or abused. Drawn from crime reports, she has created hard-hitting narratives. Holding it all together is the central character, a woman detective by the name of Adele Sòfia, who also appeared in an earlier novel, *Voci* (Voices). Her *La Nave per Kobe* (2002), based on her mother's diaries, recounts her family's time in a concentration camp for anti-fascists in Japan (she was an infant at the time).

On an altogether lighter note are the pop detective novels set in Florence by Magdalen Nabb, such as *The Marshall and The Murderer* and *Death in Autumn*. Nabb is to Florence what Donna Leon is to Venice.

MUSIC

Despite its literary achievements and flourish in fine arts, Florence has not made such illustrious contributions to the music world.

The Rome-born composer Jacopo Peri (1561–1633) moved to Florence in 1588 to serve the Medici court. He and Florentine writer Ottavio Rinuccini (1562–1621) are credited with having created the first opera in the modern sense, *Dafne*, in 1598. They and Giulio Caccini (1550–1618) also wrote *Euridice* a couple of years later. It is the oldest opera for which the complete score still exists. All three were part of a Florentine group of intellectuals known as the Camerata, which worked to revive and develop ancient Greek musical traditions in theatre.

Florence's next musical contribution was a key development, although it came at the hands of a Paduan resident on the Arno. In 1711 Bartolomeo Cristofori (1655–1731) invented the pianoforte.

Giovanni Battista Lulli (1632–87) was born in Florence. The name may not ring too many bells until we add that he moved to France where he would dominate the musical life of the court of Louis XIV as Jean-Baptiste Lully. With Molière he created new dramatic forms such as the comedy-ballet. Among his operatic works were *Alceste* and *Armide*. He also gave instrumental suites their definitive form.

Another Florentine export to Paris was the composer Luigi Cherubini (1760–1842), who somehow managed the tricky feat of keeping his head attached to his torso through the French Revolution, the Napoleonic era and the Restoration.

Top Five CDs

- *Lorenzo 1990–1995 Raccolta* Jovanotti (1996)
- *Lully: Les Divertissements de Versailles (Grandes Scènes Lyriques)* Giovanni Battista Lulli (Jean-Baptiste Lully; 2002)
- *Mondi Sommersi* Litfiba (1997)
- *Prima di Partire* Irene Grandi (2003)
- *Vecchia Toscana* Riccardo Marasco (1985)

MUSIC IN FLORENCE TODAY

The undisputed king of Tuscan folk music (yes, there is such a thing) is Riccardo Marasco, who since the 1960s has tracked down traditional material, written his own and maintained a witty and wide-ranging repertory of Tuscan music alive.

On a quite different note, one of Italy's leading rock bands, Litfiba, was originally a Florentine product, although since they started in the early 1980s they have seen a procession of changing band members – only one, Ghigo Renzulli, has remained throughout. Among their classic albums is *Mondi Sommersi* (1997), with the original lead singer, Piero Pelù, who has since embarked on a solo career. They still play live and in recent years seem to have recovered some of the original rocky oomph of the 1990s.

Florence-born Marco Masini emerged on the scene in the late 1980s with a classic of Italian pop, *Si Può Dare di Più*, actually sung by bigger stars at the time, and *Perchè lo Fai?*, which won him third place at the 1991 San Remo Song Festival. By the late 1990s he had become a fixture on the Italian stage and was touring Europe regularly.

Irene Grandi emerged from the local Florentine band scene in the early 1990s and her first solo album, *Irene Grandi* (1994), with songs by Eros Ramazzotti and rap icon Jovanotti, was a turning point. She has since toured and been associated with some of the big names of the Italian music world, such as Pino Daniele and evergreen rocker Vasco Rossi, who has written several of her songs. Her latest album, *Prima di Partire*, consists of original songs with leaving and travel as central themes.

Lorenzo Cherubini 'Jovanotti', born in Rome of Tuscan parents (from Arezzo), started his career as a DJ in Cortona and then Rome. By the early 1990s his socially critical lyrics made him the country's rap sensation. At the San Remo Song Festival in 2000, he stirred the pot by singing his 'Cancel the debt' song – cancelling of Third World debt is just one of his favourite causes.

Florence itself has all sorts of bands playing various pubs and bars around town. They include Paolo Amulfi band, which covers classic rock, heavy metal groups like Holy Sinner and such oddities as Sir Randha, a Jamaican-style ska band. One of the big local names of ragamuffin and reggae since the late 1980s is Il Generale. His third album, *In Transito…Briciole del Generale*, is one of the best. See p142 in the Entertainment chapter for tips on bars and venues for plugging into the local live scene.

CINEMA

The Italian cinema has known periods of enormous productivity and contributed some of Europe's proudest gems on film. Most people think of the postwar period of neorealism as the apogee of Italian film-making, and there is no doubting the richness of the output at that time. It didn't end there though, and Italy has continued to produce good directors ever since.

Florence, however, has had remarkably little impact on the cinematic world – used occasionally as a set and producing only rare directing or acting talent. Greatness might have come Florence's way. Filoteo Alberini had created his *kinotegrafo* in 1895, a year before the Lumière brothers patented their cinématographe in Paris. No-one in Florence was interested and Alberini moved to Rome, where he created the Cines, a production studio which would grow to command the stage in the early years of Italian cinema.

A second chance came in the 1920s when a Florentine gent by the name of Giovanni Montalbano set up studios in Rifredi to produce great historical blockbusters, which never eventuated.

An early Florentine film-maker of note was Gianni Franciolini (1910–60). After spending 10 years in France learning journalism and then film, Franciolini returned to Italy in 1940, from which time he turned out a film almost every year until his death. An early flick, *Fari Nella Nebbia* (Headlights in the Mist; 1941) shows the French influence on his ideas, but also presages the fecund period of Italian film-making that lay just around the corner – neorealism.

The biggest name to come out of Florence is Franco Zeffirelli (b 1923). His varied career took him from radio and theatre to opera productions and occasional stints as aide to Luchino Visconti on several films. His film-directing days began in earnest in the late 1970s. Some may remember his TV blockbuster *Jesus of Nazareth* (1977). Many of his productions have been non-Italian. A couple of his more interesting ones were *Young Toscanini* (1988) and *Hamlet* (1990), a British-US co-production. He visited his hometown to film *Tea with Mussolini*, starring Maggie Smith (1999).

In the genre of TV blockbusters, Franco Rossi (1919-2000) started directing films in the 1950s but moved increasingly to TV. His Italian TV films included *Il Giovane Garibaldi* (The Young Garibaldi; 1973) and *Quo Vadis?* (1984).

Neri Parenti (b 1950) started directing in 1979. Since 1980 he has been kept busy directing the comedian Paolo Villaggio in a seemingly endless stream of films starring Fantozzi, Villaggio's best-known comic character. Fantozzi is a sort of thinking man's cross between Mr Bean and Benny Hill.

Two of Italy's success stories at the moment are Tuscan if not Florentine. Light-hearted comedy is a forte of Leonardo Pieraccioni (b 1965), who directs and acts in his productions. *Il Ciclone* (The Cyclone; 1996), about the effects of the arrival of a small flamenco troupe on the lads of a small Tuscan town, was a big hit. *Il Principe e Il Pirata* (The Prince and the Pirate; 2001) has him starring as a timid Florentine school teacher who discovers at his father's funeral that his father isn't dead, just trying to avoid debts. A whole can of worms opens up in the protagonist's hitherto tranquil life.

Long established as one of Italy's favourite comedy actors, Roberto Benigni (b 1952) won three Oscars in 1999, including Best Actor, an honour rarely bestowed by Hollywood upon anyone but its own, for his *La Vita è Bella* (Life is Beautiful; 1998). The film, which he directed and starred in, is the story of an Italian Jewish family that ends up in a concentration camp, where the father tries to hide its horrors from his son by pretending it's all a game.

From the sublime to the plain scary, *Hannibal* (2001) moves the spine-tingling story of the cannibal to Florence where, since *Silence of the Lambs*, Dr Lecter has been in reclusive retirement…up to a point. Ridley Scott directed this sequel, which perhaps predictably wasn't quite up to the original.

Top Five Films

- *A Room With a View* (1986) James Ivory
- *Hannibal* (2001) Ridley Scott
- *La Vita è Bella* (*Life is Beautiful*; 2001) Roberto Benigni
- *Tea With Mussolini* (1999) Franco Zeffirelli
- *Young Toscanini* (1988) Franco Zeffirelli

THEATRE & DANCE

Florence attracts plenty of theatre and dance performances, ranging from the classics at the Teatro Verdi to more avant-garde and experimental stuff.

But the city has not had a starring role in the history of Italian theatre. True, the Florentine Giovanni Battista Fagiuoli (1660–1742) was among those who made the first tentative steps away from the *commedia dell'arte* (popular comedy), which had become something of a fixture in the Italian repertoire since the early 16th century. But it would fall to the Venetian Carlo Goldoni to work a true revolution in the theatre.

Nowadays major theatre companies from around the country, and occasionally international ones, bring high-quality performances to Florence. Local companies are a little thin on the ground. The busiest is Teatro della Limonaia (p152), which performs a lively mix of international contemporary pieces and original home-grown productions. A handful of other tiny companies struggle along, such as Kaspar Hauser, which stages the occasional musical but makes its daily bread by touring Tuscany with its version of that old fave, *The Rocky Horror Picture Show*.

The Florence Dance Festival (p10) attracts hundreds of modern dance companies from around the world to the Arno. Local dance groups, such as the Florence Dance Cultural Center and the Centro Danza Company Blu, occasionally stage contemporary pieces around town, financed by year-round courses and workshops (sometimes run by international figures) for local dance hopefuls.

Food & Drink

Food & Drink

For some, arrival in Tuscany means reaching the pearly gates of food heaven. For others, Tuscan cuisine is rather overrated.

The truth lies somewhere between these two extremes. As with many of the Mediterranean cuisines, Tuscan cookery is essentially the result of poverty. Simple, wholesome ingredients have traditionally been thrown together to produce healthy but hardly fascinating meals. Most common folk had to make do with limited ingredients. Recipes have been refined and enriched, particularly with other dishes and combinations from more far-flung parts of Italy. This region relies heavily on the quality and freshness of the ingredients, and the liberal use of herbs such as basil, thyme, parsley and rosemary.

HISTORY & CULTURE

The Tuscan traditions of today were born of the hardship and poverty of the past. The extraordinary excesses we read about of the tables of medieval barons or, later, of the Medici and their pals were not habits passed down to us through the ages. While the bulk of the population could rarely afford meat, Florence's movers and shakers gorged themselves on anything from beef to pheasant, dressed in all sorts of weird and wonderful sauces (sometimes to disguise a rancidness hard to avoid in the days without refrigerators).

Still, even without such medieval extravagance, the modern diner in Florence has a rich choice, from simple hearty local dishes through Italian regional specialities and fine dining options that often have an international air.

Dining at Da Il Latini in the Santa Maria Novella area (p130)

In Tuscany, as elsewhere in Italy, tradition still controls much of what the cook does. They can tweak and fiddle (perhaps best exemplified in a growing boldness in the preparation of pasta sauces) but generally must remain faithful to the old ways. There are those in Tuscany (and again, throughout the country) who can solemnly state exactly what kind of sauce will go with which kind of pasta – any deviation from the rules is met with scorn. Undoubtedly many of these 'rules' are sound, but at times they are merely oppressive and unimaginative.

Pasta does not occupy a place of honour in traditional Tuscan menus. Some believe it was the Arabs who introduced pasta to Sicily in the early Middle Ages and, in medieval times, it was imported from southern Italy to this region. Even today pasta dishes are not considered, strictly speaking, to be a local product.

With a few extra euros, it is possible to dine well in Florence without doing undue harm to your savings account. What you need to be especially wary of are the phalanxes of tourist rip-off restaurants that are located in the city centre and near the main tourist sights.

It is unlikely visitors will tire of Tuscan cuisine and other Italian dishes on offer in Florence. Add to your meal some of the finest wines produced in the country and you will want to come with your taste buds fully braced for action.

HOW FLORENTINES EAT

Breakfast in Florence and throughout Italy is no more than a cappuccino and pastry taken on the hop at a bar on the way to work. Lunch was, and often still is, the main meal of the day, while dinner used to be a relatively light affair. Modern work habits have changed this slightly, although the long lunch is still common.

A full Italian meal can seem a little overwhelming with starter, first course (often pasta), main (with optional vegetable side order) and dessert. Don't feel embarrassed if you can't face such an onslaught (either at lunch or dinner). Even many locals, perhaps with an eye on the waistline, now tend to skip one or more courses.

The first one to ditch are the antipasti (starters), which kill appetite and distract your attention from the mains. It is of course much more fun to have a first and main dish, as traditionally everyone once did, but you can opt for one over the other.

STAPLES & SPECIALITIES

In the dark years of the barbarian invasions of what was left of the Roman Empire, times became difficult for many Tuscans. Salt was scarce and *pane sciocco* (unsalted bread) became the basis of nutrition. Unsalted bread has remained a feature of local cooking ever since.

Locals have been cultivating the olive since Etruscan times. Harvest time is around late November, and certainly not later than the Festa di Santa Lucia (13 December). In Tuscany olives are still largely harvested by hand and sent to presses. After an initial crushing, the resulting mass is squeezed. Some of the best extra virgin olive oil, with its alluring colour, looks good enough to drink.

The main Tuscan cheese is *pecorino*, made with ewe's milk. It can be eaten fresh or after up to a year's maturing, when it has more tang.

ANTIPASTI

You have the option of starting a meal with a 'pre-meal'. The classic antipasto in Tuscany is crostini, lightly grilled slices of unsalted bread traditionally covered in a chicken-liver pâté. Other toppings have become equally popular – the diced tomato with herbs, onion and garlic is a popular version indistinguishable from the Pugliese bruschetta.

The other classic is *fettunta*, basically a slab of toasted bread rubbed with garlic and dipped in olive oil.

Another favourite, *prosciutto e melone* (cured ham and melon), is known well beyond the confines of Tuscany. Other cured meats and sausages are also popular.

PRIMI PIATTI

By the 14th century the use of pasta had definitely spread to Florence, but without displacing local favourites. A light summer dish is *panzanella*, basically a cold mixed salad with breadcrumbs. Tomato, cucumber, red onions and lettuce are tossed into a bowl with stale bread that has been soaked and broken up. This mixture is then combined with oil, vinegar and basil and refrigerated.

Hold the Parmesan!

Many people seem to believe *parmigiano* (parmesan cheese) should be scattered over *all* pasta dishes, no matter what the sauce. Nothing could be further from the truth. You should never use it with any kind of seafood sauce, for the simple reason that the cheese kills the flavour instead of enhancing it! If your waiter doesn't offer you the cheese, 99 times out of 100 there will be a perfectly good reason why not.

The winter equivalent is *ribollita*, another example of making use of every last scrap. It's basically a vegetable stew with bread mixed in, it is a hearty dish for cold winter nights. *Pappa di pomodoro* is bread and tomato paste served hot.

Tuscan pasta specialities include *pappardelle sulla lepre* (ribbon pasta with hare), *pasta e ceci* (a pasta and bean broth) and *spaghetti allo scoglio* (spaghetti with seafood – basically a national dish). Ravioli and *tortelli*, both kinds of filled pasta, are also popular.

SECONDI PIATTI

In keeping with the simplicity for which local cuisine is known, meat and fish tend to be grilled. Meat eaters will want to try *bistecca alla fiorentina*, a generous slab of Florentine steak. Traditionally the meat used for this dish was only from bovines that were raised in the Val di Chiana, but nowadays the numbers of people wanting to enjoy the meal far outweighs supply.

Cuisines born of poverty find a use for everything. Animal innards become an integral part of the local diet. *Rognone*, a large plate of kidneys, is one favourite, although you might find it a little too rich. Tripe is particularly prized by some, and you can get it at *trippaio*, or roadside stands (in the Cascine for example). *Trippa alla fiorentina* (Florentine-style tripe) is prepared with a carrot, celery, tomato and onion mix. For true tripe fans, locals distinguish between various bits of the gut – one particularly popular part of veal tripe is known as *lampredotto*, just in case you are contemplating having some on a bread roll without knowing what it is. It is boiled and liberally sprinkled in black pepper or a vaguely hot sauce.

Tuscany is hunting territory and *cinghiale* (wild boar), along with other game meats, are served at many restaurants.

Main meals are accompanied by *contorni* (side dishes). Possible choices include *fagiolini alla fiorentina*, little beans prepared with tomatoes, fennel seeds, onion and garlic.

Top Five Tuscan Foodie Reads

- *The Complete Illustrated Book of Tuscan Cookery*, Elisabetta Piazzesi (2002) A prettily illustrated book filled with specifically Tuscan cuisine, which has been translated into several languages. You can find it in bookshops in Florence.
- *The Food of Italy*, Waverley Root (1992) An acknowledged classic, which covers Italian cuisine in general.
- *Ricette di Osterie di Firenze*, Slow Food Editore publications (1999) If you read Italian, this is a wonderful source of traditional Florentine recipes.
- *Tuscan Cookbook*, Stephanie Alexander and Maggie Beer (2001) A beautifully illustrated coffee-table tome.
- *Tuscan Food and Folklore*, Jeni Wright (1997) Another book more suited to the coffee table than the kitchen.

DOLCI

Apart from the classic *gelato* (Italian ice cream), you will find no shortage of house desserts.

Tiramisu, a rich mascarpone dessert, has become something of a worldwide favourite among lovers of Italian food. It is actually a Venetian speciality, but is not too hard to stumble across in Florence.

More in the Tuscan tradition are almond-based biscuits, such as Siena's *cantucci* or *biscottini di Prato*, best chomped while you sip sweet Vin Santo. Lighter but also using almonds are *brutti ma buoni* (literally 'ugly but good') pastries. *Schiacciata con l'uva* is a flat pastry covered in crushed red grapes and is available in the late autumn months after the grape harvest.

When trawling speciality food shops, search out *cassata fiorenza*, a light wafer biscuit stuffed with almond cream and covered in a thick layer of chocolate.

DRINKS
NONALCOHOLIC DRINKS
Coffee

The first-time visitor is likely to be confused by the many ways in which the locals consume their caffeine. As in other Latin countries, Italians take their coffee seriously. Consequently they also make it complicated! See boxed text, p127.

Tea

Italians don't drink a lot of *tè* (tea) and, if they do, generally only in the late afternoon, when they might take a cup with a few *pasticcini* (small cakes). You can order tea in bars, although it will usually arrive in the form of a cup of warm water with an accompanying tea bag. If this doesn't suit your taste, ask for the water *molto caldo* or *bollente* (boiling). Good-quality packaged teas, such as Twinings tea bags and leaves, as well as packaged herbal teas like camomile are often sold in grocery stores and some bars. You can find a wide range of herbal teas in an *erboristeria* (herbalist's shop).

Granita

A drink made of crushed ice with fresh lemon or other fruit juices, or with coffee topped with fresh whipped cream, *granita* is a Sicilian speciality but you'll see it in Florence in the summer months too.

Soft Drinks

The usual range of international soft drinks is available in Florence, though they tend to be expensive. There are some local versions too, along with the rather bitter, acquired taste of Chinotto.

Water

Tap water is safe but Italians prefer *acqua minerale* (mineral water). You will be asked in restaurants and bars whether you would prefer *frizzante/gasata* (sparkling water) or *naturale/ ferma* (still). If you want a glass of tap water, ask for *acqua del rubinetto*.

Caffè latte *with a frothy smile*

ALCOHOLIC DRINKS

Wine

Of course, *vino* (wine) is an essential accompaniment to any meal, and *digestivi* (liqueurs) are a popular way to end one. Italians are justifiably proud of their wines and it would be surprising for dinner-time conversation not to touch on the subject at least for a moment.

Prices are reasonable and you will rarely pay more than €5 to €15 for a quite drinkable bottle of wine. To be sure of quality, you need to look around the €25 mark. A nice ruby-red Brunello will be yours from about €35 to €45. An exceptional *riserva* (reserve) can cost €80 to €100.

In Florence you will often see wines from other Italian regions on sale, but only rarely from outside of Italy.

Since the 1960s, Italian wine has been graded according to four main classifications, which appear on their labels. *Vino da tavola* (table wine) indicates no specific classification; IGT *(indicazione geografica tipica)* means that the wine is typical of a certain area; DOC *(denominazione di origine controllata)* wines are produced subject to certain specifications (regarding grape types and method); and DOCG *(denominazione di origine controllata e garantita)* shows the wine is subject to the same requirements as normal DOC but that it is also tested by government inspectors.

Superiore can denote DOC wines above the general standard (perhaps with greater alcohol content or longer ageing). *Riserva* is applied only to DOC or DOCG wines that have aged for a specified time.

In general, the presence or absence of such labels guarantees nothing. Many a *vino da tavola* and IGT wine is so denominated simply because its producers have chosen not to adhere to the regulations governing production. These sometimes include prestige wines.

Your average trattoria will generally stock only a limited range of bottled wines, but better restaurants present a carefully chosen selection from around Tuscany and often beyond. Wine shops, *enoteche* and some *osterie* concentrate on presenting a range of fine wines rather than on the food, which is almost seen as an accompaniment to the drink.

Generally if you simply order *vino della casa* (house wine), by the glass, half-litre or litre, you will get a perfectly acceptable table wine to accompany your food.

Bottles of olive oil and wine from the Tuscan region

Tuscan Wines

Tuscany, perhaps surprisingly to some, actually ranks third (behind the Veneto and Piedmont regions) in the production of classified wines. In total volume it comes eighth of the 20 regions, largely because the lie of the land is restrictive.

Six of Italy's DOCG wines come from Tuscany: Brunello, Carmignano, Chianti, Chianti Classico, Vernaccia di San Gimignano and Vino Nobile di Montepulciano.

There was a time when the majority of wine coming out of Tuscany was the rough and ready, if highly palatable, chianti in flasks. The Chianti region remains the heartland of Tuscan wine production but for a good generation now vintners have been concentrating on quality rather than quantity.

The best of them, Chianti Classico (a red wine), comes from seven zones in many different guises. The base for all is the Sangiovese grape, though other grape types are added in varying modest quantities to produce different styles of wine. Chianti Classico wines share the Gallo Nero (Black Cockerel) emblem that once symbolised the medieval Chianti League (a league of Chianti towns that cooperated in defence and similar matters). Chianti in general is red and dry, though ageing requirements differ from area to area and even across vineyards.

The choice doesn't stop at Chianti. Among Italy's most esteemed and priciest drops is the Brunello di Montalcino (in Siena province). Until not so long ago only a handful of established estates produced this grand old red, but now everyone seems to be at it. One reckoning counts some 60 producers turning out a good product, which as usual varies a great deal in style depending on soil, microclimate and so on. Like the Chianti reds, the Sangiovese grape is at the heart of the Brunello. It is aged in casks for four years and then for another two years in bottles. Another Sangiovese-based winner is Vino Nobile di Montepulciano, named after a hill-top town in Siena province. The grape blend and conditions here make this a quite distinctive wine too, but it is not aged for as long as the Brunello.

Tuscany is not all about reds. Easily the most widely known white is the Vernaccia di San Gimignano. Some of the best is aged in *barriques* (small barrels), while others are sometimes oaked.

An important development since the end of the 1980s has been the rise of Super Tuscans. Departing from the norms imposed by DOC and DOCG requirements, certain vineyards are finally doing the kind of thing that Australian and Californian vintners have been doing for ages – experimenting with different mixes. So now alongside the Sangiovese they are growing sauvignon, merlots and other grape varieties and mixing them with the Sangiovese. The results are some first class wines that promise to shake the wine establishment as the public is weaned off DOC–dependence. Some have been classed among the best wines in all Italy. By all means try the classics. But then experiment with these emerging wines and enjoy the difference.

A regional speciality that will appeal to the sweet tooth is *Vin Santo* (literally 'holy wine'), a dessert wine also used in Mass. Malvasia and Trebbiano grape varieties are generally used to produce a strong, aromatic and amber-coloured wine, ranging from dry to very sweet (even the dry retains a hint of sweetness). A good one will last years and is traditionally served with almond-based *cantucci* biscuits.

For hints on particular vineyards you might want to invest in a wine guide. *Burton Anderson's Best Wines of Italy* is a handy little tool to have in your back pocket.

Liqueurs

After dinner try a shot of grappa, a strong, clear brew made from grapes. It originally comes from the Grappa area in the Veneto region of northeast Italy, although plenty is also produced locally. Or you could go with an *amaro*, a dark liqueur prepared from herbs. If you prefer a sweeter liqueur, try an almond-flavoured amaretto or the sweet aniseed *sambuca*. The black version of the latter is truly heavenly.

Beer

The main Italian labels are Peroni, Dreher and Moretti, all very drinkable and cheaper than the imported varieties. If you want a local beer, ask for a *birra nazionale*. Italy also imports beers from throughout Europe and the rest of the world. You can find anything from Guinness to Australia's XXXX *alla spina* (on tap) in *birrerie* (bars specialising in beer).

VEGETARIANS & VEGANS

Vegans will only feel at home in a couple of places in Florence but less strict vegetarians will have little trouble even when eating in non-vegetarian restaurants. Pasta dishes often come with vegetable-based sauces and you can follow up with numerous vegetable side dishes.

CHILDREN

As a rule children are welcome in typical Florentine restaurants, although active infants may not be well received in some of the classier dining options. A few places offer a children's menu but it's just as easy to improvise with a tasty pasta dish.

History

History

From a garrison town built for Roman war veterans, Florence rose to become the hotbed of Renaissance creativity, one of the nerve centres in which modern Western Europe transformed itself after the Middle Ages. The city's visual splendour stands as testimony to its momentous and colourful past.

THE RECENT PAST

Florence goes quietly about its business as capital of probably the best known of Italy's 20 regions, Tuscany. Occasionally it hits the limelight, as in November 1999, when leaders from around the world gathered in Florence to discuss world affairs. The likes of US President Bill Clinton and UK Prime Minister Tony Blair gave the place a nowadays rare taste of international importance.

Normally the centre-left coalition running the town hall and headed by Leonardo Domenici since July 1999 has less headline-grabbing affairs to attend to and recently even town hall news has been shifted from the local front pages by football. The local team, AC Fiorentina, crashed down from the premier division to the lowly C2 league in 2002 due to financial scandals, but the side (with others) unexpectedly rose back to Serie B (second division) for the 2003–2004 season. Other teams boycotted the launch of the Serie B season in late August but in the end came to accept the unusual situation. Florentine fans ignored the indignation.

Although it caused much less furore than the football scandal, a national report on organised crime in 2003 showed that Italy's main crime organisations, the Sicilian Mafia, the Neapolitan Camorra and 'ndrangheta from Calabria are all increasing their activities in Tuscany. They range from drug and arms trafficking through to extortion, protection rackets and gaining control of construction contracts.

The Sicilians have been around for a while. In 1993 a massive car bomb exploded in Via dei Georgofili, killing five people and injuring 37. The blast hit the Uffizi (literally 'offices'; where the city's most important gallery is housed), where several works were ruined and others damaged in a crime attributed to the Mafia. In 2000 the renowned Mafia boss Totò Riina, long in prison for other crimes, was sentenced to still more time for his involvement.

Terrorists of the left-wing Red Brigades, famous for the assassination of the Italian former prime minister, Aldo Moro, in 1978, also brought misery to Florence when they killed Lando Conti, the city's then mayor, in 1986.

Florentine tongues still wag about the Monster of Florence. Between 1968 and 1985 six related murders took place in the city, terrifying citizens and baffling the police. A prime suspect, Pietro Pacciani, got a life sentence on flimsy evidence in 1996 and died before his appeal could get under way in 1998. Even today, the police consider Pacciani's death may itself have been murder, to stop him raising the veil on the real answer to the killings. Some believe these were carried out by a group or sect that used Pacciani as a pawn.

FROM THE BEGINNING

Neolithic tribes of Liguri from northern Italy are thought to have inhabited the Arno valley where Florence would later be founded. This narrow but navigable stretch of the river was a busy crossing point, although the Etruscans preferred the heights to the valley and

TIMELINE	c 900–1000 BC	283 BC	59 BC
	Etruscans found town of Fiesole, near Florence	Fiesole falls to Rome	Julius Caesar becomes consul and founds the barracks town of Florentia

established a settlement at Fiesole (Faesulae to the Romans), possibly as early as the 9th century BC. The origins of the Etruscans remain mysterious but by the 6th century BC a dozen or so Etruscan towns had formed a powerful league in central Italy. The small Latin town of Rome was for a while under Etruscan domination but its people turfed out their Etruscan kings in 509 BC. In the following decades this initially nondescript place began to bring neighbouring settlements under its control and soon felt the

Top Five Books

- *April Blood*, Lauro Martines (2003)
- *Florence: A Portrait*, Michael Levey (1998)
- *Florence and The Medici*, J R Hale (2001)
- *The House of Medici: Its Rise and Fall*, Christopher Hibbert (1999)
- *The Stones of Florence*, Mary McCarthy (1989)

need to move against the Etruscans. They started with Veio, which fell in 392 BC. By 265 BC all of Etruria was firmly locked into Rome's system of conquest and alliance. At that point the peninsula south from modern Tuscany and Umbria was united under Rome.

FLORENTIA

By the time Julius Caesar was made a consul in 59 BC much had changed. By force of arms and diplomacy, Rome had passed from being the head of a federation of two-thirds of the Italian peninsula to master of the greatest empire ever seen, stretching from Spain to the Middle East.

In 88 BC, civil war had induced the Empire to grant full Roman citizenship and hence substantial equality of rights to its federated Italian allies, including the Etruscan cities. The flip side was that henceforth Roman public and private law, along with the Latin language, came to dominate the peninsula. Indigenous cultures were eased out of existence.

In the year he became consul, Caesar established a garrison town for army veterans on the Arno, naming it Florentia ('the flourishing one'). The project was part of his *lex Iulia* (which allotted farm plots to veterans) and construction probably began around 30 BC. Whether or not Florentia was built on the site of a pre-existing village remains a matter of learned dispute.

Florentia lay on a strategic river crossing and was laid out in classic Roman form, with the main east–west street, the *decumanus*, intersected from north to south by the *cardo*. The first corresponds to Via del Corso and Via degli Strozzi, the latter Via Roma and Via Calimala. Piazza della Repubblica marks the site of the forum. The town walls followed Via del Proconsolo, Via de' Cerretani, Via de' Tornabuoni and, to the south, roughly a line from Piazza Santa Trinita to the Palazzo Vecchio.

The first significant urban revolution came in the 2nd century AD under Hadrian, who graced the city with baths and an amphitheatre (which occupied most of the site of the Palazzo Vecchio, Via de' Gondi and part of Palazzo Gondi). Florentia had prospered on the back of brisk maritime trade along the Arno.

Under Diocletian in the late 3rd century, Florentia became the capital of the Regio Tuscia et Umbria (the name Etruria was banned), remaining so until the end of the Empire. The first Christian churches were raised in the following century, although Greco-Syriac merchants had brought the religion to pagan Florentia as early as AD 250, when St Minias (San Miniato) was martyred here.

By now Italy and the Western Roman Empire were in deep trouble. Barbarian invasions came in swift succession in the 5th century and culminated in Theodoric the Ostrogoth's coronation as king in 493. The peace that ensued ended when Justinian, the eastern emperor in Constantinople, decided to recover Italy and so restore the heartland of the Roman Empire. The 20-year campaign and subsequent 20 years of Byzantine rule brought devastation and ruin to large tracts of Italy, and Florentia suffered with the rest.

c AD 100	AD 250	476	568
Hadrian builds baths and amphitheatre in the area around the present Palazzo Vecchio	St Minias becomes Florence's first Christian martyr	German Odovacar proclaims himself king in Rome, sealing the end of the Roman Empire	Lombards invade and occupy northern Italy, taking Florence two years later

MIDDLE AGES

After a period under Lombard rule, the duchy of Tuscia, which covered Tuscany, Umbria, much of Lazio and Corsica, passed under the control of the Holy Roman Empire, created in 800 when Charlemagne was crowned by the pope in Rome. By the end of the 11th century, particularly under the administration of Countess Matilda Canossa (see the boxed text) the duchy had achieved considerable independence. Florence, with a population of 20,000, was a robust and flourishing regional capital.

The death of Matilda spelled the end of Tuscia as a political unit. In the wake of its disintegration, more or less independent and frequently quarrelling city-states emerged in Tuscany. Florence quickly reduced Fiesole to submission in 1123. Fifty years later a new set of defensive walls was built and Florentine troops were battling Sienese soldiers in the Chianti area over boundary disputes.

Emperor Frederick Barbarossa then waltzed into the Italian labyrinth, determined to re-establish imperial control. In Florence in 1173 he decreed the city's jurisdiction limited to the city *intra muros* and installed governors in most Tuscan cities. The latter, however, took little notice and pursued their own interests.

A Woman's Touch

Duke Boniface Canossa's tendency to disregard imperial wishes did his daughter little good. On his death Matilda was packed off to Germany as a prisoner of Emperor Henry III. She clearly was not taken with her Teutonic interlude and when released returned to Florence ill-disposed to cooperate with her imperial masters. From 1069 until 1115 she ruled Florence serenely, proving to be one of the great women rulers of the Middle Ages.

When hostilities broke out between Emperor Henry IV and Pope Gregory VII, Matilda allied herself with the pope, setting a precedent that would long resonate through Florentine history. Henry tried to have the pope deposed in 1076 but instead found himself at Countess Matilda's castle at Canossa, in Emilia, imploring the pope to lift an order of excommunication. That she should be singled out as intermediary underlines the respect in which she was held by her contemporaries. It was, however, little more than a truce, and this round of the papal-imperial struggle only ended when Henry was deposed by his son, Henry V, in 1105.

By now a system of corporatist government, the *comune*, was developing, a kind of oligarchy in which the top families (increasingly a mix of landed nobility and the burgeoning merchant class) shared out the leading positions in government, or *signoria*. Powerful guilds, or *arti*, had also by now emerged. They would long play a key role in the distribution of power in Florence.

Florentine family feuding as early as the 11th century crystallised as two main factions emerged, the pro-imperial Ghibellines (Ghibellini) and the pro-papal Guelphs (Guelfi). Traditionally the spark that set off this powder keg is identified as the murder of Buondelmonte dei Buondelmonti, a Guelph, in 1216.

The Guelphs, generally wealthy merchants, sought greater independence than the Holy Roman emperor wished to countenance. The Ghibellines tended to be noble families whose sense of power rested in part on the notion of being part of the imperial order. By 1250, the Guelphs were in the ascendant in Florence and 20 years later had succeeded in having Guelph governors imposed on Siena, Pisa and other Tuscan cities.

Members of the seven senior *arti* by now furnished the city's governors, or *priori*, elected on a two-monthly rotational basis. From their ranks the *gonfaloniere* (or standard-bearer) was selected as a kind of president. Together they formed the *signoria* and resided in the Palazzo della Signoria (today known as the Palazzo Vecchio) for the duration of their mandate. Representatives of the 14 lesser guilds had no political representation and still less the remaining three-quarters of the population, most of them wage slaves in the most unpleasant of wool industry jobs, like dyeing. Florentines liked to think of this oligarchic system

1069	1115	1216	1252
Matilda Canossa becomes Countess of Tuscany, launching period of independent-minded and even-handed rule	Matilda's death brings about collapse of Tuscia (Tuscany); in Florence, an oligarchic government takes control of affairs	Buondelmonte dei Buondelmonti assassinated, unleashing protracted period of factional strife between Guelphs and Ghibellines	Florence starts minting the florin, destined to become one of Europe's most favoured currencies

as highly democratic but the city's leading families usually made sure that only candidates to their liking took up a *priore's* cap.

Renewed factional strife saw the reformist Bianchi (whites) and conservative Neri (blacks) in conflict over law proposals to block nobles' access to power in Florence. With French and Papal aid the latter prevailed and the Whites (including Dante Alighieri) were exiled.

A PLAGUE ON FLORENCE & THE PEOPLE REVOLT

In 1333 Giovanni Villani, the city's medieval chronicler, reports that a devastating flood ripped through the city, killing many and washing away the Ponte Vecchio.

Then the plague of 1348 swept across Europe and halved Florence's population. Medieval Europeans seem to have had an unlimited capacity for absorbing punishment and over the next 17 years Florence went on the warpath, bringing San Gimignano, Volterra, Pistoia, Prato and Pisa to heel.

Quiet times were rare and fleeting. In 1375 a rather nasty band of unemployed mercenaries, led by Essex man Sir John Hawkwood, descended on Florentia. In the end, Hawkwood, or Giovanni Acuto as he became known to the locals, entered the pay of Florence and remained one of its more capable soldiers.

All the blood-letting, instability, tax rises and food shortages became increasingly hard to bear and a mob revolt in 1378 left city government in the hands, briefly, of the Ciompi, as the proletariat was known. They demanded the right to create their own guilds and participate in power. They actually created three but within a few years the old oligarchy had struck back and dissolved them.

All the while, the warring went on. If Florence managed to expand its control of Tuscany by peacefully acquiring Arezzo, Livorno (or Leghorn) and Cortona, the *priori* watched aghast as Pisa slipped into Milanese control. Long years of war followed and by 1430 Florence was in control of much of Tuscany. To pay more effectively for all this, the Florentines at this time introduced the *catasto*, the world's first graduated income tax system. Tax was assessed in proportion to wealth as measured in fixed goods and income-producing potential. Of course tax avoidance and evasion in the modern sense were also born with the *catasto*!

THE RISE OF THE MEDICI

In these first decades of the 15th century, the Albizi family called most of the shots in Florence. It was by now a given that the real power lay with people behind the scenes, not directly in the hands of any one *gonfaloniere*.

Another family, however, was growing in influence. Giovanni di Bicci de' Medici had steered his bank to becoming one of the most successful investment houses in Europe. His eldest son Cosimo became paterfamilias in 1429, by which time the increasing wealth and influence of his family so upset the Albizi that they contrived to have him sent into exile in 1433.

The Albizi, however, had miscalculated. Not only were several powerful families allied to Cosimo, but he had enormous international support through his banking network. Within a year Cosimo was back and the Albizi expelled.

The Medici family crest was made up of *palle* (six balls), which must have been cause for some mirth through the years as Medici supporters would clatter down the street on horseback crying out: 'Balls! Balls! Balls!' The word has the same less than decorous meaning in Italian as it does in English.

For 30 years Cosimo de' Medici steered Florence on a course that served to increase the power and prosperity of the city. Although he chose to remain in the background he kept the government stacked with his own people. In the 1450s, Pope Pius II commented that Cosimo was 'master of all Italy'.

1260	1265	1348	1427
Siena defeats Florence at the Battle of Montaperti	Dante Alighieri born	The Black Death (bubonic plague) sweeps through the city	Florence institutes the *catasto*, an early personal income tax system applied to all classes

The Medici crest, found all over Florence

Foreign policy, however, could have been Cosimo's undoing. His unswerving allegiance to the Milanese usurper Francesco Sforza brought on Florence the enmity of Venice and the Kingdom of Naples. Cosimo remained unperturbed and the doubters were proved wrong. Venice was too concerned with threats from Turkey, and the other Italian states worried lest a French army march into Italy to aid Florence. As so often, the boys put away their toys and signed a pact in 1454 aimed at creating unity in the face of potential outside aggression.

The following 10 years were a period of rare and much appreciated peace in which the city flourished. The population reached about 70,000, taxes fell, trade blossomed and the city's leading families all felt in a position to enhance their hometown and personal reputations with grand new buildings.

The ever prudent Cosimo, who protested regularly that he was no more than a private citizen (except on those rare occasions when elected *gonfaloniere*), was not just a shrewd statesman and consummate businessman. He also had an eye for the finer things in life. Under his patronage, the artistic and intellectual life of the city exploded into a kaleidoscope of fevered activity.

Even before his rise to power, the artistic world had been in ferment. Indeed, by the time Cosimo returned to Florence from exile in 1434, the Renaissance style had largely dislodged the Gothic.

In 1436 Brunelleschi completed his extraordinary dome on the Duomo (Cathedral) and from this time on Cosimo employed artists such as Donatello, Fra Angelico and Fra Filippo Lippi on various projects. He often put up money to promote the construction or embellishment of new public buildings and churches and encouraged the work of the Platonic Academy, which translated the Greek thinker's works into Latin, making the philosophy of the ancients accessible to an emerging generation of enquiring minds.

Cosimo moved on to the next world in 1464 and he was one of the few Florentine chiefs to be genuinely mourned by his people. The *signoria* even went so far as to award Cosimo the posthumous title of pater patriae – Father of the Country.

PIERO DE' MEDICI & LORENZO THE MAGNIFICENT

Within two years of succeeding his father as head of the family, Piero de' Medici put down a revolt and altered electoral laws, effectively putting control of the elections of *priori* and *gonfalonieri* in the hands of selected people. The illusion of democracy was thus maintained (elections would continue as before) but few were in any doubt that Piero had done little else than consolidate his dynasty. Piero's successor in 1469, his 20-year-old son Lorenzo, attached the same importance to Florence's appearance as a democratic republic, but soon no-one was in doubt as to who was in charge.

The Pazzi family, rivals of the Medici and backed by the papacy, plotted to murder Lorenzo and take over the city on 26 April 1478. Lorenzo's brother Giuliano was viciously

1434	1436	1494	1513
Cosimo de' Medici returns from exile and takes effective control of the city	Brunelleschi completes the remarkable cathedral dome	Medici flee Florence ahead of French invasion; a theocratic republic declared under Dominican friar Girolamo Savonarola	Giovanni de' Medici becomes Pope Leo X, one year after Medici power restored in Florence

torn to shreds in the assassination attempt during Mass in the Duomo, but Lorenzo escaped wounded and rallied his followers, who soon gave the Pazzi troops short shrift in the Palazzo della Signoria.

No sooner had he solved the Pazzi problem than Lorenzo found himself facing an allied Papal-Neapolitan army. Lorenzo chose to negotiate in Naples and spared Florence what looked like certain defeat. He then focussed on home affairs, creating a Consiglio dei Settanta (Council of Seventy) with powers overriding those of the *signoria*. Lorenzo il Magnifico (the Magnificent), as he was by now dubbed, had the reins of power in his hands.

Lorenzo continued the promotion of the arts (the young Michelangelo came to live in the Medici household for a time) but there were some worrying signs on the horizon. Since the days of Cosimo, the Medici bank had declined significantly. Branches across Europe continued to close through mismanagement and the family fortunes dwindled. Lorenzo was often skint, although other branches of the family were still doing comparatively well.

In the momentous year of 1492 Lorenzo expired, aged 43, to be succeeded by his nasty and incompetent son Piero. He ushered in a long period of mayhem in the riverside city.

A WHIFF OF HELLFIRE

Within two years Piero was out on his ear and the Medici family in disgrace after his abject submission to the invading French army of Charles VIII. The republic was restored and the constitution again remodelled in 1494. The flavour this time was altogether novel. A city of commercial families and luxury-lovers seemed to have temporarily lost its collective nerve as it meekly submitted to the fiery theocracy of Girolamo Savonarola. The republic was organised along the lines of the Venetian model and a Consiglio dei Cinquecento (Council of 500) set up as a parliament.

Savonarola, the Dominican friar with the staring eyes, big nose and fat lips, had arrived in Florence in 1481 to preach repentance in the Chiesa di San Marco. He found a susceptible audience that, over the years, filled the church to bursting to hear his bloodcurdling warnings of horrors to come if Florentines did not repent of their ways and return to the basics.

Savonarola urged the people to renounce their evil ways and called on the government to proceed on the basis of his divine inspiration. Drinking, whoring, partying, gambling,

America, America

No-one would claim that Florence, 85km inland from the nearest sea, has a proud naval history. And yet to one of the city's sons fell the honour of having a whole new world named after him – America.

Amerigo Vespucci had been sent to Seville, in Spain, in 1491 to join a business associate of the Medici family, Giannotto Berardi. Little could he know that he would spend the rest of his days in the shipping business in Spain and Portugal. These were exciting times in Spain. The last of the Muslims were thrown out of Granada in 1492 and that same year Columbus made his first voyage to what he was convinced was Asia, but was in fact the Caribbean. Vespucci helped fit out the next two of Columbus' voyages and in 1496 became head of the Medici Seville agency.

Between 1497 and 1504 Vespucci set out on his own expeditions. On one, in which he sailed down the South American coast into Patagonia and was the first European to lay eyes on the Rio de la Plata (River Plate, between Uruguay and Argentina), Vespucci became convinced that this wasn't Asia or India, but a hitherto utterly unheard of world. In 1507 a humanist philosopher, Martin Waldseemüller, printed a treatise in which he described Amerigo as the 'inventor' of a new place called America. The name stuck, at first only to the southern continent, but later to all of what are to this day known as the Americas.

Vespucci had proved himself such a capable navigator that Spain awarded him citizenship and appointed him Pilota Mayor (Master Navigator) in 1508, with the task of organising further expeditions and coordinating the survey of the newly discovered (and conquered) territories. He remained in the post until his death in 1512.

1569	1571	1574	1600
Cosimo I named Grand Duke Cosimo of Tuscany	Cosimo I releases painters from legal obligation to belong to guilds	On death of Cosimo I, Francesco de' Medici succeeds as Grand Duke	The oldest opera for which the score still exists, *Euridice*, performed in Florence

wearing flashy clothes and other signs of wrongdoing were pushed well underground. Books, clothes, jewellery, fancy furnishings and art burned on 'bonfires of the vanities'. Bands of children marched around the city ferreting out adults still seemingly attached to their old habits and possessions.

No doubt feeling the sting of Savonarola's accusations of corruption and debauchery in the Church, Pope Alexander VI (the Borgia Pope was possibly the least religiously inclined pope of all time) was losing his cool. He demanded Savonarola be sent to Rome, and the *signoria* started to worry. Bad harvests were hurting the people, business was bad, and Savonarola seemed more outlandish with his claims of being God's special emissary.

The Franciscans, rivals of the Dominicans, had especially had enough. As 1498 wore on, street violence between the friar's supporters and opponents spread. The Franciscans challenged Savonarola to an ordeal by fire, an invitation he declined to take up, although he had no problem with sending a deputy in his stead. The trial was washed out by rain but in the ensuing riots the *signoria* finally decided to arrest Savonarola. After weeks at the hands of the city rack-master he was finally hanged and burned at the stake as a heretic, along with two supporters, in Piazza della Signoria on 22 May.

THE MEDICI STRIKE BACK

It took some time and a good deal of bloodshed, but Giovanni de' Medici returned home in 1512 backed by a Spanish-led army. He set about restoring the position of his family in Florence, which should have been further strengthened when Giovanni was elected Pope Leo X one year later.

But the Medici line seemed to have lost much of its lustre. Florence in any case was not the same city as that of Cosimo's day. Most of its banks had failed and business was bad. A series of Medici lads, culminating in the utterly useless bastards Ippolito and Alessandro, managed to so alienate Florentines that when Pope Clement VII (another Medici) was cornered in Rome by an uncompromising imperial army, the people rejoiced and threw the Medici family out.

Of course, deals were done and the imperial forces subsequently promised to reinstate the Medici in Florence if the pope recognised imperial suzerainty of all Italy. Florence, which had enjoyed a few short Medici-free years, was reduced by siege in 1530. Alessandro and Ippolito returned. Alessandro was made duke, bringing to an end even the pretence at a republic, and duly assassinated by a jealous cousin, Lorenzino, in 1537.

A GRAND DUCHY

The Medici party activists decided on Cosimo (a descendant of the first Cosimo's brother Lorenzo) as successor, hoping he would prove easy to manipulate. They got that wrong. Cosimo, who in 1569 would be officially declared grand duke of Tuscany after the definitive fall of Siena to Florence, was a tough leader who brooked no opposition. In his long reign from 1537 to 1574 he was no doubt a despot, but a comparatively enlightened one. He sorted out the city's finances and promoted economic growth across Tuscany, with irrigation programmes for agriculture and mining.

Cosimo I was a patron of the arts and sciences and he also reformed the civil service, building the Uffizi to house all government departments in one, easily controlled building. He and his family also moved into the Palazzo Pitti, which they proceeded to expand.

Cosimo's immediate successors, Francesco and Ferdinando I, between them managed to go some way to stimulating the local economy and promoting agriculture, building hospitals and bringing some relief to the poor. Cosimo II invited Galileo Galilei to Florence, where the scientist could continue his research under Tuscan protection and undisturbed by the bellyaching of the Church.

1610	1743	1769	1808
Galileo Galilei publishes a treatise on the stars, dedicated to Grand Duke Cosimo II, who later invited Galileo to reside in Florence	Anna Maria Luisa de' Medici dies, bequeathing the entire Medici art collections to the city on condition that they never leave Florence	Uffizi opened to the public	Napoleon installs his sister, Elisa Baciocchi, as Grand Duchess of Tuscany, incorporated into his empire

Ferdinando II was ineffectual if well meaning – during the three terrible years of plague that scourged Florence from 1630, he stayed behind when anyone else that could was hot-footing it to the countryside.

Next in line was Cosimo III, a dour, depressing man if ever there was one. Perhaps he had read his Savonarola. In any event, this ill-educated bigot was not a fun date. Persecution of the Jews was one of his contributions to Florentine society and he also backed the Inquisition in its opposition to virtually any kind of scientific learning. A little stretch on the rack was the prescribed tonic for extramarital sex.

Before the drunkard grand duke, Gian Gastone de' Medici, had died, the European powers had decided the issue of the 'Tuscan succession' and appointed Francis, duke of Lorraine and husband of the Austrian empress Maria Theresa, as grand duke of Tuscany. The last significant act of the Medicis came six years after the death of Gian Gastone. His sister, Anna Maria, who died in 1743, bequeathed all the Medici property and art collections to the Grand Duchy of Tuscany, on condition that they never leave Florence.

AUSTRIANS & NAPOLEON

The imperial Austrian couple visited for a three-month sojourn in Florence and liked it well enough, but from then until 1765 the city and Grand Duchy were ruled by regents.

They brought a feeling of (mostly) quiet discontent to their subjects. It is true that much-needed reforms swept away inequities in taxation, somewhat streamlined civil administration and curbed the powers of the Inquisition, but the regents' main task seemed to be the systematic plunder of Tuscany's resources in the service of the Austrian empire. The Grand Duchy of Tuscany was purportedly an independent entity, but it certainly didn't appear the case.

Things seemed to improve in 1765, when Pietro Leopoldo became grand duke and arrived from Vienna. He threw himself wholeheartedly into his task He abolished torture and the death penalty, suppressed the Inquisition, embarked on a schools building programme for the poor, busied himself with agricultural matters and prodded Florence's *comune* to clean up the city, improve lighting and introduce street names. He also made sure that some of the art and furnishings that had been removed to Austria under Grand Duke Francis were returned.

Pietro Leopoldo, as heir to the Austrian throne, had to leave Tuscany in 1790 upon the death of his brother, Emperor Josef II. His son and successor, Grand Duke Ferdinando III, was faced with Europe's new master of Blitzkrieg, Napoleon Bonaparte. In 1800 Napoleon created the Kingdom of Etruria and then in 1809, by now Emperor of France, made his sister, Elisa Baciocchi, Grand Duchess of Tuscany, and she remained so until Napoleon's defeat in 1814. This whirlwind past, Ferdinando III returned from Vienna to take up where he had left off.

Grand Duke Ferdinando III proved to be one of the more popular of the Tuscan overlords. He pushed through a raft of reforms at every level of city and grand ducal administration and by all accounts was an all-round good fellow. He eschewed many of the trappings of his position and mingled freely with his subjects.

His death in 1824 was greeted with dismay, not least because no-one knew what to expect from his gloomy son Leopoldo.

ITALIAN UNITY

Grand Duke Leopoldo II proved more able than many had anticipated. But as the years wore on the task grew steadily more onerous. The independence of the Grand Duchy was menaced not only by more direct interference from Vienna, but also by the growing calls for a united Italian state.

1823	1861	1865	1865–69
Florence Nightingale is born in …Florence	Florence hosts the first international exhibition of the now united Italy	Florence becomes capital of Italy until 1870, when Rome is finally taken	Most of the old city walls pulled down

Leopoldo took a fairly lenient line in Florence, allowing dissent and so attracting to the city intellectuals from all over the country, including writers such as Ugo Foscolo and Giacomo Leopardi. Indeed, Florence was something of a magnet for writers, activists and a fair sprinkling of dilettantes from all over the place. Since the middle of the previous century, Florence had been a favourite choice of self-imposed exile for a considerable number of Brits. Now it drew the likes of Byron and Shelley, and non-Anglos such as Chateaubriand.

Leopoldo encouraged urban development and a series of improvements, including the introduction of gas streetlighting, the widening of roads, and housing programmes for the poor.

The torment of the 1848 revolts across Europe convinced Leopoldo to repair to Vienna. Into the breach stepped a radical government among whose leaders was the key pro-unity figure of Giuseppe Mazzini. Their rule was short-lived and Leopoldo was asked back after only three months. From now on he took a more pro-Austrian stance but Florence's fate would be decided elsewhere. In 1859 a combined French and Piedmontese army defeated the Austrians in two bloody battles at Magenta and Solferino.

On 15 March 1860, the provisional government in Florence (Leopoldo had already left) announced the adhesion of the Grand Duchy to the Kingdom of Piedmont. As other parts of Italy also joined, so in 1861 a united Italy under a constitutional monarch was born.

In February 1865, King Vittorio Emanuele and the national government arrived in Florence to take up residence. Turin had been the first seat of the national parliament, but was deemed too far north to remain capital. Rome, the natural choice, was yet to be wrenched from papal hands. So an 'army' of 30,000, including bureaucrats and their families, descended on Florence, a city of around 115,000. A year later, the military hero of the Italian Risorgimento (Resurrection; the movement for a unified Italy), Giuseppe Garibaldi, was given a thunderous welcome in Florence. His 'Red Shirts' had become famous throughout the world, although their victories had been balanced by a fair share of disasters.

The incorporation of Rome into the Kingdom and the end of fighting throughout the peninsula finally came in 1870. The government shifted to Rome the following year.

In those five brief years of 'occupation' the city was given much of its present appearance. Ring roads (the broad *viali*) that follow the line of the former city walls were paved. Large new squares appeared, including Piazzale Michelangelo. The growth of whole new suburbs to the north and northwest of the centre got under way. In short, a modern middle-class Florence was born. By 1888 the first electric streetlighting was going up.

Florentines continued in large measure to live poorly. Accounts suggest that in the 1860s and '70s delinquency was rife, and poverty and begging widespread. The economic crisis of the late 1890s pushed up the price of staples and led to bread riots. An 1892 report suggested that, of a total population of 180,000, 72,000 were officially considered poor.

In the 10 years prior to the outbreak of WWI, Florence became a cultural capital in Italy. Numerous literary, political and often free-thinking newspapers and reviews came into existence at this time.

Florentine politics became more radical too. By 1914 the Socialist Party had almost 3000 party members in Florence, and the previous year, when universal male suffrage was granted, almost 30% of Tuscan votes went to them.

THE TWO WORLD WARS

Italy's decision to enter WWI on 24 May 1915 had little initial impact on Florence, tucked far away from the front lines in the north. But by the end of the struggle some 11,000 young men from Florence and its province had died in the field. By 1917 the situation on the home front had become grim too. All basic products were strictly rationed and that winter, a harsh one, heating fuel was virtually unavailable.

1866	1883	1904	1926
Giuseppe Garibaldi, whose Red Shirts were pivotal in the creation of the Kingdom of Italy, gets a hero's welcome in Florence	*L'Avventure di Pinocchio* (The Adventures of Pinocchio) published in Florence	Guccio Gucci opens a clothes store on Via Tornabuoni and so launches one of Italy's fashion dynasties	Fiorentina football club founded

Sbandieratori *(flag-throwers) in front of the Duomo (p75)*

In Florence, postwar urban plans included creating a factory zone, to include the gasworks and the Pignone smelters, in the Rifredi area northwest of the centre. This in turn aided the growth of workers' groups and support for left-wing parties and action, creating the scene for clashes between right and left.

By 1920 Benito Mussolini's Fascists had established branches in Florence. In less than two years Florence would become one of the Fascists' biggest strongholds. On 28 October 1922, Mussolini rolled the dice and marched on Rome. Had the king opposed the Fascists, it is likely they would have failed, but Mussolini emerged the victor. In Florence, 2000 Fascists took control of strategic buildings, the railway station and telecommunications posts. The police stayed pretty much out of the way.

The Florentine version of Fascism was particularly virulent. Indeed Blackshirt violence became so bad in Florence that Mussolini had to send people in to shake out local organisations and put a brake on the bloodshed.

In the following years, the opposition gradually went further underground or was suppressed altogether. For its loyalty the city got a new stadium at Campo di Marte (1932) and the train station at Santa Maria Novella (1933–35). Then in 1938 the Florentines received another gift, a joint visit in all possible pomp and circumstance by Mussolini and his new buddy with the toothbrush moustache, Adolf Hitler. The multitude duly cheered and waved Florentine lilies with Nazi swastikas. They had no idea what they were heading for.

For Italy, the tragedy began in June 1940 when Mussolini decided to take the plunge and join Hitler's European tour. Things went Germany's way for a while, but for the Italians the difficulties began almost from the outset. Florence's war clothes included asbestos blocks and sandbags, placed to protect the city's monuments.

By 8 September 1943, when Italy surrendered to the Allies, the latter's troops were about to land at Salerno, south of Naples – a long way from Florence.

1938	August 1944	1951	4 November 1966
Mussolini and Hitler pay Florence a state visit	Allied forces and Italian resistance fighters take Florence as Germans pull back, having blown all bridges but the Ponte Vecchio	Giovan Battista Giorgini organises an Italian fashion parade in Florence, taking a world dominated by French fashions by storm	Disastrous floods strike as Arno inundates Florence

Italy surrendered but not the Germans. They established their local military HQ in Piazza San Marco, while the SS (Schutzstaffel; Hitler's paramilitary forces) found a nice quiet place to carry out torture on Via Bolognese in the north of the city.

When Allied forces approached the German lines near Florence in July 1944, the German high command decided to blow up the city's bridges. They spared the Ponte Vecchio, blocking it at either end and mining its shops instead. Early in the morning of 4 August, the other bridges went up in smoke. Italian Resistance fighters harassed the Germans and later that day Allied scouts entered the city, but it would be two weeks before Florence was cleared. The last German forces finally fell back from Fiesole on 7 September. The war ended in May 1945.

AFTERMATH & THE FLOODS OF 1966

Within three months of the German exit from Florence, work began on restoration. Rebuilding bridges was paramount, and by August 1946 Ponte alla Vittoria was up. Ponte San Niccolò was finished in 1949 and Ponte alla Carraia two years later. Ponte Santa Trinita took another seven years, painstakingly reconstructed using copies of 16th-century tools.

Florentine postwar politics were dominated by the colourful, Sicilian-born *sindaco* (mayor) Giorgio La Pira, a rightwing Christian Democrat with a strong religious inspiration who vowed to govern for the poor. His first electoral victory came in 1951, after a period in which the Communists and other left-wing forces together had dominated the city.

La Pira, who had been on the committee that wrote the new national constitution promulgated in 1948, was nothing if not controversial. He requisitioned empty buildings to house the homeless, distributed bread to the poor (a stunt in questionable taste) and, oddly enough for a Christian Democrat, sided with factory workers in their struggles with employers. Such displays were all very well, but critics attacked him for not implementing a proper housing programme. In the meantime, land west of the city was turned into suburban sprawl with virtually no supervision.

Disaster struck in 1966. Torrential rain turned the Arno into a raging torrent that, in the early hours of 4 November, crashed into Florence. When the floodwaters subsided, the city was left covered in a mantle of mud, oil and slime. Some 14,000 families were left homeless and the impact on the city's art treasures was incalculable. If anything good can be said to have come of the flood, it was the great advances made in the field of art restoration.

1986	1993	1999	2003
Red Brigades assassinate mayor Lando Conti	Car bomb attributed to Mafia kills 37 and damages Uffizi	Leonardo Domenici takes over as mayor with centre-left coalition	Restorers clean Michelangelo's *David*, using a specially designed aerial platform

Quarters

Quarters

Florence is the proverbial chocolate cake in the way of 'all good things come in small packages'. Florence is jammed with monuments and sights, most of them mercifully confined to a small area. There are so many of them that, unless you stay for a few weeks, you are unlikely to digest more than a modest portion. A lot of people zip around the classics more out of a sense of obligation than because they have a profound interest in Florentine art. Before you do anything, take the time to study what there is to see and make some choices.

Not everyone is an art buff. Perhaps you'd be better off concentrating on the grand churches. You like views from on high? Then give priority to the Campanile, the Palazzo Vecchio and the dome of the Duomo. If you are curious about ancient artefacts but not too crazy on painting, skip the Uffizi and head for the Museo Archeologico. No-one is going to chastise you for *not* visiting the Uffizi!

This chapter and the review chapters are divided into a series of logical areas, loosely based on the city's traditional parishes.

> ## Top Five for Children
> - Campanile (p66)
> - Museo di Storia della Scienza (p86)
> - Museo Stibbert (p111)
> - Museo Zoologico La Specola (p108)
> - Palazzo Vecchio – Museo dei Ragazzi (p86)

ITINERARIES

You could cobble together an endless variety of itineraries. If you have the time, just wander around the city to get a feel for it. It is compact so you can easily dedicate a day to a stroll and take note of sights you'd like to come back and visit another day – unless of course you're only in town for a day!

One Day

On a flying one-day visit? You'll have to make some tough choices. You will want to get a look at the Duomo (p75) but could probably skip visiting inside. You should visit the Baptistry though, and a climb to the top of either the Duomo's dome or the Campanile (p66) is in order. After that, go for a wander down through the old city to Piazza della Signoria (p79) and on to the Ponte Vecchio (p109)– which you might then cross for some lunch in the Oltrarno (p103) area. Depending on your stamina and the time you've got left, you could, before heading across the bridge, squeeze in one of the mid-range museums: it's a toss-up between the Galleria dell'Accademia (p95), the Museo del Bargello (p85) or the Museo dell'Opera del Duomo (p77). Hard-core sightseers will then re-cross the bridge in the afternoon to tackle the Galleria degli Uffizi (p81). That should just about do you in, so from there you might like to just stroll – for instance to Piazza Santa Croce (p100) to catch the evening sunlight bathing the basilica of the same name. You could do a little leather shopping while in the area and head to one of the many tempting local eateries.

Three Days

Three days gives you at least a vague chance to get your head around the city. If you are enthusiastic about art and architecture, you should take in the sights mentioned above, and more. Consider visiting the Palazzo Pitti (p108), and Basilica di Santa Maria Novella (p89), Basilica di San Lorenzo (p92) and Basilica di Santa Croce (p100). Some specific stars worth seeking out include the Cappella Brancacci in the Basilica di Santa Maria del Carmine (p104) and Gozzoli's frescoes in the Palazzo Medici-Riccardi (p94). The Palazzo Vecchio (p86) is a strong attraction if you want to explore the city's history. Relax a little too. In summer you might want to cool off in one of the public pools (p154). Shoppers should head for Via de' Tornabuoni (p169) and drool (or you could make a day of it in the discount outlets out of town – see the boxed text, p172). Limitations on the pocket? It's always fun to slouch about the tat and leather markets, such as **Mercato Nuovo** (p85) and the stands around **San Lorenzo** (p172). Head for the Oltrarno for some soothing views of the city. You can choose between the crowded **Piazzale Michelangelo** (p109), the **Forte di Belvedere** (p107) or **Bellosguardo** (p112). A day up in **Fiesole** (p113) can be a good antidote to an impending case of Stendhalismo too (see the boxed text, p81).

One Week

OK, now we're talking. Although you could spend a month in Florence and still not feel you know it well, one week will definitely allow you to get to grips with the salient points, allowing you to mix the worthy with a little diversion. Basically take all of the above and add in your own extras. You should consider a couple of excursions out of town. Highly recommended is a day dedicated to **Siena** (p190) and one to **Pisa** (p197), which you might be able to combine with your flights in or out of the area, as well as **Lucca** (p197) and the **Chianti** area (p194) – the latter is best done with your own transport. Back in Florence, you might like to search out a few of the lesser known sights. The **Museo Archeologico** (p97) has extensive exhibits from the ancient world and the **Museo di Storia della Scienza** (p86) has all sorts of odds and ends. Art buffs looking for the unusual could search out some of the *cenacoli*, the Last Supper scenes painted in monastery refectories. Don't forget to take some time just to hang out in cafés on **Piazza della Repubblica** (p128) or in bars around **Piazza Santo Spirito** (p142).

ORGANISED TOURS

American Express and various travel agents offer tours of the city. Call into their offices for information. The **SITA** bus company (Map pp246–7; ☎ 055 21 84 44; www.sita-on-line.it, Italian only; Via Santa Caterina da Siena 15) also organises tours in and around Florence.

Associazione Mercurio (Map pp251–3; ☎ 055 26 61 41; www.mercurio-italy.org; Via Cavour 8) organises daily (except Sunday) morning walking tours of the city centre (€26), guided tours of several museums such as the Uffizi (€36) and brief walking excursions in the hills south of Piazzale Michelangelo and around Fiesole. For €55 you can join a half-day tour into the Chianti. Book at **Amici del Turismo** (Map pp251–3; ☎ 055 238 27 53; Via Cavour 36/r).

CAF Tours (Map pp251–3; ☎ 055 21 06 12; www.caftours.com; Via Roma 4; tours €34-47) offers a variety of one-day tours of the city (walking and by coach). It also offers coach tours outside Florence.

City Sightseeing (24-hour pass €20) is a hop-on-hop-off circle-line tourist bus that makes 17 stops around the historic heart of the city. You can pick up the bus just outside the train station (Map pp246–7) or any other stop on the route. Buses operate from 9am to 11pm.

Comune di Firenze tourist office (Map pp251–3; ☎ 055 21 22 45; www.comune.firenze.it; Piazza della Stazione 4) also puts on a series of guided tours to specific sights in and outside Florence. Generally they are for small groups and commentary is in Italian. You can get the latest programme and booking details from the tourist offices.

Florence by Bike (Map pp246–7; ☎ 055 48 89 92; www.florencebybike.it; Via San Zanobi 120–122/r; one-day tour €69.90) offers a Chianti tour with lunch and wine tasting.

It's Free

One week of the year (usually in spring), entry to state museums *(musei statali)* throughout Italy is made free. Since dates change, it is impossible to plan a trip around this, but keep your eyes open. Admission to all state museums is free for EU citizens under 18 and over 65. In Florence these include the Cappelle Medicee, Galleria dell'Accademia, Giardino di Boboli, Museo Archeologico, Museo del Bargello, Museo di San Marco, Opificio, Palazzo Pitti, Uffizi, and various of the *cenacoli* (refectory scenes). Admission is also free for non-EU citizens aged 12 years old and under. In some other museums, EU citizens of differing ages get discounts. For all EU-related discounts you must show your passport or national ID card. There are few discounts for non-EU citizens or nonresidents of Florence. Still, always ask to be sure.

It costs nothing to wander into the Basilica di Santa Croce, Chiesa di San Miniato al Monte, Chiesa di Orsanmichele, Duomo, some of the *cenacoli* and some of the lesser churches around Florence.

Queues at the Galleria degli Uffizi (p81)

I Bike Italy (☎ 055 234 23 71; www.ibikeitaly.com) offers reasonably full-day guided mountain-bike rides around Fiesole (US$70) and in the Chianti area (US$85), and a two-day trip down to Siena (US$280). Day tours include lunch and wine and olive oil tasting at a vineyard, while for the Siena tour a night's accommodation and meals are thrown in. All you need is a reasonable amount of energy, cash and a hardy backside.

The Accidental Tourist (Map p188; ☎ 055 69 93 76; www.accidentaltourist.com; Via Roma, San Donato in the town Collina) organises walking (€68), cycling (€74) and cooking (€78) excursions into the Chianti region from Florence. You are picked up in Florence and taken to a country estate for wine tasting and nibbling, before being let loose for a few hours of afternoon strolling or bike riding. Alternatively, you can skip the exertion and join a cooking class.

Walking Tours of Florence (Map pp251–3; ☎ 055 264 50 33; www.artviva.com; Piazza Santo de' Stefano 20; three-hour walks €20–35) organises excellent walks of the city led by specialists.

Queue Jumping

If time is more precious than money, you can skip (or at least shorten) some of the museum queues by booking ahead. In summer especially, long queues can mean a sticky wait of up to four hours! Watch 'em sweat and swan on by.

For a fee of €3 per museum, you can book a ticket in advance to any of the 13 state museums *(musei statali)* in Florence. These include the Uffizi Gallery, the various museums of Palazzo Pitti, Museo del Bargello, Galleria dell'Accademia, Museo Archeologico, Museo di San Marco, Cappelle Medicee, Museo Archeologico and the Opificio delle Pietre Dure. Simply phone Firenze Musei (☎ 055 29 48 83; www.firenzemusei.it; ☺ 8.30am-6.30pm Mon-Fri, 8.30am-12.30pm Sat). When you arrive at the site, go to the window for those with prebooked tickets, quote your booking number, pay and away you go.

For the Uffizi, you can also buy tickets in advance at the gallery itself (also €3 booking fee per ticket).

If you prefer electronic methods, Weekend a Firenze (www.weekendafirenze.com) is an online service for booking museums, galleries, shows and tours. For this you pay €6.80 on top of the normal ticket price; reserve at least three days in advance. Print out the email confirmation they send and present it on the day of your visit. You can get tickets for the Uffizi, Galleria Palatina, Museo di San Marco, Museo del Bargello, Galleria dell'Accademia, Museo Archeologico, Cappelle Medicee and the Galleria d'Arte Moderna.

Many of the bigger hotels will also book entry tickets for you.

Opening Times

Museums and monuments tend to close on Monday, although due to the hordes of tourists that pour in year-round, quite a few have made an exception to this rule – the **Azienda di Promozione Turistica** (APT; p220) has a list of them.

Opening times vary throughout the year, although many monuments stick to a vague summer/winter timetable. In the case of state museums, summer means 1 May to 31 October. For other sights it can be more like Easter to the end of September. It is impossible to be overly precise, because timetables change from year to year and from summer to winter. Museum staff frequently find out about changes only at the last minute. Get hold of the latest schedules, especially in winter (when opening times are generally less generous), from an APT office as soon as you arrive in Florence.

At most sights the ticket window shuts 30 minutes before the advertised closing time. Also, in some of these places (the Uffizi and Cappella Brancacci, to name a couple of the culprits) staff shuffle you out at least 15 minutes before closing time. Closing time means not when you have to start heading out the door, but when the door has to be bolted shut.

They can also plot all sorts of specific walks to suit your personal needs and tastes – at a price – and offer half-day guided cycle tours.

You can arrange a personal guide with the **Associazione Guide Turistiche Fiorentine** (☎ 055 422 09 01; www.florencetouristguides.com), the **Associazione Centro Guide Turismo** (☎ 055 28 84 48; www.webcom97.com/centroguide), the **Associazione Guide Turistiche e Accompagnatori** (☎ 055 448 69 71; info@agatour.it), the **Associazione Guide Turistiche della Toscana** (☎ 055 264 52 17; www.florence touristguides.com), or the **Associazione Culturale Guide Florence & Tuscany** (☎ 055 787 77 44; www .firenze-guide.com).

PIAZZA DEL DUOMO & AROUND

Eating p125; Shopping p163; Sleeping p175

Orientation

For more than 2000 years this has been the focal point of what started life as the Roman settlement of Florentia. Here, in the centre of the city and less than 500m north of the River Arno, it is believed a Roman temple once stood, replaced by a modest church after Emperor Constantine's conversion to Christianity in AD 313. As Florence emerged as one of the power centres of medieval Tuscany, so its epicentre gained in splendour. Romanesque, Gothic and Renaissance glories adorn this remarkable square.

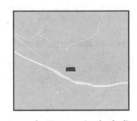

Like bees to a honey pot, tourists from all over the world converge on the Duomo (cathedral) and its surrounding sights. You will need patience to bear the queues (unless you have come in the low season or are extremely lucky) and €27 in cash to visit all the sights. It's heady stuff and will take up the better part of a full day. The area covered in this section includes Piazza del Duomo and the adjoining Piazza di San Giovanni, as well as a few surrounding streets.

BAPTISTRY (BATTISTERO) Map pp251–3

☎ 055 230 28 85; www.operaduomo.firenze.it, Italian only; Piazza di San Giovanni; admission €3;
🕙 noon-7pm Mon-Sat, 8.30am-2pm Sun & holidays;
bus 1, 6, 7, 10, 11, 14, 17, 23 & A

The Romanesque Baptistry may have been built as early as the 5th century on the site of a Roman temple. It is one of the oldest buildings in Florence and dedicated, as indeed was often the case with baptistries in Italy, to St John the Baptist (San Giovanni Battista).

Dante was among the many Florentine great and good to be baptised here. The Roman-era north gate was close to here, about where Via de' Cerretani hits Piazza di San Giovanni. That street marks the line of the Roman north wall.

The present edifice, or at least its façade, dates from about the 11th century. The white-and-green marble stripes that bedeck the octagonal structure are typical of Tuscan Romanesque style.

More striking still are the three sets of bronze doors, conceived as a series of panels in which the story of humanity and the Redemption would be told.

The earliest set of doors, now on the south flank, was completed by Andrea Pisano in 1336. The bas-reliefs on its 28 compartments deal predominantly with the life of St John the Baptist. If you take time to look at the scenes, you will see that Pisano's work is still largely rooted in the Gothic. Stiff, largely expressionless people communicate a didactic message with little or no human emotion.

Lorenzo Ghiberti tied with Brunelleschi in a competition in 1401–02 to do the north doors. Brunelleschi was so disgusted with the suggestion he share the job with Ghiberti that he flounced off in a huff to Rome, leaving his competitor to toil away for the next 20 years in an effort to get the doors just right. The top 20 panels recount episodes from the New Testament, while the eight lower ones show the four Evangelists and the four fathers of the Church.

Good as this late-Gothic effort was, Ghiberti returned almost immediately to his workshops to turn out the east doors. Made of gilded bronze, they took 28 years to complete, largely because of Ghiberti's intransigent perfectionism. The bas-reliefs on their 10 panels depict scenes from the Old Testament. So extraordinary were his exertions that, many years later, Michelangelo stood before the doors in awe and declared them fit to be the **Porta del Paradiso** (Gate of Paradise), which is how they remain known to this day. Certainly the difference between them and Pisano's doors is evidence of the extraordinary shift towards Renaissance ideals. The scenes seem more lifelike, full of movement and depth. It is instructive to spend a little time comparing the two sets of doors. The Ghiberti doors you see here are copies. Visit the Museo dell'Opera del Duomo (p77) to view eight of the original restored panels.

Inside the Baptistry one is reminded of the Pantheon in Rome. The two-coloured marble facing on the outside continues within and is made more arresting by the geometrical flourishes above the Romanesque windows. The inlaid marble designs of the floor, reminiscent of those in the Chiesa di San Miniato al Monte (p106) are equally delightful. Look in particular for the sun and zodiac designs on the side opposite the apse.

But it is the glistering golden mosaics that most leave you pinned to the spot in admiration. Those in the apse were started in 1225 and are, admittedly, looking a little worse for wear. The glittering spectacle in the dome is, however, a unique sight in Florence. For some 32 years from 1270, Venetian experts in this delicate art executed with unusual genius the designs created by Tuscan artists. Among the latter was Cimabue (c 1240–1302), credited with taking the first steps away from Gothic to more natural painting.

Around the northern, eastern and southern sides of the dome stories of the Old and New Testaments unfold, including Genesis, the Visitation, the Last Supper and the death of Christ. The western side is dominated by the figure of Christ Pantocrator enthroned. Around him takes place the Last Judgement. Anyone who has had the fortune to see the 12th- and 13th-century Byzantine mosaics in the Cattedrale di Santa Maria Assunta on the Venetian lagoon island of Torcello will notice uncanny similarities. It becomes clear that only artisans steeped in the same artistic tradition could have produced such a medieval masterpiece.

Donatello carved the tomb of Baldassare Cossa, better known as John XXIII the Antipope, which takes up the wall to the right of the apse. Despite his fall from grace, Cossa had powerful friends and Cosimo de' Medici commissioned the grand tomb for his deceased pal.

CAMPANILE Map pp251–3

☎ 055 230 28 85; www.operaduomo.firenze.it; **Piazza del Duomo; admission €6;** ⏰ 8.30am-7.30pm; **bus 1, 6, 7, 10, 11, 14, 17, 23 & A**

Soaring gracefully by the side of the Duomo is the 84.7m-high Campanile (Bell Tower). You can admire its beauty from the outside and, if you're feeling fit, head inside and climb its 414 steps for some wonderful views of the Duomo and central Florence.

Having designed the bell tower, Giotto began work on it in 1334. His death only three years later cut his contribution cruelly short, and it was left to Andrea Pisano and Francesco Talenti to continue the work. The first tier of bas-reliefs around the base, carved by Pisano but possibly designed by Giotto, depicts the *Attività Umane* (Creation of Man and the Arts and Industries). Those on the second tier depict the planets, cardinal virtues, the arts and the seven sacraments. Many of these and the sculptures of the prophets and sibyls (by Donatello and others) in the niches of the upper storeys are actually copies – the originals are in the Museo dell'Opera del Duomo.

(Continued on page 75)

1 *Catwoman strides past Hotel Botticelli (p182)* **2** *Men on their motorini (mopeds) take a break in front of the Basilica di Santa Maria Novella (p89)* **3** *Enjoying a leisurely drink at a café in the Piazza della Signoria area (p128)* **4** *People mingling outside one of Oltrarno's tempting food shops (p136)*

1 Perseus holds up Medusa's head, a work by Benvenuto Cellini, at the open-air museum in Loggia della Signoria (p84) 2 Giotto di Bondone's Campanile, or bell tower, (p66) soars gracefully by the side of the Duomo 3 Be seen at 150-year old Café Concerto Paskowski (p129) 4 Piazza della Repubblica's large triumphal arch flaunts 19th-century Italian architecture (p79)

1 The gold Last Judgement fresco glitters in the dome of the Baptistry (p65) 2 The Porta del Paradiso, or Gate of Paradise, (p66) at the Baptistry shows Lorenzo Ghiberti's perfectionism 3 Looking up from the bustling Piazza del Duomo is the striking Duomo's façade (p75) 4 Museo del Bargello (p85), once a place of torture, houses exquisite Tuscan Renaissance sculpture

1 *Officina Profumo Farmaceutica di Santa Maria Novella (p171) is one of the world's oldest pharmacies* 2 *Reading the newspaper in style outside the Museo di San Marco (p97)* 3 *The cloisters of the Basilica di Santa Maria Novella (p89)* 4 *The Basilica di Santa Maria Novella (p89) has been the temporary residence of visiting popes*

1 *Fancy some leather? The Mercato Centrale (p93) is a produce market with leather stands outside* 2 *Shopping by* motorini *(mopeds) at Piazza del Mercato Centrale (p171)* 3 *Benozzo Gozzoli's radiant* Adoration of the Magi *fresco at Museo di San Marco (p97)* 4 *Bargains galore, including T-shirts, can be found at Mercato delle Cascine (p171)*

1 *Michelangelo is just one of the celebrities buried at the Basilica di Santa Croce (p100)* 2 *Pietro Tacca's baroque fountain and the Chiesa di SS Annunziata (p95) at one of the city's loveliest piazzas* 3 *Scuola del Cuoio, or Leather School, (p174) is where to find Florentine craftsmanship at work* 4 *Statue of Dante Alighieri (p100) looks down upon the city that exiled him*

A DANTE ALIGHIERI
L' ITALIA
M · DCCC · LXV

1 Elizabeth Barrett Browning's grave at Cimitero degli Inglesi (p95), a peaceful space in the city 2 Kid gloves with silk lining? You'll find every sort in the Santa Croce area (p173) 3 Ponte alle Grazie (p103) has been built and rebuilt due to floods, war, commerce and religion 4 A glazed terracotta baby in swaddling cloth by Andrea della Robbia on the façade of the Spedale degli Innocenti, or 'hospital of the innocents' (p99)

1 *The Ponte Vecchio is located where the first stone bridge stood in 972 (p109)* 2 *The Palazzo Pitti (p108) was renovated over five centuries but the overall style is seamless* 3 *Seeing the Romanesque Chiesa di San Miniato al Monte is worth the climb up from the Piazzale Michelangelo (p109)* 4 *Finding an object of desire at the Mercato dell'Antiquariato (p171)*

(Continued from page 66)

People with heart conditions or who are otherwise unfit should not undertake the climb upstairs. There is no lift should you get into difficulties.

CASA DI DANTE Map pp251–3

☎ 055 21 94 16; Via Santa Margherita 1;
☙ closed indefinitely; bus A

Dante would doubtless be unimpressed with this little travesty. Although the poet likely lived in this part of town, this supposed House of Dante is in fact an early-20th-century structure built on a site that more or less corresponds to the location of the great poet's lodgings. In other words, it's a fake.

If it were open you would see, over several floors, a rather drab museum tracing Dante's life. It consists principally of photocopied documents, some pictorial material and a written commentary that follows Dante's peregrinations and the history of Florence. On the top floor are old copies of the *Divina Commedia* in every language from Chinese to Russian.

DUOMO Map pp251–3

☎ 055 230 28 85; Piazza Duomo; www.operaduomo.fi renze.it; admission free; ☙ 10am-5pm Mon-Wed & Fri, 10am-3.30pm Thu, 10am-4.45pm Sat, 1-4.45pm Sun, closed during Mass; bus 1, 6, 7, 10, 11, 14, 17, 23 & A

You will probably already have spotted Brunelleschi's sloping, red-tiled dome – predominant on Florence's skyline – from afar but when you first come upon the Duomo (Cathedral) from the crowded streets around its square (Piazza del Duomo), you will doubtless be taken aback by the ordered vivacity of its pink, white and green marble façade.

On 25 March 1436 the pope set off from his apartments in the monastery of Santa Maria Novella along a specially raised wooden walkway that had been laid out to the Duomo. Cardinals, bishops and the city's leading figures, including the *priori* (governors) led by the *gonfaloniere* (a kind of first minister) followed in solemn procession. They arrived at the Duomo to pay homage to Brunelleschi's remarkable feat of engineering, the dome, which had just been completed. Brunelleschi had won a public competition to design the enormous dome, the first of its kind since antiquity. Although now severely cracked and under restoration, it remains a remarkable achievement of design.

The great temple's full name is Cattedrale di Santa Maria del Fiore and it is the world's fourth-largest cathedral. It was begun in 1296 by Arnolfo di Cambio and took almost 150 years to complete. It is 153m long and 38m wide, except the transept, which extends 90m. The cathedral it replaced, dedicated to Santa Reparata, fitted into an area extending less than halfway down from the entrance to the transept.

The first 'disappointment', if you will, comes from the façade. It appears to blend perfectly well with the cathedral's flanks, the Romanesque facing of the Baptistry and the Gothic work on the Campanile (p66), but the truth of the matter is that it was raised only in the late 19th century. Its architect, Emilio de Fabris, was inspired by the design of the flanks, which largely date from the 14th century.

Arnolfo began to raise a façade before his death; it remained incomplete and was finally stripped away in 1587 because it was considered old hat. The cathedral languished, exposed, for the next three centuries, largely because no-one could decide how the façade should look, nor find the money to finance it. There was no shortage of projects down the years, including one by Bernardo Buontalenti (c 1536–1608) that would have seen the Duomo dressed up in bold classicist baroque clothes.

From the façade, do a circuit of the cathedral to take in its splendour before heading inside.

The southern flank is the oldest and most clearly Gothic. The second doorway here, the **Porta dei Canonici** (Canons' Door) is a mid-14th-century High-Gothic creation. Wander around the trio of apses, designed to appear as the flowers on the stem that is the nave of the cathedral (hence reflecting the cathedral's name, Santa Maria del Fiore – St Mary of the Flower – which refers to the lily that is the city's symbol). The first door you see on the northern flank after the apses is the early-15th-century **Porta della Mandorla** (Almond Door), so named because of the relief of the Virgin Mary contained within an almond-shaped frame (you enter here to climb up inside the dome). Much of the decorative sculpture that graced the flanks of the cathedral (especially from the original façade that was dismantled in the 16th century) was removed. Some is now on display in the Museo dell'Opera del Duomo.

The vast and spartan interior of the Duomo comes as a surprise after the visual assault outside.

Down the left aisle you will see two immense frescoes of equestrian statues dedicated to two mercenaries, or *condottieri*, who fought in the service of Florence (for lots of dosh of course). The one on the left is Niccolò da Tolentino (by

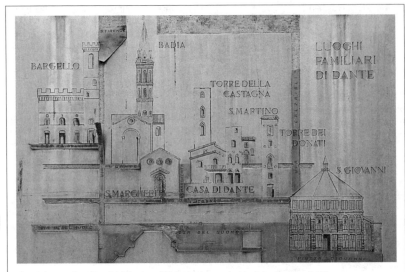

Carved map showing the location of Dante's house, behind the Duomo (p75)

Andrea del Castagno) and the other is Giovanni Acuto, better known to the English as Sir John Hawkwood (by Paolo Uccello). The Florentines made his acquaintance in rather unpleasant circumstances in 1375, when he and his merry band of bloodthirsty marauders gave Florence two options: pay a huge ransom or we'll lay waste to Tuscany. The bankers coughed up and Hawkwood, from that point on, remained the city's leading soldier.

Although Florence had exiled him, Dante's *La Divina Commedia* (The Divine Comedy) fascinated generations of Florentines. Domenico di Michelino's *Dante ei Suoi Mondi* (Dante and His Worlds), the next painting along the left aisle, is one of the most reproduced images of the poet and his verse masterpiece.

The festival of colour and images that greets you as you arrive beneath Brunelleschi's dome is the work of Giorgio Vasari and Federico Zuccari. The fresco series depicts *Il Giudizio Universale* (The Last Judgement). Below that is the octagonal *coro* (choirstalls). Its low marble 'fence' also encloses the altar, above which hangs a crucifix by Benedetto da Maiano.

From the choirstalls, the two wings of the transept and the rear apse spread out, each containing five chapels. The pillars delimiting the entrance into each wing and the apse are fronted by statues of apostles, as are the two hefty pillars just west of the choirstalls.

Between the left (northern) arm of the transept and the apse is the **Sagrestia delle Messe** (Mass Sacristy), whose panelling is a marvel of inlaid wood created by Benedetto and Giuliano da Maiano. The fine bronze doors were executed by Luca della Robbia, showing he could turn his hand to other materials as well as glazed terracotta. That said, the top of the doorway is decorated with one of his *robbiane*, as is the **Sagrestia Nuova** (New Sacristy) by the right transept (no access). It was through della Robbia's doors that Lorenzo de' Medici fled in the uproar following the assassination by the Pazzi conspirators of his brother Giuliano during Mass in 1478.

Some of the finest stained-glass windows in Italy, by Donatello, Andrea del Castagno, Paolo Uccello and Lorenzo Ghiberti, adorn the windows.

A stairway near the main entrance of the Duomo leads down to the **crypt** (admission €3; 10am-5pm Mon-Fri, 10am-4.45pm Sat, closed during Mass), which is the site where excavations (which began in 1965) have unearthed parts of the 8th-century Chiesa di Santa Reparata. Brunelleschi's tomb is also in here (turn left into the bookshop rather than right into the main excavated area). Apart from the surviving floor mosaics, typical of early Christian churches in Italy and recalling their Roman heritage, the spurs and sword of

Giovanni de' Medici were dug up here. Otherwise the remains give only a vague idea of what the Romanesque church might have been like, and a still dimmer clue of what the church's Roman predecessor might have been.

You can climb up into the **dome** (admission €6; 🕐 8.30am-7pm Mon-Fri, 8.30am-5.40pm Sat) to get a closer look at Brunelleschi's engineering feat. You enter by the Porta della Mandorla from outside the north flank of the cathedral. The view from the summit over Florence is breathtaking. Be aware that you must climb 463 stairs – there is no lift. As with the Campanile, people with heart conditions should think twice about this climb.

On 8 September every year, a walkway that stretches around the sides and façade of the dome is opened to the public. You access it by the same entrance as to the dome.

LOGGIA DEL BIGALLO Map pp251–3
🕿 055 230 28 85; Piazza di San Giovanni; admission €3; 🕐 8.30am-noon Mon, 4-6pm Thu; bus 1, 6, 7, 10, 11, 14, 17, 23 & A

This elegant marble loggia was built in the second half of the 14th century for the Compagnia (or Confraternita) di Santa Maria della Misericordia, which had been formed in 1244 to aid the elderly, the sick and orphans. Lost and abandoned children were customarily placed here so that they could be reclaimed by their families or put into the care of foster mothers. In the meantime, the orphans were lodged upstairs. The members of the fraternity transported the ill to hospital and buried the dead in times of plague. In 1425 the fraternity was fused with another that had been founded by the same person, the Confraternita del Bigallo. The fusion lasted for a century, after which the Misericordia moved to its present position on Piazza del Duomo, from where to this day they continue their ambulance vocation.

The loggia houses a small museum containing a limited collection of artworks belonging to the two fraternities. Of particular interest are the two frescoes in the last room. One, by Niccolò di Pietro Gerini (active 1368–1415) depicts the 'captains' of the Misericordia fraternity assigning orphans to their new mothers (for which the latter were paid). The other, Bernardo Daddi's La Madonna della Misericordia, is interesting above all for the view of Florence at the feet of Our Lady. It is the earliest-known depiction of the city and shows the nearby Duomo with its (at the time) incomplete façade.

MUSEO DELL'OPERA DEL DUOMO
Map pp251–3
🕿 055 230 28 85; Piazza del Duomo 9; admission €6; 🕐 9am-7.30pm Mon-Sat, 9am-1.40pm Sun; bus 14 & 23

Lurking modestly behind the cathedral is the treasure chest of sculptures that once adorned the Duomo, Baptistry and Campanile.

As you enter you see several 3rd-century marble fragments from funerary urns and sarcophagi. These are followed by some sculptural groups from the Baptistry and then various statues (ranging from 1335 to the 1380s) that once adorned the doorways of the Duomo.

You then enter the first main hall, devoted to statuary that graced Arnolfo di Cambio's original Gothic façade, which was never completed. Among the pieces, which, after the façade was dismantled in the 16th century, were scattered about churches and gardens across Florence, are some masterpieces, including several by Arnolfo himself. They include representations of Pope Boniface VIII, the Virgin and Child, and Santa Reparata. The long flowing beard of Donatello's St John stands out among the four mighty statues of the Evangelists.

Out in the courtyard are displayed eight of the original 10 panels of Ghiberti's masterpiece, the *Porta del Paradiso* of the Baptistry (what you see at the Baptistry itself are copies). They were damaged in the 1966 floods and needed urgent restoration. It has taken a while but the result is worth it.

As you head up the stairs you approach what is the museum's best-known piece, Michelangelo's *Pietà*, which he intended for his own tomb and was moved here from the Duomo in 1980. Vasari recorded in his *Lives of the Artists* that, unsatisfied with the quality of the marble or his own work, Michelangelo broke up the unfinished sculpture, destroying the arm and left leg of the figure of Christ. A student of Michelangelo later restored the arm and completed the figure of Mary Magdalene.

Continue upstairs to the next main hall, which is dominated by the two extraordinary *cantorie*, or choir lofts (one by Donatello and the other by Luca della Robbia) that once adorned the Sagrestie in the Duomo. The panels of Luca della Robbia's *cantoria* have been removed and placed at eye level for closer inspection. They display children in joyous song and dance, and playing musical instruments, in what is one of the most remarkable pieces of Renaissance sculpture you are likely to see. In the same hall is Donatello's carving

Relaxing in front of the Hotel Savoy (p179)

of the prophet Habakkuk (taken from the Campanile and now under restoration) and, in an adjoining room, his wooden impression of Mary Magdalene (formerly in the Baptistry) – another masterpiece, tense with the stress and emotion of a woman who has submitted herself to fasting and penitence.

Another room of the hall with the *cantorie* is filled with original medallions from the Campanile, principally by Andrea and Nino Pisano, as well as others by Luca della Robbia and Maso di Banco. From there the display takes you past some of the scaffolding and tools from the work site of Brunelleschi's dome, the architect's death mask and several models of plans for the Duomo's new façade (which was only finalised in the 19th century).

MUSEO STORICO-TOPOGRAFICO 'FIRENZE COM'ERA' Map pp248–50

☎ 055 261 65 45; Via dell'Oriuolo 24; admission €2.70; ⏱ 9am-2pm Fri-Wed; bus 14 & 23

The mildly interesting 'Florence as it was' museum, behind the Duomo, charts the city's development, particularly from the Renaissance to the modern day. Paintings, models, topographical drawings (the earliest dating from 1594) and prints help explain the history of the city. The sketches and other pictures of the Mercato Vecchio (Old Market) and the old Jewish ghetto area are intriguing (and a little

sad), showing as they do something of what was the bustling heart of the city before the town fathers had it all torn down to make way for the Piazza della Repubblica. A fine diorama and some maps complete the picture of destruction.

Another of the sections is dedicated to the evolution of the site from the times of the earliest-known settlement to Roman days, also providing information on what excavations have revealed about the city. Interspersed between explanatory panels is a sparse collection of Roman and Etruscan remains dug up in and around Florence.

The entire collection is a somewhat makeshift affair, as plans are afoot to create (one day!) the Museo della Città (Museum of the City) in the Palazzo Vecchio.

PALAZZO NONFINITO Map pp251–3

☎ 055 239 64 49; Via del Proconsolo 12; admission €3; ⏱ 9am-1pm Mon-Wed & Thu-Fri; bus 14, 23 & A

Bernardo Buontalenti started work on this residence for the Strozzi family in 1593. The area had been occupied by smaller houses, all swept aside for the grand new structure. Buontalenti and others completed the Palladian-style 1st floor and courtyard but the upper floors were never completely finished, hence the building's name. Buontalenti's window designs and other details constitute a mannerist touch that take the building beyond the classicist rigour of the Renaissance. The obscure **Museo dell'Antropologia e Etnologia** is housed here. It contains all sorts of oddments, ranging from ancient crania to arms, boats and other objects from various indigenous peoples around the world. The fusty displays are sorted roughly by regions (Africa, America, Asia, India and Oceania).

PIAZZA DELLA REPUBBLICA Map pp251–3
bus A

On first sight this broad, breezy square seems perfectly acceptable as squares go, but the longer you look the more you realise that it probably isn't an ancient public space. Ever since this square was ruthlessly gouged from the city centre in the years following Italian unity in 1861, all and sundry have continued to execrate it.

On the western flank of the square a huge memorial plaque atop a bombastic triumphal arch proclaims stridently *l'antico centro della città da secolare squallore a nuova vita restituito* ('the ancient city centre returned to new life after centuries of squalor'). A polite way of saying: 'Hey, look! We've managed to rip out the heart of the old city and replace it with a soulless void!' Even today more sensitive Florentines remain embarrassed by this masterstroke of middle-class 19th-century arrogance.

To create the piazza and restructure the surrounding areas, 26 ancient streets and a further 18 lanes disappeared, along with 341 residential buildings, 451 shops, 173 warehouses and other buildings and services, while 5822 residents were forcibly relocated to other parts of the city. The entire Mercato Vecchio, which had inherited its function as a central market from the Roman forum, and the nearby lanes of the small Jewish ghetto were simply wiped from the map.

Just off the northwest tip of Piazza della Repubblica, where the Cinema Gambrinus is, excavators found a Roman ramp leading down to what must have been one of the Roman town's main cisterns, from which the populace would have drawn its fresh water.

If you want to get some idea of what this part of town looked like before the 'squalor' was wiped away, the Museo Storico-Topografico 'Firenze Com'Era' (opposite) has a model, maps and late-19th-century pictures of the area.

PIAZZA DELLA SIGNORIA & AROUND
Eating p125; Shopping p163; Sleeping p175

Orientation

The hub of the city's political life through the centuries and surrounded by some of its most celebrated buildings, the piazza has the appearance of an outdoor sculpture gallery. Just to the east, stretching in a semicircle from Via de' Gondi to the junction of Via de' Castellani and Via dei Neri, was Roman Florentia's first theatre, built in the 1st century AD.

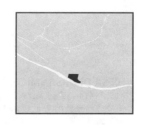

Whenever Florence entered one of its innumerable political crises, the people would be called here as a *parlamento* to rubber-stamp decisions that frequently meant ruin for some ruling families and victory for others. Often one side or the other would make sure the square was cordoned off with loyal troops, just to hint in which direction votes should go. Here too the Ciompi (working class, or *popolo minuto*) rampaged in Florence's only true proletarian uprising in the 14th century. Scenes of great pomp and circumstance alternated with others of terrible suffering – the puritan preacher Savonarola was hanged and fried along with two supporters here in 1498. A bronze plaque towards the middle of the piazza marks the spot of his execution.

The Palazzo Vecchio, with its crenellated walls and slender bell tower, stands watch over the square and the whole city. Seat of republican government and later of less democratic rule, it serves today as the mayoral offices. Directly connected are the Uffizi, built under Cosimo I to house his Grand Duchy's public servants, and today is the city's most important art gallery.

The square itself is something of an art gallery. Bartolomeo Ammanati's huge Fontana di Netuno (Neptune Fountain) sits beside the Palazzo Vecchio. Although the bronze satyrs and divinities frolicking about the edges of the fountain are quite delightful, *Il Biancone* (The Big White Thing), as locals derisively refer to it, is pretty universally considered a flop. Michelangelo couldn't believe Ammannati (1511–92) had ruined such a nice block of marble.

Flanking the entrance to the palace are copies of Michelangelo's *David* (the original is in the Galleria dell'Accademia) and Donatello's *Marzocco*, the heraldic Florentine lion (the original is in the Museo del Bargello). To the latter's right is a 1980 copy of Donatello's bronze *Giuditta e Oloferne* (Judith Slays Holofernes) – the original is in the Sala dei Gigli inside the palace.

A bronze equestrian statue of Cosimo I de' Medici, rendered by Giambologna in 1594–98, stands towards the centre of the piazza.

The piazza lies at the core of the area covered in this section, which spreads south to the river, north to Via del Corso, east to Via dei Leoni and Piazza San Firenze and west to Piazza Santa Trinita.

BADIA FIORENTINA Map pp251–3
Via del Proconsolo; admission free; 3-6pm Mon; bus 14, 23 & A

The 10th-century Badia Fiorentina (Florence Abbey) was built on the orders of Willa, mother of one of the early margraves of Tuscany, Ugo. Willa was inspired to this act by calls for greater piety in the Church, which at the time was coming under hefty attack from some quarters for corruption. Ugo continued the work of his mother, investing considerably in the Benedictine monastery and church. He was eventually buried here.

This is one of several places where they say Dante first espied the object of his unrequited love, Beatrice. It is particularly worth visiting to see Filippino Lippi's *Apparizione della Madonna a San Bernardo* (Appearance of the Virgin to St Bernard), which is to the left as you enter the church through the small (and scaffolding-cluttered) Renaissance cloister.

At the left end of the transept is the monument to Margrave Ugo by Mino da Fiesole (1429–84).

CHIESA DI ORSANMICHELE Map pp251–3
☎ 055 28 49 44; Via dell'Arte della Lana; admission free; 9am-noon & 4-6pm, closed 1st & last Mon of month; bus A

Originally a grain market, the church was formed when the arcades of the granary building were walled in during the 14th century and the granary moved elsewhere. The granary was built on a spot known as Orsanmichele, a contraction of Orto di San Michele (St Michael's Garden). Under the Lombards a small church dedicated to St Michael and an adjacent Benedictine convent had indeed been graced with a pleasant garden. The *signoria* (the city's government) cleared the lot to have the granary built. It was destroyed by fire 20 years later and a finer replacement constructed. This was

considered too good to be a mere granary, so it was converted into a church.

The *signoria* ordered the guilds to finance the decoration of the oddly shaped house of worship, and they proceeded to commission sculptors to erect statues of their patron saints in tabernacles placed around the building's façades.

The statues, commissioned over the 15th and 16th centuries, represent the work of some of the Renaissance's greatest artists. Some of the statues are now in the Museo del Bargello. Many splendid pieces remain, however, including Giambologna's *San Luca* (St Luke; third on the right on Via de' Calzaiuoli), a copy of Donatello's *San Giorgio* (St George; last on the right on Via Orsanmichele), and Ghiberti's bronze *San Matteo* (St Matthew; first on the left on Via dell'Arte della Lana).

The main feature of the interior is the splendid Gothic tabernacle, decorated with coloured marble, by Andrea Orcagna. It is an extraordinary item; to look at the convulsed, twisting columns, you would swear you were looking at a scale prototype for the cathedral in Orvieto (Umbria). Classical music recitals are held here occasionally.

Eventually (but no-one knows when) the remaining statues outside will be replaced by copies and the originals exhibited in a museum inside Orsanmichele.

CHIESA DI SAN FIRENZE Map pp251–3
Piazza San Firenze; bus 14, 23 & A

From as early as 1645, the Oratorian Fathers wanted to expand the small parish church of San Firenze. For the next century, architects and finances came and went, and the design continued to change. The original church, which stood on the right flank of the present building, was to have a chapel and convent added. In the end, a new church, dedicated to

St Philip Neri, was built on the left flank and the San Firenze church was reduced to an oratory. The two were then linked and the whole complex became known, erroneously, as Chiesa di San Firenze. The late-baroque façade that unites the buildings was completed in 1775. Today most of the building is occupied by law courts, although if you get lucky you may be able to enter the church.

CORRIDOIO VASARIANO Map pp251–3
☎ 055 265 43 21; Galleria degli Uffizi; ⏱ irregular; bus B

When Cosimo I de' Medici's wife bought the Palazzo Pitti and the family moved into their new digs, they wanted to maintain their link – literally – with what from now on would be known as the Palazzo Vecchio. And so Cosimo commissioned Vasari to build an enclosed walkway between the two palaces that would allow the Medicis to wander between the two without having to deal with the public. Vasari's original project envisaged that it would take five years to complete. But Cosimo had other ideas. His son Francesco was to be married and father wanted everything ready sooner. Vasari always boasted about being fast with a canvas. Now he and his workshop managed to turn out this singular architectural feat in just five months – the kind of efficiency Florentines can only dream about nowadays.

The corridor, lined with phalanxes of largely minor art works, has changed considerably over the years. Its present aspect dates to 1923, but it is possible that many of the paintings hung here will be moved to the Nuovi Uffizi (see the boxed text, p84) in the coming years.

At various times since 1999 the corridor has been opened up to the public. When or whether it does seems completely random – the only way to find out is to call. If it does open, visitors should note that the art on display is fairly minor stuff and the amount requested for a guided tour frequently exorbitant (approximately €30 a head). To appreciate it you will want to have a genuine interest in Florentine history or a hunger for relatively obscure art.

You may find yourself on a guided tour from Palazzo Vecchio, where from the Quartiere di Eleonora (after much unbolting of doors and ceremony) you are ushered in through the first part of the corridor (which houses offices) across to the Uffizi, where you will plunge into the main stretch of the corridor, following its twists and turns along the Arno, over the Ponte

A Recipe for Stendhalismo

Any list of 'must sees' in Florence is going to incite cries of protest. How can you recommend that a tour cover the Uffizi, the Duomo and the Baptistry, without including the Museo del Bargello, the Convento di San Marco and the churches of Santa Maria Novella, Santa Croce and SS Annunziata? And what about Masaccio's fresco cycle in Basilica di Santa Maria del Carmine? Or Michelangelo's *David* in the Galleria dell'Accademia and his Medici tombs in the family chapel attached to the Basilica di San Lorenzo?

Plan carefully, or you could end up with a severe case of *Stendhalismo*. Stendhal, the 19th-century French writer, was so dazzled by the magnificence of the Basilica di Santa Croce that he was barely able to walk for faintness. He is apparently not the only one to have felt thus overwhelmed by the beauty of Florence – they say Florentine doctors treat a dozen cases of *Stendhalismo*, or *sindrome di Stendhal* (Stendhal syndrome), a year.

Oh, and make sure you carry plenty of small change for the machines to illuminate the frescoes in the churches!

Vecchio, around the Torre dei Mannelli (whose owners refused to allow Cosimo I to bulldoze through the medieval tower house), across the road and past the Chiesa di Santa Felicita (where an enclosed balcony allowed the Medici to hear Mass without being seen) and then into the Palazzo Pitti, where you emerge by the Grotta del Buontalenti in the Giardino di Boboli. Along the way you can peer out for unusual views of Florence, and various paintings are explained. A long corridor of self-portraits of artists starts with one of Leonardo (at least it is believed to be genuine) and continues through to one by Chagall. But for most of us the paintings are a little yawn inducing. Apart from a couple of Rubens and a Dürer, there is precious little in the way of first-class art on view.

GALLERIA DEGLI UFFIZI Map pp251–3
☎ 055 238 86 51; Piazza degli Uffizi 6; admission €6.50 (plus €2 for advance booking); ☎ 8.15am-6.50pm Tue-Sun; bus B

Designed and built by Vasari in the second half of the 16th century at the request of Cosimo I de' Medici, the Palazzo degli Uffizi, south of the Palazzo Vecchio, originally housed the city's administrators, judiciary and guilds. It was, in effect, a government office building (*uffizi* means offices).

Vasari designed the private corridor, Corridoio Vasariano (see the previous entry), linking Palazzo Vecchio with Palazzo Pitti, through the Uffizi and across the Ponte Vecchio.

Cosimo I's successor, Francesco I, commissioned the architect Buontalenti to modify the upper floor of the Palazzo degli Uffizi to house the Medicis' growing art collection. Thus, indirectly, the first steps were taken to turn it into an art gallery. It was first opened to selected public visits in 1591 – making it one of Europe's first functioning museums. Francesco also had a roof garden created – now converted into the gallery's cafeteria.

The Uffizi Gallery today houses the family's private collection, bequeathed to the city in 1743 by the last of the Medici family, Anna Maria Ludovica, on condition that it never leave the city. Over the years parts of the collection have been moved to the Museo del Bargello and the city's Museo Archeologico. In compensation, other collections, such as that of Count Augusto Contini-Bonacossi, put together in the 1930s, have joined the core group. Paintings from Florence's churches have also been moved to the gallery. It houses the world's single greatest collection of Italian and Florentine art.

It has to be said that, especially when crowded in summer, visiting the Uffizi can be unpleasant. The gallery tends to be hot and stuffy and the crowds render the chances of enjoying anything of what is on display a challenge, to say the least. To queue and then suffer inside seems more like a modern-day act of religious abnegation than a desirable opportunity to contemplate beautiful art. On the other hand, the queuing is in part due to an effort to limit the maximum number inside at any time to 780 people.

Try to arrive in the morning when the gallery first opens, or during lunchtime or the late afternoon. Alternatively, book ahead (see the boxed text, p64). In high season especially, queuing can mean waits of three or more hours.

Before heading upstairs to the gallery, visit the restored remains of the 11th-century **Chiesa di San Piero Scheraggio**. The church's apse was incorporated into the structure of the palace but most of the rest was destroyed. If it is closed (as it has been for some years now), you can get a fractional idea from what remains on the exterior of the northern wall of the palace.

On the 1st floor is the small **Galleria dei Disegni e delle Stampe** (Drawing and Print Gallery), in which initial draughts and sketches by the great masters are often shown. They tend to rotate the display frequently, as prolonged exposure can damage the drawings.

Upstairs in the gallery proper, you pass through two vestibules, the first with busts

Portraiture outside the Galleria degli Uffizi (p81)

of several of the Medici clan and other grand dukes, the second with some Roman statuary.

The long corridor has been arranged much as it appeared in the 16th century. Below the frescoed ceilings is a series of small portraits of great and good men, interspersed with larger portraits, often of Medici family members or intimates. The statuary, much of it collected in Rome by the Medicis' agents, is either Roman or at least thought to be. **Room 1** (which used to hold archaeological treasures) is closed.

The first accessible rooms feature works by Tuscan masters of the 13th and early 14th centuries. **Room 2** is dominated by three paintings of the *Madonna in Maestà* by Duccio di Buoninsegna, Cimabue and Giotto. All three were altarpieces in Florentine churches before being placed in the gallery. To look at them in this order is to appreciate the transition from Gothic to the precursor of the Renaissance. Also in the room is Giotto's polyptych *Madonna col Bambino Gesù, Santi e Angeli* (Madonna with Baby Jesus, Saints and Angels).

Room 3 traces the Sienese school of the 14th century. Of particular note is Simone Martini's shimmering *Annunciazione* (Annunciation), considered a masterpiece of the school, and Ambrogio Lorenzetti's triptych *Madonna col Bambino e Santi* (Madonna with Child and Saints). **Room 4** contains works of the Florentine 14th century.

Rooms 5 and **6** house examples of the International Gothic style, among them Gentile da Fabriano's *Adorazione dei Magi* (Adoration of the Magi).

Room 7 features works by painters of the early-15th-century Florentine school, which pioneered the Renaissance. There is one panel (the other two are in the Louvre and London's National Gallery) from Paolo Uccello's striking *La Battaglia di San Romano* (Battle of San Romano). In his efforts to create perspective, he directs the lances, horses and soldiers to a central disappearing point. Other works include Piero della Francesca's portraits of *Battista Sforza* and *Federico da Montefeltro*, and a *Madonna col Bambino* painted jointly by Masaccio and Masolino. In the next room, devoted to a collection of works by Fra Filippo Lippi and Filippino Lippi, is Fra Filippo's delightful *Madonna col Bambino e due Angeli* (Madonna with Child and Two Angels). One of those angels has the cheekiest little grin.

Room 9 is devoted largely to Antonio de Pollaiuolo. His series of six virtues is followed by an addition (*Fortezza* – Strength) by Botticelli. The clarity of line and light, and the

humanity in the face set the painting apart from Pollaiuolo's work and is a taster for the **Botticelli Room**, **Nos 10** to **14**, which is considered the gallery's most spectacular. Highlights are the *La Nascita di Venere* (Birth of Venus) and *Allegoria della Primavera* (Allegory of Spring). *Calunnia* (Calumny) is a disturbing reflection of Botticelli's loss of faith in human potential that came in later life.

Room 15 features da Vinci's *Annunciazione*, Annunciation) painted when he was a student of Verrocchio. Perhaps more intriguing is his unfinished *Adorazione dei Magi*. **Room 16** (blocked off, although you can peer in) contained old maps.

Room 18, known as the **Tribuna**, houses the celebrated Medici *Venus*, a copy from the 1st century BC of a 4th-century-BC sculpture by the Greek sculptor, Praxiteles. The room also contains portraits of various members of the Medici family.

The great Umbrian painter, Perugino, who studied under Piero della Francesca and later became Raphael's master, is represented in **Room 19**, as well as Luca Signorelli. Piero di Cosimo's *Perseo Libera Andromeda* is full of fantastical whimsy with beasts and flying heroes. **Room 20** features works from the German Renaissance, including Dürer's *Adorazione dei Magi*. His depictions of Adam and Eve are mirrored by those of Lucas Cranach. **Room 21**, with a heavily Venetian leaning, has works by Giovanni Bellini and his pupil, Giorgione, along with a few by Vittorio Carpaccio.

In **Room 22**, given over to various German and Flemish Renaissance artists, you can see a small self-portrait by Hans Holbein. The following room takes us back to the Veneto region in Italy's northeast with paintings mainly by Andrea Mantegna and Correggio. Peek into **Room 24** to see the 15th- to 19th-century works in the **Miniatures Room** and then cross into the west wing, which houses works of Italian masters dating from the 16th century.

The star of **Room 25** is Michelangelo's dazzling *Tondo Doni*, which depicts the Holy Family. The composition is highly unusual, with Joseph holding Jesus on Mary's shoulder as she twists around to watch him. The colours are so vibrant and the lines so clear as to seem almost photographic. This masterpiece of the High Renaissance seems to leap out at you as you enter, demanding attention.

In **Room 26** are works by Raphael, including his *Leo X* and *Madonna del Cardellino* (actually a copy as the original is being restored). The former is remarkable for the richness of colour (especially the reds) and detail. Also on

An Old Story at the New Uffizi

When, oh when will the Nuovi Uffizi (New Uffizi) open its doors? For decades they have been contemplating the expansion of the museum into largely unused space and the modernisation of its installations. This became more urgent when the Mafia bombing in 1993 damaged part of the west wing. More importantly, the rise in the number of visitors (from 100,000 in 1950 to the current number of more than 1.5 million a year) has made such changes a matter of urgency.

The floors below the present gallery have been cleared of state archives and the Japanese architect Arata Isozaki is ready to go ahead with his controversial project for a starkly modern portico exit on to Piazza de' Castellani on the east side of the gallery. He won the 1998 competition for the job but his project has whipped up a storm of protest from many Florentines (including film director Franco Zeffirelli) who feel his monumental way out of the museum will be an equally monstrous eyesore in the heart of medieval Florence.

The town's authorities are more concerned about getting the thing finally under way. A complex alliance of public and private forces (including Benetton, which will open a restaurant and stores on Piazza de' Castellani) are putting up the €57 million for the project and archaeological investigation got started in late 2003. The whole thing was supposed to be finished in late 2004 but is unlikely to be ready before the end of 2006. Even that date seems increasingly optimistic.

When the Nuovi Uffizi finally do open, many works now in storage, as well as a sizable archaeological collection and temporary exhibitions, will all be part of the new gallery. Already the occasional temporary exhibit is put on in the lower floors. Visiting is an opportunity to see just how much work is still left to be done!

display are some works by Andrea del Sarto. **Room 27** is dominated by the at times disquieting works of Florence's two main mannerist masters, Pontormo and Il Rosso Fiorentino.

Room 28 boasts eight Titians, including *Venere d'Urbino* (Venus of Urbino). His presence signals a shift in the weighting here to representatives of the Venetian school. **Rooms 29** and **30** contain works by comparatively minor painters from northern Italy, but **Room 31** is dominated above all by Venice's Paolo Veronese, including his *Sacra Famiglia e Santa Barbara* (Holy Family and St Barbara).

In **Room 32** it is Tintoretto's turn. He is accompanied by a few Jacopo Bassano canvasses. **Room 33** is named the Corridor of the 16th Century and contains works by a mix of lesser-known artists. A couple of pieces by Vasari appear, along with an unexpected foreign contribution, El Greco's *I Santi San Giovanni Evangelista e San Francesco* (Saints John the Evangelist and Francis). The following room is filled mainly with 16th-century works by Lombard painters, although somehow the Venetian Lorenzo Lotto managed to sneak in with three paintings.

Next door comes as a bit of a shock as you are confronted with the enormous and sumptuous canvasses of Federico Barocci (1535–1612) of Urbino. **Rooms 36** and **37** are part of the exit, while the adjoining **Room 38** at the moment houses the extraordinary restored *Annunciazione* (Annunciation) by Siena's Simone Martini and Lippo Memmi.

For some reason the counting starts at No **41** after this. This room is given over mostly to non-Italian masters such as Rubens, Van Dyck and Spain's Diego Velázquez. There are two enormous tableaux by Rubens, sweeping with violence and power, representing the French King Henri IV at the Battle of Ivry and his triumphal march into Paris. The beautifully designed **Room 42**, with its exquisite coffered ceiling and splendid dome, is filled with Roman statues.

Caravaggio dominates **Room 43** with his play of light and shade (look for *Il Sacrificio d'Isacco*), while Rembrandt features in **Room 44**. **Room 45** takes us back to Venice, with 18th-century works by Canaletto, Guardi, Tiepolo, the two Longhi, and Crespi, along with a couple of stray pieces by the Spaniard Goya.

Between Rooms 25 and 34 is an entrance (not generally open to the public) that leads down a staircase into the Corridoio Vasariano.

LOGGIA DELLA SIGNORIA Map pp251–3
Piazza della Signoria; bus B

Built in the late 14th century as a platform for public ceremonies, this loggia in Piazza della Signoria eventually became a showcase for sculptures. It also became known as the Loggia dei Lanzi, as Cosimo I used to station his Swiss mercenaries (or *Landsknechte*), armed with lances, in it to remind people who was in charge around here.

To the left of the steps stands Benvenuto Cellini's magnificent bronze statue of Perseus holding aloft the head of Medusa. To the right is Giambologna's mannerist *Ratto delle Sabine* (Rape of the Sabine Women), his final work. Inside the loggia proper is another of Giambologna's works, *Ercole col Centauro Nesso* (Hercules with the Centaur Nessus), in which the centaur definitely appears to be coming off second best. The statue originally stood near the southern end of the Ponte Vecchio. Among the other statues (some of which are being restored) are Roman representations of women.

MERCATO NUOVO Map pp251–3
Bus B

Leather goods of varying quality compete with trashy trinkets and tourist gewgaws at the 'New Market'. The loggia was built in the 16th century to cover the merchandise (including wool, silk and gold) traded here in the days of Cosimo I.

The **Fontana del Porcellino** (Piglet's Fountain) at the southern side of the market is a bit of a misnomer. This life-size bronze of a wild boar is supposed to have particular powers over those who chuck a coin into the small basin and rub the critter's shiny snout. Those who do this will, it is said, inevitably one day return to Florence. The statue is an early-17th-century copy of the Greek marble original that is now in the Uffizi. If the local environmental group, Legambiente, had anything to say in the matter, no-one would come back because touching and clambering on the poor old 'piglet' would be made illegal.

Smack in the middle of the market is a stone symbol in the shape of a cartwheel in the pavement (visible if it has not been covered up with bags and other junk). In times of war, the city's old medieval war cart *(carroccio)* was placed here as a symbol of impending hostilities. On a less serious note (except perhaps for those on the receiving end), this was also the spot where dodgy merchants were punished. According to the law they were to drop their trousers, 'exposing the pudenda', and receive a sound thrashing on the bare buttocks. No doubt some disgruntled shoppers will wish the law were still on the books today.

MUSEO DEL BARGELLO Map pp251–3
☎ 055 238 86 06; Via del Proconsolo 4; admission €4; ⏰ 8.30am-1.50pm Tue-Sat, also alternating Sun & Mon; bus 14, 23 & A

Begun in 1254, the Palazzo del Bargello, also known as the Palazzo del Podestà, was originally the residence of the chief magistrate and then a police station. During its days as a police complex, many people were tortured near the well in the centre of the medieval courtyard. Indeed, for a long time the city's prisons were located here.

It now houses the most comprehensive collection of Tuscan Renaissance sculpture in Italy. The museum is absolutely not to be missed. It is less popular than the Galleria dell'Accademia and Uffizi and attracts smaller crowds.

You enter the courtyard from Via Ghibellina and turn right into the ticket office. From here you end up into the ground-floor **Sala del Cinquecento** (16th-Century Room), dominated by early works by Michelangelo. His drunken *Bacco* (Bacchus), executed when the artist was 22, a marble bust of Brutus, and a tondo of the *Madonna col Bambino* (Madonna and Child) are among his best here. Other works of particular interest are Benvenuto Cellini's rather camp marble *Ganimede* (Ganymede) and *Narciso* (Narcissus), along with Giambologna's *Mercurio Volante* (Winged Mercury).

Among the statues lining the courtyard is Giambologna's powerful *Oceano* (on the Via della Vigna Vecchia side). Cross the courtyard to the small **Sala del Trecento** (14th-Century Room) where, among other pieces, you can see Arnolfo's very Gothic group of *Acoliti* (Acolytes).

Head now up the grand staircase to the 1st floor. In the gallery (which, in the days when the building was a prison, was closed off and divided into cells) are a series of statues and bronzes destined for fountains and gardens. They include a series of animal and bird bronzes by Giambologna.

Turn right into the majestic **Salone del Consiglio Generale** (Hall of the General Council). At the far end, housed in a tabernacle, is Donatello's famed *San Giorgio* (St George), which once graced the Chiesa di Orsanmichele. *David* (as in David and Goliath) was a favourite subject for sculptors. In this hall you can see both a marble version by Donatello and the fabled bronze he executed in later years. The latter is extraordinary – more so when you consider it was the first freestanding naked statue sculpted since classical times. This David doesn't appear terribly warrior-like. He looks rather like he is mincing up to the bar for a drinkie.

Another Donatello of note here is the *Marzocco*, the lion propping up the standard of Florence (a red lily on a white background). This originally stood on Piazza della Signoria, where it has been replaced with a copy.

From this hall you pass into a room given over to Islamic tapestries, ceramics and other items. There follows the Carrand collection, a mixed bag of items collected by a 19th-century French antiquarian in Florence. At the far end of this hall is the **Cappella di Santa Maria Maddalena** (Mary Magdalene's Chapel). The frescoes were created around 1340 by Giotto's workshop. The back-wall fresco depicting *Paradiso* (Heaven) includes a portrait of Dante.

You head back into the Carrand hall and then left into a room containing exquisite ivory pieces, some dating from Carolingian times. The closer you look at these miniature sculptures, the more astounding the workmanship appears.

Up on the 2nd floor you arrive in a room filled with glazed terracotta sculptures by the della Robbia family and others. The simplest and yet most captivating is the bust of a *Fanciullo* (Boy) in the annexe room to the left.

From that room you enter another filled with small bronzes. Among them, the two masterpieces are Antonio Pollaiuolo's *Ercole e Anteo* (Hercules and Anteus) and Cellini's *Ganimede*. Backtrack through the small room with the *Fanciullo* and continue into the next hall. Reliefs and sculptures by Mino da Fiesole and others play second fiddle to Verrocchio, among whose best efforts here is the *Madonna del Mazzolino*.

MUSEO DI STORIA DELLA SCIENZA

Map pp251–3

☎ 055 26 53 11; Piazza de' Giudici 1; admission €6.50; 9.30am-5pm Mon & Wed-Fri, 9.30am-1pm Tue & Sat Jun-Sep; 9.30am-5pm Mon & Wed-Sat, 9.30am-1pm Tue, 10am-1pm 2nd Sun of every month Oct-May; bus 23 & B

Telescopes that look more like works of art; the most extraordinarily complex-looking instruments for the measurement of distance, time and space; and a room full of wax and plastic cutaway models of the various stages of childbirth are among the highlights in the odd collection that makes up this Museum of the History of Science.

If you have a genuine interest in the history of science, then you will almost certainly find at least some of the exhibits intriguing. Many, such as Samuel Morland's mechanical calculator, are from other parts of Europe. Indeed, after the golden age personified by the likes of Galileo, science in Florence and the rest of Tuscany declined in spite of occasional efforts on the part of the Medici and their successors to encourage research.

The centre of **Room VIII**, filled with globes of the world, is occupied by a huge solar-system globe with earth at the centre and the moon, sun and other known planets, as well as astrological symbols, represented by wooden rotating 'spheres'.

Also on display in 21 rooms over two floors are astrolabes, clocks, pumps, microscopes and surgical instruments.

PALAZZO DAVANZATI Map pp251–3

☎ 055 238 86 10; Via Porta Rossa 13; closed for restoration since 1995; bus A

This remarkable 14th-century mansion has survived intact in its medieval state largely due to the intervention of an antiquarian, Elia Volpi, who bought the building in 1904. By that time it had come down in the world, having been divided into small flats and shops and been reduced to a pathetic state. Volpi had it restored to its former glory and it eventually became the seat of the **Museo dell'Antica Casa Fiorentina**, which aims to transmit an idea of what life was like in a medieval Florentine mansion. As the work of restoration proceeds slowly, all you can see is a small display on the house in the foyer, open 8.15am–1.45pm every 1st, 3rd and 5th Sunday and each 2nd and 4th Monday of the month.

PALAZZO VECCHIO Map pp251–3

☎ 055 276 82 24; Piazza della Signoria; admission €6 (combined ticket with Cappella Brancacci €8); 9am-7pm Fri-Wed, 9am-2pm Thu; bus B

Formerly known as the Palazzo della Signoria and built by Arnolfo di Cambio between 1298 and 1314, this palace is the traditional seat of Florentine government. Its **Torre d'Arnolfo** is 94m

The Urge to Discover

In keeping with Cosimo I de' Medici's avid interest in the arts and sciences, the Medici family finally sponsored the creation, in 1657, of the Accademia del Cimento. Founded three years before the Royal Society in London, it was Europe's first research centre. Laudable though the idea was, the feverish activity – some 600 recorded experiments – carried out by its members lasted only 10 years. One area in which significant progress was made was in the study of vacuums. A long-held belief that nature abhorred vacuums was definitively put to rest. The Accademia folded in 1667 but the Royal Society proved somewhat more durable.

Neptune's fountain in Piazza della Signoria

high and, with its striking crenellations, is as much a symbol of the city as the Duomo.

Built for the *priori* (governors) who ruled Florence in two-month turns, the mansion came to be known as the Palazzo della Signoria as the government took on this name. The fortress-like pile is a strange rhomboid shape, in part due to a government decree that nothing should be built on the razed land (now part of Piazza della Signoria near the palace) on which the Uberti family's residences had stood. The Uberti had been declared traitors.

In 1540 Cosimo I de' Medici moved from the Palazzo Medici into this building, making it the ducal residence and centre of government. Cosimo commissioned Vasari to renovate the interior, creating new apartments and decorating the lot. In a sense it was all in vain, because Cosimo's wife, Eleonora de Toledo, was not so keen on it and bought Palazzo Pitti.

The latter took a while to expand and fit out as Eleonora wanted (she died before the work was finished), but the Medici family moved in anyway in 1549. Thus the Palazzo Ducale (or della Signoria for those with a nostalgic bent) came to be called the Palazzo Vecchio (Old Palace) as it still is today. It remains the seat of the city's power, as this is where the mayor is located.

Coming in from Piazza della Signoria, you arrive first in the courtyard, reworked in early Renaissance style by Michelozzo in 1453. The decoration came more than a century later when Francesco de' Medici married Joanna of Austria. The cities depicted are jewels in the Austrian imperial crown. The poor woman was much neglected by her unpleasant husband, who made no secret of his preference for various mistresses. The thin, pale and haughty Joanna, not much liked by anyone in Florence, died in this bitter gilded cage at the age of 30.

From here you pass into the **Cortile della Dogana** (Customs Courtyard), off which you'll find the ticket office.

A stairway leads upstairs to the magnificent **Salone dei Cinquecento**, also known more simply as the Sala Grande (Big Hall). It was created within the original building in the 1490s to accommodate the Consiglio dei Cinquecento (Council of 500), called into being in the republic under Savonarola. Cosimo I de' Medici turned the hall, whose council had symbolised the end of Medici family rule, into a splendid expression of his own power. The elevated tribune at one end was where Cosimo held audiences. Vasari added the decorations, operating with a vast workshop of apprentices, and boasted of the speed with which he could turn out paintings, frescoes and whatever else might be required. Michelangelo once quipped that you could tell by the results.

Vasari and Co slapped on the two sets of three panels depicting famous battles between Florence and Pisa (on the side you enter the hall) and Siena (on the opposite side). On the same side as the Siena painting is a statue, *Genio della Vittoria* (Genius of Victory), by the acid-tongued Michelangelo.

On the same side as the entrance, another door leads off to the windowless **Studiolo di Francesco I de' Medici** (Francesco's 'Little Study'), a mannerist gem whose design was also directed by Vasari. The best you can hope for is to peek inside if a museum employee leaves the door open (or by joining the small guided groups). Francesco lived in the shadow of his autocratic papa and sought solace in his little hideaway.

Opposite the studiolo, you enter the **Quartiere di Leone X** by another door. The so-called 'Leo X Area' is named after the Medici pope. You can only see the one room as the others are given over to offices. Upstairs is the **Quartiere degli Elementi** (Elements Area), a series of rooms and terraces dedicated to pagan deities. The original *Putto col Delfino* (Cupid with Dolphin) sculpture by Verrocchio (a copy graces the courtyard of the building) is in the **Sala di Giunone**. Have a look at Vasari's *Venere* (Venus) in the central **Sala degli Elementi** and compare it with Botticelli's version. Michelangelo might have had a point.

From here a walkway takes you across the top of the Salone dei Cinquecento into the **Quartiere di Eleonora**, the apartments of Cosimo I's wife. The room most likely to catch your attention is Eleonora's chapel just off to the right as you enter the apartments. Il Bronzino's decoration represents the acme of his painting career (pity this is a copy of the original).

You pass through several more rooms until you reach the **Sala dell'Udienza** (Audience Room), where the *priori* administered medieval Florentine justice. The following room is the **Sala dei Gigli**, named after the lilies of the French monarchy that decorate three of the walls (the French were traditionally well disposed to Florence). Domenico Ghirlandaio's fresco on the far wall was to be matched by others. Donatello's restored bronze of *Giuditta e Oloferne* stands in here. A small, bare study off this hall is the chancery, where Machiavelli worked for a while. The other room off the hall is a wonderful map room. The walls are covered by 16th-century maps of the known world.

Climb the stairs outside the Sala dei Gigli to the **battlements**, for views of the city. By following the stairs down towards the exit you'll see, at the mezzanine level, the **Loeser collection** of minor Tuscan art from the 14th to 16th centuries.

But there's more. By paying a little extra you can join in small guided groups to explore the *percorsi segreti* (secret ways), or head for the **Museo dei Ragazzi** (Children's Museum). The former consist of several options, including the possibility of visiting the Studiolo di Francesco and the nearby treasury of Cosimo I. Another walk takes you into the roof of the Salone dei Cinquecento.

In the **Museo dei Ragazzi**, kids and families can hang out with actors dressed up as Cosimo I and Eleonora di Toledo – kids are invited to dress up as their kids (Bia and Garcia) and play with the kinds of toys the two grand-ducal imps used to enjoy. Other available activities include building and taking apart models of the Palazzo Vecchio and of bridges (for those children with an engineering bent), and peering through a remake of Michelangelo's binoculars. Another possibility is to follow around Giorgio Vasari (or rather a lookalike) for a personal explanation of his architectural and artistic work in the Palazzo. A multimedia show on the palace's history can also be seen (maximum 30 people) on a big screen.

For any one of these options and the standard visit you pay €8. If you want to add on more of the extras, each one costs an additional €1. Family tickets for two adults and two to three children (€20/22) are also available. Tickets and information on all these extra activities can be found in a room just back from the main ticket area.

RACCOLTA D'ARTE CONTEMPORANEA ALBERTO DELLA RAGIONE

Map pp251–3

☎ 055 28 30 78; Piazza della Signoria 5; ☺ closed at the time of writing; bus B

This collection *(raccolta)* of contemporary art may awaken mild interest in art buffs with a passion for the Italian 20th century. Most of the painters on show worked in the first half of the century. A few Giorgio Morandis in **Room IX** are worth a quick look. There's even a modest De Chirico in the same room. Fans of Carlo Levi's classic book, *Cristo si è Fermato ad Eboli* (Christ Stopped at Eboli), may be curious to see the trio of paintings he did while in exile in southern Italy (on the 1st floor). Mario Mafai, Ottone Rosai (among whose works figure some dreamscapes of Florence) and Virgilio Guidi are well represented. The collection was donated to Florence by the Genoese collector Alberto della Ragione on his death in 1970.

SANTA MARIA NOVELLA & AROUND

Eating p125; Shopping p163; Sleeping p175

Orientation

As you wander out of the Santa Maria Novella train station, you find yourself before the Basilica di Santa Maria Novella, one of the most important of Florence's churches, the Dominican headquarters and often temporary residence of visiting popes. For the purposes of this book, the area stretches north to Viale Fratelli Rosselli, south to the Arno, west to the Cascine park and as far east as Via de' Tornabuoni.

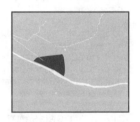

BASILICA DI SANTA MARIA NOVELLA

Map pp251–3

☎ 055 21 59 18; Piazza di Santa Maria Novella; adult/child €2.50/1.50; ☼ 9am-5pm Mon-Thu & Sat, 1-5pm Fri, Sun & holidays; bus 1, 7, 10, 11, 14, 17, 22, 23, 36, 37 & A

Just south of the main train station, Stazione di Santa Maria Novella, this church was begun in the late 13th century as the Florentine base for the Dominican order. Although mostly completed by around 1360, work on its façade and the embellishment of its interior continued well into the 15th century.

The lower section of the green-and-white marble façade is transitional from Romanesque to Gothic, while the upper section and main doorway were designed by Alberti and completed in around 1470. The highlight of the interior is Masaccio's superb fresco (restored 2000) of *La Trinità* (The Trinity; 1428), one of the first artworks to use the then newly discovered techniques of perspective and proportion. It is about halfway along the northern aisle.

The first chapel to the right of the choir, the **Cappella di Filippo Strozzi**, features lively frescoes by Filippino Lippi depicting the lives of St John the Evangelist and St Philip the Apostle. Recent restoration has infused the frescoes with renewed vibrancy. Another important work is Domenico Ghirlandaio's series of frescoes behind the main altar, painted with the help of artists who may have included the young student Michelangelo. Relating the lives of the Virgin Mary, St John the Baptist and others, the frescoes are notable for their depiction of Florentine life during the Renaissance. In the **Cappella Gondi**, the first chapel on the left of the choir, Brunelleschi's crucifix hangs above the altar.

The large painted wooden crucifix hanging from the ceiling in the middle of the central nave is a recently restored Giotto masterpiece.

To reach the **Chiostro Verde** (Green Cloister), exit the church and follow the signs to the 'Museo'. The porticoes' arches are propped by massive octagonal pillars. Three of the four walls are decorated with fading frescoes recounting Genesis. The cloister takes its name from the green earth base used for the frescoes. The most interesting artistically are those, by Paolo Uccello, on the party wall with the church, particularly *Il Diluvio Universale* (The Great Flood).

Off the next side of the cloister is the **Cappellone degli Spagnoli**, or Spanish Chapel, which was set aside for the Spanish retinue that accompanied Eleonora de Toledo, Cosimo I's wife, to Florence. It contains well-preserved frescoes by Andrea di Bonaiuto and his helpers. On the western side of the cloister is the **museum** (☎ 055 28 21 87; admission €2.70; ☼ 9am-5pm Mon-Sat, 9am-2pm Sun & holidays) in two rooms that used to be the convent's foyer and refectory, contains vestments, relics and some art belonging to the Dominicans.

CASA GALLERIA Map pp248–50

Borgo Ognissanti 26; ☼ closed to the public; bus A

Giovanni Micheluzzi breathed a rare moment of originality into Florentine architecture in the 20th century with a couple of town houses. This one, a few doors east of Chiesa di Ognissanti, is a pleasing Art Nouveau house whose façade, liberally laced with glass and iron, has striking curves and circular features. Most other buildings and villas built around Florence at this time have since been pulled down.

CENACOLO DI FOLIGNO Map pp246–7

☎ 055 28 69 82; Via Faenza 42; admission by donation; ☼ 9am-noon Mon, Tue & Sat (ring the doorbell); bus 4, 12, 25, 31, 32 & 33

Discovered in what had been a convent until the early 19th century, this Last Supper scene is thought to have been done around the end of the 15th century by students of the Umbrian Renaissance artist Il Perugino (1445–1523) to his design. The organisation of the scene is classic, with Judas (*sans* halo) sitting on the wrong side of the table, grasping the sack of coins (his reward for betraying Christ), and St John snoozing at Christ's side. Unusual are the light, bright colours, the decorated architectural scheme that frames the scene and the portrayal in the background of Christ praying in the Garden of Gethsemane while the Apostles sleep.

CHIESA DI OGNISSANTI Map pp248–50
☎ 055 239 68 02; Piazza d'Ognissanti; admission free; ☺ 9am-noon Mon, Tue & Sat; bus A

This 13th-century church was much altered in the 17th century and has a baroque façade, but inside are 15th-century works by Domenico Ghirlandaio and Sandro Botticelli. Of interest is Ghirlandaio's fresco above the second altar on the right of the *Madonna della Misericordia*, protector of the Vespucci family. Amerigo Vespucci, who gave his name to the American continent (see the boxed text, p55), is supposedly the young boy whose head appears between the Madonna and the old man.

Ghirlandaio's masterpiece, however, is *L'Ultima Cena* (Last Supper) that covers most of a wall in the former monastery's **cenacolo** (refectory; entrance Borgo Ognissanti 42; admission free; ☺ 9am-noon Mon, Tue & Sat). You go through the cloister (lined with a fresco cycle on the life of St Francis of Assisi) to get to the refectory. It is an all too human scene, and touches like the transparent glasses and wine bottles are indicative of Ghirlandaio's eye. Art historians see in this work the main precedent set for Leonardo da Vinci's extraordinary Last Supper scene in Milan. When work was done to restore Ghirlandaio's fresco, a rare opportunity was seized to remove from the layer below, revealing the *sinopia*, or red-earth pigment sketch that the artist used as a guide when slapping on the layers of wet plaster upon which he painted. The *sinopia* is on display on a side wall.

CHIESA DI SAN PANCRAZIO & MUSEO MARINO MARINI Map pp251–3
☎ 055 21 94 32; Piazza San Pancrazio 1; admission €7.50; ☺ 10am-5pm Mon & Wed-Sat; bus A

As early as the 9th century a church stood here. The shabby-looking version you see today is

what remains of the building from the 14th and 15th centuries. The church, deconsecrated in the 19th century, now houses the Museo Marino Marini. Donated to the city by the Pistoia-born sculptor Marino Marini (1901–80), the cost of admission is rather a lot unless you are particularly taken with this guy.

Among the 200 works the artist left behind are sculptures, portraits and drawings. The overwhelmingly recurring theme appears to be man and horse, or rather man on horse. The figures are, in some cases, simple-looking chaps in various poses suggesting rapture or extreme frustration; the horses too seem to express a gamut of emotion. At times, man and horse seem barely distinguishable from one another.

CHIESA DI SANTA TRINITA Map pp251–3
☎ 055 21 69 12; Piazza Santa Trinita; admission free; ☺ 8am-noon & 4-6pm Mon-Sat, 4-6pm Sun & holidays; bus 6, 11, 36, 37 & A

Although rebuilt in the Gothic style and later graced with a mannerist façade of indifferent taste, you can still get some idea of what the Romanesque original looked like by contemplating the façade wall from the inside. Among its more eye-catching artworks are the frescoes depicting the life of St Francis of Assisi by Domenico Ghirlandaio in the **Cappella Sassetti** (in the right transept). The altarpiece of the *Annunziazione* (Annunciation) in the fourth chapel of the southern aisle is by Lorenzo Monaco, who was Fra Angelico's master. Monaco also painted the frescoes on the walls of the chapel.

Piazza Santa Trinita itself is faced by **Palazzo Buondelmonti**. The Buondelmonte family was at the heart of the Guelph–Ghibelline feud in Florence (see p52). More imposing is the **Palazzo Bartolini-Salimbeni**, an example of High Renaissance with a Roman touch (columns flanking the main door and triangular tympana).

CHIESA DI SS MICHELE E GAETANO
Map pp251–3
Via de' Tornabuoni; admission free; ☺ 1.30-5.30pm; bus 6, 11, 22, 36, 37 & A

A church has stood on this site since the 11th century but from 1604 it underwent a complete overhaul, resulting in the *pietra forte* (strong stone) baroque façade (completed in 1683) you see today. More commonly known simply as San Gaetano, it is one of the most outstanding churches to be raised in 17th-century Florence. Whether or not you find it open could be a matter of luck, as restoration work is intermittently in progress.

A Bridge for All Seasons

Cosimo I de' Medici put Vasari in charge of the Ponte Santa Trinità project, and he in turn asked Michelangelo for advice. In the end, the job was handed to Ammannati, who finished it in 1567. The statues of the seasons are by Pietro Francavilla. The bridge was one of those blown up by the Germans as they retreated in 1944. Rather than throw some slapdash number back over the river, engineers rebuilt it as it had been, using copies of 16th-century tools and stone from the Boboli quarry. The statues were fished out of the Arno and the bridge completed in 1958.

All that was missing was the head from Francavilla's *Primavera* (Spring) statue on the northern bank. The fate of the head was long a source of anguished debate in Florence. Some eyewitnesses swore they had seen an Allied soldier make off with it after the city was liberated. Ads were even placed in New Zealand newspapers (New Zealanders were among the first Allied troops to enter the city in 1944) asking for whoever had made off with the head to send it back – no questions asked and a US$3000 reward! Needless to say, no-one owned up. Then, three years later, the missing head was discovered by chance in the Arno riverbed and finally restored to its rightful place.

LE CASCINE Map pp244–5
Bus 1, 9, 12, 13, 16, 26, 27, 80 & B

Before we turn our steps back to the centre of Florence, you might want to bear in mind that about 10 minutes' walk to the west along Borgo Ognissanti brings you to the **Porta al Prato**, part of the walls that were knocked down in the late 19th century to make way for the ring of boulevards that still surrounds the city. Through this gate many a Medici bride arrived in Florence in festive parade on her way to the Palazzo Vecchio or Palazzo Pitti down through the centuries.

A short walk south from here towards the Arno brings you to the eastern tip of Florence's great green lung, the Cascine. The Medici dukes made this a private hunting reserve, but Pietro Leopoldo opened it to the public in 1776, with boulevards, fountains and bird sanctuaries (Le Pavoniere, now a swimming pool). In the late 19th century horse racing began here (a British import it seems, since the locals referred to the sport as *le corse inglesi* – the English races). Queen Victoria was a fan of Florence and toddled along to the Cascine during her stays.

At the extreme western end of the park is a monument to Rajaram Cuttiputti, an Indian maharajah who, while holidaying in Florence in 1870, managed to get a severe bout of gastro-enteritis and died. His retinue requested, and surprisingly obtained, permission to cremate him by the river. This was quite a spectacle for the locals, who didn't understand a word of the ritual but were thoroughly fascinated by it. Four years later he got a statue and memorial designed by British artisans. At its opening the British imperial anthem sounded across the green expanses. To this day, the spot is called Piazzetta dell'Indiano. The nearby bridge is named after him too.

MUSEO SALVATORE FERRAGAMO
Map pp251–3

☎ 055 336 04 56; www.salvatoreferragamo.it; Via de' Tornabuoni 2; admission free; ⏲ 9am-1pm & 2-6pm Mon-Fri; bus 6, 11, 36, 37 & A

The forbidding **Palazzo Spini-Ferroni** was built in the 14th century with Guelph battlements and is owned by the Ferragamo shoe empire (see the boxed text, p169). The building is now just as intimidating as for all the high-class fashion it exudes. If you don't feel like a pauper when entering the 2nd-floor shoe museum in your jeans and sandals, you never will! Although the museum advises booking by phone at least 10 days ahead, you may get lucky if you just wander and climb the two floors of red-carpeted stairs. On display is a wide variety of some of Ferragamo's classic shoes, many worn by princesses and film stars. The *forme* (wooden model feet upon which tailor-made shoes were crafted) of everyone from Katherine Hepburn to Madonna are there to be seen.

Via de' Tornabuoni, often called the 'Salotto di Firenze' (Florence's Drawing Room) and the most seriously chic shopping boulevard in Florence, follows the original course of the Mugnone tributary into the Arno. The Mugnone was diverted to the present-day Via dei Fossi and then again to the Cascine park.

PALAZZO CORSINI Map pp251–3

☎ 055 21 28 80; www.palazzocorsini.it; Via del Parione 11; admission free; ⏲ 9am-1pm & 4-7pm Mon-Fri; bus A & B

For the best view of the Arno-side of this grandiose late-baroque edifice, head across to the south side of the Arno. It may seem a trifle curious, given that the U-shaped courtyard isn't in the middle. It would have been had the project been completed. The wing nearest Ponte alla Carraia (Map pp248–50) was originally supposed to mirror the right wing. The building had belonged to the Medici family but they sold it in 1640. From then until 1735 work on the exterior (the mighty façade on Via del Parione is a worthy counterpoint to the Arno frontage) dragged on at a snail's pace. By the time it was completed, the Corsini family was in the ascendant, with Lorenzo Corsini in the driving seat in Rome as Pope Clement XII. The most interesting feature inside the building is the spiral staircase known as the *lumaca* (literally 'slug'). You can take a look at it by entering the building at Via del Parione 11/b. Turn left after entering the building and there it is. About the only way you'll see any more of this sumptuous pile is to take a virtual tour on the palace's website, although if you call it is possible to organise private visits.

PALAZZO RUCELLAI Map pp251–3
Via della Vigna Nuova; bus 6 & A
Designed by Alberti, the Palazzo Rucellai houses a photographic museum dedicated to the vast collection compiled by the Alinari brothers. The

façade is curious for a few reasons, not least for the seating originally intended for employees of the Rucellai family but now quite handy for anyone passing by. Across the small triangular square is the family loggia, also by Alberti and now used for occasional exhibits. Any family worth its salt aimed to have a loggia in addition to the family residence.

PALAZZO STROZZI Map pp251–3
Piazza degli Strozzi; admission depends on exhibition; ☺ **depends on exhibitions; bus 6, 11, 22, 36, 37 & A**
By far the most impressive of the Renaissance mansions is this earth-coloured palace, a great colossus of rusticated *pietra forte*. The Strozzi family rivalled the Medici, but Filippo Strozzi was no fool. Before setting about the building of a structure greater than the Medici residence, he consulted Lorenzo de' Medici on some rather modest plans. Lorenzo advised Filippo to go for something grander, more befitting his family and the city. Filippo took this as carte blanche to massage his own ego – so began the construction of the city's greatest, if only in dimensions, Renaissance residence. It now houses offices and occasional art exhibitions.

SAN LORENZO AREA
Eating p125; Shopping p163; Sleeping p175

Orientation
The parish of the San Lorenzo (St Laurence) was synonymous with Medici power. The basilica itself was heavily funded by Florence's top family, who eventually lavished upon it the glories of their family chapel and mausoleum. Strange that they never managed to find the funds to give the church a decent façade! Only a few blocks away is the Renaissance family mansion commissioned by Cosimo de' Medici, while a short hop to the north you strike the ebullient bustle of the city's 19th-century central produce market. For this area, we take

it north to Viale Filippo Strozzi, south to Via de' Cerretani, east to Via de' Martelli and its continuation Via Cavour, and west to Via Faenza.

BASILICA DI SAN LORENZO Map pp251–3
Piazza San Lorenzo; admission €2.50; ☺ **10am-5pm Mon-Sat; bus 1, 6, 7, 10, 11, 14, 17, 23 & A**
The Medici family commissioned Brunelleschi to rebuild this church in 1425, on the site of a 4th-century basilica. It is considered one of the most harmonious examples of Florentine Renaissance architecture. Michelangelo prepared a design for the façade that was never executed, which is why this, as so many other Florentine churches, appears unfinished from

the outside. Many of the Medici family are buried in this, the family's parish church.

The church is a masterstroke of Brunelleschi's individual style. The nave is separated from the two aisles by columns in *pietra serena* (grey 'tranquil stone') and crowned with Corinthian capitals. It is interesting to visit this church in conjunction with a visit to the Basilica di Santo Spirito (see p105), as Brunelleschi designed both of these buildings. The materials used for both are the same, as is the maintenance of spartan, classical harmony in the proportions in each. The differences are also noteworthy. The beautiful coffered ceiling here is mirrored in Santo Spirito by a frescoed trompe l'oeil 'fake'. The latter is admirable, but the real thing splendid.

The inside façade was done by Michelangelo, and above the main entrance is the Medici family coat of arms with the six balls. Il Rosso Fiorentino's *Sposalizio della Vergine* (Marriage of the Virgin Mary) dominates the second chapel on the right aisle after you enter. As you approach the transept, you will see two pulpits, or *pergami* (they look like treasure chests on Ionic columns), in what appears to be dark bronze. Some of the panels on each have been attributed to Donatello. Others, added later, are supposedly made of wood (money was obviously running short) made to seem like bronze.

You enter the **Sagrestia Vecchia** (Old Sacristy) to the left of the altar. It was designed by Brunelleschi and mostly decorated by Donatello.

From another entrance off Piazza San Lorenzo you can also enter the peaceful **cloisters**, off the first of which a staircase leads up to the **Biblioteca Medicea Laurenziana** (admission €2.50; ☎ 8.30am-1.30pm Mon-Sat). This was commissioned by Cosimo I de' Medici to house the Medici library and contains 10,000 volumes. The real attraction is Michelangelo's magnificent vestibule and staircase. They are executed in grey *pietra serena* and the curvaceous steps are a sign of the master's move towards mannerism from the stricter bounds of Renaissance architecture and design. Michelangelo wasn't around to oversee the execution of the project, which was entrusted to Florence's then leading resident architect, Bartolommeo Ammannati. He followed the design but had the masterstroke of using stone rather than Michelangelo's preferred walnut.

Michelangelo also designed the main reading hall, covered by a magnificently carved timber ceiling, but the project would have been more striking still had he been able to finish it.

CAPPELLE MEDICEE Map pp251–3

☎ 055 238 86 02; Piazza Madonna degli Aldobrandini; admission €6; ☒ 8.15am-5pm Tue-Sat, plus alternate Sun & Mon; bus 1, 6, 7, 10, 11, 14, 17, 23 & A

It seems odd that the Medici chapels, built to balance the Brunelleschi sacristy on the other side of the church, have for organisational purposes been hived off from the church itself. Visitors are obliged to enter from another point behind the church rather than from inside. It

would also allow people to understand how the chapels fit in with the rest of the complex.

You first enter a crypt after buying your ticket for the Medici chapels. The stairs from this take you up to the **Cappella dei Principi** (Princes' Chapel). The so-called chapel is rather the triumphalist mausoleum of some of the Medici rulers.

It is sumptuously decorated top to bottom with various kinds of marble, granite and other stone, and there are decorative tableaux made from painstakingly chosen and cut semiprecious stones, or *pietre dure*. It was for the purpose of decorating the chapel that Ferdinando I ordered the creation of the Opificio delle Pietre Dure (see p98).

Statues of the grand men were supposed to be placed in the still-empty niches, but only the bronze of Ferdinando I and partly gilt bronze of Cosimo II were done. The chapel's unfinished state lends it a gloomy air. Had the remaining statues been created, the chapel would no doubt have all the grandeur of the great royal pantheons.

A corridor leads from the Cappella dei Principi to the **Sagrestia Nuova** (New Sacristy), so-called to distinguish it from the Sagrestia Vecchia. It was in fact the Medicis' funeral chapel.

It was here that Michelangelo came nearest to finishing an architectural commission. His haunting sculptures, *Notte e Giorno* (Night and Day), *Aurora e Crepusculo* (Dawn and Dusk) and the *Madonna col Bambino* (Madonna and Child), adorn Medici tombs including that of Lorenzo the Magnificent. Michelangelo's sculptures are interesting for many reasons. In *Notte e Giorno*, whose face remains barely hinted at, Michelangelo goes to town in his study of human musculature. He liked boys so much that the female figures were modelled by lads. In the case of *Notte*, this is especially evident in the upper torso – the breasts seem to have been added as an afterthought. Still, as has been pointed out by art experts, it was incredibly daring to place nude female figures in a holy location like this. The statues of two Roman-looking princes (apparently representative of two of the Medici clan) was another surprise – a classical pagan element in church!

MERCATO CENTRALE Map pp248–50

Piazza del Mercato Centrale; admission free; ☒ 7am-2pm Mon-Sat; bus 4, 12, 25, 31, 32 & 33

Built in 1874, the city's central produce market seems to disappear amid the confusion of makeshift stands of the clothes and leather market that fill the surrounding square and streets during the day. At night all of this disappears, replaced instead by the contented munching of punters at the various eateries (which vary considerably in quality). The iron-and-glass architecture was something of a novelty in Florence when the market was first built.

PALAZZO MEDICI-RICCARDI Map pp246–7
☎ 055 276 03 40; Via Cavour 3; admission €4;
🕒 9am-7pm Thu-Tue; bus 1, 6, 7, 10, 11 & 17

When Cosimo de' Medici felt fairly sure of his position in Florence, he decided it was time to move house. He asked Brunelleschi to design him a new residence, but rejected the result as too ostentatious. Cosimo had learned that the secret to long life in the politically fickle atmosphere of Florence was to keep a modest profile. With this in mind, he entrusted Michelozzo with the design in 1444. This palace is the result.

What Michelozzo came up with was groundbreaking and greatly influenced the construction of family residences in Florence. The fortress town houses with their towers that characterised Gothic Florence were no longer necessary. Cosimo's power was more or less undisputed. Instead Michelozzo created a self-assured, stout but not inelegant pile on three storeys.

The ground floor is characterised by the bulbous, rough surface (known as rustication) in *pietra forte*. The upper two storeys maintain restrained classical lines, which were already a feature of an emerging Renaissance canon, and topped with a heavy timber roof whose eaves protrude well out over the street below.

The Medicis stayed here until 1540, and the building was finally acquired and somewhat remodelled by the Riccardi family in the 17th century.

You can wander inside to the courtyard and to some of the rooms upstairs, although much of the building is now given over to public administration offices. The 1st-floor **Galleria** is a rather sumptuous example of late baroque, designed for the Riccardi family. The room glistens with gold leaf and curvaceous figures loom out at you, especially from the ceiling frescoes by Luca Giordano (after whom the room is now usually named – **Sala Luca Giordano**).

The highlight and a real jewel, however, is the **Cappella dei Magi**, a chapel with striking frescoes by Benozzo Gozzoli. Staff rotate 15 people through the chapel every 15 minutes as it is rather squeezy inside.

Gozzoli never got a break like this again. Although he worked at a time when the Renaissance had taken off in Florence, he remained rooted in the International Gothic style. This magnificent fresco depicting the arrival of the Wise Men and a procession of the faithful to adore the newborn Christ betrays all sorts of jarring qualities.

On the rear wall he captures the natural essence of the Tuscan countryside (despite the subject, this is a very Florentine painting, filled with Medici family members and medieval dress), and yet on the lateral walls that same countryside seems bizarrely unreal. His characters mostly lack the realism and movement you might expect from greater Renaissance painters, and yet some of them are strikingly human.

The men in the lower right-hand corner on the left wall as you enter are exquisitely rendered, particularly the one with creased brow and quizzical expression. The colours are joyful and Gozzoli ensures immortality by penning his own name on one of the citizens' caps. He's the one looking straight out at you towards the back of the procession on the left side of the right-hand wall.

SAN MARCO AREA
Eating p125; Shopping p163; Sleeping p175

Orientation
Once the stalking ground of the fiery friar, Savonarola, the area around the former church and monastery of St Mark has some big artistic hitters. The Museo di San Marco, inside the former monastery, is a treasure chest of Fra (Beato) Angelico's works and people will want to get a gander at Michelangelo's *David* in the nearby Galleria dell'Accademia. Also close by is one of Italy's most important archaeological museums, with Egyptian and Etruscan collections. For the purposes of this guide, the area stretches to the north and east to the area around Piazza della Libertà and the Cimitero degli Inglesi.

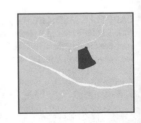

CENACOLO DI SANT'APOLLONIA

Map pp246–7

☎ 055 238 86 07; Via XXVII Aprile 1; admission free; ☼ 8.15am-1.50pm Tue-Sat & alternate Mon & Sun; bus 7, 10, 20, 25, 31, 32 & 33

Seek out the refectory (raised in the Renaissance style in 1445) of the former Benedictine convent that stands here. It is decorated with a remarkable fresco of the Last Supper, which is dominated by shades of red, blue and purple, by Andrea del Castagno (done in 1447). Its existence had long been forgotten until the convent was suppressed and the nuns turfed out in 1860. Three further frescoes above the Last Supper, depicting the crucifixion, burial and resurrection of Christ, had been whitewashed by some inspired fellow. Careful removal of the whitewash finally revealed the three frescoes, which include a rare image of a beardless Christ crucified. The backdrop of the dining hall has been made to look like grand slabs of veined and multicoloured marble. Also in the refectory are the *sinopie*, or preparatory sketches, done for the three upper frescoes. To get to these, the frescoes had to be stripped off, then the *sinopie* removed, and the frescoes put back.

CHIESA DI SS ANNUNZIATA Map pp246–7

☎ 055 26 61 81; Piazza della SS Annunziata; admission free; ☼ 7.30am-12.30pm & 4-6.30pm; bus 6, 31, 32 & C

Dedicated to the Virgin Mary, this church was established in 1250 by the founders of the Servite order and rebuilt by Michelozzo and others in the mid-15th century. In the ornate tabernacle, to your left as you enter the church from the atrium, is what is believed by the faithful to be a miraculous painting of the Virgin.

The painting, which is no longer on public view, is attributed to a 14th-century friar, but legend has it that an angel popped down from the heavens to add the finishing touches. Also of note are frescoes by Andrea del Castagno in the first two chapels on the left of the church, a fresco by Perugino in the fifth chapel and the frescoes in Michelozzo's atrium, particularly the *Nascita della Vergine* (Birth of the Virgin) by Andrea del Sarto and *La Visitazione* by Jacopo Pontormo.

The square itself is one of the city's loveliest (a view shared by a handful of Florence's nocturnal junkies). Commanding from the centre is Giambologna's equestrian statue of Grand Duke Ferdinando I de' Medici (it was actually largely created by Pietro Tacca on his master's design).

CHIESA E CONVENTO DI SANTA MARIA MADDALENA DE' PAZZI

Map pp246–7

☎ 055 247 84 20; Borgo Pinti 58; admission free; ☼ 9am-noon & 5-7pm Mon-Sat

A convent was first raised on this site in 1257, where a variety of orders occupied it in turn. The Carmelites were turfed out when the present late-15th century building (built by Giuliano da Sangallo) was expropriated and converted into a high school in 1888. In 1493–96 Pietro Perugino executed a fine fresco in the chapter house *(sala capitolare)* in three parts depicting the crucifixion of Christ. To Christ's left appear the Virgin Mary with St Bernard and to the right St John and St Benedict.

CIMITERO DEGLI INGLESI Map pp246–7

☎ 055 232 14 77; Piazzale Donatello 38; admission by donation; ☼ 9am-noon Mon, 2-5pm Tue-Fri; bus 8 & 80

If you are a little sick of museums and need some air and a bit of a change of speed, you might consider heading east for the so-called English Cemetery. Located outside what were the city walls in 1828, and now effectively forming a large traffic island around which swarm thousands of hectic Florentine commuters, it is more accurately a Protestant cemetery and Swiss property. Several notable foreigners rest in (relative) peace here, including Elizabeth Barrett Browning and Walter Savage Landor, part of the Percy Shelley/Lord Byron clique of Anglo writers that made Florence home.

GALLERIA DELL'ACCADEMIA

Map pp246–7

☎ 055 238 86 09; Via Ricasoli 60; admission €6.50; ☼ 8.15am-6.50pm Tue-Sun; bus C

You've seen the postcards and may feel you've already seen all you need of one of the greatest of all the Renaissance's sculptures, Michelangelo's *David*. Wrong. Make a date with this gallery, which is filled with all sorts of other intriguing items. The gallery occupies what were once a hospital and adjoining convent, converted into the seat of the Accademia di Belle Arti (Fine Arts Academy) under Grand Duke Pietro Leopoldo.

After collecting your ticket you enter the grand **Sala del Colosso**, dominated by a plaster model of Giambologna's *Il Ratto delle Sabine* (Rape of Sabine) and lined by several interesting paintings. The latter include a fresco of the *Pietà* by Andrea del Sarto, a couple of pieces by

Fra Bartolommeo and a *Deposizione* started by Filippino Lippi and finished by Il Perugino.

Immediately to the left off this first room a doorway leads into a long hall, at the end of which you can make out *David*. Try to contain the urge to hurtle off in the giant-slayer's general direction and have a look at the four in the *Prigioni* (prisoners or slaves) series and the statue of San Matteo (St Matthew) between the two *Prigioni* on the right. The latter was sculpted about 1506, and the four others in 1530.

The *Prigioni* were supposed to decorate the tomb of Pope Julius II, but ended up in the Giardino di Boboli. After the *Prigioni* comes another piece sometimes attributed to Michelangelo. It is an unfinished *Pietà* whose odd proportions have led several scholars to ascribe it to a not-so-successful employee of Michelangelo's.

All these pieces have in common the feature of not being completed. In the case of Michelangelo in particular, it is said he left many works 'unfinished' deliberately. Thus the observer is engaged in the process of creation, being obliged to 'complete' the work left undone by the master. It has been said that with Michelangelo this was in part due to his perfectionism. He could stop working on a project, but never truly finish.

Whatever you make of all these arguments, they are interesting if only because they show us a little of how the artist went about extracting such beauty from lumps of marble. Some of us will continue to think the sculptures are unfinished, if only because old Michelangelo had a tendency to abandon blocks of stone he considered bungled or in any way deficient.

David, however, is finished. Carved from one block of marble and weighing in at 19 tonnes, it's an exquisite, powerful figure that beggars description. While the statue still stood in Piazza della Signoria (it took four days in May 1504 to transport it on greased rollers from the Duomo, where it was carved and originally destined to stay, to its spot in Piazza della Signoria – and was only unveiled in September), the left arm was hacked off during a riot and killed a peasant. Cosimo I de' Medici happened to be there at the time and is said to have been rather taken aback by the whole incident. You can see the break still, as well as one on the middle finger of the right hand (which was fixed in 1813). Over the centuries, *David* has also suffered a couple of broken toes – the last one at the hands of a hammer attack carried out by a slightly emotional individual in 1991. The statue was moved to the gallery from Piazza della Signoria in 1873. In 2003 a storm in a teacup broke out as to whether or not *David* needed a good bath – in the end it was decided that the answer was yes (see the boxed text, p34). In the wing to the right of *David*

Buying roasted chestnuts from a street stall

are paintings by Florentine contemporaries of Michelangelo, including some by Botticelli.

In the wing to the left are more paintings of secondary importance. At the end of that wing, a hall hosts the **Gipsoteca Bartolini**. Lorenzo Bartolini was a major Italian sculptor of the 19th century. The works in here are plaster models created to help with the production of sculptures.

Another series of rooms off the left wing contains 13th- and 14th-century works of art. A triptych by Andrea Orcagna, which once hung in the Chiesa degli SS Apostoli, is particularly striking. From here you are led out into a small courtyard towards the exit. Just before you leave the building you can climb to the next floor to view mostly 14th-century Tuscan works, all with a religious theme. In among there is a small collection of 13th- and 14th-century art and Russian icons.

Another ground floor area is sometimes opened up for temporary exhibitions.

MUSEO ARCHEOLOGICO Map pp246–7

☎ 055 2 35 75; Via della Colonna 38; admission €4; 🕑 2-7pm Mon, 8.30am-7pm Tue & Thu, 8.30am-2pm Wed & Fri-Sun; bus 6, 31, 32 & C

A good deal of the Medici family's hoard of antiquities ended up here, in what would become one of Italy's most extensive archaeological museums. Further collections have been added in the centuries since. In each room you will find detailed explanatory sheets in several languages. You'd have the beginnings of a book if you were to take a copy of each home – which, in the interests of saving paper, you might perhaps refrain from doing. The museum offers a surprisingly rich collection of antiquities, in spite of the damage to some items during the 1966 funds.

On the 1st floor you can either head left into the ancient Egyptian collection (the second in importance in Italy to Turin's Museo Egizio), or right into the section on Etruscan and Greco-Roman art.

The former is an impressive collection of tablets inscribed with hieroglyphics, statues and other sculpture, various coffins and a remarkable array of everyday objects – it is extraordinary to ponder how sandals, baskets and all sorts of other odds and ends have survived to this day.

In the Etruscan section you pass first through two rooms dominated by funerary urns. Particularly noteworthy is the marble *Sarcofago delle Amazzoni* (Amazons' Tomb) from Tarquinia and the alabaster *Sarcofago*

dell'Obeso (Fat Man's Tomb) from Chiusi. It is interesting to note the differences between Etruscan and Roman art. If you study the scenes on many of the Etruscan urns, you will notice an oriental touch in the depiction of battle and other scenes. Frequently the appearance of the characters and their attire is anything but Roman or classical. Even from the early days of Roman expansion, there had been cross-fertilisation between the Greeks, Romans and Etruscans. The Etruscans clearly took many of their artistic cues from the Greeks, and the Romans after them tended to follow suit.

From the funerary urns you pass into a hall dedicated to bronze sculptures, ranging from miniatures depicting mythical beasts through to the life-size *Arringatore* (Orator). Dating from the 1st century BC, the figure, draped in clearly Roman garb, illustrates the extent to which the empire had come to dominate the Etruscans at this point. By the time the statue was made, Etruria had been under the Roman thumb for a good 200 years. Other outstanding works include the statue of Minerva from Arezzo, a Roman copy of a Greek original, and the Chimera, a beast of classical mythology.

From this display you enter an enclosed corridor lined on one side by ancient rings, pendants and amulets, many made of chalcedony. When you reach the end, you swing left and walk back along another corridor with windows overlooking the museum's gardens. Here you can admire a selection of the museum's treasure of ancient gold jewellery.

There is space downstairs for temporary exhibits.

The 2nd floor is taken up with an extensive collection of Greek (in large part the characteristically red-and-black Attic type) pottery from various epochs. Again it is surprising for its sheer extent. Although most of the exhibits have had to be meticulously reassembled from the shards discovered on excavation sites, the collection is varied and certainly intriguing to anyone interested in this kind of thing.

MUSEO DI SAN MARCO Map pp246–7

☎ 055 238 86 08; Piazza San Marco 1; admission €6; 🕑 8.30am-1.50pm Tue-Fri, 8.30am-6.50pm Sat, 8.30am-1.50pm alternate Mon & Sun; bus 6, 7, 10, 20, 25, 31, 32, 33 & C

In the centre of the university area, this museum is housed in the now deconsecrated Dominican convent and the Chiesa di San Marco. The church was founded in 1299, rebuilt by Michelozzo in 1437, and again remodelled by Giambologna some years later. It features several paintings, but they pale in comparison with the treasures contained in the adjoining convent.

Famous Florentines who called the convent home include the painters Fra (or Beato) Angelico and Fra Bartolommeo. Fra Angelico, who painted the radiant frescoes on the convent walls, was of the Dominican order. Almost 30 years after Fra Angelico's death in 1455, the rather ugly and intense little Dominican friar, Girolamo Savonarola, turned up in Florence with a post as lector at the Chiesa di San Marco (see p55 for more details).

The convent now serves as a museum of Fra Angelico's works, many of which were moved there in the 1860s, and should be up there on every art lover's top-priority list.

You find yourself in the **Chiostro di Sant'Antonio** (St Anthony's Cloisters), designed by Michelozzo in 1440, when you first enter the museum. Turn immediately to the right and enter the **Sala dell'Ospizio**. Paintings by Fra Angelico that once hung in the Galleria dell'Accademia and the Uffizi have been brought together here. Among the better-known works are *La Deposizione di Cristo* (Deposition of Christ) and the Pala di San Marco, an altarpiece for the church paid for by the Medici family. It did not fare well as a result of 19th-century restoration.

More of Angelico's works, including a Crocifissione, are on display in the **Sala del Capitolo** (Chapter House) on the opposite side of the cloister. In here is also La Piagnona, the bell rung the night Savonarola was arrested on 8 April 1498.

The east wing of the cloister, formerly the monks' rectory, contains works by various artists from the 14th to the 17th centuries. Paintings by Fra Bartolommeo are on display in a small annexe off the refectory rooms. Among them is a celebrated portrait of Savonarola.

You reach the upper floor by passing through the bookshop. This is, in a sense, the real treat. Fra Angelico was invited to decorate the monks' cells with devotional frescoes aimed as a guide to the friars' mediation. Some were done by Fra Angelico, others by aides under his supervision including Bennozo Gozzoli. You can peer into them today and wonder what sort of thoughts would swim through the minds of the monks as they prayed before these images.

The true masterpieces up here are, however, on the walls in the corridors. Already at the top of the stairs you climbed to the 1st floor is an *Annunciazione* (Annunciation),

faced on the opposite wall with a *crocifisso* (crucifix) featuring St Dominic (San Domenico). One of Fra Angelico's most famous works is the *Madonna delle Ombre* (Madonna of the Shadows), to the right of cell No 25.

OPIFICIO DELLE PIETRE DURE
Map pp246–7

☎ 055 26 51 11; Via degli Alfani 78; admission €2;
🕑 8.15am-2pm Mon-Wed, Fri & Sat, 8.15am-7pm Thu; bus C

For centuries a workshop that took pride of place in Florence's high-class handicrafts industry, the Opificio was established in 1588 in the Uffizi by Ferdinando I to create decorative pieces in *pietre dure* for the Cappella dei Principi in the Basilica di San Lorenzo. These pieces were such a hit that demand began to spread well beyond the private needs of the Medici family. Soon artisans were making everything from tabletops to sculptures, and so called 'paintings in stone' (by the 17th century mostly still lifes of flower vases) for sale in Florence and export across Europe.

The Opificio moved to its present home in the 18th century, and in 1975 was fused with the Laboratori di Restauro in 1975 to become, officially at least, the Istituto Specializzato per il Restauro (Specialised Institute for Restoration). It remains known to most as the Opificio, and has developed a worldwide reputation for its instruction in art restoration. Specialist students from around the world flock here.

In the museum you can see a broad range of items in *pietre dure*, or *scagliola*, a method that produces results similar in appearance.

ORTO BOTANICO Map pp246–7

☎ 055 275 74 38; Via Pier Antonio Micheli 3;
adult/child €3/1.50; 🕑 9am-1pm Mon-Fri;
bus 1, 7, 10, 11, 17, 20, 25 & 33

Also known as the Giardino dei Semplici, this small botanical garden was the Medici herb garden, where all sorts of medicinal plants were grown for the city's pharmacies. It now belongs to the university and is an unexpectedly curious green patch in this part of the city. You can see a good deal of the garden from Via Giorgio la Pira.

ROTONDA DEL BRUNELLESCHI
Map pp246–7
Piazza Brunelleschi; bus C

If you walk down towards the Duomo from Piazza della SS Annunziata along Via dei Fibbiai,

Glazed terracotta babies in swaddling cloth on façade of Spedale degli Innocenti (below)

you will come across this rather sad-looking hexagonal building. It was going to be the Rotonda di Santa Maria degli Angioli and, lined with chapels, would have been one of the architect's most original buildings had money not run out. What stands today was finished off in 1936 so that the building might at least be usable. The university now has offices here.

SPEDALE DEGLI INNOCENTI Map pp246–7
☎ 055 249 17 08; Piazza della SS Annunziata 12; admission €2.60; ⏰ 8.30am-2pm Thu-Tue; bus 6, 31, 32 & C

For the bulk of medieval Florence's poorer people, and indeed those of all Europe, having children was frequently a charge too onerous to bear. Many of the newborn ended up abandoned and so orphanages began to spring up in cities across Europe. Among the first was this 'hospital of the innocents', founded on the southeast side of the piazza in 1421.

Brunelleschi designed the portico, which Andrea della Robbia then decorated with terracotta medallions of a baby in swaddling cloths. Under the portico to the left of the entrance is the small revolving door where unwanted children were left. A good number

of people in Florence with surnames such as degli Innocenti, Innocenti and Nocentini, can trace their family tree only as far back as the orphanage. Undoubtedly life inside was no picnic, but the Spedale's avowed aim was to care for and educate its wards until they turned 18.

A small gallery on the 2nd floor features works by Florentine artists. If you are already overdosing on the seemingly endless diet of art in Florence, you could skip this stop. Those truly interested will find it worthwhile.

The most striking piece is Domenico Ghirlandaio's *L'Adorazione dei Magi* (Adoration of the Magi) at the right end of the hall. This is one of those paintings that truly repays close inspection. The main image of the Wise Men come to adore the Christ child distracts most observers from such secondary scenes as Herod's massacre of the innocents. The city and port detail in the background is remarkable.

Also in here is a *Madonna in Trono col Bambino e Santi* (Madonna and Child with Saints and Angels) by Piero Cosimo and a glazed terracotta *Madonna col Bambino* (Madonna and Child) by Luca della Robbia. Watch out also for the muted tones of Botticelli's *Madonna col Bambino e un Angelo* (Madonna and Child with an Angel).

SANTA CROCE AREA

Eating p125; Shopping p163; Sleeping p175

Orientation

Spread out to the east of the old city centre and north of Ponte alle Grazie, Piazza Santa Croce is an unusually large space that was opened out before the Franciscan basilica of the same name to accommodate hordes of the Sunday faithful who could not cram inside the church (Mass must have been quite an event in those days). It was perhaps inevitable that such a square would become a multifunctional public domain. From the 14th century it was the stage for all sorts of festivals, jousts and other merriment. On a more sober note, it came in handy for the execution of heretics in Savonarola's day.

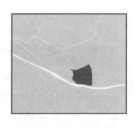

Most curious of all were the ancient matches of *calcio storico* – a combination of football (soccer) and rugby with no rules. They still play it today (see p11). Below the gaily frescoed façade of the Palazzo dell'Antella, on the south side of the piazza, is a marble stone embedded in the wall – it marks the halfway line on this, one of the oldest football pitches in the world. Today the square is lined with the inevitable souvenir shops.

The Romans used to have fun in much the same area centuries before. The city's 2nd-century amphitheatre took up the area facing the western end of Piazza di Santa Croce. To this day, Piazza de' Peruzzi, Via Bentaccordi and Via Torta mark the oval outline of the theatre's northern, western and southern sides.

To the north and east, long, narrow streets spin out to the busy boulevards that mark the line of the former city walls. Attractions range from Florence's synagogue to Michelangelo's House.

BASILICA DI SANTA CROCE Map pp248–50

☎ 055 246 61 05; Piazza di Santa Croce 16;
adult/child €4/2; ⏰ 9.30am-5.30pm Mon-Sat
& 1-5.30pm Sun & holidays; bus C

Attributed to Arnolfo di Cambio, Santa Croce was started in 1294 on the site of a Franciscan chapel but not completed until 1385. The name stems from a splinter of the Holy Cross donated to the Franciscans by King Louis of France in 1258. Today the church is known as much for the celebrities buried here as its captivating artistic gems.

The magnificent façade is actually a neo-Gothic addition of the 19th century, as indeed is the bell tower. The architect, Niccola Matas, had a hard time even getting his façade design passed. Rather austere compared with the contemporary job done on the Duomo, the main source of jollity is the variety of colour in the different types of marble used. A commission set up in 1837 to study the urgent question of dressing the front of the church, apparently loath to make any decision, was finally moved to do so when Matas produced the old designs for a façade by Il Cronaca, found in the church's archives. Matas was a clever fellow, for it seems he created these designs in the hope of finally getting some action, and it worked!

Brooding at the foot of the left side of the church (as you gaze upon the façade) is a dazzling white statue of Dante. It is as though his ghost had returned to the ungrateful city that exiled him. There he stands with crumpled brow, contemplating the ebb and flow of the crowds of his fellow citizens across the square with acid gaze.

The church's massive interior is divided into a nave and two aisles by solid octagonal pillars. The ceiling is a fine example of the timber A-frame style used occasionally in Italy's Gothic churches.

The protagonists of EM Forster's *A Room with a View* stumbled across one another beneath the silent vaults in here. Today you'll be lucky to squeeze through the seemingly endless hordes that mill at the front end of the church before being raced through by their tour guides. Try to get here early in the morning or leave it till late in the day – you could easily spend an hour or more wandering around inside.

The celebrity roll call of those buried or at least commemorated here is quite impressive. Heading down the right aisle you will see, between the first and second altar, Michelangelo's tomb, designed by Vasari.

The three muses below it represent his three principal gifts – sculpting, painting and architecture. Next up is a cenotaph to the memory of Dante, followed by a monument to the memory of the 18th-century poet Vittorio Alfieri sculpted by Antonio Canova in 1810. After the fourth altar is Machiavelli's tomb.

Following the next is Donatello's extraordinary sculpture of *L'Annunciazione* (Annunciation). You won't see many other sculptures in grey *pietra serena*, brightened here by some gilding. Between the sixth and seventh altars you can peer out the doorway into the cloister for a look at Brunelleschi's Cappella de' Pazzi (see the end of this entry).

Dogleg round to the right as you approach the transept and you find yourself before the delightful frescoes by Agnolo Gaddi in the **Cappella Castellani** (in all, the church is covered in more than 2500 sq metres of frescoes). Taddeo Gaddi created the frescoes, depicting the life of the Virgin, and the stained-glass window in the adjacent **Cappella Baroncelli**. Next, a doorway designed by Michelozzo leads into a corridor off which is the **Sagrestia**, an enchanting 14th-century room dominated on the right by Taddeo Gaddi's fresco of *La Crocifissione* (Crucifixion).

Through the next room, now serving as a bookshop, you can get to the **Scuola del Cuoio**, (School of Leather; see p174). At the end of the Michelozzo corridor is a Medici chapel, featuring a large altarpiece by Andrea della Robbia.

Back in the church, the transept is lined by five minor chapels on either side of the **Cappella Maggiore** (Main Chapel). The two chapels nearest the right side of the Cappella Maggiore, belonging to the Bardi and Peruzzi clans, are decorated with partly fragmented frescoes by Giotto. In the ninth chapel along, there's a glazed terracotta altarpiece by Giovanni della Robbia, while the final chapel is frescoed by Maso di Banco. These frescoes, among them *Miracolo del Santo che Chiude la Fauci del Drago e Risuscita due Maghi Uccisi dall'Alito del Mostro* (Miracle of the Saint who Shuts the Dragon's Jaws and Brings Back to Life the Magi Killed by the Monster's Breath) burst with life.

In the central chapel of the northern transept (also a Bardi chapel) hangs a wooden crucifix by Donatello. Brunelleschi thought it ugly and, to get his point across, went and sculpted another for the Basilica di Santa Maria Novella.

From the entrance, the first tomb in the left aisle is Galileo Galilei's. You will also have noticed by now that the floor is paved with the tombstones of famous Florentines of the past 500 years. Monuments to the particularly notable were added along the walls from the mid-16th century.

Brunelleschi designed the serene **cloisters** just before his death in 1446. His **Cappella de' Pazzi**, at the end of the first cloister, is a masterpiece of Renaissance architecture. Also off the first cloister is the **Museo dell'Opera di Santa Croce**, which features a partially restored crucifix by Cimabue, which was badly damaged during the disastrous 1966 flood, when the Santa Croce area was inundated. Donatello's gilded bronze statue of *San Ludovico di Tolosa* (St Ludovich of Toulouse) was originally placed in a tabernacle on the Orsanmichele façade. Also on view is Taddeo Gaddi's somewhat faded Last Supper fresco, surmounted by a more intriguing one depicting Christ crucified on the background of the Tree of Life.

CASA BUONARROTI Map pp248–50

☎ 055 24 17 52; Via Ghibellina 70; admission €6.50;
🕙 9.30am-2pm Wed-Mon; bus 14

Michelangelo bought himself this rather nice residence in Florence but never lived in it. Upon his death, it went to his nephew and eventually became a museum in the mid-1850s.

Although not uninteresting, the collections are a little disappointing given what you pay to get in. On the ground floor on the left is a series of rooms used for temporary exhibitions, usually held once a year from May to September. To the right of the ticket window is a small archaeological display. The Buonarroti family collected about 150 pieces over the years, many of which were for a long time in the Museo Archeologico (see p97). The last of them were returned to this house in 1996. The most interesting items are the Etruscan urns – though if you have seen the collection in the Museo Archeologico you don't really need to come here.

Beyond this room are some paintings done in imitation of Michelangelo's style, along with some fine glazed terracotta pieces by the della Robbia family.

Upstairs you can admire a detailed model of Michelangelo's design for the façade of the Basilica di San Lorenzo – as close as the church came to ever getting one. Also by Michelangelo are a couple of marble bas-reliefs and a crucifix. Of the reliefs, *Madonna della Scala* (Madonna of the Steps) is thought to be his earliest work.

Otherwise, a series of rooms designed by Michelangelo Il Giovane, the genius' grand-nephew, are intriguing. The first is full of

Footpath outside Teatro Verdi (opposite)

paintings and frescoes that together amount to a kind of apotheosis of the great man. Portraits of Michelangelo meeting VIPs of his time predominate.

CHIESA DI SANT'AMBROGIO

Map pp248–50

Piazza Sant'Ambrogio; ⏲ **for Mass only; bus C**

A rather dull 18th-century façade hides centuries of church history on this site. The first church here was raised in the 10th century, but what you see inside is a mix of 13th-century Gothic and 15th-century refurbishment. The name comes from the powerful 4th-century archbishop of Milan, Sant'Ambrogio (St Ambrose), who stayed in an earlier convent on this site when he visited Florence. The church is something of an artists' graveyard too. Among those who rest in peace here are Mino da Fiesole, Il Verrocchio and Il Cronaca. Nearby is the local produce market, **Mercato di Sant'Ambrogio**, on Piazza Ghiberti.

MUSEO HORNE Map pp248–50

☎ 055 24 46 61; Via de' Benci 6; admission €5;
⏲ 9am-1pm Mon-Sat; bus 13, 23, B & C

Herbert Percy Horne was one of those eccentric 'Brits abroad' with cash. He bought this building on Via de' Benci in the early 1900s and installed his eclectic collection of 14th- and 15th-century Italian paintings, sculptures, ceramics, coins and other odds and ends, creating this museum. Horne renovated the house in an effort to recreate a Renaissance ambience. Although the occasional big name pops up among the artworks, such as Giotto, Luca Signorelli and Giambologna, most of the stuff is minor. Perhaps more interesting than many of the paintings is the furniture, some of which is exquisite. On the top floor is the original kitchen. Kitchens tended to be on the top floor to reduce the risk of fire spreading through the whole building.

PIAZZA DEI CIOMPI Map pp248–50

Bus A & C

Cleared in the 1930s, the square was named after the textile workers who used to meet in secret in the Santa Croce area and whose 14th-century revolt, which had seemed so full of promise, came to nothing. Nowadays it is the scene of a busy flea market called **Mercato dei Pulci** (see p171). The **Loggia del Pesce**, the Fish Market, was designed by Vasari on the orders of Cosimo I de' Medici for the Mercato Vecchio (Old Market), which was at the heart of what is now Piazza della Repubblica. The loggia was at first moved to the convent at San Marco when the Mercato Vecchio was wiped out, then set up here in 1955.

PONTE ALLE GRAZIE Map pp248–50
Piazza Carlo Goldini; bus 23 & C

In 1237, Giovanni Villani tells us, Messer Ruba-conte da Mandella, a Milanese then serving as external martial (*podestà*) in Florence, had this bridge built. It was swept away in 1333 and on its replacement were raised chapels, one of them dubbed Madonna alle Grazie (Our Lady of the Graces), from which the bridge then took its name. Eventually the chapel, at one end of the bridge, was expanded into a small convent whose Benedictine nuns lived in isolation. Their food was passed to them through a small window and so the nuns became known as Le Mu-rate (The Walled-in Ones). In 1424 they left for larger premises on Via dell'Agnolo, which took on their name, Le Murate (Map pp251–3). Much later that building was turned into a women's prison and nowadays is used in summer as a giant open-air bar (see the boxed text, p147).

The bridge, in the meantime, had filled up with chapels, shops and other buildings much in the manner of the Ponte Vecchio. These were demolished in 1876 to allow street-widening across it. The Germans then blew up the bridge in 1944, and the present version was constructed in 1957.

SINAGOGA & MUSEO DI STORIA E ARTE EBRAICA Map pp248–50
☎ 055 24 52 52; Via Luigi Carlo Farini 4; synagogue & museum adult/child €4/2; ☼ 10am-6pm Sun-Thu & 10am-2pm Fri Jun-Aug; 10am-5pm Sun-Thu & 10am-2pm Fri Apr-May & Sep-Oct; 10am-3pm Sun-Thu & 10am-2pm Fri Nov-Mar; bus C

This late-19th-century synagogue is a fanci-ful structure with playful Moorish and even Byzantine elements. Although Florence was home to a Jewish community since at least the 14th century, serious discussion on the building of an appropriate temple only began around 1850, after the town authori-ties had definitively dropped all discrimin-atory regulations against the Jews.

The playfulness of the exterior of the syna-gogue that resulted is matched inside by the prayer hall, sumptuously (if a little gloomily) decorated with Arabesques and held together by Moorish-style arches. Up on the top floor is the small museum. You can see Jewish cere-monial objects and some old codices, as well as follow the story of Florence's Jews down through the centuries. There are also various photos and models that transmit something of the appearance of the old centre of town, which was destroyed to make way for Piazza della Repubblica – it was in this area that Florence's ghetto had long been located. The local Jewish community today amounts to about 1000 people.

TEATRO VERDI Map pp248–50
Via Giuseppe Verdi; bus 14 & A

Heading north from the Arno river along Via de' Benci (which after Piazza di Santa Croce becomes Via Giuseppe Verdi), you come across this 19th-century theatre at the inter-section with Via Ghibellina. It stands on the site of the 14th-century prison, Le Stinche, which had also been used as a horse-riding school. Building work on the theatre began in 1838 and it was finally inaugurated in 1854. Even today some of the cells from the former prisons remain below the service. It is still going strong (see p152).

Quarters – Oltrarno

OLTRARNO
Eating p125; Shopping p163; Sleeping p175

Orientation

Literally 'beyond the Arno', the Oltrarno encompasses the part of the city that lies south of the river. Protected from much (but not all!) of the chaos north of the river, it is in some regards the most charming side of Florence. Green and hilly, in parts it gives the impression that you have already left the city behind. It bristles with restaurants and bars (for those in need of a break from the sightseeing) and more than a respectable clutch of important churches and art. And be-yond the monuments and crowds come to see them, you get the feeling something of the real Florence lives on, especially around Borgo San Frediano. Wander the lanes and feel the pulse…

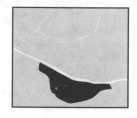

BASILICA DI SANTA MARIA DEL CARMINE Map pp248–50

☎ 055 238 21 95, compulsory bookings for Cappella Brancacci ☎ 055 276 82 24; Via Santa Monaca; admission free (church), €4 (Cappella Brancacci) or €8 combined ticket with Palazzo Vecchio; ⏱ 10am-5pm Wed-Mon, 1-5pm Sun & holidays; bus D

West from Piazza Santo Spirito is Piazza del Carmine, an unkempt square used as a car park. On its southern flank stands this church, high on many art-lovers' Florentine list of must-sees because of the **Cappella Brancacci**.

This chapel is a treasure of paintings by Masolino da Panicale, Masaccio and Filippino Lippi. Above all, the frescoes by Masaccio are considered among his greatest works, representing a definitive break with Gothic art and a plunge into new worlds of expression in the early stages of the Renaissance. His *Cacciata dei Progenitori* (Expulsion of Adam and Eve), on the left side of the chapel, is the best-known work. His depiction of Eve's anguish in particular lends the image a human touch hitherto little seen in European painting. In times gone by prudish church authorities had Adam and Eve's privates covered up. Masaccio painted these frescoes in his early twenties and interrupted the task to go to Rome, where he died aged only 28. The cycle was completed some 60 years later by Filippino Lippi.

That you can even see these frescoes today is little short of miraculous. The 13th-century church was nearly destroyed by a fire in the late 18th century. About the only thing the fire spared was the chapel.

The church interior is something of a saccharine baroque bomb. Take a look up at the barrel-vaulted ceiling above the single nave. There is an excessive architectural trompe l'oeil fresco painting, with arches, pillars, columns and tympana all crammed in together. Opposite the Cappella Brancacci is the **Cappella Corsini**, one of the first (and few) examples of the extremes of billowing Roman baroque executed in Florence. It is not to everyone's taste but that does not justify its complete neglect – you'll have it all to yourself as thousands file past through Brancacci chapel across the nave. The fresco in the cupola after the statuary is by Luca Giordano.

You enter Cappella Brancacci by a side door that takes you through the cloister. Should you arrive after it has closed but find the church open, you can wander in and get a distant look at it from behind barriers – but a close-up inspection is what you need to appreciate the staggering detail.

There are several ways to deepen your appreciation of the chapel. A 40-minute computer graphics film, a guided visit by a Giorgio

People talking outside Cabiria café in Piazza Santo Spirito on market day

Vasari lookalike and a tour of parts of the basilica normally closed to the public (including sacristy, chapels and refectory) are all possible for a small extra fee (€1 to €2).

BASILICA DI SANTO SPIRITO
Map pp248–50

Piazza Santa Spirito; admission free; ◷ **10am-noon Mon-Fri & 4-5.30pm Thu-Tue; bus 11, 36, 37 & D**

It's a shame the authorities concerned could never get their act together sufficiently to provide this fine church with a dignified front, but don't let this put you off. The inside is a masterpiece of Florentine Renaissance design.

The church was one of Brunelleschi's last commissions. Its entire length inside is lined by a series of 40 semicircular chapels. The architects who succeeded the master were unfortunately not entirely faithful to his design. He wanted the chapels to form a shell of little apses right around the church, which clearly would have been a revolutionary step. Instead they chose to hide them behind a rather ad hoc–looking wall, flattening off the flanks of the church in an unsatisfying and untidy fashion.

More than the chapels, the colonnade of 35 columns in *pietra serena* is particularly striking inside. Not only do they separate the aisles from the nave, they continue round into the transept, creating the optical impression of a grey-stone forest. Look closely at the high 'coffered' ceiling above the nave. It is simply painted, a trompe l'oeil 'fake' (funds were limited). Remember the similar-looking ceiling in the Basilica di San Lorenzo? There the coffered effect is real.

One of the most noteworthy works of art is Filippino Lippi's *Madonna col Bambino e Santi* (Madonna and Child with Saints) in one of the chapels in the right transept. The main altar, beneath the central dome, is a voluptuous baroque flourish rather out of place in the spare setting of Brunelleschi's church. The sacristy *(sagrestia)* on the left side of the church is worth a look, particularly for its barrel-vaulted vestibule.

BORGO SAN FREDIANO Map pp248–50
Bus 6 & D

Just north of Piazza del Carmine stretches Borgo San Frediano. The street and surrounding area have, to a degree, retained their feel of a working-class quarter where small-scale artisans have beavered away over the centuries. Many continue to do so.

At the western end of the street stands the lonely **Porta San Frediano**, one of the old city gates left in place when the walls were demolished in the 19th century. Before you reach the gate, you'll notice the unpolished feel of the area neatly reflected in the unadorned brick walls of the **Chiesa di San Frediano in Cestello** (Piazza di Cestello; admission free; ☎ 9am-11.30am & 4.30-6pm Mon-Fri, 5-6.30pm Sun & holidays), whose incomplete façade hides a restrained version of a baroque interior. The western side of Piazza di Cestello is occupied by granaries built under Cosimo III de' Medici.

CASA GUIDI Map pp248–50
☎ **055 35 44 57; Piazza San Felice 8; admission free (donation appreciated);** ◷ **3-6pm Mon, Wed & Fri Apr-Nov; bus 11, 36, 37 & D**

Welcome to chez Browning. Robert and Elizabeth Barrett rented this house in 1847 and lived and scribbled here for many years. Elizabeth died here in 1861. The house, run by Eton College and the Landmark Trust, has been restored in 19th-century style and some of the furnishings belonged to the poetic couple. If you like it enough you can stay (see p185).

CENACOLO DI SANTO SPIRITO
Map pp248–50

☎ **055 28 70 34; Piazza Santo Spirito 29; admission €2.20;** ◷ **9am-2pm Tue-Sun Apr-Nov, 10.30am-1.30pm Tue-Sun Dec-Mar; bus D**

Housed in a refectory next door to the basilica of the same name, the Cenacolo is a grand fresco depicting the Last Supper and Crucifixion by Andrea Orcagna. In 1946 the building was enriched by the creation of the Fondazione Romano when the Neapolitan collector Salvatore Romano left his horde of sculpture to Florence's town council. Among the most intriguing pieces are rare pre-Romanesque sculptures and works by Jacopo della Quercia and Donatello. It will be most interesting to those with a genuine interest in Romanesque and pre-Romanesque sculptures.

CHIESA DI SAN FELICE Map pp248–50
☎ **055 22 17 06; Piazza San Felice;** ◷ **8am-11am Mon-Sat, 6.30pm Sun for Mass; bus 11, 36, 37 & D**

This unprepossessing church has been made over several times since the Romanesque original was ruined in 1066. The simple Renaissance façade is by Michelozzo. Inside you can admire an extraordinary early 14th-century crucifix by Giotto's workshop. This giant cross dominates the altar area by its sheer size and colour.

CHIESA DI SAN MINIATO AL MONTE

Map pp248–50

☎ 055 234 27 31; Via delle Porte Sante; admission free; ⊙ 8am-7.30pm May-Oct, 8am-1pm & 2.30-6pm Nov-Apr; bus 12 & 13

A steep climb up from Piazzale Michelangelo will bring you to this wonderful Romanesque church, surely the best surviving example of the genre in Florence. The church is dedicated to San Miniato (St Minius), an early Christian martyr in Florence who is said to have flown to this spot after his death down in the town.

The church, started in the early 11th century, has a typically Tuscan marble façade featuring a mosaic depicting Christ with the Virgin and St Minius added 200 years later. The eagle at the top represents the Arte di Calimala, the guild that financed the construction.

Inside you will see 13th- to 15th-century frescoes on the right wall, intricate inlaid marble designs down the length of the nave and a fine Romanesque crypt at the back, below the unusual raised *presbiterio* (presbytery). The latter boasts a fine marble pulpit replete with intriguing geometrical designs. The sacristy, to the right of the church (they suggest you make a small donation to get in), features marvellously bright frescoes. The four figures in the cross vault are the Evangelists.

The **Cappella del Cardinale del Portogallo** (Chapel of the Portuguese Cardinal), to the left side of the church, features a tomb by Antonio Rossellino and a striking ceiling decorated in terracotta by Luca della Robbia. The chapel was created for the Portuguese Prince James, who also happened to be a cardinal. Caught ill and dying in Florence, he requested (and no doubt paid for) a suitably regal burial place.

It is possible to wander through the cemetery outside. Some of Michelangelo's battlements remain standing around here too.

CHIESA DI SANTA FELICITA Map pp251–3

Via de' Guicciardini; admission free; ⊙ 9am-noon & 3-6pm Mon-Fri, 9am-1pm Sun & holidays; bus D

The most captivating thing about the façade of this 18th-century remake of what had been Florence's oldest (4th-century) church is the

---

The World Turns

'Eppur si muove', Galileo is supposed to have muttered after having been compelled to recant his teachings on astronomy before the Inquisition in Rome in 1633. 'And yet it *does* move.' He was referring to the earth, whose exalted position at the centre of the universe he so inconveniently maintained was a falsehood. The earth, along with other planets, rotated around the sun, just as Copernicus had sustained.

As long ago as 1616 he had been ordered not to push this theory, which Vatican conservatives, not overly well disposed to the 'new learning', saw as a potential threat to the Church. If teachings long held dear about the position of the world in God's universe were accepted as balderdash, it could lead to further uncertainty. The capacity to reveal what makes things tick, rather than simply remaining awestruck by divine majesty, threatened those intent on maintaining the Church's position of pre-eminence in worldly and spiritual affairs.

Galileo was born in Pisa on 15 February 1564, the son of a musician. He received his early education at the monastery of Vallombrosa near Florence and later studied medicine at the University of Pisa. During his time there he became fascinated by mathematics and the study of motion, so much so that he is regarded as the founder of experimental physics. He became teacher of mathematics in Pisa and then moved to Padua for 18 years to teach and research there.

Having heard of the invention of the telescope in 1609, he set about making his own, the first used to scan the night skies. In the coming years he made discoveries that led him to confirm Copernicus' theory that the planets revolve around the sun. In 1610 he moved to Florence, where the grand duke had offered him permanent residence to continue his research. Galileo had many supporters, but not enough to prevent his works on the subject being placed on the 1616 index of banned books.

For the next seven years he continued his studies in Florence, where he lived mainly at Bellosguardo (see p112). The 1616 edict declaring his teachings on astronomy blasphemous was softened in 1624 to the extent that he was given permission to write an 'objective study' of the various proposed systems. His study was a triumph of argumentation in favour of his own theory, culminating nevertheless in the obligatory disclaimer that remained imposed on him. It was in the wake of this that the Inquisition summoned him to Rome in 1632. From then on he was confined to exile within Florence until his death in 1642, when he was buried in the Basilica di Santa Croce. Until his last days, even after blindness had beset him in 1637, he continued to study, experiment, correspond with other scientists across Europe and write books. No doubt he was touched (in spirit) when, only 350 years after his death, the Pope acknowledged that, actually, Galileo's theories had largely been correct.

fact that the Corridoio Vasariano passes right across it. The Medici could drop by and hear Mass without being seen by anyone!

Inside, the main interest is in the small **Cappella Barbadori**, designed by Brunelleschi, immediately on the right as you enter. Here Pontormo left his disquieting mark with a fresco of the Annunciation and a Deposizione. The latter depicts the taking down of Christ from the Cross in disturbingly surreal colours. The people engaged in this operation look almost as if they have been given a fright by the prying eyes of the onlooker.

The good thing about coming into a 'minor' church like this is that you'll probably find it empty, with one or two seniors perhaps muttering a few prayers in the silence. Shame it's not like that all over town!

FORTE DI BELVEDERE Map pp248–50

Costa di San Giorgio; admission €8 (€6.50 if you enter from Giardino di Boboli), includes temporary art exhibition; ☾ 9am-dusk; bus D & C + walk

Bernardo Buontalenti helped design the rambling fortifications here for Grand Duke Ferdinando I towards the end of the 16th century. From this massive bulwark soldiers could keep watch on four fronts, and indeed it was designed with internal security in mind as much as foreign attack. Set high on a hill, the views across the city are, for this writer's money, better than the much-touted ones from Piazzale Michelangelo (see p109).

The main entrance is near **Porta San Giorgio**, and you can approach from the east along the walls or by taking Costa di San Giorgio up from near the Ponte Vecchio. If you take the latter, you will pass, at Nos 17 to 21, one of the houses where **Galileo Galilei** lived while in Florence. You can also visit the fort from the Giardino di Boboli.

As you take in the sweep of the view south of the fort, you can identify clearly the marble Romanesque façade of the Chiesa di San Miniato al Monte (opposite) to the southeast. More or less directly south on a distant height you can make out what appears to be another fort with watchtower. Known as the **Torre del Gallo** (Map pp244–5), it belonged to the Galli clan, a Ghibelline family. They say Galileo carried out his astronomical observations from the tower here. What you see today is a bit of a travesty – a medieval-style reconstruction built in 1906.

Inside the Forte di Belvedere you will find a bar-restaurant, and the site is used for open-air cinema screenings in summer (see p151). At the time of writing it was not known whether the fort would remain open year-round or only for temporary exhibitions.

If you feel like a long walk, you could follow Via di San Leonardo south to Viale Galileo Galilei, about 1.5km, turning left to head another couple of kilometres towards the Chiesa di San Miniato al Monte (or catch a bus back into the centre of town). Along Via di San Leonardo you'll pass the medieval **Chiesa di San Leonardo** (Map pp248–50), whose 13th-century marble pulpit was taken from another church, San Piero Scheraggio (largely demolished to make way for the Uffizi). They say the likes of Dante and Boccaccio spoke from that pulpit. The church only opens for occasional services. Shortly before you reach Viale Galileo Galilei, you pass a villa (Map pp244–5) on your right where Tchaikovsky resided for a while.

GIARDINO DI BOBOLI Map pp248–50

☎ 055 265 15 18; Piazza Pitti; admission €4, includes Museo delle Porcellane & Museo degli Argenti; ☾ 8.15am-7.30pm Jun-Aug, 8.15am-6.30pm Apr-May & Sep-Oct, 8.15am-5.30pm Mar, 8.15am-4.30pm Nov-Feb; closed 1st and last Mon of each month; bus D

A relaxing antidote to cultural overdose in the Palazzo Pitti (see p108) is a stroll in the palace's Renaissance Giardino di Boboli (called Boboli Gardens in English). The garden was laid out in the mid-16th century and based on a design by the architect known as Il Tribolo. Buontalenti's noted artificial grotto, the **Grotta del Buontalenti**, with *Venere* (Venus) by Giambologna, is curious. In June, concerts of classical music are sometimes held in the gardens.

Before you leave, you can visit the **Museo degli Argenti** in the north wing of Palazzo Pitti on the same ticket. It contains collections of glassware, silver, ivory and amber objects (mostly imported from Germany in the 17th century), *pietre dure* from the Medici collections and those of the Dukes of Lorraine who succeeded the Medici as Grand Dukes of Tuscany. Cosimo Medici got the ball rolling in the 15th century. His successors, especially starting with the first Grand Duke Cosimo I, actively sponsored an industry in the 'minor arts', promoting the ingenious work of jewellers, goldsmiths and others, and so hording this endless array of expensive trinkets.

At the southeastern end of the garden is the **Museo delle Porcellane**, housing a varied collection of fine porcelain collected over the centuries by the illustrious tenants of Palazzo Pitti, from Cosimo I de' Medici and Eleonora de Toledo onwards. The exhibits include some exquisite Sèvres and Vincennes pieces, as well as Meissen, Vienna and local collections from Doccia.

The views south from the museum give a wonderful bucolic flavour to your Florentine experience; the hilly country at your feet is dotted with olive trees and cypresses – you can hardly get more rustic Tuscan than that.

You can get into the **Forte di Belvedere** (see p107) from the southeast end of the garden. Also near here is the **Kaffeehaus**, a 19th-century conceit installed by Grand Duke Pietro Leopoldo. Until recently you could get an expensive cuppa here.

MUSEO ZOOLOGICO LA SPECOLA
Map pp248–50
☎ 055 228 82 51; Via Romana 17; adult/child €5/2.50; ✆ 9am-1pm Thu-Tue; bus 11, 36, 37 & D

A little further down Via Romana from Piazza San Felice, this a rather fusty old but fascinating museum. On the top floor are hundreds of stuffed animals and all sorts of other critters. The range is extraordinary, from giant South American insects to a rhinoceros, from crocodiles to emus, from sharks and sea mammals to Prince Vittorio Emanuele's African hunting trophies. There are even gorillas. People are not left out either. Easily the highlight of the collection are the late-18th-century wax models of assorted bits of human anatomy. The life-size human bodies, laid out as if taking a liedown and stripped back to muscles, organs and veins, are particularly gruesome. The section devoted to the genitals is enough to put you off sex forever. Created as teaching aids for doctors in training, they certainly make for an offbeat diversion from all that art! Downstairs in the courtyard is a skeleton collection, including kids' favourites like whales, an elephant and a giraffe. The animals and bug section is also bound to fascinate youngsters. Whether or not they'll like the chamber of medical wax horrors is another matter.

PALAZZO PITTI Map pp248–50
☎ 055 238 86 14; Piazza de' Pitti 1; admission €10.50 for combined ticket to all galleries & museums, €7.75 after 4pm (see the following sights for single-entry costs); ✆ 8.15am-6.50pm Tue-Sun (Galleria Palatina); 8.15am-1.50pm Tue-Sat & alternating Sun & Mon (Galleria d'Arte Moderna & Galleria del Costume); 8.15am-7.30pm Jun-Aug, 8.15am-6.30pm Apr-May & Sep-Oct, 8.15am-5.30pm Mar, 8.15am-4.30pm Nov-Feb; closed 1st & last Mon of each month (Museo degli Argenti, Museo delle Porcellane & Giardino di Boboli); bus D

When the Pitti, a wealthy merchant family, asked Brunelleschi to design the family home,

they did not have modesty in mind. Great rivals of the Medici, there is not a little irony in the fact that their grandiloquence would one day be sacrificed to the bank account.

Begun in 1458, the original nucleus of the palace took up the space encompassing the seven sets of windows on the 2nd and 3rd storeys.

In 1549 Eleonora de Toledo, wife of Cosimo I de' Medici, finding Palazzo Vecchio too claustrophobic, acquired the palace from a by-now rather skint Pitti family. She launched the extension work, which ended up crawling along until 1839! Through all that time the original design was respected and today you would be hard-pressed to distinguish the various phases of construction.

After the demise of the Medici dynasty, the palace remained the residence of the city's rulers, the dukes of Lorraine and their Austrian and (briefly) Napoleonic successors.

When Florence was made capital of the nascent Kingdom of Italy in 1865, it became a residence of the Savoy royal family, who graciously presented it to the state in 1919.

The palace houses five museums. The **Galleria Palatina** (Palatine Gallery; admission €8.50, including Appartamenti Reali, €4 after 4pm) has paintings from the 16th to 18th centuries, hung in lavishly decorated rooms. The works were collected mostly by the Medici and their grand ducal successors.

After getting your ticket, head up a grand staircase to the gallery floor. The first rooms you pass through are a seemingly haphazard mix of the odd painting, sculpture and period furniture.

The gallery proper starts after the **Sala della Musica** (Music Room, created under the short reign of Elisa Baciocchi as a reception room for her brother, the Emperor Napoleon – he never had the time to come and try it out). The paintings hung in the succeeding rooms are not in any particular order. Among Tuscan masters you can see work by Fra Filippo Lippi, Sandro Botticelli, Giorgio Vasari and Andrea del Sarto (who is represented in just about every room!). The collection also boasts some important works by other Italian and foreign painters. Foremost among them are those by Raphael, especially in the **Sala di Saturno**. A close second is Titian (especially in the **Sala di Marte**), one of the greatest of the Venetian school. Other important artists represented include Tintoretto, Paolo Veronese, Jose Ribera, Bravo Murillo, Peter Paul Rubens and Van Dyck. Caravaggio is represented with the striking *Amore Dormiente* (Love Sleeping) inside the

Absorbing the atmosphere near a fountain on Palazzo Pitti (opposite)

Sala dell'Educazione di Giove. Although probably overwhelmed by all the art hanging on the walls, you should scrape together some energy for the ceilings too – many of the wonderfully airy frescoes are by Pietro da Cortona, who came from Rome to do the job.

From the gallery you can pass into the **Appartamenti Reali**, a series of rather sickeningly furnished and decorated rooms, where the Medici grand dukes and their successors slept, received guests and generally hung about. It was redecorated by the Hapsburgs: the style and division of tasks assigned to each room is reminiscent of Spanish royal palaces, all heavily bedecked with curtains, silk, chandeliers and so on. Each room has a colour theme, ranging from aqua green to deep wine red and dusty mellow yellow.

The other galleries are also worth a look if you have plenty of time at hand. The **Galleria d'Arte Moderna** (Gallery of Modern Art; admission €5 combined with Galleria del Costume) covers mostly Tuscan works from the 18th to the mid-20th century (including numerous works by the Macchiaioli), while the **Galleria del Costume** (Costume Gallery) features high-class ballroom threads from the 19th century and curious outfits from as late at the 1960s, including ones worn by Jacqui Onassis and Audrey Hepburn. The gallery is housed in the Meridiana, a low-slung neoclassical addition to the Palazzo Pitti made under the Habsburg Pietro Leopoldo.

The **Museo delle Carrozze** contains ducal coaches and the like but has been closed for years and shows no signs of reopening any time soon.

From Palazzo Pitti you also access the Giardino di Boboli, beautifully maintained gardens that spread east of the palace. From the garden you can access two more museums dedicated to silverware and porcelain collections. See the separate Giardino di Boboli entry (p107).

PIAZZALE MICHELANGELO Map pp248–50
Bus 12 & 13
Since its creation in the 19th century, this grand viewpoint-cum-carpark has been a favourite with locals and visitors alike for gazing down over the Arno and city. It is dominated by a bronze copy of Michelangelo's *David* and littered with snack bars and cafés. You can get up here by following the winding paths up from Piazza Giuseppe Poggi (marked by the medieval gate tower, the Porta San Niccolò). Buses arriving from Siena often pass this way, and for those who are arriving in Florence for the first time, this initial glimpse of the place usually elicits a little leap of joy in even the hardest of hearts.

PONTE VECCHIO Map pp248–50
Via de Guicciardino; bus B, C & D
The first documentation of a stone bridge here, at the narrowest crossing point along the entire length of the Arno, dates from 972. The Arno

looks placid enough but when it gets mean, it gets very mean. Floods in 1177 and 1333 destroyed the bridge, and in 1966 it came close again. Newspaper reports of the time highlight how dangerous the situation was. One couple who owned a jewellery shop on the bridge described the crashing of the waters just below the floorboards as they tried to salvage some of their goods. *Carabinieri* (military police) on the river bank excitedly warned them to get off, but they retorted that the forces of law and order should do something. They did get off in the end, fearful they'd be swept away by the torrential onslaught.

Those jewellers were among several on the bridge who inherited the traditional business in the 16th century when Grand Duke Ferdinando I de' Medici ordered a replacement to the rather malodorous presence of the town butchers. The latter tended to jettison unwanted leftovers into the river.

The bridge as it stands was built in 1345, and those of us who get the chance to admire it can thank...well, someone...that it wasn't blown to smithereens in August 1944. Retreating German forces blew up all the other bridges on the Arno, but someone among them must have decided that sending the Ponte Vecchio to the bottom would have been going too far! Instead they mined the areas on either side of the bridge. As you reach the southern bank, this becomes obvious. Take a look at the buildings around Via de' Guicciardini and Borgo San Jacopo – they aren't exactly ancient heritage sites.

It was on this side of the bridge that Buondelmonte dei Buondelmonti was assassinated beneath the statue of Mars that stood here then, sparking the conflict between the Guelphs and Ghibellines that subsequently tore the city and Tuscany apart. Mars was washed away by the 1333 flood.

Among the buildings to survive the Nazis' mines are two medieval towers. The first, **Torre dei Mannelli**, just on the southern end of the bridge,

looks very odd, as the Corridoio Vasariano was built around it, not simply straight through it as the Medici would have preferred. Across Via de' Bardi as your eye follows the Corridoio you espy **Torre degli Ubriachi** (Drunks' Tower). On the intersection of Borgo San Jacopo and Via de' Guicciardini you will see an unassuming fountain, the **Fontana di Bacco** (Bacchus Fountain). Giambologna's *Ercole col Centauro Nesso* (Hercules with the Centaur) statue was here until transported to the Loggia della Signoria (see p84).

PORTA ROMANA Map pp248–50
Via Romana; bus 11, 36 & 37
Pilgrims to Rome headed down Via Romana leaving Florence behind them. The end of the road is marked by the Porta Romana, an imposing gate that was part of the outer circle of city walls knocked down in the 19th century. A strip of this wall still stretches to the north from the gate. If you head along the inside of this wall (the area is now a car park), you will soon come across an entrance that allows you to get to the top of the Porta Romana.

The square below was traditionally a fairground for peasants in the surrounding county *(contado)*. By far the most curious of these fairs was the *Fiera dei Contratti* (Contracts Fair), when country folk from near and far dragged sons and daughters along to contract marriage. They would haggle keenly over dowries and, much to the amusement of the not-too-respectful city folk who had taken the day off to come and gawk, compel prospective brides to walk up the hill towards the Poggio Imperiale (see p112) to see how well they swayed their hips!

VIA MAGGIO Map pp248–50
Bus 11, 36, 37 & D
No, it doesn't mean May St, but rather Via Maggiore (Main St). In the 16th century this was a rather posh address, as the line-up of fine Renaissance mansions duly attests. **Palazzo di Bianca Cappello**, at No 26, has the most eye-catching façade, covered as it is in graffiti designs. Bianca Cappello was Francesco I de' Medici's lover and eventually became his wife. Across the street, a series of imposing mansions more or less follow the same Renaissance or Renaissance-inspired style. They include the **Palazzo Ricasoli-Ridolfi** at No 7, **Palazzo Martellini** at No 9, **Palazzo Michelozzi** at No 11, **Palazzo Zanchini** at No 13 and **Palazzo di Cosimo Ridolfi** at No 15. All were built and fiddled around with over the 14th, 15th and 16th centuries. Another impressive one is the **Palazzo Corsini-Suarez** at No 42.

Transport

ATAF's No 13 circular line bus runs from Stazione di Santa Maria Novella to Piazzale Michelangelo Via Ponte alle Grazie, past the Chiesa di San Miniato al Monte and on to Porta Romana before turning north again for the station via Ponte al Prato. Minibus D runs back and forth between the train station and Oltrarno, ranging between Ponte di Vespucci and Piazza Ferrucci on its travels.

NORTH OF THE OLD CITY

Eating p125; Sleeping p175

Orientation

Florentine traffic is at its splutter-inducing heaviest in the maze of boulevards that swirl around the back of the train station. Just nearby glowers the hulk of Alessandro de' Medici's fortress. Otherwise there are a couple of quite curious surprises in this northern end of town. The gleaming onion-shaped domes of the Russian Orthodox church is one, while the more distant hill-top caprice-turned-museum, the Museo Stibbert, could be worth the effort for kids and war buffs.

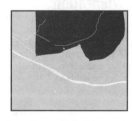

CHIESA RUSSA ORTODOSSA

Map pp246–7

☎ 055 49 01 48; Viale Giovanni Milton; admission free; ☒ 3.30pm 3rd Sun of month for service; bus 4, 8, 13 & 20

The onion-shaped domes are a bit of a give-away on this Russian Orthodox church. Built in 1902 for the Russian populace resident here, it was designed in the northern Russian style, with two interior levels decorated in part by Florentine artists but mostly by Russians expert in iconography.

FORTEZZA DA BASSO Map pp246–7

Viale Filippo Strozzi; bus 4, 12, 13, 14, 20, 23, 28, 33 & 80

Alessandro de' Medici ordered this huge defensive fortress built in 1534, and the task went to a Florentine living in Rome, Antonio da Sangallo il Giovane. The Medici family in general and Alessandro in particular were not flavour of the month in Florence at the time, and construction of the fortress was an ominous sign of oppression. It was not designed to protect the city from invasion – Alessandro had recently been put back in the saddle after a siege by papal-imperial forces. The idea of this fort was to keep a watchful eye over the Florentines themselves. Nowadays it is used for trade fairs, exhibitions and cultural events.

MUSEO STIBBERT Map pp244–5

☎ 055 47 55 20; Via F Stibbert 26; admission €5, gardens free; ☒ 10am-2pm Mon-Wed, 10am-6pm Fri-Sun, gardens 10am-dusk; bus 4

Frederick Stibbert (1838–1906) was one of the big wheeler-dealers on the European antiquities market in the 19th century and unsurprisingly had quite a collection himself. Born in Florence to an officer of the Coldstream Guards and a Florentine mother, Stibbert was forced through the English public school system and

at 20 inherited a huge fortune from his grandfather. He bought and expanded the Villa di Montughi with the intention of creating a museum-home. His obsessions (apart from fast women and parties) revolved around the study of costume and armour. And so he built up a unique collection of European and Middle Eastern armour. The centrepiece of the display is the **Sala della Cavalcata** (Parade Room), with life-size mannequins of mounted knights, more than a dozen of them, on parade in German, French, Italian and Turkish armour. It is a unique sight and the hall is topped at one end with a figure of St George slaying the dragon – the latter is made of hundreds of snakeskins!

The exhibits, which spread out over a seeming infinity of rooms, also include clothes, furnishings, tapestries, ceramics and paintings (among them a good dose of Flemish and Dutch works) from the 16th to the 19th centuries. One of the most important items is the ceremonial cape in which Napoleon had himself crowned King of Italy (a short-lived honour as it turned out). It cost Stibbert 800 lire at auction.

Set in magnificent gardens, the museum lies about 1.5km north of the Fortezza da Basso.

13th-century doors of the Baptistry (p65)

SOUTH OF THE OLD CITY
Sleeping p175

Orientation
Beyond the settled and busy area of Oltrarno, Florence's urban landscape is quickly replaced by verdant Tuscan hills. The countryside has largely impeded urban sprawl, except to some extent along the main roads south, in particular the Via Senese. The main attraction is the grand Certosa monastery at Galluzzo, but a couple of other spots merit a detour.

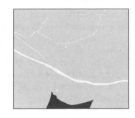

Quarters – South of the Old City

BELLOSGUARDO Map pp244–5
A favourite spot for 19th-century landscape painters was the hill of Bellosguardo (Beautiful View), southwest of the city centre. A narrow winding road leads up past a couple of villas from Piazza Tasso to Piazza Bellosguardo. You can't see anything from here, but if you wander along Via Roti Michelozzi into the grounds of the Albergo Torre di Bellosguardo, you'll see what the fuss was about. The hotel is the latest guise of what was once a 14th-century castle.

Try to get a look before you are not-so-kindly requested to be on your way. The hotel is great if you are staying there (p186), but otherwise they won't even let you spend money at the bar.

CERTOSA DI GALLUZZO Map p254
☎ 055 204 92 26; admission by donation; ⏰ 9am-noon & 3-6pm Tue-Sun May-Oct, 9am-noon & 3-5pm Tue-Sun Nov-Apr; bus 37
Dominating the village of Galluzzo, about 3km south along Via Senese from Porta Romana is this quite remarkable 14th-century monastery, the Certosa. The Carthusian order of monks once had 50 monasteries in Italy. Of these, only two are now inhabited by monks of that order. The Certosa di Galluzzo passed into Cistercian hands in 1955.

Door knockers near the Duomo (p75)

The Certosa can only be visited with a guide (reckon on about 45 minutes) who will take you first to the Gothic hall of the **Palazzo degli Studi**, now graced by a small collection of art, including five somewhat weathered frescoes by Pontormo. It is a little depressing to think that, until Napoleon's troops looted the place in the early 19th century, more than 500 important works of art graced the monastery. The **Basilica di San Lorenzo**, with 14th-century origins, has a Renaissance exterior. To one side of it is the **Colloquio**, a narrow hall with benches. Here the Carthusian monks were permitted to break their vow of silence once a week (they got a second chance on Mondays when they were allowed to leave the monastery grounds for a gentle stroll). You end up in the **Chiostro Grande**, the biggest of the complex's three cloisters. It is flanked by 18 monks' cells and decorated with busts from the della Robbia workshop.

POGGIO IMPERIALE Map p254
Bus 38
From Porta Romana a straight boulevard, Viale del Poggio Imperiale, leads directly to this once-grand Medici residence, the 'Imperial Hill'. The neoclassical appearance is due to changes wrought in the 18th and 19th centuries. It is now home to a high school and girls boarding school. If you turn up alone you will probably be able to wander around this somewhat neglected site.

Transport
No buses run to Bellosguardo – you need your own wheels or the patience to walk for an hour or so from central Florence. ATAF bus No 37 runs from Stazione di Santa Maria Novella to Galluzzo and No 38 from Porta Romana to Poggio Imperiale.

EAST OF THE OLD CITY

Orientation

To cool yourself down after a day's enjoyment of sights , you can enjoy the city's most favoured swimming pool which is situated in this area. Alternatively, for an art-history experience so characteristic of Florence, there are some magnificent frescoes of the Last Supper that are worth seeking out.

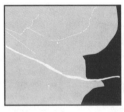

CENACOLO DI SAN SALVI Map pp244–5

☎ 055 238 86 03; Via San Salvi 16; admission free; ⏰ 8.15am-1.50pm Tue-Sun; bus 3, 6, 20 & 34

Dominating the refectory wall in what was once a part of the San Salvi monastery is one of Andrea del Sarto's most extraordinary frescoes (1527). In this scene of the Last Supper, the diners gather at an austere table beneath a grand trompe l'oeil vault. Curiously, the tavern owner and an employee are peering at the proceedings from a window above and behind them. They watch as Jesus hands Judas Iscariot (who sits among the apostles and not customarily alone on the other side) a piece of bread to indicate that he is the apostle who will betray him. There is a collection of other works by Andrea del Sarto's contemporaries on show. You are more than likely to have the place to yourself.

OUTSKIRTS OF FLORENCE

Eating p125; Shopping p163; Sleeping p175

Orientation

About 5km northeast of the old city centre lies the hillside town of Fiesole, a cool and pretty escape hatch for Florentines and foreigners with cash. Those that can afford it enjoy their grand residences up here, far from the madding crowds below. The Etruscans liked it too, and probably never understood why the Romans built Florentia down in the river valley below. Still, Romans weren't silly, and they soon had a theatre built in Fiesole with panoramic views.

FIESOLE Map p254

Founded at the latest in the 5th century BC, Fiesole had a five-century head start on Florence. The main northern Etruscan settlement, Fiesole was in many respects a far more pleasant site for a town than the sweaty malarial river valley in which Roman Florentia was founded. As the stoic Romans set about building their town, the Etruscans sat back and probably regarded them with considerable ambivalence.

Then, as now, the view over the Roman city is a drawcard. Add the olive groves and pretty valleys and you can understand why the likes of Boccaccio, Marcel Proust, Gertrude Stein and Frank Lloyd Wright (it's unlikely they have anything else in common!) have resided here.

The **tourist office** (☎ 055 59 87 20; www.co mune.fiesole.fi.it; Via Portigiani 3; ⏰ 9am-6pm Mon-Sat, 10am-1pm & 2-6pm Sun Mar-Oct; 9am-5pm Mon-Sat, 10am-4pm Sun Nov-Feb) is just off Piazza Mino da Fiesole, the heart of the village. In the piazza itself is the **cathedral** (admission free; ⏰ 7.30am-noon & 3-6pm). Much of its medieval splendour was lovingly erased by 19th-century renovation. Behind it, the **Museo Bandini** (☎ 055 5 94 77; Via Duprè 1; admission €6.50, including Zona Archeologica; ⏰ 9.30am-7pm May-Sept, 9.30am-6pm Mar & Oct, 9.30am-5pm Wed-Mon Nov-Feb) features an impressive collection of Tuscan artwork, most of it pre-dating the early Renaissance period. Among the paintings is also a collection of ceramics from the Della Robbia clan.

Opposite the entrance to the museum is the **Zona Archeologica** (Map p254; ☎ 055 5 94 77; Via Portigiana 1; admission €6.50, including Museo Bandini; ⏰ 9.30am-7pm May-Oct, 9.30am-5pm Wed-Mon Nov-Apr). At its centre is the 1st-century-BC Roman theatre – built not long after the Romans took the

Etruscan settlement and still used from June to August for the Estate Fiesolana, a series of summer concerts and performances. Also in the complex are a small Etruscan temple, Roman baths and a small archaeological museum containing finds ranging from Etruscan funeral stones through Greek-era ceramics and on to Lombard tombs.

Far in time and style from the Renaissance splendours of the valley below, the **Museo Primo Conti** (☎ 055 59 70 95; Via Dupré 18; admission €2.60; ☺ 9am-1pm Mon-Fri, 2nd & 3rd Sat each month), a five-minute walk north of Piazza Mino da Fiesole, was the home of the eponymous avant-garde 20th-century artist and houses over 60 of his paintings. His style was eclectic but always bursting with colour, as these works show.

MEDICI VILLAS Map p254

The Medicis built several opulent villas in the countryside around Florence as their wealth and prosperity grew during the 15th and 16th centuries. Most of the villas are now enclosed by the city's suburbs and industrial sprawl, and are easily reached by bus.

One of the finest of the Medici villas is **Villa Medicea La Petraia** (☎ 055 45 26 91; Via della Petraia 40; admission €2, also valid for Villa Medicea di Castello; ☺ 8.15am-7.30pm Jun-Aug, 8.15am-6.30pm Apr-May & Sep, 8.15am-5.30pm Mar & Oct, 8.15am-4.30pm Nov-Feb; closed 2nd & 3rd Mon each month). Commissioned by Cardinal Ferdinando de' Medici in 1576, this former fortress, about 3.5km north of the city, was converted by Buontalenti and features a magnificent sculpted garden from where you can take in the entire Florentine plain (it is easy to see why there was a fort

Transport

ATAF bus No 7 from Stazione di Santa Maria Novella connects with Piazza Mino da Fiesole in Fiesole. If you are driving, find your way to Piazza della Libertà in Florence and follow signs to Fiesole. ATAF bus No 28 from Stazione di Santa Maria Novella runs to the Villa Medicea La Petraia and Villa Medicea di Castello. No 14C, which you can pick up at Piazza C Beccaria (Map pp248–50), the Duomo or Stazione di Santa Maria Novella, runs past Villa Careggi.

The easiest way to reach Villa di Poggio a Caiano without your own transport is with the COPIT bus service running between Florence and Pistoia (€3.75, 30 minutes). There is a bus stop right outside the villa.

here). Brunelleschi's dome and Giotto's Campanile are perfectly visible, as are the planes taking off from Florence's airport. Inside, the bulk of what you see was redecorated in the time of King Vittorio Emanuele's rule, when the Italian capital shifted temporarily to Florence in 1865. The most stunning aspect is the first entry into the fresco-plastered former courtyard. Vittorio Emanuele had any wall space not already frescoed covered with more. Then he had a glass and metal roof built to cover the area so that his guests could use it as a ballroom under the stars. His morganatic wife, the Duchess of Mirafiori, took up residence here.

Barely 1km west is **Villa Medicea di Castello** (☎ 055 45 47 91; Via di Castello 47; admission €2, also valid for Villa Medicea La Petraia; ☺ 8.15am-7.30pm Jun-Aug, 8.15am-6.30pm Apr-May & Sep, 8.15am-5.30pm Mar & Oct, 8.15am-4.30pm Nov-Feb, closed 2nd & 3rd Mon each month). Also known as the Villa Reale, it was Lorenzo the Magnificent's favoured summer retreat. You can visit the gardens only. Again, take bus No 28.

Villa Careggi (☎ 055 427 97 55; Viale Pieraccini 17; admission free; ☺ 9am-6pm Mon-Fri, 9am-1pm Sat). Access to this villa, where Lorenzo the Magnificent breathed his last in 1492, is limited as it is used as administrative offices for the local hospital. You can wander about outside the villa and visit two halls, one of them with 18th-century frescoes. The villa has been sold to Tuscan regional government and will eventually be handed over, restored and opened as a museum, although hospital staff expect to remain until 2006.

Another Medici getaway was the **Villa di Poggio a Caiano** (Map p188; ☎ 055 87 70 12; Piazza dei Medici 12; admission €2.50, grounds free; inside visits every hour 9.30am-6.30pm Jun-Aug, 9.30am-5.30pm Apr-May & Sep, 9am-4.30pm Mar & Oct, 9am-3.30pm Nov-Feb). About 15km from Florence on the road to Pistoia, and set in magnificent sprawling gardens, the interior of the villa is sumptuously decorated with frescoes and furnished much as it was early in the 20th century as a royal residence of the Savoys. Work began on the villa in 1445 and continued, with interruptions, until 1520. It became the family's main summer residence from the early 16th century and scene of big family events, such as the marriage of Cosimo I to his Spanish bride Eleonora de Toledo. They say that Napoleon's sister, Elisa Baciocchi, whom he had made Grand Duchess of Tuscany in 1809, had a love affair with the violinist Nicolò Paganini here.

Walking Tours

Walking Tours

The Florence of our dreams is a compact place and you will rarely find yourself wanting to hop onto to a bus, except perhaps to return to a central point after a long meander. In this chapter, a selection of possible walks is suggested, from general discoveries to specific thematic searches. However you choose to wander this town, the used shoe leather will pay wonderful dividends.

THE DUOMO TO PIAZZA DELLA SIGNORIA

What follows is a serpentine route across old Florence from its religious to its political heart. The big sights are dealt with in detail in the Quarters chapter. Here we explore another, less obvious face of the medieval centre.

From the apse of the **Duomo** 1 (p75) head south down Via del Proconsolo. The first grand mansion on your left is the **Palazzo Nonfinito** 2 (p78). Across Borgo degli Albizi from it stands the equally impressive **Palazzo dei Pazzi** 3, which was completed a century earlier than the

> ### Walk Facts
> **Start** Duomo
> **Finish** Piazza della Signoria
> **Distance** 1.5km

Palazzo Nonfinito and is influenced by the Palazzo Medici-Riccardi. The striking difference is in the sumptuous sculpting of the cornices on the windows, a departure that places the building's design, attributed to Giuliano da Maiano, in the late 15th century. It now houses offices but you can wander into the courtyard. Diagonally across from Palazzo dei Pazzi is one of the oldest churches in Florence, the **Badia Fiorentina** 4 (p80), fronted by the one-time seat of the city prison and now a grand museum, the **Palazzo del Bargello** 5 (p85). A block east of the latter is **Palazzo Borghese** 6. This long, low building is an early-19th-century neoclassical pile built for the family of the same name.

A few metres further south we arrive in Piazza San Firenze, dominated by the law courts made up of two churches in one, most commonly known as the **Chiesa di San Firenze** 7 (p80). Across the piazza (on the west side) is the main façade of **Palazzo Gondi** 8, once the site of the merchants' tribunal, a court set up to deal with their quarrels. Off Via de' Gondi you can enter a beautiful courtyard with fountain and staircase in *pietra serena* (grey 'tranquil stone'). The whole courtyard is crammed with tourist tat in the shops that have nested in the ground floor. What would Leonardo da Vinci, who as a young lad was apprenticed to a painter's workshop here before Palazzo Gondi was built, think of it all?

From Piazza San Firenze, turn west along Via della Condotta, which in medieval times was one of the main fashion shopping streets. Take Via dei Magazzini north and you'll arrive at Via Dante Alighieri. On the corner of this street and Via Santa Margherita is what is touted as the **Casa di Dante** 9 (Dante's House; p75).

Opposite the house is the **Torre della Castagna** 10, all that remains of the *palazzo* where the medieval republic's leaders, the *priori*, met until the Palazzo della Signoria (nowadays the Palazzo Vecchio) was built. Facing the tower across Via dei Magazzini is the **Oratorio di San Martino** 11, a chapel on the site of the former Chiesa di San Martino, Dante's parish church.

Just up Via Santa Margherita from Dante's alleged place is the small **Chiesa di Santa Margherita** 12, which dates at least from 1032. Some say that it was in this small single-nave church that Dante met his muse, Beatrice Portinari, although he himself claimed that he bumped into her in the Badia. However, he may have married Gemma Donati in this church. Members of both families, and conceivably Beatrice and Gemma themselves, are buried here.

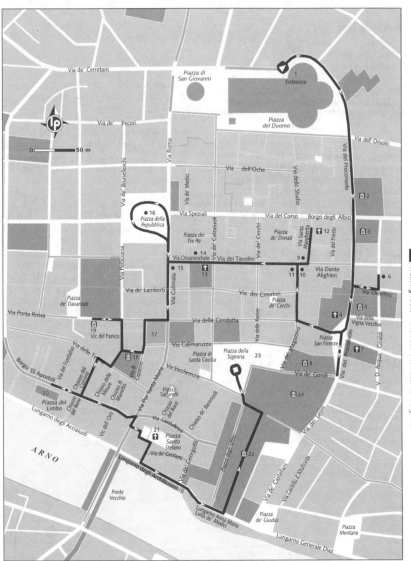

Continuing along Via Dante Alighieri, which leads into Via dei Tavolini, you come across the **Chiesa di Orsanmichele 13** (p80) and opposite it the **Arte dei Beccai 14**, the 14th-century headquarters of the Butchers' Guild. Far more important was the Wool Guild or **Arte della Lana 15**, the medieval headquarters of which still stand proudly on the corner of Via Orsanmichele and Via Calimala. It is made up of a tower-house, echoing that Florentine preoccupation with self-defence that clearly affected the guilds as much as it did feuding families.

Just south of where Via Calimaruzza runs into Via Calimala is where the Roman city's south gate stood. By the way, some think the name 'Calimala' was a distortion

Along the Way

Along this route you are spoilt for choice for rest and lunch stops. Special mention should be made of the grand cafés on Piazza della Repubblica, like **Gilli** (p129) and **Giubbe Rose** (p129). Or you could hold out until you emerge in Piazza della Signoria and sit down for a cup of sticky chocolate at **Rivoire** (p129).

of *callis maius*, itself a badly pronounced version of the Roman *cardo maximus*, the standard main cross street in a Roman garrison town.

A short way north along Via Calimala is **Piazza della Repubblica 16** (p79). If you stroll back south down Via Calimala you arrive at the **Mercato Nuovo**, or Newmarket **17** (p85). Just off to the southwest of the Mercato Nuovo, **Palazzo dei Capitani di Parte Guelfa 18** (Palace of the Guelph Faction's Captains) was built in the early 13th century and later tinkered with by Brunelleschi and Vasari. The leaders of the Guelph faction raised this fortified building in 1265, taking up land and houses that had been confiscated from the Ghibellines (for more on this medieval faction-fighting, see p52). About a block west is a remarkable leftover from the 14th century, **Palazzo Davanzati 19** (p86).

The modest 11th-century **Chiesa degli SS Apostoli 20** is dwarfed by the houses built on and around it in Piazza del Limbo. The plain exposed brick of the Romanesque façade is complemented by a Renaissance entrance. Inside, columns of green Prato marble set apart two aisles from the considerably higher central nave. At the end of the left aisle is a glazed terracotta tabernacle by Giovanni della Robbia.

If you hike back east to Via Por Santa Maria, cross into the little square presided over by the part-Romanesque, part-Gothic façade of the now deconsecrated **Chiesa di Santo Stefano 21**. It's only ever open when concerts are held, in which case you could get a look at the rather heady baroque interior. From here wind on to Lungarno degli Archibusieri and then between the wings of the **Galleria degli Uffizi 22** (p81) into **Piazza della Signoria 23** (p79), dominated by the fortified hulk of the **Palazzo Vecchio 24** (p86).

AN OLTRARNO STROLL

When you come off the **Ponte Vecchio 1** (p109) on the Oltrarno side of the river you are in Via de' Guicciardini. This street has had its fair share of VIP residents. At No 18, is **Machiavelli's home 2**. Exiled for a time, he ended up back in Florence and breathed his last here.

Walk Facts

Start Ponte Vecchio
Finish Porta San Miniato
Distance 2.8km

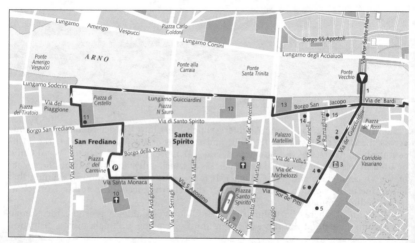

At No 15 is **Palazzo Guicciardini 3**, one of several mansions belonging to the family of the same name. In this one the 16th-century intriguer and historian, Francesco, had his home. At **No 22 Piazza de' Pitti 4**, Russian novelist **Fyodor Dostoyevsky** stayed to write *The Idiot* in 1868–69. A few doors down, opposite **Palazzo Pitti 5** (p108), was the **home of Paolo dal Pozzo Toscanelli 6** (1397–1482), cosmographer, scientist, engineer and all-round extremely clever chap. They say Columbus used his theoretical maps on the explorations that led to the discovery of the Americas.

Dogleg west down Via Sor de' Pitti, cross Via Maggio and head along Via de' Michelozzi to reach **Piazza Santo Spirito 7**. If you wander into the square late on a summer afternoon you could almost be in Spain. The bars are grunge cool, attracting a mixed and largely local crowd of students, layabouts, artists, misfits and the odd foreigner. The feel is laid-back in the bars with their tables tumbling out on to the square, and music always humming from one corner or another. It gets more animated as the night sets in.

Along the Way

The best options for eating and drinking are found at either end of this walk. The bars and restaurants on and around Piazza Santo Spirito could be used to fuel up at lunchtime before setting off. Or, at the end of your exertions, you could opt for one of the places around Porta San Miniato, like **Enoteca Fuoriporta** (p131) or **La Beppa** (p137).

During WWII, the Deutsches Institut (German Institute) had its offices and library in a building on this square. The staff had a risky habit of sheltering anti-Fascists in its library.

At its northern end, the square is fronted by the flaking façade of the **Basilica di Santo Spirito 8** (p105). As you walk south across Piazza Santo Spirito you will notice a fine Renaissance residence, the **Palazzo Guadagni 9**, on the southeast corner.

West from Piazza Santo Spirito you wind up in Piazza del Carmine, whose star attraction is the **Cappella Brancacci** in the **Basilica di Santa Maria del Carmine 10** (p104). To the north runs Borgo San Frediano, a busy street dotted with workshops ranging from shoemakers to jewellers. Nip around baroque **Chiesa di San Frediano 11** (p105) to reach the Arno again. Here you turn right (east) and head back towards the Ponte Vecchio. Along the way you pass several grand family mansions, including **Palazzo Guicciardini 12** at Lungarno Guicciardini 7 and the 13th-century **Palazzo Frescobaldi 13** in Piazza de' Frescobaldi. The latter played host to Charles de Valois in 1301, when he came to mediate peace between the Bianchi and Neri in one of Florence's interminable squabbles.

Round this palazzo you continue east along Borgo San Jacopo, on which still stand two 12th-century towers, the **Torre dei Marsili 14** and **Torre de' Belfredelli 15**. On Via de' Ramaglianti once stood the old Jewish synagogue.

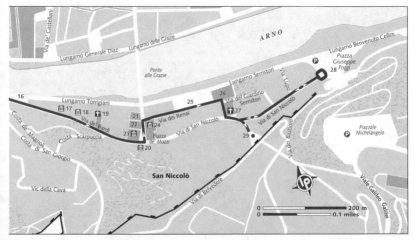

119

Continuing east away from the Ponte Vecchio, the first stretch of Via de' Bardi shows clear signs of its recent history. The entire area was flattened by German mines in 1944 and hastily rebuilt in questionable taste after the war. The street spills into **Piazza di Santa Maria Soprarno 16**, which takes its name from a church that has long ceased to exist. Follow the narrow Via de' Bardi (the right fork) away from the square and you enter a pleasantly quieter corner of Florence. The Bardi family once owned all the houses along this street, but by the time the chubby Cosimo de' Medici married Contessina de' Bardi in 1415, the latter's family was in decline. They were among the banking dynasties ruined by the habit that debtors, such as England's King Edward III, had of defaulting on huge loans. Cosimo and Contessina moved into a Bardi mansion on this street, but it was later pulled down. Buying up the street had clearly been a medieval bargain – until the de' Bardi family built their mansions the street had been known as Borgo Pidiglioso (Flea St), one of the city's poorest quarters.

A couple of 15th-century mansions on the left, the **Palazzo Capponi delle Rovinate 17** at Via de' Bardi 36 and **Palazzo Canigiani 18** at No 28, are typically Renaissance structures with heavy *pietra forte* ('strong stone') façades and jutting eaves. A little further on, the **Chiesa di Santa Lucia dei Magnoli 19** has a striking glazed terracotta relief above the portal of Santa Lucia in the style of the della Robbia workshop.

Via de' Bardi expires in Piazza de' Mozzi, which is also surrounded by the sturdy façades of grand residences belonging to the high and mighty. The southern flank of the piazza is occupied by the **Palazzi de' Mozzi 20** (Piazza de' Mozzi 2), where Pope Gregory X stayed when brokering peace between the Guelphs and Ghibellines. The western side is lined by the 15th-century **Palazzo Lensi-Nencioni 21**, **Palazzo Torrigiani-Nasi 22** (with the graffiti ornamentation) and **Palazzo Torrigiani 23**.

Across the square, the long façade of the **Museo Bardini 24** is the result of an eclectic 19th-century building project by its owner, the collector Stefano Bardini. The collection itself has been closed for years.

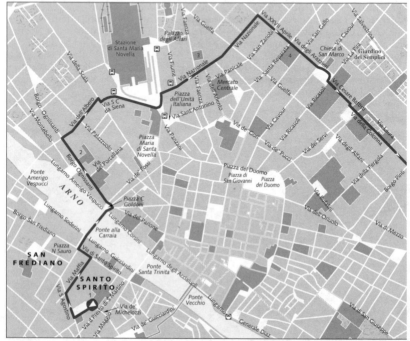

From here turn east down Via dei Renai past the leafy **Piazza Demidoff 25**, which is dedicated to Nicola Demidoff, a 19th-century Russian philanthropist who lived nearby in Via di San Niccolò. The 16th-century **Palazzo Serristori 26** in Via dei Renai was home to Joseph Bonaparte in the last years of his life (he died in 1844). At the height of his career he had been made king of Spain under Napoleon.

Turn right and you end up in Via di San Niccolò. Here, the bland-looking **Chiesa di San Niccolò Oltrarno 27** is interesting if for nothing else than the plaque indicating how high the 1966 flood waters reached – about 4m. East along Via San Niccolò you emerge at the tower marking the **Porta San Niccolò 28**, all that is left of the medieval city gate here.

To get an idea of what the old walls were like, walk south from the Chiesa di San Niccolò Oltrarno through **Porta San Miniato 29**. The wall extends a short way to the east and quite a deal further west up a steep hill that leads to the **Forte di Belvedere** (see p107). Less strenuous are the back roads, such as Via dell'Erta Canina, that wend southwards into a paradise of olive groves and vineyards. Those who live in the few villas scattered about in what is virtually Florence's back garden must know people in the right places to keep developers out!

THE LAST SUPPER TRAIL

In the convents and monasteries of medieval Italy, and indeed much later, it was customary to decorate the *cenacolo* (refectory), or dining hall, with a scene of *L'Ultima Cena* (Last Supper). In this way, dining friars or sisters could contemplate the importance of physical *and* spiritual nutrition. From the early 14th century on

Walk Facts

Start Piazza Santo Spirito
Finish Via di San Salvi
Distance 5km

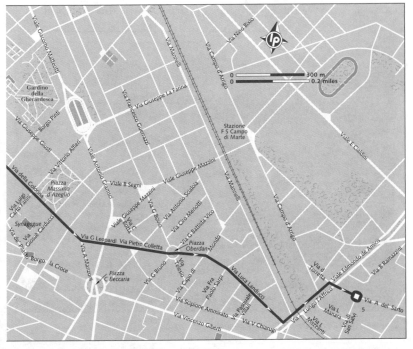

Along the Way

You could have your day's breakfast at one of the lively bar-eateries on Piazza Santo Spirito before embarking on this walk, which could leave you feeling hungry again, given the constant supper theme! **Cabiria** (p136) or **Caffè Ricchi** (p138) are both good choices. If peckish by the time you exit the Cenacolo di Foligno, pop down to **Da Nerbone** (p133) in the Marcato Centrale for a *lampredotto* (tripe) roll.

the standard model for the scene had Christ seated between St Peter and a sleeping St John. Alone on the other side of the table, with his back to the observers of the fresco, was a furtive Judas Iscariot. On rare occasions artists elected to abandon that scheme (as in the Cenacolo di San Salvi).

Although many of Florence's religious houses were shut down in the course of the 19th century and the buildings handed over to public institutions (such as schools) or sold to private entrepreneurs, some fine examples of these frescoes have survived (most have had to be restored). A tour of these, aside from the pleasure of contemplating fine works of art, brings the added joy of being able to do so in peace (hardly anyone bothers to seek these sights out), almost with a sense of discovering the unknown, and (with one modest exception) for free. Most open only in the morning, so you need to get off to an early start if you want to digest the lot in one day!

Start in the Oltrarno, with **Cenacolo di Santo Spirito 1** (p105), in which the central scene by Andrea Orcagna is accompanied by a museum display of sculpture. This is the only time you'll need to pull out a few euros on the length of the tour. From here head across Ponte alla Carraia to Piazza C Goldoni. Turn left and make for the **Chiesa di Ognissanti 2** (p90), in whose refectory you will find an extraordinary fresco of the Last Supper by Domenico Ghirlandaio. You pass through the equally fresco-rich cloister to reach the refectory.

From here, stroll another block west and then swing around to the northeast, past the front of the train station and down Via Nazionale. Turn left (north) into Via Faenza for the least known and visited of the city's *cenacoli*, **Cenacolo di Foligno 3** (p89), a delightful scene

The view over Florence from Piazzale Michelangelo (p109)

carried out at the very end of the 15th century by Il Perugino's workshop. Thereafter it's a short stroll up Via Nazionale and right along Via XXVII Aprile Via degli Arazzieri to Andrea del Castagno's startling **Cenacolo di Sant'Apollonia 4** (p95). To reach the final stage of this tour, you can catch a bus No 20 heading east along Via XXVII Aprile degli Arazzieri or opt for a longish walk to Andrea del Sarto's **Cenacolo di San Salvi 5** (p113).

SUNSET VIEWS & A COUNTRY MILE

From **Ponte Vecchio 1** (p109), walk along Via de' Guicciardini then take a quick left and along the left flank of **Chiesa di Santa Felicita 2** (p106), under the Corridoio Vasariano. Stroll up central Florence's only hill, Costa di San Giorgio, lined with lovely small *palazzi*, and take in the city view at the intersection of Costa Scarpuccia. A little further, at No 19, is the beautifully restored former **home of Galileo 3** (p106). At the top is the 13th-century city gate, **Porta di San Giorgio 4** (p107). Passing the entrance

Walk Facts

Start Ponte Vecchio
Finish Piazza Santa Felicita
Distance 5km

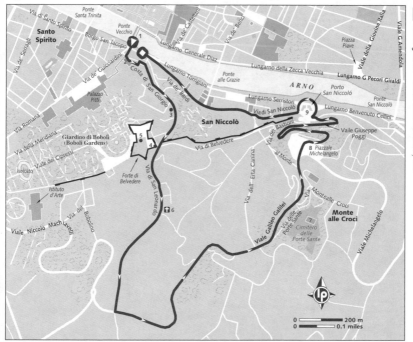

Along the Way

If you pay to enter Forte di Belvedere, you could take a weight off early in your trek and enjoy a cuppa in the fort's bar. Otherwise wait until you reach **Piazzale Michelangelo** (p109) and drink in the views at one of several cafés. If you're feeling hungry, hang on until you get down to Porta San Niccolò – a quick stroll west will bring you to a gaggle of eating and drinking options, including **Osteria Antica Mescita San Niccolò** (p137) and the youthful **Zoe** (p147).

to **Forte di Belvedere 5** (p107) on your right, walk along Via di San Leonardo – lined with villas, olive groves and cypresses – to the 11th-century **Chiesa di San Leonardo 6** (p107). Turn left into the tree-lined Viale Galileo Galilei for 800m of views, before climbing the steps on your right to the captivating **Chiesa di San Miniato 7** (p106). If your timing is right, it will gently resound to the monks' Gregorian chanting. With the sun setting, rejoin tourist Florence at **Piazzale Michelangelo 8** (p109) for refreshments and more stunning views. Take the western steps and winding path down to **Porta San Niccolò 9** and head back along the Arno to **Piazza Santa Felicita 2**.

Eating

Eating

Florence presents plenty of opportunity to wrap your mandibles around fine local food and to savour the exquisite fruit of the Tuscan vine. Tourist traps abound in the city centre, but even there you will discover cosy little trattorias, snack bars and fancier restaurants. Edge just a little way from the central pole of the Duomo and Piazza della Signoria and you will soon turn up all sorts of goodies.

Opening Hours & Meal Times

Italians rarely eat a sit-down *colazione* (breakfast). They tend to drink a cappuccino and eat a *cornetto* (croissant) or other type of pastry (generically known as a brioche) at a bar.

For *pranzo* (lunch), restaurants usually open from 12.30pm to 3pm. Few take orders after 2pm. Traditionally lunch is the main meal of the day and many shops and businesses close for two or three hours to accommodate it.

A full meal will include some type of antipasto, which can vary from a classic dish, such as *prosciutto e melone* (cured ham and melon) to crostini. After this comes the *primo piatto*, generally a pasta or risotto, followed by the *secondo piatto* of meat or fish. This is not usually accompanied with vegetables and Italians will order a *contorno* (vegetable dish) to go with it. *Insalate* (salads) have a strange position in the order. They are usually ordered as separate dishes and, in some cases, serve as a replacement for the *primo piatto* – although there is nothing to stop you ordering a salad as a side order to a *secondo*.

Opening hours for *cena* (dinner) vary, but people start sitting down around 8.30pm. With a few exceptions, you'll be hard pressed to find a place still serving after 10.30pm. The evening meal follows a similar pattern to lunch. It was once a simpler affair, but habits are changing because of the inconvenience of travelling home or going out for lunch every day.

Rivoire café on Piazza della Signoria (p129)

Restaurants and bars are generally closed one day each week; the day varies depending on the establishment. Closing days where applicable are listed but opening times are only mentioned where they vary substantially from the norm.

Cafés and bars that serve sandwiches and other snacks generally open from 7.30am to 8pm, although some stay open after 8pm and turn into pub-style drinking and meeting places.

A lot of restaurants close for part or all of August. This is especially the case with some of the homier trattorias – with all their customers on holidays, there's little point in them opening. This is yet another excellent reason for steering clear of Florence at this stifling time of year.

How Much?

Florence offers a broad range of eating options in terms of quality and price. Although it can be an expensive business, all sorts of curious little eateries will feed you well at a reasonable cost.

A few bars serve filling snacks with lunch-time and predinner drinks. At others you can pick up reasonable *panini* (filled rolls or sandwiches). These can cost from €2 to €3.50 if you eat them standing up or takeaway. Otherwise snack food is more the preserve of the *trippai* and occasional *vinai* (see the boxed text, p131). You'll also find numerous outlets where you can buy pizza *a taglio* (by the slice) for not more than a couple of euros.

For a sit-down meal there are several options. Numerous restaurants offer a *menù turistico* or *menù a prezzo fisso*, a set-price lunch costing around €9 to €15 excluding drinks. Generally, choice is limited and the food is unspectacular (there are exceptions). In some cases it is downright awful (see the boxed text, p128). From your taste buds' point of view and as long as you are not overly hungry, you'd be better off settling for a plate of pasta, some salad and wine at a decent restaurant.

Prices throughout this guide are given for a full meal, by which we mean a *primo*, a *secondo*, a dessert and some house wine. You could also add an antipasto (starter) at the front end of your meal but these are generally expensive and will simply stunt your appetite. At modest restaurants a full meal is unlikely to cost less than €25 a head. Any place where you have a good chance of paying €20 or less for a full meal, or places where you would mainly eat pizza, have generally been classified as 'cheap eats'. At good mid-range places expect to part with €35 to €50 a head. Much depends on your choice of dish and wine. You can easily hit €80 to €100 and more in the top-flight joints.

Even many Italians are breaking with the habit of the full meal, preferring instead, say, a *secondo* with a side dish, although curiously the change in Italian habits is one reason cited by restaurateurs for the rise in prices (not to mention introduction of the euro) over the past few years.

Booking Tables

For much of the year, Florence is full of visitors, so you should consider booking ahead. You can often get a table when you walk in off the street, but you can by no means bank on it.

Confused over Coffee

Coffee in Italy is complex. An espresso is a small cup of strong black coffee. A *doppio espresso* is a double. A *caffè lungo* is more watery, and an approximation of bland filter coffee is a *caffè americano*.

A *caffè latte* is coffee with milk. Cappuccino is a frothy version. You can ask for it *senza schiuma* (without froth), in which case the froth is scraped off the top. It tends to come lukewarm, so if you want it hot, ask for it to be *molto caldo*. Both are breakfast drinks to Italians. *Caffè macchiato* is an espresso with a dash of frothy milk. In summer you can opt for a *caffè freddo*, a long glass of cold coffee with ice cubes. Good on winter afternoons is a *corretto* – an *espresso* 'corrected' with grappa or other hard liquor.

After lunch and dinner it wouldn't occur to Italians to order either *caffè latte* or a cappuccino – an espresso, macchiato or *corretto* are all perfectly acceptable. If you want a cappuccino there's no problem – but you might have to repeat your request a couple of times to convince disbelieving waiters that they have heard correctly.

An espresso at a regular bar costs €0.80 to €0.90. It costs up to €3.50 if you opt to sit at one of the grand café terraces, such as Gilli or Giubbe Rosse.

Where Not to Eat

You may not wish to know this but many of the touristy restaurants – especially in the centre of town – have a rather ruthless attitude to food, their customers and their employees. How does it make you feel to know that a number of pizzerias employ foreigners without papers at slave rates to churn out prepacked pizzas? The base and sauce are ready to go, just tip tinned mushrooms on the top, heat and serve. Delicious. The process with other dishes in some trattorias is similar. Mountains of precooked pasta is reheated – you can be sure most of the ingredients are canned and your hosts will do their best to make sure the elements of your salad have been well aged.

We didn't want to spoil your appetite, but this is the state of affairs. How do you recognise these places before it's too late? Many of the places on the most touristed squares and streets, especially if they have outdoor dining, tend to fall roughly into this category. If no locals are eating in the place you are considering, ask yourself why. If you see tour groups gobbling down identical meals – stay away! Places that need to advertise themselves loudly or that display menus in a variety of languages are often suspect. Unfortunately there are some noble exceptions to these rules, so you need something of a sixth sense and a small portion of good luck.

Tipping

Most eating establishments have a cover charge, ranging from €1 up to €6. You have to factor in the service charge of 10% to 15%. Since most places include this, further tipping is strictly optional. Most locals don't bother adding any more unless they have been particularly overwhelmed by service and quality. Remember this if you are presented a credit card receipt with space to add in the tip. In any case, it is always preferable to leave a tip in cash for the person who has waited your table.

Self-catering

Making your own snacks is the cheapest way to keep body and soul together. For salami, cheese and wine, shop in *alimentary, salumerie* or *pizzicherie*, which are a cross between grocery stores and delicatessens. Fresh bread is available at a *forno* or *panetteria*, bakeries that sell bread, pastries and sometimes groceries.

You will find small shops, produce markets and small supermarkets throughout Florence. **Standa** (Map pp248–50; ☎ 055 234 78 56; Via Pietrapiana 42-44; ⏱ 8am-9pm Mon-Sat & 9am-8pm Sun) is a handy central supermarket.

PIAZZA DEL DUOMO & AROUND

There's no shortage of eateries to be found immediately near the Duomo but few of real quality. As a rule, it is worth investing a little shoe leather to track down better trattorias a little further from the epicentre of old Florence.

CAFFÈ COQUINARIUS

Map pp251–3 *Wine Bar*
☎ 055 230 21 53; Via dell' Oche 15/r; ⏱ 9am-midnight, food available noon-11pm; bus A

An excellent choice outside rigid meal times, this laid-back and comfy café in a former stables has light and substantial dishes of crostini, salads, pastas and the usual meaty mains as well as more than a dozen wines by the glass.

Cheap Eats

RISTORANTE SELF-SERVICE
LEONARDO Map pp251–3 *Italian*
☎ 055 28 44 46; Via de' Pecori 35/r; pasta €3.30 & mains €4-5; ⏱ 11.45am-2.45pm & 6.45-9.45pm Sun-Fri; bus A

When it comes to eating a full meal while you pinch pennies, it's hard to beat this refectory-style spot. Queue up with a tray and choose from a limited range of *primi* and *secondi* and wash it down with a simple Tuscan tipple – it beats McDonald's every day of the week.

PIAZZA DELLA SIGNORIA & AROUND

You won't find anything much right on this square at the heart of Florence's long turbulent political life but hidden away in various surrounding streets and lanes are a few eating dens that reward a little hunting. Piazza della Signoria *does* host one of the city's great cafés. And just a caffeine-induced hop, skip and jump away are the grand cafés of Piazza della Repubblica.

ANGELS Map pp251–3   *Modern Tuscan*
☎ 055 239 87 62; www.ristoranteangels.it; Via del Proconsolo 29-31r; meal €40; ⌚ daily; bus A
Here is a chic restaurant, with dark tables and white seats, all hard angles and expansive windows. Elegantly presented Tuscan faves with a few twists on national dishes are the main fare. Or drop by for its light buffet lunch (€12).

CAFFÈ ITALIANO Map pp251–3   *Italian*
☎ 055 28 90 20; Via della Condotta 56/r; salad €7.50, meal €20-25 ⌚ 8am-8.30pm Mon-Sat; bus A
Full of glamorous locals and a few savvy tourists who see beyond the stand-up bar, upstairs here is a lovely relaxed café with small antique tables, velvet sofas and soft lighting. The food – tangy soufflés, pastas, and hearty salads – is a light alternative to the norm and the coffee will make you linger. It's a lunch option only.

EITO Map pp251–3   *Japanese*
☎ 055 21 09 40; Via dei Neri 72/r; meal €25-30; ⌚ Tue-Sun; bus B

One of the first and better Japanese eateries in Florence, Eito welcomes you into a down-to-earth atmosphere. In addition to sushi and sashimi in various guises, you can go for lightly deep-fried tempura options. All is best washed down with Kirin or Sapporo beer.

TRATTORIA DA BENVENUTO
Map pp251–3   *Tuscan*
☎ 055 21 48 33; Via della Mosca 16/r; meal €25; ⌚ Mon-Sat; bus B
Eating here, on the corner of Via dei Neri, is hardly an ambient experience, but the food is reliable and modestly priced. Mains include some Florentine favourites, including *lampredotto* and *bistecca*, while the pasta dishes are innovative, such as *rigatoni alla siciliana* (with a slightly spicy Sicilian sauce). It is wise to reserve a table.

Cheap Eats
OSTERIA DEL GATTO E LA VOLPE
Map pp248–50   *Tuscan*
☎ 055 28 92 64; Via Ghibellina 151/r; meal €20; ⌚ Tue-Sun; bus 14 & A
On the corner of Via de' Giraldi, this is a small and welcoming spot where the food is reasonable and the prices are stable. It gets its fair share of tourists but this hasn't yet ruined what's on offer. Pizzas are reliable too.

Top Five Cafés

- **Café Concerto Paskowski** (Map pp251–3; ☎ 055 21 02 36; Piazza della Repubblica 31-35/r; cappuccino on the square €4.50; ⌚ 7am-2am Tue-Sun; bus A) With more than 150 years of history, this is one of the class café acts of the city and makes a stylish way to start the day. Prices are similar to those in Gilli and it is worth making the trip to the square for the café's interior, even if it's a little out of your way.
- **Colle Bereto** (Map pp251–3; ☎ 055 28 31 56; Piazza Strozzi 5/r; ⌚ 8am-9pm daily; bus A) A grand new café over two floors in the heart of chic Florence, this place is run by a Chianti wine producer. You can have sweet pastries for breakfast, a light snack and fine wine during the day or early evening. Gaze out through the giant window panes. You could even stop for lunch, as it has a nice Tuscan menu.
- **Gilli** (Map pp251–3; ☎ 055 21 38 96; Piazza della Repubblica 39/r; coffee at the bar €0.90, at a table outside €3.50; ⌚ 8am-1am Wed-Sun; bus A) This is one of the city's finest cafés.
- **Giubbe Rosse** (Map pp251–3; ☎ 055 21 22 80; Piazza della Repubblica 13-14/r; cappuccino at outside table €4.50; ⌚ 8am-2am; bus A) The early-20th-century futurist movement, despite not making as big an impact in Florence as elsewhere in Italy, nevertheless had its following – and this is where its die-hard members used to drink and debate. Inside, long vaulted halls lined with old photos, sketches and artwork make a great place for coffee over the papers – some of which you'll find hanging up for the customers' use. The red jackets of the place's name are still in evidence on the waiting staff, along with red shirts and tablecloths.
- **Rivoire** (Map pp251–3; ☎ 055 21 44 12; Piazza della Signoria 4/r; coffee at a table outside €3.50; ⌚ Tue-Sun; bus B) Founded in 1872 by a chocolate-maker from Turin, Enrico Rivoire, it is inevitably somewhat touristy because of its position, but if only once this is the place to sip on a cup of sticky *cioccolata* (€5.50) after overdosing on art in the Uffizi.

SANTA MARIA NOVELLA & AROUND

It's quite a mixed bag around here. There's no end of cheap and cheerful Italian diners, where you can load up on filling but unexciting fare, in streets like Via della Scala and Via Palazzuolo, near the train station. A few of these are quite good. They get more interesting to the south and southeast of the basilica, with some of the city's more popular nooks and crannies frequented by Florentines with a nose for good value and quality.

CANTINETTA ANTINORI

Map pp251–3 *Tuscan*

☎ 055 29 22 34; Piazza degli Antinori 3; meal €35-40; ☽ daily, lunch only Sat & Sun; bus 6, 11, 22, 36, 37 & A

Feeling posh? This might be the place for you. The *enoteca* (speciality wine shop/bar) and restaurant on the ground floor of 15th-century Palazzo Antinori offers a reasonable meal along with some fine wines – it is for the latter that most people come here. It's not a bad choice if you have to impress a suit or two.

DA IL LATINI Map pp251–3 *Tuscan*

☎ 055 21 09 16; Via dei Palchetti 6/r; meal €20-30; ☽ Tue-Sat; bus 6 & A

Hiding away just off Via del Moro, this place remains something of a classic for Florentines in spite of the queues. The food is largely Tuscan but the dining area has a singularly Spanish touch – all those legs of ham dangling off the ceiling! It doesn't take reservations and the place can get packed. So many locals can't be wrong.

MASA Map pp248–50 *Japanese*

☎ 055 29 09 78; Borgo Ognissanti 1/r; meal €40-50; ☽ Wed eve-Mon; bus A

For a more refined, business-like atmosphere than in Eito (see p129), try this place for carefully prepared Japanese food. You head downstairs to the almost fussily efficient dining room. All hushed chat and serious concentration on good grub. You'll probably feel a little underdressed without a tie.

OSTARIA DEI CENTO POVERI

Map pp246–7 *Tuscan*

☎ 055 21 88 46; Via Palazzuolo 31/r; meal €35-40; ☽ Wed-Sun; bus 11, 36, 37 & A

A congenial spot in a not-so-congenial part of town, the 'hostel of the hundred poor people' sits apart from most other places around here as a quality dining option. Tuck in to creative Tuscan food in a down-to-earth setting.

PROCACCI Map pp251–3 *International*

☎ 055 21 16 56; Via de' Tornabuoni 64/r; ☽ Tue-Sat; bus 6, 11, 22, 36, 37 & A

For a century the chefs here have been tickling Florentine (and quite a few foreign) palates with its *panini tartufati*. Not so much a nutritional exercise as a ritual, these tasty little numbers can be accompanied by a drop of Tuscan wine or even a cup of tea. The green marble used for the bar and table tops is the same used in the city's great monuments. Genteel locals sometimes take a bottle to one of the said tables, order some nibbles and generally have a cosy time. It's definitely more of a winter scene, when it stays open until about 9pm (no later than 8pm in the warmer months). You can also buy wine and foodstuffs, including truffles, to take away (see p171).

SOSTANZA Map pp248–50 *Tuscan*

☎ 055 21 26 91; Via del Porcellana 25r; meal €20-25; ☽ noon-2pm & 7-9.45pm Mon-Fri; bus A

This traditional Tuscan eatery is a good spot for *bistecca alla fiorentina* if you are not fussy about your surrounds. A no-nonsense approach dominates. The minestrone (€5.50) is also good. Locals know it as Il Troia – the (Male) Slut – because they say its 19th-century owner had the habit of touching up his guests. Don't worry, he's long gone.

TRATTORIA COCO LEZZONE

Map pp251–3 *Tuscan*

☎ 055 28 71 78; Via Parioncino 26/r; meal €30-40; ☽ Mon-Sat; bus A

This tiny place tucked away off Via del Purgatorio is a cheerful, down-to-earth spot where you can find yourself rubbing shoulders with out-of-towners and local businesspeople seeking old-fashioned, genuine home-cooking. *Ribollita* is the house speciality, but it will do you a *bistecca alla fiorentina* for €40 (enough for two in most cases) if you book it ahead. One oddity, though, is that it doesn't serve coffee.

TRATTORIA DEI 13 GOBBI

Map pp251–3 *Tuscan*

☎ 055 21 32 04; Via del Porcellana 9/r; meal €25-30; ☽ Tue-Sat; bus A

There is an almost bucolic feeling inside this trattoria, especially in the plant-filled courtyard out the back. Inside, hunker down with the locals under the low ceilings to typical Tuscan treats. Beef and pork lead the way here so don't expect a light meal.

Cheap Eats

AMON   Map pp248–50   *Egyptian*
☎ 055 29 31 46; Via Palazzuolo 26-28/r; sandwiches €2.50-3.50; ☽ Tue-Sun; bus 11, 36, 37 & A
If you don't want to spend much, here you can pick up Egyptian sandwiches such as felafel or *foul* (fava beans) – a couple of these will fill most reasonable paunches.

TRATTORIA IL CONTADINO
Map pp246–7   *Italian*
☎ 055 238 26 73; Via Palazzuolo 71/r; set menu with wine €10.50; ☽ Mon-Sat; bus 11, 36, 37 & A

The set menu price says it all. Don't expect marvellous food, but if you need to fill up without inflicting fiscal damage, this is one place to do it. It is one of several cheapies around here.

SAN LORENZO AREA

The Mercato Centrale is naturally a hub in this part of town. Trattorias of all sorts cater to the tourist trade and market workers. The whole gamut is run, from trusty, good value institutions that locals still pile into at lunchtime through to the worst of all limp-lettuce traps for the unsuspecting.

I' TOZZO...DI PANE
Map pp246–7   *Tuscan*
☎ 055 47 57 53; Via Guelfa 94/r; meal €25; ☽ Mon dinner-Sat; bus 4, 12, 25 & 33
A young, friendly team run this simple neighbourhood place, where cool jazz warbles in

---

Fast Food Florence-Style

Some habits die hard. When Florentines feel like a fast snack instead of a sit-down lunch, they might well stop by a *trippaio* (often just a mobile stand) for a nice tripe burger (well, tripe on a bread roll). It may sound a little nauseating to the uninitiated but it's really not that bad. McDonald's has very definitely arrived in Florence, but it has yet to snuff out local preferences. Who knows what a generation fed on the Big Mac might think of tripe rolls in years to come?

Savouring fine wines is one of the great pleasures of the palate in Florence, and for many there is nothing better than a couple of glasses of a good drop accompanied by simple local snacks – sausage meats, cheeses, *ribollita* (vegetable stew) and the like. And the good news is that the tradition of the *vinaio* (wine bar) has won new life in the past few years in Florence. You may never see the word 'vinaio' on the doorway, but the idea remains the same. The old traditional places still exist – often dark little grog shops where you can get a bite to eat too. Look out for the sign 'Mescita di Vini' (roughly, 'wine outlet'). You could start your search with the following:

Enoteca Baldovino (Map pp248–50; ☎ 055 234 72 00; Via di San Giuseppe 18/r; ☽ Tue-Sat; bus C) A recent addition to the wine-sampling scene in Florence, this place is in a pleasant location, with footpath seating and in the shadow of Santa Croce. You can taste fine wines accompanied by sophisticated snacks and salads. If you like what you sip, you can then buy a bottle.

Enoteca Fuoriporta (Map pp248–50; ☎ 055 234 24 83; Via del Monte alle Croci 10/r; dishes around €5-10; ☽ Mon-Sat; bus 13, 23 & C) In this fine *enoteca*, lovingly carved out of what was once just a simple local bar and now an obligatory stop on any wine-lover's stay in Florence, the wine list comprises hundreds of different drops (and an impressive roll call of whiskies and other liquors). You can order from a limited list of *primi piatti* for a pleasant evening meal. The desserts are also good.

Le Volpi e l'Uva (Map pp251–3; ☎ 055 239 81 32; Piazza de' Rossi 1/r; snacks €2-4; ☽ 11am-8pm Mon-Sat; bus D) At 'The Foxes and the Grape', hidden away off the Oltrarno end of the Ponte Vecchio, you can sample from an impressive stock of cheeses, have a gourmet *tramezzino* (sandwich triangle) and try out new wines that the owners have discovered in the vast backyard that is Tuscany (along with a few from further afield in Italy and even France).

Vini e Vecchi Sapori (Map pp251–3; ☎ 055 29 30 45; Via dei Magazzini 3/r; meal €20-25; ☽ 1-11pm Tue-Sat & Sun lunch; bus A) It seems barely conceivable that within about 10 seconds' walk of Piazza della Signoria, which is lined with tourist rip-off restaurants, one of the city centre's last surviving, more or less genuine, *osterie* should remain. Inside this little den of 'wines and old tastes' there is barely room to swing a Florentine rat, but you can eat decently and taste some solid local wines at low prices. It also imports *fragolino*, a strawberry-flavoured wine made in the northeast of Italy.

the background. For starters, go for the *zuppa toscana*, a thick gruel of vegetables and barley. Although not to all tastes, the *trippa alla fiorentina* (tripe) follows on a treat. The small rear garden is a pleasant retreat from the street in summer.

MARIO Map pp246–7 *Tuscan*
☎ 055 21 85 50; Via Rosina 2/r; meal €15-20;
lunch only Mon-Sat; bus 1, 6, 7, 10, 11 & 17

For an eternity Mario has been serving up plentiful, hearty lunches to market workers and a host of passers-by. It has become something of a culinary icon. It attracts a mix of foreign strays and local workers, who chow down in close company. A limited series of pasta options and Tuscan classics are followed by a few meat-dominated mains, including a passable *bistecca alla fiorentina* if you are willing to shell out a little extra. In spite of growing popularity with tourists it remains faithful to its unpretentious, no-nonsense formula.

RISTORANTE LOBS
Map pp246–7 *Seafood*
☎ 055 21 24 78; Via Faenza 75-77/r; meal €40-50;
daily; bus 4, 12, 25, 31, 32 & 33

This superb fish restaurant offers always fresh, exclusively Mediterranean fish and seafood

(most mains cost €25). There's a nonsmoking area at the rear and the setting is cosy with maritime frescoes and, appropriately, salmon-pink walls. At midday, it does a selection of spaghetti specials (€7). Sluice it all down with its Soave wine from the country's northeast.

RISTORANTE ZÀZÀ Map pp246–7 *Italian*
☎ 055 21 54 11; Piazza del Mercato Centrale 20; meal €20-25; Mon-Sat; bus 1, 6, 7, 10, 11 & 17

This place gets its produce fresh from the covered market, just across the square. It's a great spot for combining outdoor dining and a little people-watching. In winter head inside for some exposed-brick cosiness. The menu changes regularly and often presents imaginative dishes.

Cheap Eats
CAFÉ CARACOL Map pp251–3 *Mexican*
☎ 055 21 14 27; Via de' Ginori 10/r; dishes around €8;
6pm-2am Tue-Sun; bus 1, 6, 7, 10, 11 & 17

For a slightly cheesy Tex-Mex atmosphere you could drop by for a plateful of nachos, fajitas and other Mexican flavours. It's not going to win any food prizes, but there aren't many places in Florence where you can get corn chips and salsa, and the atmosphere is jolly enough.

Interior of Gilli café on Piazza della Repubblica (p129)

DA NERBONE Map pp246-7 *Tuscan*

☎ 055 21 99 49; Mercato Centrale; meal €15-20;
🕐 7am-2pm Mon-Sat; bus 1, 6, 7, 10, 11 & 17

Way back in 1872 this corner stall was set up in the market as a snack stop for toiling market workers. They still pile in for breakfast on market days and are joined at lunch by a growing troupe of curious outsiders. Breakfast at Da Nerbone means a *lampredotto* roll but at lunch you can fill up on soups and boiled meats, among other things. Friday is fish day.

SAN MARCO AREA

The pickings are fairly slim around Savonarola's old haunts and things don't get much better as you proceed further away from the centre to the north, east and west. A couple of exceptions confirm the rule.

DIONISO Map pp246-7 *Greek*

☎ 055 21 78 82; Via San Gallo 16/r; meal €15;
🕐 daily; bus 1, 6, 7, 10, 11 & 17

Feel like a big Greek salad full of feta (€5.50)? Or perhaps some taramasalata and other similar dips to accompany typical meat dishes like souvlakia? Dioniso can be a lively and filling stop. On Fridays and Saturdays it stays open until 3am, taking on more the air of a bar with snacks available.

IL VEGETARIANO

Map pp246-7 *Vegetarian*

☎ 055 47 50 30; Via delle Ruote 30/r; meal €15;
🕐 Tue-Sun (dinner only Sat & Sun); bus 4, 12 & 20

One of the few restaurants to seriously cater to vegetarian needs, this is an unassuming locale with a great selection of fresh food, salads and mains.

SANTA CROCE AREA

Several of the city's finest restaurants await discovery in the streets east of the centre and around Piazza Santa Croce. But the area is full of diversity too. You can just as easily spend €100 or more at one of the top establishments or simply enjoy a quick felafel or Indian takeaway.

ANTICO NOÈ Map pp248-50 *Tuscan*

☎ 055 234 08 38; Arco di San Piero 6r; panini €2.50-5, meal €25-30; 🕐 10am-8pm Tue-Sun; bus 14 & 23

This legendary sandwich bar, just off Piazza San Pier Maggiore, is a good option for a light

lunch. It has two sections. The sandwich bar is takeaway only, but next door there's a cosy restaurant where you can enjoy fine cooking to slow jazz and blues tunes. Don't let the loitering drunks outside bother you as they're generally pretty harmless.

BOCCADAMA Map pp248-50 *Italian*

☎ 055 24 36 40; www.boccadama.it, Italian only; Piazza di Santa Croce 25-26/r; meal €25-30; 🕐 Mon-Sat; bus C

Located inside the medieval Palazzo dell'Antella is this surprise packet. Sweep away the lunch time tourists and underneath you find a quality restaurant with a classy wine list. The menu is very limited and changes regularly. One good way to accompany your choice of wine is to opt for the cold meat platter, perhaps with a selection of Italian and French cheeses.

CAFFELLATTE Map pp246-7 *Italian*

☎ 055 47 88 78; Via degli Alfani 39/r; meal €10-15; 🕐 8am-8pm Mon-Sat; bus C

A tiny, charming place for a long *caffè latte* (or indeed a cappuccino if your prefer) over the paper or a tasty lunch, such as *crema di zucca* (pumpkin soup). This is a health-food haven and it doesn't serve alcohol, so you can feel virtuous while you eat.

DANNY ROCK Map pp248-50 *Pizzeria*

☎ 055 234 03 07; Via de' Pandolfini 13/r; meal €20-25; 🕐 7pm-3am daily; bus A

This place does not sound promising, but inside is an immensely popular place for pizza, pasta and, perhaps best of all, its *insalatoni* (huge salads) for €6.50. One of the latter with a drink or two could make a filling and ultra-healthy meal. Be prepared to queue for a bit.

Eating – San Marco Area

DOLCI E DOLCEZZE Map pp248–50 *Cakes*
☎ 055 234 54 58; Piazza Beccaria 8/r; ⏰ 8.30am-8pm Tue-Sat, 9am-1pm & 4.30-7pm Sun; bus 8, 12, 13, 14, 31, 32, 33, 80 & A

This place claims its *torta di cioccolato* (chocolate cake) is 'best in the world'. Hyperbole aside, it's damned good, made with fine Swiss and Belgian ingredients and creamy Maremma butter. There are no tables so it's takeaway.

ENOTECA PINCHIORRI
Map pp248–50 *Italian*
☎ 055 24 27 77; www.enotecapinchiorri.com; Via Ghibellina 87; meal €120-150; ⏰ Tue-Sat; bus 14

Glide upstairs to the grand foyer that fronts Florence's premier address for food buffs. Here your wallet will have a date with destiny but every now and then you just have to do it. Elegant dress is your preferred sartorial option for this excursion into Italian nouvelle cuisine. What about lightly grilled lobster with a crust of bread and capers? You can book online.

LA BARAONDA
Map pp248–50 *Modern Tuscan*
☎ 055 234 11 71; www.labaraonda.net; Via Ghibellina 67/r; meal €30-35; ⏰ 7.30-10.30pm Mon, 12.30-2.30pm & 7.30-10.30pm Tue-Sat; bus 14 & A

As the name implies, a 'convivial chaos' prevails at this handsome trattoria where the friendly owner floats between three connecting dining rooms articulating the seasonal Tuscan menu for tourists. Spare his voice box and order the *polpettone* (meatloaf). It also hosts cooking classes.

And Then There Was Brunch

Brunch has arrived in Florence. It's a bit of a show, as much about being seen the day after in as good form as the night before. **Ristorante Beccofino** (p138) leads the way with its Great Sunday Lunch – muffins, banana bread, maple syrup or more substantial offerings will help deal with the night before. Feeling classier still? The **Hotel Excelsior** (p181) puts on a €35 spread including bubbly. **Gallery Hotel Art** (p179) stages its Fashion Brunch in the hotel bar of the same name, while the nearby chichi bar of the moment, **Slowly** (p146), sees its punters of the night before come back for more – eggs in all their forms, ham, asparagus and mushrooms and soft drinks thrown in for €20.

LA PENTOLA DELL'ORO
Map pp248–50 *Modern Tuscan*
☎ 055 24 18 08; Via di Mezzo 24/r; meal €50-60; ⏰ Mon-Sat; bus A

Long a guarded secret among serious Florentine food-lovers, this place is a one-off that in the past few years has started to advertise itself. Guiseppe Alessi is a man of encyclopaedic learning who spends much of his time studying medieval recipes and transforming them into the most remarkable meals. The menu is largely up to his whim, and can involve all sorts of mixes, such as beef prepared with black pepper in a pear sauce. Alessi swears Brunelleschi came up with this dish to keep his workers well nourished as they worked away on the scary, scaffolding-free dome project for the Duomo. There is no sign outside and there was a time when it was for members only.

OSTERIA CAFFÈ ITALIANO
Map pp248–50 *Tuscan*
☎ 055 28 93 68; Via Isola delle Stinche 11-13/r; meal €20-25; ⏰ Tue-Sun; bus A

The old-time lettering on the windows invites you to peer in to the welcoming restaurant, the dark timber tables of which are scattered about spaciously. An ever-changing daily menu such as *sformata di verdure* (vegetable pie) keeps you on your toes. Cold meat platters are good and the wines chosen with care.

OSTERIA CIBRÈO Map pp248–50 *Tuscan*
☎ 055 234 11 00; Via de' Macci 122/r; meal €35-40; ⏰ Tue-Sat; bus C

This is a true delight to the palate, located next door to the much more expensive restaurant of the same name (see Ristorante Cibrèo, opposite). It offers no pasta at all, but some enticing first courses such as *sformato di patate e ricotta* (oven-cooked potato and white cheese). There follows a variety of seafood and meat options for the main course. As in the restaurant next door, the atmosphere is of a slightly dated elegance, with lots of wood panelling and frosted glass. You can't book here, so it's first come, first served.

OSTERIA DE' BENCI Map pp248–50 *Tuscan*
☎ 055 234 49 23; Via de' Benci 13/r; meal €30; ⏰ Mon-Sat; bus 13, 23, B & C

This wonderful little *osteria* is a consistently good bet. The menu changes frequently, although it serves up a few core dishes regularly. The young team serves up generous slabs of *carbonata di chianina* (1kg for two costs €35) – more tender and succulent than the ubiquitous *bistecca alla fiorentina*. The food is well prepared, the feel is cosy and prices moderate.

RISTORANTE ALLE MURATE

Map pp248–50   *Mediterranean*
☎ 055 24 06 18; Via Ghibellina 64; meal €80;
🕑 7pm-11pm Tues-Sun; bus 14
Enter a low-lit ambience for creative, light home-made pasta dishes and seafood mains (particularly in winter, when fish rules here). A special emphasis is laid on the preparation of vegetables and side dishes. All are accompanied by classy wines from Tuscany and further afield.

RISTORANTE CIBRÈO

Map pp248–50   *Italian*
☎ 055 234 11 00; Via de' Macci 118/r; meal €75-90;
🕑 Tue-Sat; bus C
Over the years, this quietly elegant but unpretentious locale has made an international name for itself. Warm timber dominates the décor but the table settings are a notable sign of the class that this place exudes. The dishes are, to say the least, curious. What about *collo di pollo con maionese* (chicken neck with mayonnaise)? It offers more mainstream options too!

TRATTORIA BALDOVINO

Map pp248–50   *Tuscan & Pizzeria*
☎ 055 24 17 73; Via di San Giuseppe 22r; pizza €6-10, meal €30; 🕑 11am-3pm & 7pm-1am Tue-Sun; bus C
Spread over several interlocking dining areas, each of a different hue, this is a delightful spot for a Neapolitan wood-oven pizza or a selection of cold meats and cheeses. A handful of more expensive Tuscan dishes are also available.

Cheap Eats

CAFFETTERIA PIANSA

Map pp248–50   *Italian*
☎ 055 234 23 62; Borgo Pinti 18/r; set lunch €10.50;
🕑 for lunch only Mon-Sat; bus 14 & 23
At this ebullient, vaulted local workers' diner, you basically point and choose from a limited number of cheap and tasty first and main courses. Get in early as it's all over by 2.30pm.

IL NILO
Map pp248–50   *Egyptian*
☎ 055 24 16 99; Arco di San Piero 9/r; *shawarma* & felafel sandwiches €2.50-3.50; 🕑 noon-10pm Mon-Sat; bus 14 & 23

A Bakery with No Name

Need a pastry at 4am? A couple of bakeries open to sell their wares straight out of the oven. One without a name or street number is at **Via del Canto Rivolto** (Map pp248–50), just north of Via dei Neri. As you will see the people want you to be quiet and get out quickly. Should the neighbours become vexed by the street noise, it may have to stop the practice.

Revellers, dropouts and a host of other weird and wonderful beings wander in here in the course of the evening for a takeaway felafel. Some hang about and eat it here, although there's nowhere to sit.

RAMRAJ
Map pp248–50   *Indian*
☎ 055 24 09 99; Via Ghibellina 61r; meal €12;
🕑 Tue-Sun; bus 14
If you feel like a cheap taste of the subcontinent, drop in here for tandoori and other Indian specialities. You can take away or eat at the bench if you want. The food's OK if unspectacular, but quick and modestly priced.

RUTH'S
Map pp248–50   *Middle Eastern Kosher*
☎ 055 248 08 88; Via Luigi Carlo Farini 2a; meal €12-15; 🕑 Sun-Fri; bus C
For something a little different, try out this place by the synagogue. It serves tasty kosher food bearing a strong resemblance to other Middle Eastern cuisine. It makes a good choice for vegetarians. You can have a plate of mixed dips with couscous, felafel, filo pastry pie and potato salad, quite filling in itself (€9). The *fattoush*, a finely chopped and liquidy salad mixed with pita croutons, is a tad bitter.

SEDANO ALLEGRO
Map pp248–50   *Vegetarian*
☎ 055 234 55 05; Borgo della Croce 20/r; meal €18-25; 🕑 Tue-Sun; bus A
Clearly not that many vegans are circulating in Florence, as this vegetarian hangout has found it necessary to add a fish and seafood menu to its vegetarian specials (many of which don't meet vegan needs either). If you don't want fish you could try a *filetto di formaggio al whisky* (cheese 'fillet' done in whisky...). There is a pleasant, shady courtyard out back.

Eating – Santa Croce Area

135

OLTRARNO

Piazza Santo Spirito (Map pp248–50) is one of the most attractive squares in the city and clustered on and around it is a nice range of restaurants, snack places and café-bars. This is the headquarters of laid-back Florentines. Heading east you will find several other spots on the way to Ponte Vecchio (Map pp248–50) and then, much further east again near Porta San Niccolò (Map pp248–50) is another cluster of places well worth seeking out.

ALL'ANTICO RISTORO DI CAMBI
Map pp248–50 _Tuscan_
☎ 055 21 71 34; Via Sant'Onofrio 1; meal €25-30; ☺ Mon-Sat; bus 6 & D

The food here is traditional Tuscan and the _bistecca alla fiorentina_ is succulent. This is one of those places a local might take a newcomer to impress with its local knowledge. You can eat inside or out on the square. Don't come looking for fish unless it's cod you're after.

ASHOKA Map pp244–5 _Indian_
☎ 055 22 44 46; Via Pisana 86/r; meal €20; ☺ 7pm-midnight daily; bus 6

For fine Indian dining at comparatively reasonable prices it is hard to surpass this place, one of the very few Indian options in Florence. A reasonable range of predictable dishes, from tandoori to biryanis and korma can be washed down with cold Kingfisher.

BORGO ANTICO Map pp248–50 _Pizzeria_
☎ 055 21 04 37; Piazza Santo Spirito 6/r; meal €20-25; ☺ daily; bus D

This pizzeria and restaurant is a great location in summer, when you can sit at an outside table and enjoy the atmosphere in the square. If you decide to go for the expensive menu, which changes daily, you can get some surprisingly good meals. Try the big salads or plates of pasta for €6.

CABIRIA Map pp248–50 _Italian_
☎ 055 21 57 32; Piazza Santo Spirito 4/r; meal €20-25; ☺ Wed-Mon; bus D

This is a cool bar, café and restaurant. Some of the pasta dishes on offer are good and the terrace on the square is a very pleasant place to eat them. Otherwise, just hang around the bar inside (see p143).

DILADDARNO Map pp248–50 _Tuscan_
☎ 055 22 50 01; Via de' Serragli 108/r; meal €25-30; ☺ Tue-Sun; bus 11, 36 & 37

Wander into this very yellow locals' eatery, with benches lining the walls that lead out to a pergola courtyard. The menu is brief, the dishes hearty and there's not a whiff of fish. The _spaghetti alla chitarra con pomodorini, mozzarella e basilico_ (a square-sided spaghetti with cherry tomatoes, mozza and basil) is great for starters.

HEMINGWAY Map pp248–50 _Sweets_
☎ 055 28 47 81; Piazza Piattellina 9/r; ☺ Tue-Sun; bus D

This is a chocolate-lover's haven. You can choose from all sorts of goodies to take home and munch in private. Or sit down for a glorious cup of hot chocolate.

IL SANTO BEVITORE Map pp248–50 _Tuscan_
☎ 055 21 12 64; Via di Spirito Santo 64-66/r; meal €25-30; ☺ Mon-Sat; bus 6 & D

Beneath the vast vaults of this young, bustling _enoteca_, settle in at the spaciously-set dark timber tables for a bottle of fine Tuscan wine and then choose from a limited list of generous dishes to go with it. The thick, hearty _pappa al pomodoro_ (tomato and bread soup) would be enough to eat for a limited appetite. The

A waiter emerging from a café on Piazza della Signoria (p128)

hungry might follow with a *tartare di chianina* of top-grade minced Tuscan beef.

I TAROCCHI Map pp248–50   *Pizzeria*

☎ 055 234 39 12; Via dei Renai 12-14/r; pizzas around €6-8, meal €20-25; ☺ Tue-Fri & Sat-Sun dinner only; bus 13, 23 & C

Most people drop by here for the excellent pizzas. In summer you can gobble one up on the pavement terrace (if you can find a seat, no easy feat), or squeeze in along the benches inside. Aside from the pizza, the kitchen churns out immensely filling pasta dishes and a handful of main courses (only those with an abyss opening up inside them will be capable of ingesting pasta *and* main!). The menu changes daily.

LA BEPPA Map pp248–50   *Italian*

☎ 055 234 76 81; Via dell'Erta Canina 6/r; meal €30-35; ☺ Wed-Mon; bus 13, 23 & C

For some inventive Italian cooking in what feels like the countryside, La Beppa is worth going the extra mile. For an almost sweet-and-sour effect, try the *spaghetti alle acciughe e pomodorini* (spaghetti with anchovies and baby tomatoes). After your meal, it's worth taking a stroll along this back lane through vineyards guarded by retiring villas. You feel as though you're already deep in Chianti country.

L'BRINDELLONE

Map pp248–50   *Tuscan & Vegetarian*

☎ 055 21 78 79; Piazza Piattellina 10-11/r; meal €20-25; ☺ dinner only Thu-Tue; bus D

Surrounded by dangling garlic strands and old chianti bottles, this is a truly Tuscan spot with a slightly vegetarian bent too. Alongside such classics as *vitello tonnato* (veal in a tuna sauce) you can get vegetable couscous. The house red is good and the atmosphere welcoming with soft lighting.

MOMOYAMA Map pp248–50   *Japanese*

☎ 055 29 18 40; Borgo San Frediano 10r; meal €30-40; ☺ Tues-Sun; bus 6 & D

Technically operating as a club, this place touts itself as a sushi bar offering 'inventive food'. When you come the first time you fill out a form and may have to show some form of ID to become a member. It is an offbeat dining experience for Florence, with its bare minimalist ochre-coloured decor and tables spread over floors reaching well into the back. As you

---

Mr Sandman

The *renai* in the street name Via dei Renai (Map pp248–50) refers to the burly *renaioli* (sandmen) who, in the second half of the 19th century, found employment by trawling the depths of the Arno for sand. What previously had been a dredging exercise turned into something more profitable with the building boom that came around the 1860s as the city was drastically restructured. Sand (*rena* to the locals) was in big demand as an essential construction ingredient. The Florentine writer Vasco Pratolini later wrote that they sold sand like bread in those busy days. Not that the *renaioli* lived in luxury. Working from dawn to dusk, your average sandman collected two cubic metres of sand, enough to earn him his daily bread.

---

enter you will see a Japanese chef preparing some of the dishes right in front of you.

OSTERIA ANTICA MESCITA SAN NICCOLÒ Map pp248–50   *Tuscan*

☎ 055 234 28 36; Via di San Niccolò 60/r; meal €25; ☺ Mon-Sat; bus 13, 23 & C

A limited but tasty range of home-style local cooking awaits in this wine den. Sit down at the timber tables, choose from an endless range of Tuscan tipples and place your order. In summer this *osteria* has a few tables set up outside. Alongside the many great wines it also offers some very tasty cured meats and related savoury nibbles if you don't want a full meal.

OSTERIA SANTO SPIRITO

Map pp248–50   *Tuscan*

☎ 055 238 23 83; Piazza Santo Spirito 16/r; meal €30-35; ☺ daily; bus D

If you prefer a slightly higher-quality meal than in the bustling locales across the square and the occasional non-Italian surprise dish, this restaurant, set over two cosy floors, is the place. Try the tangy *tagliata di salmone con curry e cocco* (salmon steak with curry and coconut) for €15.

PANE E VINO

Map pp248–50   *Modern Tuscan*

☎ 055 247 69 56; Via di San Niccolò 70; meal €30; ☺ 7.30pm-1am Mon-Fri & Sat evening; bus 12, 13, 23 & C

Trust the waiters at this wonderful, informal and late-opening former *enoteca*, where superb wines and a seven-course *menu desgutazione* of classic Tuscan treats such as *porcini* mousse and chicken-liver crepes may well be the highlight of your trip. Bizarrely, the air-con is set up like a tabernacle at the end of the room.

🦋 RISTORANTE BECCOFINO

Map pp248–50 *Modern Italian*
☎ 055 29 00 76; Piazza degli Scarlatti 1/r; meal €50; 🕑 Tue-Sun; bus 6

This place is one of a rare breed. The grub is pricey and the surroundings nouveau chic – (check out the stainless steel, floor-lit loos!). You can sip at the bar and then try a vaguely adventurous style of cooking. Pasta dishes in particular represent a departure from tradition – try the *gnocchetti* with sweet onions. The wine list is impressive; this is a good opportunity to try some lesser-known but fine blends – the so-called Super Tuscans that thumb their noses at the DOC establishment.

RISTORANTE RICCHI

Map pp248–50 *Seafood*
☎ 055 21 58 64; Piazza Santo Spirito 8-9/r; meal €25-30; 🕑 Mon-Sat; bus D

For a sybarite's seafood experience at reasonable prices, drop into this long, narrow eatery

(next door to one of town's top *gelaterie*) on Florence's funkiest piazza. Old favourites like *spaghetti alle vongole* (with clams) are done with panache. You could try a spot in the little courtyard out the back.

TRATTORIA CAVOLO NERO

Map pp248–50 *International*
☎ 055 29 47 44; Via dell'Ardiglione 22; meal €30-35; 🕑 Tue-Sat; bus 11, 36 & 37

Hidden away in a back street, the 'Black Cabbage' is a gem. Try the entrecôte of Angus steak prepared with assorted herbs, but it's probably best to skip the house wine. Soups and tarts are also tempting. Homemade desserts by Michela are worth the extra notch in your belt.

TRATTORIA I RADDI

Map pp248–50 *Tuscan*
☎ 055 21 10 72; Via dell'Ardiglione 47/r; meal €30; 🕑 Mon-Sat; bus 11, 36 & 37

Just near Via de' Serragli, this trattoria serves traditional Florentine meals in an intimate and quiet location. Generous slabs of meat in the form of *bistecca* (steak) or hashed up as *peposo* (a hearty, peppery beef stew) leads the way in this carnivore's paradise.

Enjoying the relaxing atmosphere in one of the trattorias

Cheap Eats

AL TRANVAI Map pp248–50 *Tuscan*
☎ 055 22 51 97; Piazza Torquato Tasso 14/r; meal €20-25; ☺ Mon-Fri; bus 12, 13 & D

If you don't mind eating elbow to elbow with complete (local) strangers on benches set up along the walls, this is a wonderful rustic Tuscan eatery. It serves a limited range of pastas as *primi*, along with classics like *pappa al pomodoro* and *ribollita*. It also specialises in animal innards, including *trippa alla fiorentina*. If that doesn't attract, there are some meat alternatives.

CAFFÈ LA TORRE Map pp251–3 *Snacks*
☎ 055 68 06 43, Lungarno Benvenuto Cellini 65/r; meal €10-15; ☺ 8.30am-3am daily; bus 13, 23 & C

If you are in need of snack food of indifferent quality in the wee hours of the morning or a meal as late as 3am, this is about the only choice you have. It is also a busy bar and a great deal of fun (see p143).

TRATTORIA CASALINGA
Map pp248–50 *Tuscan*
☎ 055 21 86 24; Via de' Michelozzi 9/r; meal €15-20; ☺ Mon-Sat; bus 11, 36 & 37

People jostle into this cheerfully bustling eatery. What you get are standard Florentine mainstays at bargain basement prices. Don't expect to linger over a meal, as there is usually a queue of people waiting for your table.

NORTH OF THE OLD CITY

Little of interest for foodophiles awaits you in the mostly residential area arching around the north of the old centre. On the other hand, the places you stumble across are far less likely to populated by out-of-towners, which is already an advantage in some respects. And while high-class elegance and subtle culinary adventures may not be the order of day, you will find the occasional spot serving good, solid meals – after all, few Italians settle for rubbish.

EDI HOUSE Map pp246–7 *Pizzeria*
☎ 055 58 88 86; Piazza Savonarola 8/r; pizza €5-8, meal €25; ☺ 7pm-1.30am daily; bus 13 & 33

Out on its own to the north of the city centre, this big bright place is a lighthouse for starving locals. They mainly come to feast on the broad variety of pizzas and focaccia (how about the one with *gamberetti* – tiny prawns – and

pesto?), preferably on the pavement terrace in the warmer months.

OUTSKIRTS OF FLORENCE

In summer especially, choking Florentines seek escape and solace in the marginally cooler hill area of Fiesole. Around the central Piazza San Tommaseo you'll find no end of pizzerias, terraces and other eateries, all of them perfectly cheerful. A couple of quality restaurants with a penchant for slabs of meat are well worth the effort of traipsing out here in any season.

LA CAPPONCINA Map p254 *Tuscan*
☎ 055 69 70 37; Via San Romano 17/r, Settignano; meal €40; ☺ 7.30pm-midnight Tue-Sun; bus 10 & 67

Up in the hills overlooking Florence from the northeast, Florentines gather for a bit of a splurge on the restaurant's *tagliata di manzo*, succulent beef fillets sliced up and served on a bed of rocket lettuce. Sitting in the garden is a true pleasure in summer, when you are sure of being several degrees cooler than in town.

The restaurant is a few steps off Piazza San Tommaseo, where the bus terminates.

TRATTORIA CAVE DI MAIANO

Map p254   *Tuscan*
☎ 055 5 91 33; Via Cave di Maiano 16, Fiesole; meal €30; ☽ daily except Mon lunch; bus 7 plus taxi

This place is not dissimilar in terms of price, atmosphere and clientele to La Capponcina. Tables are arranged across a variety of inter-connected dining rooms and out on terraces. Getting here without a car is tricky as the restaurant is actually in Maiano, a *frazione* (division) of Fiesole, and off the bus routes. You could try getting a taxi from central Fiesole.

Entertainment

Entertainment

For a provincial capital, Florence has a variegated palette of entertainment. Bars of all sorts, from wine outlets to cool cocktail coves, keep the young and not-so-young of Florence in tipples. A wide mixture of live music (from jazz to rock) and clubs will keep you jiving through the wee hours. Theatre, the occasional opera and cinema are also on hand.

In summer, the scene changes somewhat. The city organises open-air concerts (located in places like the ever-convivial Piazza di Spirito Santo), theatre and modern dance cycles. Several outdoor cinemas are set up (although none with films in the original language).

Information

The tourist office produces a bimonthly publication, *Turismonotizie* (which is nominally €0.50 but often available free), a free monthly events flyer, *Eventi*, and an annual brochure, *Avvenimenti,* covering major events in and around the city. There is also the monthly freebie *Informacittà* – check out its website (www.informacittafirenze.it, Italian only) for the latest updates.

Firenze Spettacolo, the city's definitive entertainment publication, is available monthly for €1.55 at newsstands. Posters at the tourist offices, the university and in Piazza della Repubblica advertise concerts and other events.

DRINKING

We're far from London and New York but Florence has a pleasing array of watering holes that fall into all sorts of categories. Inveterate bar-hoppers and night owls will find plenty to fill their wee hours over a couple of weeks. You can sip on endless selections of fine Tuscan wine in an *enoteca* (wine bar), perhaps over a tasty snack or two.

Cabiria café on Piazza Santo Spirito (p143)

At the other end of the scale, you might choose from one of several UK-style pubs. The latter are a reflection of a double phenomenon in Florence: the considerable Anglo-Saxon presence in town (whether language students or travellers) and a certain Italian fondness for bars dressed up as Anglo-Irish pubs. These latter offer everything from UK football games live onscreen through to mostly Italian punters sipping on pints of McCaffreys in genteel fashion.

Otherwise bars are distinctive in their own style. They range from a chintzy one-time brothel (all leopard skins and puffy cushions at Montecarla) to low-lit cocktail bars.

Many bars and pubs tend to shut by 1am or 2am, but there are enough exceptions (especially on Fridays and Saturdays) to this rule to keep you going to 3am and, on a few occasions, later.

Drink prices don't vary as much as you might expect. A good rule of thumb is €4 to €5 for a pint-sized glass of beer on tap, while mixed drinks and cocktails typically cost around €6 to €8. In some clubs and discos you may pay more.

Be aware that, starting in late May, quite a few bars in Florence shut for the long summer break and don't open their doors again until September.

ART BAR Map pp248–50

☎ 055 28 76 61; Via del Moro 4/r; ◷ 7pm-1am Sun-Thu, 7pm-2am Fri & Sat; bus A

Once known as the Antico Caffè del Moro (the sign remains), this tiny establishment has the air of a spring-cleaned Bohemian hide-out. The metallic clutter (sewing machines, old film projectors and other extraneous bits of decor) notwithstanding, it is an appealing locale to slip into for a fruity cocktail.

ASTOR CAFFÈ Map pp251–3

☎ 055 239 90 00; Piazza del Duomo 5/r; ◷ 10am-3am; bus 14 & 23

You can have breakfast here but the nocturnal folk gather around for loud music and cocktails both inside and out, right by the solemn walls of the Duomo. You can keep an eye on the big red clock to see how near it is to closing time.

BLOB Map pp251–3

☎ 055 21 12 09; Via Vinegia 21/r; ◷ 8pm-3.30am; bus B

This tiny place is tucked away in the shadow of Palazzo Vecchio. With a bar, some cramped upstairs lounge seating and a rather mixed music selection (tending to techno), it can be a cosy nook to hang out. Blob will ask you to organise a *tessera* (membership card) for €8 (and you may not be able to collect it and use it until the following day) – hang on to it for future visits.

CABIRIA Map pp248–50

☎ 055 21 57 32; Piazza Santo Spirito 4/r; ◷ 11am-2am Wed-Mon; bus D

This popular café by day converts into a busy music bar by night. In summer the buzz ex-

Top Five Drinking Establishments

- **Mayday** (p145)
- **Rex Caffè** (p145)
- **Joshua Tree** (p144)
- **Universale** (p147)
- **Zoe** (p147)

tends onto Piazza Santo Spirito, which itself becomes a stage for an outdoor bar and regular free concerts.

CAFFÈ LA TORRE Map pp248–50

☎ 055 68 06 43; Lungarno Benvenuto Cellini 65/r; mixed drinks around €5.50; ◷ 8.30am-3am; bus 12, 13, 23 & C

Hang out into the wee hours drinking and listening to all kinds of music – from cool jazz to Latin rhythms – in the largely red-lit ambience inside this bar (or outside on the terrace). Drinks are reasonable, and this is one of the only places in Florence where you can snack after midnight. It's a bit of a cult fave with Florentines.

CAFFÈ MEGARA Map pp251–3

☎ 055 21 18 37; Via della Spada 13-15/r; cocktails €5.50; ◷ 8am-2am; bus A

By day a pleasing breakfast or snack stop, this place turns into a buzzy little bar at night, with punters crowded inside the microscopic locale dominated by an almost life-size replica of the Red Baron's tri-wing fighter plane in deep dive. In the sweatier months go for a seat outside and sip a cocktail.

CAPOCACCIA Map pp248–50
☎ 055 21 07 51; Lungarno Corsini 12-14/r; ✆ noon-1am Tue-Sun; bus B

The fashion set of Florence gathers here, especially on a balmy spring or summer evening, for a riverside nibble and cocktail before heading onto dinner and clubs. Dress up a little to avoid feeling like a hick from the sticks and it can be a curious exercise in people-watching. Tuesday is sushi night and the DJ takes over at 11pm, Wednesday to Sunday.

CHEQUERS PUB Map pp246–7
☎ 055 28 75 88; Via della Scala 7-9/r; bus 11, 36, 37 & A

Mainly foreigners hang out in this big and busy UK-style pub, although Italians sometimes frequent here. In the background the big-screen TV will feature anything from European football to American basketball.

CLURICANE PUB Map pp251–3
☎ 055 28 45 09; Piazza dell'Olio 2; ✆ 2pm-2am; bus A

Touting itself as a Guinness bar, it is really a warm, dark drinking cubicle with a fan over the bar and Latin music. But the Guinness (warm and cold) and Kilkenny are there. A handful of tables are set up outside in the warmer months.

EBY'S LATIN BAR Map pp248–50
☎ 055 24 00 27; Via dell'Oriuolo 5r; burritos etc €3.50, cocktails €5.50; ✆ noon-3am Mon-Sat; bus C

Bright blues and reds in a festive Mexican fashion greet you in this lively new Latin bar. Cocktails are good, the music tropical and the place is a hit with locals.

GATE PUB Map pp248–50
☎ 055 29 51 81; Borgo San Frediano 102/r; ✆ 8pm-2am; bus 6 & D

In a rarely visited corner of the Oltrarno, this is another quite pleasant, low-key example of the UK-style pub that so densely populates the city.

H2O2 Map pp248–50
☎ 055 24 32 39; Via Ghibellina 47/r; cocktails around €6; ✆ 9pm-1am Thu-Tue Oct-May; bus 14 & A

This is a cruisy spot for a pre-club tipple, frequented by locals and also a sprinkling of out-of-towners. The music is mostly house.

IL RIFRULLO Map pp248–50
☎ 055 234 26 21; Via di San Niccolò 55/r; ✆ 9am-1am; bus 12, 13, 23 & C

A cool corner bar nicely placed off the main tourist trail. The bar snacks are generous and the evening cocktails good. You can sit by the bar or wind your way out to the back garden on summer nights.

JAMES JOYCE Map pp248–50
☎ 055 658 08 56; Lungarno Benvenuto Cellini 1/r; ✆ 6pm-1am; bus 12, 13, 23 & C

This is a rather pleasant version of the UK-pub theme, with a beer garden and largely local punters, if only because it's a bridge too far for most interlopers. Beamish is the main drop on tap, which you can mix with Florence-style bar snacks.

JJ CATHEDRAL Map pp251–3
☎ 055 28 02 60; Piazza San Giovanni 44/r; ✆ 11am-1am; bus 1, 6, 7, 10, 11, 14, 17 & 23

Get here early if you want the balcony table overlooking the Baptistry, which is the most coveted drinking spot in Florence. Otherwise make do with the narrow interior cluttered with ripped wallpaper and fiddly bits of Irish paraphernalia. Usually filled with heavy-smoking international students.

JOSHUA TREE Map pp246–7
Via della Scala 41; ✆ 4pm-1am; bus 11, 36, 37 & A

A dark, conspiratorial air pervades the place, with U2 reminders scattered about. The crowd is mixed although you can expect a predominance of young foreigners.

KIKUYA PUB Map pp248–50
☎ 055 234 48 79; Via de' Benci 43/r; cocktails €6; ✆ 7pm-3am; bus 13, 23, B & C

The cocktails in Kikuya are unusually generous and happy hour runs from 6pm to 9pm. You can also hear live music here occasionally. It invites a predominantly foreign crowd, but it at least avoids the overtly UK-style-pub identity. Indeed it is a strange mix with Brazilian bar staff and a rocky ambience. If you get hungry the staff can provide you with some nachos (well, corn crisps and two sauces).

LA DOLCE VITA Map pp248–50
☎ 055 28 45 95; Piazza del Carmine 6/r; ✆ 8pm-1am Mon-Thu, 8pm-3am Fri-Sun; bus D

Just a piazza away from Santo Spirito, this place attracts very voguish people. During the week it's a tame affair, with the clientele looking carefully dressy over a cocktail. Things get busier from Thursday night on.

LA ROTONDA Map pp246–7

☎ 055 265 46 44; Via il Prato 10-16; ☼ 7.30pm-1am; bus 1, 2, 9, 16, 17, 26, 27, 29, 30, 35 & D

This cavernous place spreads over two floors. Part pub, part music bar, and sometimes with live action, it offers simple grub and attracts a largely Italian crowd as the foreign student brigade doesn't seem to migrate this far.

LION'S FOUNTAIN Map pp248–50

☎ 055 234 44 12; Borgo degli Albizi 34/r; ☼ 6pm-2am; bus A

This pub tends to attract a young, rowdy and substantially English-speaking crowd that, as it spews out into the streets towards closing time, is highly reminiscent of 11pm closing.

LOCHNESS Map pp248–50

www.lochnessclub.com; Via de' Benci 19/r; ☼ 10pm-5am Sep-May; bus 13, 23, B & C

Look for the green door. Loonees' patrons (see the next entry) often end up here. You'll need to pay a one-off membership fee of €8. Those with unlimited drinking capacity but short on cash could combine the Loonees happy hour from 8pm to 10pm with a follow-up until 11pm at Lochness.

LOONEES Map pp251–3

☎ 055 21 22 49; Via Porta Rossa 15; ☼ 8pm-3am; bus A

You wouldn't know this place existed if you had not been told. Walk into the building and the door is to the left of the staircase. It's a fairly small 'club' – basically just a bar with an expat bent and occasional live music of dubious taste. Still it's a personable enough spot for a pint. If you've found this place you may well be put on to the Lochness, with which it's connected (see previous entry).

MAYDAY Map pp251–3 ●

☎ 055 238 12 90; Via Dante Alighieri 16/r; ☼ 8pm-2am; bus A

This stylish lounge bar, often the scene of art exhibitions, is primarily the funky stage for an evening out, with great music and even the occasional live show.

MONTECARLA Map pp248–50

☎ 055 234 02 59; Via de' Bardi 2; mixed drinks around €7; ☼ 8pm-4am Thu-Tue; bus 13, 23 & C

This is one of the weirder locations to get a late-night cocktail (and an indifferent pizza if you have the munchies). It has remained faithful to the baroque kitsch aesthetic that inspired Montecarla's supposed originator – a prostitute of some fame in years gone by (hence the feminine version of the bar's name). It's all leopard skins, gaudy cushions, plush drapes and moody corners: warm and cosy on a winter's evening. It operates a 'membership' policy, but you should be able to get away with filling out a card as a pro forma operation.

NEGRONI Map pp248–50

☎ 055 24 36 47; Via dei Renai 17/r; ☼ 9am-2am Mon-Sat, 6pm-2am Sun; bus 12, 13, 23 & C

A smart bar named after a cocktail and serving plenty of them, Negroni adds a touch of metropolitan bar class to this pretty corner of the city. In summer, in conjunction with its more youthful but equally attractive neighbour, Zoe (see p147), bar staff set up outdoor kiosks in the leafy shade of Piazza Demidoff. Parking around here has never been so fraught!

PICCOLO CAFÉ Map pp248–50

☎ 055 200 10 57; Borgo Santa Croce 23/r; ☼ 5pm-2am; bus C

This is a relaxed little place to hang out and get acquainted with the city's gay scene. Although leaning towards a male clientele, the bar is by no means exclusive; lesbians and straights are equally welcome. You also might want to pop by for the buffet between 6.30pm and 9pm.

✎ REX CAFFÈ Map pp248–50

☎ 055 248 03 31; Via Fiesolana 25/r; ☼ 5pm-3am; bus C

A top stop on the cocktail circuit and a hip place to slip into for your favourite mixed concoction. Occasionally you'll strike live music and when it's vinyl the taste is eclectic. You get a mixed crowd, including an arty, grunge crowd as well as students and a sprinkling of the fashion set. Take a martini at the luridly lit central bar or a quiet beer sitting at one of the metallic tables.

ROBIN HOOD'S TAVERN Map pp248–50

☎ 055 24 45 79; Via dell'Oriuolo 58/r; ☼ 11am-2am Sun-Thu, 11am-3am Fri & Sat; bus 14 & 23

At this, one of the city's Irish contingent, Thursday is 'ladies' night'. Just walking past makes you think you have time-warped out of Italy. Clearly not many locals make it here. The food is fairly cheap but it's not astounding and happy hour lasts from 6pm to 11.30pm.

ROSE'S Map pp251–3

☎ 055 28 70 90; Via del Parione 26/r; ⏰ 7am-1am Mon-Sat; bus A & B

A casual and smoke-free New York–style café with salads and pastas during the day, Rose's undergoes a metamorphosis after dark when it turns into a hip and lively sushi bar and fills up with a trendy crowd.

SALAMANCA Map pp248–50

☎ 055 234 54 52; Via Ghibellina 80/r; ⏰ 7.30pm-2am; bus 14

The tapas here have a vaguely Italian flavour about them but otherwise the place manages to exude an almost convincing pseudo-Spanish atmosphere with plenty of hearty flamenco rock and South American sounds to keep punters returning to the bar for more – it's a favourite with Latin Americans living in Florence. Sangria and Latin American cocktails predominate.

SANT'AMBROGIO CAFFÈ Map pp248–50

☎ 055 24 10 35; Piazza Sant'Ambrogio 7/r; cocktails €6; ⏰ 9am-2am Mon-Sat; bus C

A good source of snacks, Sant'Ambrogio Caffè is especially dedicated to the sipping of cocktails. On summer nights tables are set up outside and the place is popular with a mix of Italian students and arty types.

SLOWLY Map pp251–3

☎ 055 264 53 54; Via Porta Rossa 63/r; ⏰ 11am-2.30am Mon-Sat; bus A

Frizzy-haired ladies with euro-trash wardrobes trip their way in on high heels while brillo'd Don Giovannis check out the talent from behind their designer shades. The barman has a heavy hand with the cocktails. Sunday evening is the king of *aperitivo* time, featuring oysters and champagne.

TARTAN JOCK Map pp248–50

☎ 055 247 83 05; Corso dei Tintori 41/r; ⏰ 6pm-2am; bus 13, B & C

The Scots must have felt left out as the tide of English and Irish pubs rose in Florence and thus this tartan whim was opened. It is a perfectly acceptable watering hole frequented by Italians and foreigners alike, although

Patrons at Porto di Mare (p148)

Summer Frolics

While some clubs and bars close for a month or more in summer, all sorts of places spring to life to keep Florentines occupied through the hot months (mid-June to early September). There are some great nightlife options.

The centuries-old former convent and women's prison called **Le Murate** (Map pp248–50; ☎ 328 176 71 98; Via dell'Agnolo; admission free) becomes the scene of nightly organised fun known as **Vie di Fuga** (Escape Routes) from June to September. Music, films projected on a huge screen, and other events are staged each night, although many locals use it as a place to kick on to after other bars have closed. Most nights it stays open until around 3am.

Just off Piazza della Libertà, the rather odd-looking collection of buildings and performance spaces known as **Parterre** (Map pp246–7) comes to life as a kind of all-in-one entertainment scene. Nightly performances of music of all types, theatre (for adults and kids) and so on are the order of the evening. Scattered about are a pizzeria, a gelateria, bars and shops. It goes from 8pm to 1am.

In **Piazza Santo Spirito** (Map pp248–50) a bar is set up in the middle of the square every night for **Notti d'Estate** (Summer Nights) and frequent live-music acts keep punters coming. The fun (free) lasts from 8pm to 1am. **Jazz & Co** keeps Piazza della SS Annunziata (Map pp246–7) humming. Get hold of a programme from the tourist office to find out who's performing. An open-air bar also operates here and the activity winds up by 1am.

Rime Rampanti (free) is a mixed programme of music and theatre on Piazza Giuseppe Poggi by the Porta San Niccolò in Oltrarno (Map pp251–3). Again, temporary bars and snack stands are put in place and the activity runs from 7pm to 2am.

Teatro dell'Acqua (Map pp248–50; ☎ 055 234 34 60; Lungarno G Pecori Giraldi 1) opens up for fun and music in the summer months (mid-May to September). It attracts a mixed crowd and you can also get a bite to eat at the restaurant and pizzeria. You have to pay €4 for a *tessera* (membership card) the first time you go – just remember to take it along if you decide to go back another time. Virtually on top of this place is **Lidò** (Map pp248–50; ☎ 055 234 27 26), a similar deal which is fun for early evening open-air riverside cocktails – they often put on some free munchies, including pasta, to nibble on from around 7pm to 9pm.

much more low-key than the nearby William (see following).

THE WILLIAM Map pp248–50
☎ 055 246 98 00; Via Magliabechi 7/r;
🕙 6pm-2am; bus C
This is a loud UK-style pub but it has found quite a following among twenty-something Florentines in search of a pint of ale, rather than Anglos in search of six.

UNIVERSALE Map pp244–5
☎ 055 22 11 22; Via Pisana 77/r; admission €10-15 (includes first drink); 🕙 8pm-3am Wed-Sun Sep-May; bus 6
The owners have converted this old cinema which now has a restaurant upstairs and a bar in the middle of the downstairs area, around which gathers a mixed set of locals tending towards a very fashionable crowd. In the background a screen plays clips from classic black-and-white movies.

Y.A.G. BAR Map pp248–50
☎ 055 246 90 22; Via de' Macci 8/r; 🕙 5pm-2am; bus C
Barely a stone's throw away from the Piccolo Café, this gay bar is another relaxed and mixed

location. It claims to be the largest gay bar in Florence and is upfront about its identity. If you don't want to chat, there are some computer terminals for going online and playing video games.

ZOE Map pp248–50
☎ 055 24 31 11; Via dei Renai 13/r; 🕙 3pm-2am Apr-Oct, 6pm-2am Tue-Sun Nov-Mar; bus 12, 13, 23 & C
Twenty-something Florentines converge on this hopping Oltrarno bar from all corners of town. They spill out on to the street amid a friendly atmosphere. Although the bar attracts a mixed crowd, the majority tend to be aged 25 or younger.

ZONA 15 Map pp246–7
☎ 055 21 16 78; Via del Castellaccio 53-55/r;
🕙 11am-3am; bus C
Shimmy up to Zona's rectangular bar for a taste of one or two of about 200 Italian and French wines – by the glass or by the bottle. In this low-lit, casually elegant wine bar environment you'll be tempted to hang around for a snack or two as well. Sunday nights from 7pm you'll likely find live jazz here as well.

LIVE MUSIC

In some cases you may be asked to pay for membership – this is effectively like paying a one-off cover charge. If you are staying in Florence for any length of time give a local address so that you receive your card – generally valid for a year.

Sometimes people just talk their way into a place. 'Yes, I'm a member but I left my membership card at home,' must be one of the most oft-used lines in Florence. In some places the request is a formality anyway and if you can't produce a card you will be asked to fill out a new one, or some kind of replacement form. Establishments do this to keep their noses clean with the law and maintain their status as 'clubs', which brings tax breaks.

See p151 for venues which also present live music on occasion. Also, check out *Firenze Spettacolo* to see what's happening where.

JAZZ

Several bars provide Florentines with a regular diet of the sounds of jazz. The Jazz Club is the main bastion for the genre, and a couple of other locales occasionally chime in.

BEBOP Map pp246–7

☎ 055 239 65 44; Via dei Servi 76/r; admission free-€10; ☯ 8pm-2am Mon-Sat; bus C

A mellow, underground music cavern, this is a spot to catch a little jazz, blues or whatever else they might come up with – the programme can be quite eclectic. Basically the music consists of light covers but can be quite pleasant, and the place doesn't seem to get too crowded. On Monday and Wednesday nights every draught beer you buy gets you a free shot (oh dear).

JAZZ CLUB Map pp246–7

☎ 055 247 97 00; Via Nuova de' Caccini 3; admission €5 (for a year's membership), drinks around €7; ☯ 9.30pm-1am Sun-Thu, 9.30pm-2am Fri & Sat; bus C

The name says it all. This is Florence's top jazz venue and it gets some quality acts, both local and from out of town. The atmosphere is low-lit and the music to be enjoyed without necessarily killing the conversation – a good mix. At the weekend you should book a table if you are going in a group. A bottle of unspectacular chianti will cost around €20.

PINOCCHIO CLUB Map pp244–5

☎ 055 68 33 88; Via Donato Giannotti 13; admission €5-12; bus 23, 31, 32, 33 & 71 (night bus)

You can often hear quality jazz here on Friday and Saturday. Call ahead to make sure something is on, as the place is out of the way, south of Piazza Gavinana in the area of the same name southeast of the centre and across the Arno.

ROCK & OTHER

A handful of big venues host the headlining concerts at various times through the year. Otherwise, to hear a little live music you must dig around a handful of spots spread thinly around town.

AUDITORIUM FLOG Map pp244–5

☎ 055 49 04 37; www.flog.it; Via M Mercati 24b; admission free-€10, mixed drinks around €6; ☯ 10pm-4am; bus 4, 8, 14, 20 & 28

A major venue for bands that was born out of a workers' society created in 1945, Flog is in the Rifredi area, quite a way north of the centre. It has a reasonable stage and dance area, and a swimming pool sometimes operates in summer.

PORTO DI MARE Map pp244–5

☎ 055 71 57 94; Via Pisana 128; admission €5.20 (membership); ☯ 8pm-3am; bus 6, 13, 26, 27 & 80

Those who arrive here earlier in the evening generally do so to eat, which is not such a bad idea in this spacious 'port'. The owners are into music, however, and the live jamming (which can be anything from world music to blues and jazz to emerging acts) takes place downstairs.

TENAX Map p254

☎ 055 30 81 60; www.tenax.org, Italian only; Via Pratese 46; admission free-€10.40, mixed drinks around €5.20; ☯ 10pm-4am Tue-Sun; bus 29 & 30

Located well northwest of the centre, Tenax has been staging big local and international acts since the early 1980s. Although the emphasis has moved to clubbing in recent years, Tenax still attracts live shows by noted performers, such as Bob Geldof and Grace Jones. Keep an eye on its programme.

CLUBBING

An odd mix of little dance clubs is scattered across the city. You can get down to Latin rhythms, squeeze up in dance clubs no bigger than your average bathroom or join the glitzy things in a couple of good old-fashioned meat markets in central Florence.

Two of the city's main clubs, Central Park and Rio Grande, are in the Cascine park. They are fun without exactly being the last word in European nightlife. In both you will be given a card on entry. You use this to get drinks (and food if you want). It is swiped on your way out, which is when

you will be obliged to pay for at least one drink whether you have one or not – this is effectively your admission charge. A word of warning about the Cascine – it is a haunt for prostitutes, pimps and other interesting folk. A taxi is probably not a bad idea when you head home.

The pay-on-your-way-out system operates in some other clubs as well so bear this in mind. Beware of places claiming that entrance is free. Literally this may be true, but the exit generally won't be! Often you will get a chit on ordering your first drink – you must have (and pay for) this chit (with all subsequent drinks also totted up) to leave.

Gay & Lesbian Options

Florence isn't memorable for gay nightlife but the scene has improved marginally over the years and there is a handful of possibilities, including the **clubs** listed here. A couple of relaxed bars to commence your gay pilgrimage include **Piccolo Café** (p145) and **Y.A.G. Bar** (p147). In summer especially, Florence's gays head for the clubs of Viareggio on the coast instead.

CENTRAL PARK Map pp244–5

☎ 055 35 35 05; Via Fosso Macinante 2; drinks around €8; ⏰ 10pm-6am Tue-Sun; bus 1, 9, 12, 13, 16, 26, 27, 80 & B

What kind of music you hear in this club, one of the city's most popular, will depend partly on the night, although as you wander from one dance area to another (there are five) you can expect a general range from Latin and pop through to house. Thursday is a big night out in Florence and moves to hip-hop and reggae classics. In summer you can dance inside or under the stars.

CRISCO Map pp248–50

☎ 055 248 05 80; Via Sant'Egidio 43/r; ⏰ 8pm-4am Sun-Mon & Wed-Thu, 8pm-6am Fri & Sat; bus 14 & 23

A somewhat furtive air seems to reign in this strictly men-only club. After a few warm-up tipples and body-grinding dance, explore the dark rooms.

CRUISING Z Map pp248–50

☎ 055 246 63 87; Via dell'Oriuolo 19-21/r; ⏰ 4pm-4am Tue-Sun; bus 14 & 23

Florence's first full-on gay sex bar is barely a stumble from the area's senior gay club, Crisco. After sipping a few drinks at the bar, head off for games of erotic hide-and-seek

in the labyrinth. The discrete entry is simply marked 19-21r.

FULL UP Map pp248–50

☎ 055 29 30 06; Via della Vigna Vecchia 23-25/r; ⏰ 10pm-4am Wed-Sat; bus 14 & A

Full-up by name and, you guessed it, this tiny venue is very popular with a largely Florentine crowd made up of Fabios and the skimpily-clad objects of their desire. A good place to go if you're looking for a Mediterranean orgasm (and we're not talking cocktails).

JARAGUA Map pp248–50

☎ 055 234 36 00; Via dell'Erta Canina 12/r; admission free; ⏰ 8pm-3am; bus 12, 13, 23 & C

Somewhat hidden from the main tourist stream, this is a cool Latin locale where you can admire some slick dance moves or join in – definitely the place to practice your salsa and merengue. Sip on a Banana Mama, Jaragua or Culo Bello ('Nice Ass'). The whole Latin thing is extremely popular with Florentines.

MARAMAO Map pp248–50

☎ 055 24 43 41; Via de' Macci 79/r; admission with 1 drink €10; ⏰ 8pm-3am Wed-Sun Oct-May; bus A

It has all the appearance of a bar but stays open late and the DJs keep the music suitably deafening so that you can at least imagine

DJs and dancing – essential ingredients for a night on the town

you're in a club. A fairly narrow place with a minuscule dance area on what could be described as the poop deck at the back, it can get packed beyond comfort at the weekend. This is one of those places where you are given a card on entry that is then exchanged for a different one when you purchase a drink – you need this to get back out.

RIO GRANDE Map pp244–5

☎ 055 33 13 71; Viale degli Olmi; admission €16-20; 10pm-5am Tue-Sat; bus 1, 9, 12, 13, 16, 26, 27, 80 & B

Three dance spaces offer house, funk and mainstream music to appeal to a fairly broad range of tastes. The main dance floor is dominated by go-go dancers – presumably its mission is to get people shaking their booty. From here you can meander your way through the other dance floors. Rio puts on regular theme nights; Thursday is usually salsa and Caribbean. On a Brazilian note, on most nights you can dine at the *churrascaria* (which means sizzling slabs of meat).

SOULCIETY CLUB Map pp246–7

☎ 055 830 35 13; Via San Zanobi 114a; admission €6; 11pm-4am Tue-Sun Oct-May; bus 4, 12 & 20

Just when you thought there were no good 'music' clubs in Florence, you happen upon this low-key gem serving up juicy slabs of deep house, funk and soul in a party atmosphere – an oversubscribed one at weekends.

SILVER STUD Map pp248–50

☎ 055 68 84 46; Via della Fornace 9; 9pm-5am Mon-Sat; bus 12, 13, 23 & C

This exclusively gay men's club is a no-nonsense cruising bar with dark room. The bar occasion-ally organises fairly in-your-face live erotic shows too, just in case you need a little warming up.

TABASCO Map pp251–3

☎ 055 21 30 00; Piazza di Santa Cecilia 3/r; admission free, drinks €6-7; 8pm-4am, disco until 6am Tue, Fri & Sat; bus A

For some time, this place stood alone as Florence's only serious gay club (indeed it was Italy's first gay disco) where you could dance through the wee hours. It remains one of the best options for a good dance night out, although if you are more directly hunting for sex, some of the more recent arrivals (see elsewhere in this section) may be more to your liking. In a building dating to the 16th century, you dance beneath stone vaults and among ageing statues. The old well still works! Here you have a space for dancing, a cocktail bar and dark room. Wednesday is leather night. You are obliged to have at least one drink.

TENAX Map p254

☎ 055 30 81 60; www.tenax.org, Italian only; Via Pratese 46; admission up to €25; 10pm-4am Tue-Sun; bus 29 & 30

Tenax isn't just the main venue for major live bands; it is also one of the hottest and longest-standing clubs in town. It still gets plenty of live acts, but in recent years the emphasis has shifted to clubbing and dance theme parties. Upstairs you'll find a cool wine bar and chill-out area as well as MUM, a club within the club featuring DJs from around Europe. On Friday night clubbers go behind the bars for The Cage, while Saturday is run by DJs, such as Alex Neri, of Nobody's Perfect – basically a house night.

XO Map pp248–50

☎ 055 234 78 80; Via Giuseppe Verdi 59/r; admission with 1 drink €7.50-10; ☺ 9pm-4am Wed-Sun Oct-May; bus 14, 23 & A

New life has been breathed into this local Santa Croce dance dive. At its best it can get seriously hopping, occasionally with a live act until midnight followed by deep dancing with Deep House, trip hop and so on. Don't leave it until the last half-hour as the music and thinning crowd of punters can be a disappointment.

YAB Map pp251–3

☎ 055 21 51 60; Via de' Sassetti 15; ☺ Mon-Sat Oct-late May; bus 6 & A

Remember those '80s disco years? In some respects Yab never moved on. With a famous local reputation as a meat market, it grinds on with a hormonally charged crowd of local dons and gals, and a mixture of tipsy out-of-towners. Music is a middle-of-the-road mix of rock and house and the key point in its favour is its central location.

CINEMA

There are a few venues that show films in the *versione originale* (original language). This generally means films in English with Italian subtitles. At most cinemas there are three or four sessions daily, the latest starting between 10pm and 10.45pm. Wednesday is cheap cinema day, when tickets cost €5. Normally they cost around €7.20.

BRITISH INSTITUTE Map pp248–50

☎ 055 26 77 82; Lungarno Guicciardini 9; bus 6 & D
The British Institute will sometimes put on English-language films in its library.

CINEMA FULGOR Map pp246–7

☎ 055 238 18 81; Via Maso Finiguerra 22/r
You'll find films in English screened here on Thursday evenings.

ODEON CINEHALL Map pp251–3

☎ 055 21 40 68; www.cinehall.it; Piazza degli Strozzi; bus 6 & A

This is the main location for seeing subtitled films, screened on Mondays, Tuesdays and Thursdays. The Odeon chain has cinemas spread all over town, but this is the best for original English version films.

Cinema under the Stars

From mid-June to early September several places set up outdoor cinemas (programmes are available from tourist offices) as most indoor cinemas shut for the summer break. Tickets generally cost €5. Among them are:

Arena Chiardiluna (Map pp244–5; ☎ 055 233 70 42; Via Monte Uliveto 1; bus 12 & 13)

Arena di Marte (Map pp244–5; ☎ 055 67 88 41; Viale Paoli, Terrazza Palasport at Campo di Marte; bus 10)

Arena Villa Vittoria (Map pp246–7; ☎ 055 497 32 22; Via Valfonda, Palazzo dei Congressi; bus 7, 10, 12, 13, 31 & 32)

Cinema Sotto Le Stelle (Map pp244–5; ☎ 055 200 14 86; Forte di Belvedere, Via San Leonardo; bus C & D + walk) Cinema classics.

CLASSICAL MUSIC & OPERA

From October to April the city's main theatres provide Florentines with a programme of opera and classical music. Come the warmer months, special performances and music festivals take over the scene (see p9). In summer especially, concerts of chamber music are held in churches across the city. Keep an eye out for programmes of the Orchestra da Camera Fiorentina (Florentine Chamber Orchestra), whose performance season runs from March to October.

Tickets & Reservations

A handy central ticket outlet is **Box Office** (Map pp246–7; ☎ 055 21 08 04; www.boxoffice.it; Via Luigi Alamanni 39; ☺ 3.30-7.30pm Mon, 10am-7pm Tues-Sat). You can call by the office or book events online. Another Web ticket service, **Ticket One** (www.ticketone.it), allows you to book tickets for theatre, football and other events on the Internet.

CHIESA SANTA MARIA DE' RICCI
CONCERTI Map pp251–3
☎ 055 28 93 67; Via del Corso; admission €11;
🕒 9.15pm; bus A

Although they can sometimes be a little cheesy, the concerts of baroque and classical music staged in this church (the proceeds go, in part at least, to the church's restoration), may be your only chance to get in a little musical culture while in Florence. The whole affair is low-key, with no touts or other annoying elements that usually go hand-in-hand with such performances (like in Venice and Vienna). Quality is variable, but on the whole a night of faves (such as *The Four Seasons*, a little Bach or Paganini) can make for a pleasant evening out.

TEATRO COMUNALE Map pp244–5
☎ 800 11 22 11; Corso Italia 12; bus B
Concerts, opera and dance are performed at various times of the year here, on the northern bank of the Arno. In May and June the theatre hosts **Maggio Musicale Fiorentina** (www.maggiofiorentino.com), an international concert festival. Contact the theatre's box office.

TEATRO DELLA PERGOLA Map pp246–7
☎ 055 247 96 51; Via della Pergola 18; bus C
The **Amici della Musica** (☎ 055 60 84 20) organises classical music concerts and recitals, often featuring prestigious international performers, in this theatre from January to April and October to December.

TEATRO VERDI Map pp248–50
☎ 055 21 23 20; www.teatroverdifirenze.it; Via Ghibellina 101; tickets €7-12 for classical music concerts; 🕒 Oct-Apr; bus 14 & A
For decades this classic 19th-century theatre has been the focal point of classical music, drama, opera, and dance. It is the permanent home of the Orchestra della Toscana. Most performances start around 8.30pm.

THEATRE & DANCE

The theatre season runs from October into April/May. Which is not to say that Florence comes to a standstill, but many of the main stages stay quiet while more festive cultural events take centre billing in summer. See p9 and the boxed text, p147.

The theatres mentioned in the Classical Music & Opera section also frequently stage drama. You will find productions at these and several other smaller theatres dotted about town advertised in *Firenze Spettacolo*. Most theatre is in Italian.

EX-STAZIONE LEOPOLDA Map p254
☎ 055 247 83 32; Viale Fratelli Rosselli 5; bus 1, 9, 12, 13, 16, 26, 27, 80 & B
One of the council's smarter ideas some years back was to convert this former train station (near the Cascine) into several performance spaces. Mostly avant-garde theatre is featured, although occasionally concerts are put on too. It comes into full swing in summer. For programmes and tickets go to Box Office (see p151) or any of the tourist offices in Florence.

TEATRO DELLA LIMONAIA Map p254
☎ 055 44 08 52; www.teatro-limonaia.fi.it, Italian only; Via Gramsci 426, Sesto Fiorentino; admission €6-10; bus 2 & 28A
This place, well beyond the centre of Florence, is one of the leading avant-garde theatres in Italy. It puts on a wide variety of new drama (pretty much all in Italian) and also runs a series of small theatre spaces elsewhere in the city. Take the bus from Stazione di Santa Maria Novella.

SPORTS, HEALTH & FITNESS

Travellers may not be flocking to Florence for sports games, but to watch the local football team in action, you can purchase tickets at the footbal stadium, Chiosco degli Sportivi (see p153) or Ticket One (p151).

CYCLING

Cycling around Florence and across Tuscany is becoming increasingly popular. In Florence, ask for a copy of *Viaggio in Toscana – Discovering Tuscany by Bike* at the APT office. For details of where to rent a bike see p205, or for bike tours outside of Florence, see p63.

Rowing towards Ponte Vecchio

FOOTBALL

Your average Florentine is as passionate about football as the next Italian, but their side, **AC Fiorentina** (which only recently re-acquired its traditional name after the club's scandal-ridden collapse in 2002), has known more downs than ups recently. Relegated to Serie B (second division), the club is slowly trying to climb back into the black and the big league. For more on the club's story, see Sport in the City Life chapter (p15).

If, in spite of the team's poor fortunes, you wish to see a game, tickets are available directly at the **Stadio Comunale Artemio Franchi** (Map pp244–5; ☎ 055 58 78 58; Campo di Marte) or at the **Chiosco degli Sportivi** ticket outlet (Map pp251–3; ☎ 055 29 23 63; Via Anselmi, just off Piazza della Repubblica; ☺ 9am-1pm & 3pm-6pm Mon, Tue & Thu, 9am-7.30pm Wed, 9am-7pm Fri, 9am-1pm & 3pm-8pm Sat, 10am-12.30pm Sun). While you're at it you can have a flutter on the Totocalcio, or football pools.

GYM

A handful of gyms around central Florence will allow you to work off a little extra sweat.

PALESTRA RICCIARDI Map pp246–7
☎ 055 247 84 62; Borgo Pinti 75; admission €10; ☺ 9am-10pm Mon-Fri, 9.30am-6pm Sat (4.30-9.30pm Mon-Fri Aug); bus C
Pump weights, attach yourself to exercise machines or join a class at this central gym.

ROWING

Should you wind up staying in Florence for any length of time, a wonderful way to keep fit and meet locals is to join one of the city's rowing clubs. The cost of joining either of the main clubs that indulge in river activities is prohibitive if you don't plan to stay in the city for at least a couple of months.

SOCIETÀ CANOTTIERI FIRENZE
Map pp251–3
☎ 055 28 21 30; www.canottierifirenze.it, Italian only; Lungarno Anna Marisa Luisa de' Medici 8; ☺ office 10am-1pm & 2pm-5pm Mon-Fri; bus B
Of the two clubs, this one is handier for the centre, with impressive installations virtually under the Uffizi. Apart from joining rowing classes, you can use its small pool and gym if you become a full member (a rather costly exercise). A four-month rowing course costs €160.

SOCIETÀ CANOTTIERI COMUNALI

Map pp244–5

☎ 055 681 21 51; www.canottiericomunalifirenze.it; Lungarno Francesco Ferrucci 6; ⏰ office 3pm-6pm Tue & Thu; bus 12, 13, 23 & C

Nonresidents can take out a three-month membership for €200 (renewable once). Courses in skull-rowing are available for beginners, as are canoeing courses. You can use the canoes and skulls as well as the club facilities (showers etc).

SWIMMING POOLS

In the scorching summer months a dip in a pool can come as welcome relief. From mid-September to June is winter for Florentine pools and gaining access becomes rather complicated. You have to take out one-month (or longer) subscriptions and access is restricted to certain times on no more than four days a week. Pathetic, as most Florentines would agree.

PISCINA LE PAVONIERE Map pp244–5

☎ 055 36 22 33; Viale della Catena 2; admission €7; ⏰ 10am-6pm Jun–mid-Sep; bus 1, 9, 12, 13, 16, 26, 27, 80 & B

The pool, Florence's most attractive, opens late into the night on some summer evenings and has a pizzeria and bar.

PISCINA NANNINI Map pp244–5

☎ 055 67 75 21; Lungarno Aldo Moro 6; adult €6.50 or book of 10 tickets €45; ⏰ 10am-6.30pm & 8-11.30pm Jun-Aug; bus 14 & 34

In summer, when they pull back the movable roof over the Olympic-size pool, it becomes a watery haven on those torrid Florentine days. Opening times tend to change from month to month; it's a good idea to ring up and check.

TENNIS

CAMPO SPORTIVO ASSI Map pp248–50

☎ 055 68 78 58, Viale Michelangelo 64; €12.50 per hour; 8am-10.30pm Mon-Fri, 8am-7pm Sat, 8am-2pm Sun; bus 12 & 13

This is a pleasant spot to book a court (but not equipment) for a bit of therapeutic ball bashing – a great antidote for *stendhalismo*.

1 Combining two of Florence's great loves, the Galleria degli Uffizi (p81) and a football match on the river bank **2** The calmness of the River Arno, towards Ponte Santa Trinita, disguises its dramatic history (p17) **3** Chilling out with a book at the Ponte Vecchio (p109) **4** Like bees to a honey pot, visitors flock to the Duomo (p75)

1 One of Florence's best cafés, Rivoire (p129), is situated at Piazza della Signoria 2 A tantalizing selection of wines from the Chianti region (pp167) 3 Fast-food Florence style is a lampredotto (boiled veal tripe on a bread roll) bought at a mobile stand called a trippaio (p131) 4 Assorted sweet tooth temptations at Gilli (p129), one of the grand café terraces

1 Da Il Latini (p130) is the place to eat for Tuscan food 2 An impressive range of cheeses is just one of the delicacies to be enjoyed in Florence (p128) 3 Having a relaxing pranzo (lunch) at the limitless choice of restaurants 4 Gelateria Vivoli even serves rice-pudding flavoured gelati (p139)

1 Dining alfresco and people-watching go hand in hand
2 Piazza Santo Spirito (p142) is the headquarters of laid-back Florentines **3** Shakin' all over at Capocaccia (p144) **4** Cycling around the sights of Florence (p152)

1 Football team AC Fiorentina's scandalous history resembles an Italian opera (p14) **2** Porto di Mare bar hosts live gigs ranging from jazz to world music (p148)
3 Arty Rex Caffè is a hip place to be for the cocktail set (p145)
4 Playing a football match (p153) on the banks of the River Arno

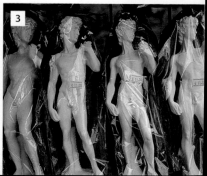

1 Florence is renowned for its elegant stationery and paper products (p167) 2 Fare bella figure ('to look good') is ensured at the best fashion boutiques 3 A chorus line of Michelangelo's David at Mercato Nuovo (p171) 4 At shopping strips near the Piazza del Duomo, sophistication and retail are synonymous

1 Treasure chests of gold jewellery are available in the Ponte Vecchio shops (p167) 2 Contemplating items on offer at the daily markets of San Lorenzo (p171) 3 The shop with the famous surname, Luca della Robbia (p168), has opened its doors since the 19th century 4 Baroque-style crafts can be found around Sante Croce (p173)

1 The Siena Duomo (p192) is one of Italy's great Gothic churches 2 Picturesque vineyards near Greve in Chianti (p194) 3 The exterior Romanesque mosaic on Chiesa di San Frediano in Lucca (p199) is spectacular 4 Experts reckon the Leaning Tower (Torre Pendente) of Pisa (p197) is safe for another 300 years

Shopping

Shopping

Your credit-card Geiger counter is likely to start pulsating in alarming fashion as you near Florence. Suckers for style and lovers of luxury are going to have a hard time resisting the goodies on display in all those alluring shop windows. Name-droppers and label-seekers may well find themselves permanently distracted from all the Renaissance art and architecture and spend most of their time paying homage in Florence's many temples of high fashion.

As a rule, the experience doesn't come cheap. Italians from other parts of the country can be heard sighing, with much shaking of heads, as they bemoan Florentine prices. Florence is one of Italy's homes of fashion and any label worth its name from other parts of the country has also made sure it has a presence here. The quality is undoubtedly good and the prices generally match. Still, hunting around the markets for leather items can sometimes turn up a bargain, as might a trip to the increasingly popular discount outlets outside Florence.

What to Buy

Clothes, shoes, accessories and leather goods lead the way to your retail undoing. Local boys Gucci, Pucci and Ferragamo are joined by a host of labels you'll recognise (and some you might not). One thing you should not expect is outrageous or avant-garde threads. Florentines are a fairly conservative lot at heart and prefer classic style over zany innovation. If you are of a similar mind, you can come away from the Arno with a suitcase full of clobber that will last through the vagaries of transient trends.

The same goes for shoes and leather. Whether you seek out your footwear in a workshop in Oltrarno or at a high fashion store around Via de' Tornabuoni, you can be sure your new shoes are made to last. That said, each season in Italy brings some new and at times slightly off-the-wall novelty and soon lots of people are wearing the latest look in shoes. You can join them if you will, but beware that the year after it will be seen as last year's oddity rather than a fashion statement.

As Florence tried to pick itself up by the bootstraps in the wake of WWII, local leather workshops began to crank out all sorts of goods. The process accelerated with the increase in tourism in the 1960s and for a while the city had a name for low-priced, high-quality leather goods. At the top end of the market the quality remains exceptional but the bargain days are largely a matter of wistful memory. However, the city *is* jammed with leather. If only for the sheer quantity and choice it is worth looking around. And it can be fun to hunt in the leather markets, such as Mercato Nuovo and around San Lorenzo (p171), and the shops of Santa Croce (p173), as you can sometimes turn up a reasonable deal. Make like you're in a Middle Eastern *souq* and always bargain (prices in the markets drop considerably under the merest whiff of bargaining pressure) and keep your eyes peeled for defects in the production.

It's Sale Time

The serious shopper will find a greater range and probably better prices in Milan, the real fashion capital of the country. Those who don't have the time or inclination to include Milan in their trip should watch out for the sales. The winter sales start shortly after New Year and can go on into February. The summer sales start in July, with stores trying to entice Florentines to part with one last wad of euros before they flood out of the city on holiday in August. Some shops prolong their sales to the end of August.

For those with unlimited bank accounts, gold and jewellery might be an option. Back in 1563, Grand Duke Ferdinando I ordered that goldsmiths install themselves in the shops of the Ponte Vecchio. He had decided that enough was enough – for centuries butchers and greengrocers had sold meat and veggies to the good citizens of Florence on the bridge (and dumped rubbish in the river below) but now they had to go. The stench and rotting mess of dead flesh was not for central Florence, rather the glamour of all that glitters. The gold merchants haven't budged since.

Souvenirs from Florence

In line with its reputation for style, Florence has a name for elegant stationery and paper products. This could be the place to look if you want to turn back the clock and do a little high-class letter writing.

Florence is graced with a fair sprinkling of private art galleries, but many deal in a staid diet of typical 'Tuscan' scenes and the like. Don't expect to run into anything particularly forward-looking.

Ceramics are also worth considering. Various shops about the city turn out highly distinctive pottery and porcelain, from practical vases to purely decorative items. Florence itself is not particularly known for its ceramics, but in the nearby town of Montelupo, west along the Arno, the locals have been pottering about since the Middle Ages. A good deal of their stuff makes its way to Florentine stores.

And the food and drink! Gourmet lovers should trail around some of the specialist food and wine stores. Florence offers a cornucopia of goods designed to tantalise the palate, as you may have already noticed at the city's dinner tables. For your personal supply of Brunello, truffles and homemade pasta, how can you pass up an opportunity like this?

Finally, there is no shortage of tourist tat. Some of us are suckers for the stuff. Anything from I Love Florence T-shirts to snow-scenes (those little models of the Duomo encased in plastic that you turn upside down to make it snow) can be picked up in shops around the centre of town. Or what about your very own David statuette-cum-pencil-sharpener?

Shopping Areas

The medieval heart of Florence is mainly dedicated to fashion, with the streets of **Via de' Tornabuoni** and **Via della Vigna Nuova** (Map pp251–3) the altar of *haute couture*. There you'll find more designer shops than you could shake a gold card at.

Many Florentines head to **Borgo San Lorenzo** (Map pp251–3) for their shoes, although you will also find some quality shoe stores on another major shopping street, **Via Roma** (Map pp251–3). Santa Croce is the heart of the leather merchants' district (see the **Scuola del Cuoio**, p174). Streets near **Piazza della Signoria**, **Borgo de' Greci** and **Via de' Gondi** (pp167–9) in particular are lined with leather shops and stands of every possible description (and quality). Leather stands are also abundant in the outdoor market around the **Basilica di San Lorenzo** and at **Mercato Nuovo** (p171) – buyer beware.

Borgo Ognissanti, Via de' Fossi and Via Maggio (Map pp248–50) are the antique strips, while the whole area of Oltrarno abounds with traditional artisans' shops and studios, cherished by locals and turning out everything from shoes to jewels.

Ponte Vecchio (Map pp251–3) is laden with gold and jewellery stores, although goldsmiths no longer actually work in them. To find higher quality jewellers and artisans, you'll need to get off the bridge and search about; a few options appear in this chapter.

Top Five Shopping Areas

- **Antiques** Borgo Ognissanti & Around (Map pp248–50)
- **Gold** Ponte Vecchio & Around (Map pp251–3)
- **High Fashion** Via de' Tornabuoni & Around (Map pp251–3)
- **Leather** Santa Croce (Map pp248–50)
- **Shoes** Borgo San Lorenzo & Oltrarno (Maps pp248–50 & pp251–3)

How to Shop

Florentine shopkeepers will try to sell you anything they can, from extreme kitsch to serious art. One basic rule applies to all purchases – shop around before making your mind up.

When shopping in the markets, haggle. Paying the asking price is not only bad karma but makes things tougher for everyone else! Haggling won't get you anywhere in a department store but you'd be surprised how often you can wangle a discount in many fashion stores. Just asking 'is that the best price you can do?' will sometimes produce surprising effects. In many central Florence stores you can go ahead and do so in English as at least some shop employees speak it well enough to more than fully understand such market banter.

If you're dizzy at the fashion boutique prices but would still like to invest in some clothes, there are a couple of options. Do what many locals do and visit the department stores, like La Rinascente (p168) and COIN (p168). These don't necessarily carry many big label items but you can often find good quality clothing at quite reasonable prices. Another fun option is to explore the so-called 'stock houses', loaded with brand name cast-offs.

Heavy, cumbersome and fragile items (such as ceramics and some antiques) need to be shipped home. Many stores will take care of this for you and include the costs of shipping in the price. Ask before you buy as shipping it yourself can be a pain. If you do find yourself with something that you need to ship, head for the central post office (Map pp251–3).

Opening Hours

In general, shops are open 9am to 1pm and 3.30pm to 7.30pm (or 4pm to 8pm) Monday to Saturday. Many shops remain closed on Monday morning (which can mean until about 4pm). Others close on Wednesday and/or Saturday afternoon. Laws on opening hours are fairly flexible so shopkeepers have a large degree of discretion. Although the summer sales keep many shops busy through July and into early August, many take off at least part of the latter month.

Department stores such as La Rinascente, COIN and most supermarkets are open around 9.30am to 7.30pm Monday to Saturday. Some even open 9am to 1pm on Sunday.

PIAZZA DEL DUOMO & AROUND

Only a few steps from the grand cathedral, spend your hard-earned on classic watches, fine food and ceramics.

ARTE CRETA Map pp251–3   *Ceramics*
☎ 055 28 43 41; Via del Proconsolo 63/r; bus 14, 23 & A
Elisabetta di Costanzo turns out some original work, breaking with tradition in her use of pre-

dominantly green floral scenes on the majority of the objects for sale. They make a refreshing change from the usual stuff.

CARNICELLI
Map pp251–3   *Photographic Equipment*
☎ 055 21 43 52; Piazza del Duomo 4r; bus 1, 6, 7, 10, 11, 14, 17, 23 & A
For serious photography needs, traditional and digital, you could try this central camera emporium. It also provides the standard services.

DISNEY STORE Map pp251–3 *Toys*
☎ 055 29 16 33; Via de' Calzaiuoli 69/r; bus A

Probably shouldn't mention this highly un-Italian shop, but kids seem to love it. If you need to mollify the little darlings, perhaps this is one method of bribery that will work.

EDISON Map pp251–3 *Books*
☎ 055 21 31 10; Piazza della Repubblica 27/r;
🕐 9am-11pm; bus A

A grand array of Italian literature on Florence and Tuscany and some foreign-language books arranged over three floors and open extra-long hours.

EXPERIMENTA Map pp251–3 *Perfume*
☎ 055 21 03 94; Via dello Studio 25/r; bus A

Fancy a chocolate or coffee wash? Get your tasty-smelling bath foam, and other less unusual perfume products here.

FRATELLI ROSSETTI Map pp251–3 *Shoes*
☎ 055 21 66 56; Piazza della Repubblica 43-45; bus A

For one of the last words in classic elegant footwear made to last a lifetime, you should have a browse here.

LA GALLERIA DEL CHIANTI
Map pp251–3 *Wine*
☎ 055 29 14 40; Via del Corso 41/r; bus A

In spite of the name, this shop has on its shelves a selection of fine wines from around Tuscany, as well as top-quality drops (such as Poli Grappa from Bassano del Grappa in the Veneto region) from other parts of the country.

LUISA Map pp251–3 *Clothes*
☎ 055 21 78 26; Via Roma 19-21/r; bus A

For quality men's and women's clothing of a none-too-daring but classic and self-assuring cut, this is a regular stop on Florence's shopping circuit.

OFFICINE PANERAI
Map pp251–3 *Watches*
☎ 055 21 57 95; Piazza San Giovanni 16/r; bus 1, 6, 7, 10, 11, 14, 17, 23 & A

This purveyor of watches has a special place in Italian hearts. The watches were first produced for Italy's navy divers in WWII. Nowadays the chunky nautical timepieces are collectors' items that can easily cost €3000. Upstairs from the store is a small archive with WWII photos of Italian navy commandos and their deadly (often for their crew) little manned torpedos.

PEGNA Map pp251–3 *Food & Drink*
☎ 055 28 27 01; Via dello Studio 26/r; bus A

Pegna's has an interesting selection of Tuscan wines and Italian produce, such as bottled *ribollita* (vegetable stew). It's pricey, so don't go buying your De Cecco pasta (which you can get in any supermarket) here.

RASPINI Map pp251–3 *Clothes*
☎ 055 21 30 77; Via Roma 25-29/r; bus A

A classic Florentine purveyor of fine footwear, with an enticing range of quality fashion for both sexes. There are branches elsewhere too.

RICORDI MEDIASTORE
Map pp251–3 *Music*
☎ 055 21 41 04; Via de' Brunelleschi 8/r; bus A

This nationwide chain store is Italy's vague equivalent of Virgin or HMV. It stocks a solid range of Italian and international CDs and tapes. It also stocks sheet music.

SERGIO ROSSI Map pp251–3 *Shoes*
☎ 055 29 48 73; Via Roma 15; bus A

For women after footwear that's adventurous (but not outrageous), this is the place to visit. Extra pointy, impossibly high and a sometimes aggressive cut can make a statement about the person attached to the feet in the shoes.

PIAZZA DELLA SIGNORIA & AROUND

A mixed bag of shops is scattered around the medieval streets surrounding Piazza della Signoria. Everything from camera equipment through food and wine to jewellery and stationery wait to be discovered.

BARTOLUCCI Map pp251–3 *Crafts*
☎ 055 21 17 73; www.bartolucci.com; Via della Condotta 12/r; bus A

The Bartolucci clan uses pine to create a remarkable range of toys, models and trinkets that may appeal as much to adults as to kids.

BOTTEGA DELL'OLIO
Map pp251–3 *Olive Oil Products*
☎ 055 26704 68; Piazza del Limbo 2/r; bus A

Only the best of central Italy's extra virgin olive oil arrives in this tiny store tucked away in an equally tiny square. There is also aromatic oils, olive soap (the best imported from Aleppo, Syria) and balsamic vinegar.

Taking Stock

Vertigo-inducing prices can take the fun out of fashion. If you can't afford the name shops and can't be bothered heading out of town to the discount outlets, you have another option. Lots of fallen-off-the-back-of-a-rack clothing is crammed into so-called stockhouses, real rag-trade stores stuffed to the rafters in generally disorderly fashion with all sorts of goodies. Finding something you like can take a little time but that can be part of the fun. A couple of handy stores are:

Stockhouse Il Giglio (Map pp246–7; ☎ 055 21 75 96; Borgo Ognissanti 86/r; bus A) Cheap is a relative term in Florence, but you can pick up some interesting men's and women's fashion items here and occasionally turn up some genuine bargains. Name labels can come in at a considerable discount. Florentines consider it one of the best 'stockhouses' for picking up labelled items at off-the-back-of-a-lorry rates.

Stockhouse Il Guardaroba (Map pp248–50; ☎ 055 234 02 71; Borgo Albizi 78/r; bus A) Across town, this is another spot worth dropping by, although the range is not as great. The place is arranged more like a standard fashion boutique than a higgledy-piggledy threads lucky dip. There is another branch at Via Giuseppe Verdi 28/r (Map pp248–50).

Stockhouse One Price (Map pp248–50; ☎ 055 28 46 74; Borgo Ognissanti 74/r; bus A) Although more densely stocked (in a smaller space) than the others, the idea basically remains the same.

COIN Map pp251–3   *Department Store*
☎ 055 28 05 31; Via de' Calzaiuoli 56/r; bus A
A slightly downmarket version of La Rinascente, this is the place for practical shopping that most visitors probably won't need to do while in Florence. You could look at the clothes department. It's strictly standard stuff, but the standards are Italian and you can find some quality gear at prices Marks & Spencer could not afford to consider.

ENOTECA ROMANO GAMBI
Map pp251–3   *Food & Drink*
☎ 055 29 26 46; Borgo SS Apostoli 21-23/r; bus B
A quality foodstuffs and wine outlet, this *enoteca* claims to sell the 'best Tuscan biscuits', among a broad selection of other products ranging from wine and olive oil to chocolate. The prices are not exactly rock bottom, but the place is at least worth a browse.

EPT Map pp251–3   *Books*
☎ 055 29 45 51; Via della Condotta 42/r; bus A
In the centre of town this shop has a fair range of travel books, maps and so on, with tons of stuff on Florence and Tuscany. .

FESTINA LENTE EDIZIONI
Map pp251–3   *Paper & Stationery*
☎ 055 29 26 12; Via della Condotta 18/r; bus A
For unusual stationery and postcards, including exercise books with silk-print covers, this is a curious stop.

IL GATTO BIANCO Map pp251–3   *Jewellery*
☎ 055 28 29 89; Borgo dei SS Apostoli 12/r; bus B

Get off the Ponte Vecchio and you can do better by your bank manager. Here at the White Cat, an attractive back-street jewellery workshop, you can pick up all sorts of wonderful and affordable jewellery. Contemporary designs incorporate gold, silver and semiprecious stones.

LANZO CAFFÈ Map p252–3   *Food & Drink*
☎ 055 29 08 34; Via dei Neri 69r; bus B
This shop offers a mix of attractively packaged foodstuffs, such as *panforte* ('strong bread', made of almonds, candied fruit, spices and honey) and various regional products like honey – as well as a wine selection from Tuscany and beyond.

LA RINASCENTE
Map pp251–3   *Department Store*
☎ 055 239 85 44; Piazza della Repubblica 1; bus A
The prince of Italian department stores, the Florence branch is rather modest but worth a look around for fashion, perfumes and similar items.

LUCA DELLA ROBBIA
Map pp251–3   *Ceramics*
☎ 055 28 35 32; Via del Proconsolo 19/r; bus 14, 23 & A
Since the end of the 19th century this shop with the famous surname has been creating handmade reproductions of *robbiane* (terracotta medallions). They also offer a broader range of more general ceramics.

MANETTI & MASINI Map pp251–3 *Ceramics*
☎ 055 21 22 54; Borgo SS Apostoli 45/r; bus B
Since 1948 this classic ceramic store has been producing top-quality porcelain, specialising

in reproduction antique majolica and restoring the genuine articles. Tucked away just off chic Via de' Tornabuoni, you could easily miss it.

PINEIDER
Map pp251–3   *Paper & Stationery*
☎ 055 28 46 55; Piazza della Signoria 13/r; bus B
Purveyors of paper and related products, Pineider has been in business since 1774. If you want to purchase a gift of stationery, this is the city's class act. In an age where handwriting is a rapidly dying art, the store has extended its range into all sorts of quality office materials.

VETTORI Map pp251–3   *Gold & Jewellery*
☎ 055 28 20 30; Ponte Vecchio 37/r; bus B, C & D
One of the big names weighing down the Ponte Vecchio with its treasure chests of gold. You can order pieces to be handcrafted but be aware that none of the Ponte Vecchio stores is a workshop any more – they buy and sell the stuff and generally have the work done elsewhere. Look for other off-bridge jewellers mentioned in this chapter for some creative inspiration (see p168 and p173).

SANTA MARIA NOVELLA & AROUND
The area between the basilica and the Arno is a particularly rich hunting ground. Via de' Tornabuoni is at the heart of high-fashion shopping – all your favourite names cluster here. If you get sick of threads, you can inject a little variety by checking out the purveyors of classy leather goods, antiques, gourmet snacks and a couple of good bookshops.

BIAGIOTTI Map pp251–3   *Art Gallery*
☎ 055 29 42 65; Via delle Belle Donne 39/r; bus A
For truly adventurous art exhibitions, this place, tucked away in a street named after the one-time trade in pearly-hawking that went on here, is well worth checking out.

BM BOOKSHOP Map pp251–3   *Books*
☎ 055 29 45 75; Borgo Ognissanti 4/r; bus A
This bookshop claims to have the broadest range of books in English in town and it may be true. You can find a fair spread of books on Florence and Tuscany, as well as speciality books on art and fiction.

The Ferragamos' Fluctuating Fortunes
Born in 1898 outside Naples, Salvatore Ferragamo made his first pair of shoes for his sister's first communion at the age of nine. They must have been good, because four years later he was already in charge of a shoe shop with six workers.

Ferragamo was hoping for bigger things and he moved to the USA in 1914. After a brief stint in Boston with his brothers, he headed across to Hollywood, where he started designing shoes and boots for the film industry – everything from Egyptian sandals to cowboy boots. From there it was a short step to making footwear for the stars when they were off the screen, and he began to build up an elite clientele, from Mary Pickford to John Barrymore.

When he returned to Italy in the early 1930s, Ferragamo set up a 'factory' in Via Mannelli in Florence with 60 employees all making certain parts of the shoes by hand. Ferragamo designed and created the shoes in Florence and sold them in the USA. That all went fine until the Great Depression hit and brought bankruptcy in 1933. By the time he had business up and running again, his clientele had become largely local. He was still creating new designs, including the cork wedge, which he patented in 1936.

In 1938 Ferragamo bought the Palazzo Spini-Ferroni on Via de' Tornabuoni, where he had already moved his shop. The war years were difficult and Ferragamo did not resume exporting beyond Italy until 1947. By the 1950s he had 700 employees producing 350 pairs of shoes per day entirely by hand. The glitterati, Italian and foreign, were again flocking to his store. Everyone from Audrey Hepburn to Sophia Loren was wearing Ferragamo's designs.

Salvatore died in 1960 and his wife, Wanda, took over. Under her and Fiamma, the eldest of their six children, the Ferragamo label was attached to a growing range of women's fashion accessories. Fiamma in particular was responsible for the expansion of production. She abandoned the policy of producing the shoes by hand. By the time Fiamma died in 1998, the company had a turnover of more than US$500 million.

In the years since, the Ferragamo family has not sat on its laurels. After launching a line in children's fashion, the big news was the opening of flagship stores in Tokyo and, shortly after, New York's Fifth Ave.

BOJOLA Map pp248–50   *Leather*
☎ 055 21 11 55; Via de' Rondinelli 25/r; bus 6, 11, 22, 36, 37 & A
For more than 150 years Bojola has been turning out high-quality items for the discerning

Boots and T-shirts at San Lorenzo Market (p171)

Shopping – Santa Maria Novella & Around

psychedelic colours, pop into the shop. Just looking at his women's fashions and accessories (anything from swimwear to umbrellas) will make you think you have dropped acid.

FERRAGAMO Map pp251–3   *Clothes*
☎ 055 29 21 23; Via de' Tornabuoni 14/r; bus 6, 11, 36, 37 & A

Another grand Florentine name (see the boxed text, p169), the one-time shoe specialist now turns out a range of clothes and accessories for the serious fashion aficionado, man, woman or child. It also has a curious shoe museum – see p91.

GALLERIA TORNABUONI
Map pp251–3   *Art Gallery*
☎ 055 28 47 20; Via de' Tornabuoni 74/r; bus 6, 11, 22, 36, 37 & A

Although it doesn't completely turn its back on mainstream tastes, this art gallery on Florence's chic street occasionally lets its hair down a little with curious contemporary work.

GUCCI Map pp251–3   *Clothes*
☎ 055 26 40 11; Via de' Tornabuoni 73/r; bus 6, 11, 22, 36, 37 & A

Only the name remains of the great Florentine fashion house. Of course the soap-opera family saga has put a lot of spice into Gucci (see the boxed text, p13) but the fashion-conscious take little notice and keep on buying. The Japanese especially can be seen lining up to pay homage.

HOUSE OF FLORENCE Map pp251–3 *Clothes*
☎ 055 28 81 62; Via de' Tornabuoni 6; bus 6, 11, 36, 37 & A

Here you can spend upwards of €60 on a leather belt or silk tie and other conservative handmade clothes and accessories for the well-lined. In fact you are warned of this as you reach the heart of the shop by a little sign reminding you that one never forgets quality but soon forgets the price paid for it.

IL BISONTE Map pp251–3   *Leather*
☎ 055 21 57 22; Via del Parione 31/r; bus A

Here the concentration is on accessories, ranging from elegant bags in natural leather to distinguished desktop items, leather-bound notebooks, briefcases etc.

LIBRAIRIE FRANÇAISE
Map pp248–50   *Books*
☎ 055 21 26 59; Piazza d'Ognissanti 1/r; bus A

lover of animal hides. From classic belts and wallets (which start at around €40) to classy travel bags, this is one of Florence's top stops in the search for fine leather gifts.

CASADEI Map pp251–3   *Shoes*
☎ 055 28 72 40; Via de' Tornabuoni 33/r; bus 6, 11, 22, 36, 37 & A

An interesting one for ladies on the lookout for shoes. You can go to town with the plastic on classically stylish knee-high boots or let your imagination fly a little on all sorts of shoes in a surprising (for this fairly conservative town) range of primary colours and angular design.

DESMO Map pp251–3   *Leather*
☎ 055 29 23 95; Piazza de' Rucellai 10; bus 6 & A

For those with full wallets, and perhaps the desire to replace them with a new one, this is a good address for leather accessories and a range of clothes as well.

EMILIO PUCCI Map pp251–3   *Clothes*
☎ 055 29 40 28; Via de' Tornabuoni 20-22; bus 6, 11, 22, 36, 37 & A

The marquis Emilio Pucci is not only a Florentine aristocrat but was a big clothes designer for the jet set back in the 1960s. Since the 1990s the name has again been up among the bright lights of Italian fashion. He keeps his *haute couture* stuff at home but for his 1960s-revisited

Housed within the city's French cultural institute, this is easily the best place for French texts, with a range of books on Florence and Tuscany and a welter of Gallic prose.

L'IPPOGRIFO Map pp251–3   *Books*
☎ 055 29 08 05; Via della Vigna Nuova 5/r; bus 6 & A
Lovers of old and rare books, maps and manuscripts should mosey around here. You may not want to buy but the place is laden with curios redolent of other, less frenetic times.

LORETTA CAPONI Map pp251–3   *Clothes*
☎ 055 21 36 68; Piazza degli Antinori 4/r; bus 6, 11, 22, 36, 37 & A
If nothing is too good for your infant or small child, particularly girls, this store sells exquisite small persons' clothing (and a few things for big people too), some of it finely embroidered. Your three-year-old may not fully appreciate it, but be assured they will be dressed to impress when they leave here.

NEUBER Map pp251–3   *Clothes*
☎ 055 21 57 63; Via de' Tornabuoni 17; bus 6, 11, 22, 36, 37 & A
Here is another Mecca of Florentine class for men and women who want to cut an elegant swathe through life. Cuts are classic and will last through many a swanky night out.

OFFICINA PROFUMO FARMACEUTICA DI SANTA MARIA NOVELLA
Map pp246–7   *Pharmacy & Perfumes*
☎ 055 21 62 76; Via della Scala 16; bus 11, 36, 37 & A
This ancient pharmacy, set up by Dominican monks in the 13th century, opened to the public in the 17th century. When Napoleon confiscated Church property early in the 19th century, the business went into private hands, in which it has continued to prosper. All sorts of traditional and herbal potions made to recipes handed down by the monks through to the present owners treat everything from sore feet to bad breath. Need any *amamelide* (witch hazel) or *iperico* (St John's Wort)? Extract of heliotrope? This is the place for you. From the entrance you pass through a long hall to the 'pharmacy', a magnificent room with a high vaulted and frescoed ceiling. Here you buy mainly essences and perfumes. Pass on to the *erboristeria* (natural medicine shop), which backs onto the cloister of the Basilica di Santa Maria Novella, for your herbal remedies.

PROCACCI Map pp251–3   *Food & Drink*
☎ 055 21 16 56; Via de' Tornabuoni 64/r; bus 6, 11, 22, 36, 37 & A
Come to nibble and sip (see p130) or buy stuff to take away, from fine Tuscan wines to homemade honey and jams. The star is the truffle.

Milling in Markets

The daily markets of **San Lorenzo** (Map pp252–3; Piazza San Lorenzo) and **Il Mercato Nuovo** (Map pp251–3; also known as Mercato del Porcellino, or Piglet's Market) are the most visible in town, and the curious but uncommitted shopper can enjoy a rather tacky browse at either any day of the week. Next to the predictable stocks of cheap (and sometimes nasty) leather gear are phalanxes of tourist tat and other far-from-useful paraphernalia. To get the feel for a real Florentine market, you need to look elsewhere.

Mercato Centrale (Piazza del Mercato Centrale; Map pp246–7; ☺ 7am-2pm Mon-Sat) This, the main daily-produce market, is under cover in the 19th-century market hall. Outside are all the leather and tat stalls of San Lorenzo.

Mercato dei Pulci (Piazza dei Ciompi; Map pp248–50; ☺ Mon-Sat & last Sun of the month) This flea market is where the townsfolk gather to poke about amid the mountains of junk and bric-a-brac that every self-respecting household should be able to cough up sooner or later. From antique furniture to ancient comic books, all sorts of junk turns up here. It's fun for a browse and occasionally you'll find genuinely interesting little items.

Mercato dell'Antiquariato (Piazza Santo Spirito; Map pp248–50; ☺ 2nd Sun of the month) A cheerful little antiques market with all sorts of odds and ends is held in this delightful square.

Mercato delle Cascine (The Cascine, Viale Abramo Lincoln; Map pp244–5; ☺ 8am-noon Tue) This is Florence's only all-in-one market. Sufficiently far from the city centre to put most tourists off, it specialises in off-the-back-of-a-lorry clothes and fabrics, along with other household products and a modest produce section. Some Florentines come here in search of bargains.

Mercato di Sant'Ambrogio (Piazza Ghiberti; Map pp248–50; ☺ 7am-2pm Mon-Sat) Buzzy and without the tourist-tat element, this produce market is the best place to do your daily hunting for fresh products, from fruit and veg to all sorts of local cheeses, sausages and other goodies.

You can obtain white truffles here in season or content yourself with a *panino tartufato* (little bread roll with truffle spread).

SHOWROOM FRATELLI ALINARI

Map pp251–3   *Photography, Old Prints & Books*

☎ 055 2 39 51; www.alinari.com; Largo Fratelli Alinari 15; bus 4, 12, 25 & 33

Head down the arcaded lane to get to the showroom of Florence's fathers of photography. The Alinari brothers got the world's first photographic store up and running in 1852.

Today you can get a hold of grand coffee-table books featuring photos of 19th-century Florence and other locations around Italy. It also stocks wonderful prints.

SAN LORENZO AREA

The main shopping attraction is the stands set up just outside the basilica. If you dare, bargain for a leather jacket of potentially dubious origins and quality, or just have fun watching others haggle. A couple of interesting speciality stores are worth checking out.

Outlets for Your Every Desire...

Champagne tastes on a beer budget? If you want the high-fashion look of central Florence without the price tag, you may be able to satisfy your modish retail cravings if you flee the metropolis. Southeast of Florence are clustered several discount outlets for big names in fashion. These basically sell off last year's fashion at more reasonable prices than you can hope to find in their Florence stores. The ranges are not always wonderful but you can come away with bargains on name goods. The phenomenon has grown over the years and you can find information on the following and more still on www.outlet-firenze.com.

Dolce & Gabbana (☎ 055 833 13 00; Località Santa Maria Maddalena, Via Piana dell'Isola 49, Rignano sull'Arno; ☺ 9am-7pm Mon-Sat, 3-7pm Sun) Mostly interesting for accessories, it is really only worth coming here if you have your own transport, as it is close to The Mall. In itself, it does not warrant the effort from Florence if you are relying on public transport. Less than 1km south of Leccio, turn right (follow the Fendi Outlet signs) and you arrive at a T-junction. On your left is a long building with no signs whatsoever. This is the Dolce & Gabbana outlet. If you do want to do it by public transport, catch a train to Rignano sull'Arno. From there it is about 4km south (see the directions for Fendi below).

Fendi (☎ 055 83 49 81; Via Pian dell'Isola 66/33, Rignano sull'Arno; ☺ 9.30am-6.30pm Mon-Sat, 2.30-6.30pm Sun) For bags, belts and other fashion extras, this can be a worthwhile option to browse through. At the same address you'll also find Celine and Loewe (☎ 055 833 13 00), for a similar range of articles. On the whole, however, the offerings are a little thin. To get here by car (assuming you have hit The Mall first, which you should), you turn right (north) at the T-junction where you find Dolce & Gabbana (see above) and head north for 1km – follow the Fendi Outlet signs. It is located in a *zona industriale* (industrial estate) 3km south of Rignano sull'Arno. You can get a train to the latter and then a taxi.

Prada (Map 000; ☎ 055 9 19 01; Località Levanella, Montevarchi; ☺ 9.30am-7pm Mon-Sat, 3-7pm Sun) This outlet, although set in an industrial estate just outside the village of Levanella, has the elegance of a high-street store with a café and taxis waiting. It's best for women's accessories and classic suits for men. The women's clothing can be disappointing and mostly comes in small sizes. A queuing ticket system operates so you may find yourself waiting in line. By car you could follow the SS69 south from Leccio (see The Mall below) to Montevarchi (28km). As you edge south through this sprawling town you will enter Levanella (no signs and virtually soldered onto Montevarchi), whose southern end is an industrial estate. Turn left at Via Levanella Becorpi and pass the warehouses to the car park at the end of the street. If you pass under the rail bridge on the SS69, you have overshot the turn off by a few hundred metres. Alternatively, if you want to come here direct from Florence, take the A1 motorway and exit at Montevarchi. From the exit it's 7km to the outlet, following the same directions. Otherwise take an Arezzo-bound train from Florence, get off at Montevarchi and grab a cab.

The Mall (☎ 055 865 77 75; Via Europa 8, Leccio; ☺ 9am-7pm Mon-Sat, 3-7pm Sun) Gucci leads the way at this mixed-bag emporium, by far the most serious of the outlets and looking more like a regular fashion store. Gucci accessories, from belts and bags to shoes and sunglasses are well worth sifting through. Also represented here are Yves Saint Laurent, Sergio Rossi, Armani, Ferragamo, Valentino, Loro Piana and Bottega Veneta. Clothes tend to be from the previous season but can be good value. Check out the Armani suits. Take a train to Rignano sull'Arno and then a 10-minute taxi ride; the Mall also runs a daily shuttle bus from Florence – call for details. If driving, follow the SS69 east out of Florence, following the signs for Arezzo. The Mall and its car park are off to the right as you enter the village of Leccio. If coming from the south, you'll see it signposted. It's about a 40-minute drive from Florence (depending on traffic).

CECCHERINI & CO

Map pp251–3   *Musical Instruments*
☎ 055 21 00 31; Via de' Ginori 31/r; bus 1, 6, 7, 10, 11, 14, 17, 23 & A

Florentines with cash flow and a musical bent converge on this classic store in search of guitars and most other imaginable instruments. Or you could just pick up some replacement strings.

DREONI Map pp251–3   *Toys*
☎ 055 21 66 11; Via Cavour 33/r; bus 1, 6, 7, 10, 11, 14, 17, 23 & A

Florence's leading toy store ain't exactly Manhattan's FAO Schwarz, but it's full of fun stuff for kids and also has models that seem to attract just as many adults (well, blokes).

FELTRINELLI INTERNATIONAL

Map pp251–3   *Books*
☎ 055 21 95 24; Via Cavour 12/r; bus 1, 6, 7, 10, 11, 14, 17, 23 & A

This place has a good selection of books in English, French, German, Spanish, Portuguese and Russian, as well as a reasonable travel section and plenty of Italian literature.

SAN MARCO AREA

There's not a lot of serious shopping action in this part of town, although we have picked one exception to prove that rule!

STEFANO ALINARI

Map pp246–7   *Gold & Jewellery*
☎ 055 28 49 96; Via San Zanobi 24/r; bus 1, 6, 7, 10, 11, 14, 17, 23 & A

Mr Alinari is a craftsman in the old mould. He creates his pieces with all the temperament of a great sculptor and the results are often extraordinary. Be prepared to pay prices that match that individualised skill.

SANTA CROCE AREA

Traditionally the heart of Florence's leather production, Santa Croce is also home to other curious shops. A useful second-hand book exchange is located in the area.

ANDREINI Map pp248–50   *Ceramics*
☎ 055 234 08 23; Borgo degli Albizi 63/r; bus A

A century ago the statues and ceramics crafted here adorned the gardens of Tuscan nobility. Today you'd need a lot of money to afford most of the work on show in this workshop-gallery. It

Display of crockery

is tempting to imagine that in this kind of place lies the heritage of the great Renaissance sculptors' workshops. For those eager to add a special touch to their houses, this is where to come for a fine copy of a David or Venus. If nothing else, it is worth dropping by for a browse in this wonderful relic of another epoch.

FILISTRUCCHI

Map pp248–50   *Masks & Theatre*
☎ 055 234 49 01; Via Giuseppe Verdi 9; bus 14, 23 & A

Need a wig or other theatrical devices? This has been the place to come for masks and theatre accessories since the early 18th century.

LIBRERIA DELLE DONNE

Map pp248–50   *Books*
☎ 055 24 03 84; Via Fiesolana 2b; bus 14, 23 & A

Florence's main women's bookshop is also something of a lesbian info centre. Most of the literature is in Italian, but you may find the listings on the notice board useful.

PERUZZI Map pp248–50   *Leather*
☎ 055 28 90 39; Borgo de' Greci 8-20/r; bus 14, 23 & A

This barn-like leather emporium has been selling everything from cheap accessories to high-quality shoes since the end of WWII. Its sheer size alone makes it an interesting one-stop leather shop, even if only browsing for an idea of pricing. It also carries name-brand accessories.

SCUOLA DEL CUOIO

Map pp248-50   *Leather*

☎ 055 24 45 33; www.leatherschool.com; Piazza di Santa Croce 16; bus C

If you're lucky you will see apprentices beavering away at some hide here. It is also not a bad place to get some measure of quality-price ratios and the products are good (and only sold here). The Franciscans decided to set up and house the school in 1950, at a time when the lads of Santa Croce were hungry for any work they could get. Access is through the Basilica di Santa Croce or through an entrance behind the basilica at Via di San Giuseppe 5/r.

THE PAPERBACK EXCHANGE

Map pp246-7   *Books*

☎ 055 247 81 54; Via Fiesolana 31/r; ☺ Mon-Sat; bus C

This is the place to track down bargains in English. The store has a vast selection of new and second-hand books in English, including classics, contemporary literature, reference and bestsellers, as well as travel guides.

OLTRARNO

Wandering around on the south bank of the river you cannot help being charmed by the small boutiques and, especially around Borgo San Frediano, craftsmen's workshops. In these modest and often seemingly half-hidden spots you can come across anything from fine gold jewellery to top-quality handcrafted shoes.

ALESSANDRO DARI

Map pp248-50   *Jewellery*

☎ 055 24 47 47; Via San Niccolò 115/r; bus 12, 13, 23 & C

This master craftsman turns out remarkable castellated rings and some at times rather over-the-top pieces of jewellery that not everyone would dare to don. The quality of the handiwork is, however, high.

BELVEDERE GIOIELLI

Map pp251-3   *Jewellery*

☎ 055 234 10 16; www.belvederegioielli.com, Italian only; Piazza Santa Maria Soprarno 1/r; bus C & D

Marina approaches jewellery as though it were sculpture, creating little works of art of semi-precious and precious stones in, for example, startling square silver settings. Pendants, necklaces, earrings – nothing is beyond reach.

CAFISSI Map pp248-50   *Crafts*

☎ 055 29 21 64; Borgo San Jacopo 80/r; bus D

From tables to animals, hand-turned items in wood are the curiosity here. It might be an expensive way to furnish your place, but a little browsing can't hurt. And who knows, you might just be tempted by one of the little wooden ducks.

FRANCESCO DA FIRENZE

Map pp248-50   *Shoes*

☎ 055 21 24 28; Via di Santo Spirito 62/r; bus D

If only every shoemaker made shoes this way. Hand-stitched leather is the key to this tiny family business. You should expect to pay a fair amount for your footwear here, but the investment will pay off as your shoes and sandals will be made to your specifications.

MADOVA Map pp251-3   *Gloves*

☎ 055 239 65 26; www.madova.com; Via de' Guicciardini 1/r; bus D

Dreaming of an elegant pair of leather gloves? This is the place. They come in all sorts of colours and styles, lined with anything from cashmere to silk and prices ranging from €45 to €245.

LA BOTTEGA DI LEONARDO

Map pp251-3   *Crafts*

☎ 055 21 75 05; Via de' Guicciardini 45/r; bus D

This compact shop sells odds and ends aimed at the passing tourist trade, but the kids might be interested in the Leokits – unique wooden models of some of Leonardo da Vinci's wacky inventions.

STEFANO BEMER Map pp248-50   *Shoes*

☎ 055 21 13 56; Borgo San Frediano 143/r; bus 6 & D

Want handmade shoes to fit you fit like a glove? This could be the place if you have €1000 or so for the job. They will make a model of your feet (the *forma*) and then choose the materials to create a shoe to your taste and specifications. It all takes quite a while – you mustn't rush a craftsman!

Sleeping

Sleeping

Styles of Accommodation

The city has hundreds of hotels in all categories and a good range of alternatives, including hostels and private rooms. There are more than 200 one- and two-star hotels in Florence, so even in the peak season it is generally possible – although not always easy – to find a *camera* (room).

The APT office has a list of houses and apartments offering bed & breakfast accommodation – this is an option rapidly growing in popularity and more open up all the time. In general they only offer a couple of rooms. They can, however, be a pleasant and cheaper alternative to hotels, with a more 'at home' feeling. You could also check **Bed & Breakfast Italia** (www.bbitalia.it). The more traditional version is the *affittacamere* (room rental), basically the same deal in private houses but without the breakfast.

Hotels go by various names. An *albergo* is a hotel. A *pensione* is generally a smaller, simpler, family-run establishment, although frequently there is little to distinguish them from lower-end hotels. The great majority of these places are housed within buildings that date back several centuries and often have no more than a dozen or so rooms.

Hotels and *pensioni* are concentrated in three areas: near Stazione di Santa Maria Novella, near Piazza di Santa Maria Novella and in the old city between the Duomo and the Arno. Budget travellers have the choice of several youth hostels scattered about the city.

Many hotels boast parking but few actually offer it on site. More often than not they have a discount deal with a nearby garage, but it can still be a costly addition – easily €20 a day. Those hotels listed as having Internet access often have the sockets for you to plug in your laptop, so don't expect to find a terminal on site. Also, the sockets provided may not necessarily be compatible with your machine.

Price Ranges

Even in the low season, you're unlikely to pay less than €45 for a single (or €70 for a double) without private bathroom. In the high season, only a handful of cheapies offer such prices. Expect to pay €80 to €130 for a budget double, sometimes with bathroom (which often means shower, washbasin and toilet). For good mid-range places you can be looking at €125 for singles (or €200 for doubles). We have included some 'cheap sleeps' in this chapter, by which we mean places where you pay less than €70 for a single or (€100 for a double) in high season. Some of these places have more expensive doubles with own bathroom. Many places, especially at the lower end, offer triples and quads as well as the standard *singola/ doppia* (single/double) arrangement. If you are travelling in a group of three or four, these bigger rooms are generally the best value. Be aware that a *doppia* (double) usually means two single beds. If you want a cosy bed for two, ask for a *matrimoniale*.

Lone travellers are particularly penalised. Most hotels have few, if any, single rooms. When they do, such rooms are often rather poky. Otherwise you may be offered a double at two-thirds to three-quarters of the price two people would pay.

Most hotel proprietors pad out the bill by including a compulsory breakfast. The (in)famous continental breakfast in these cases generally consists of a lavishly laid-out stale bread roll, accompanied by little packets of butter and jam and a pot of weak instant coffee. If you have the cash, you may as well view this as an optional arrangement and get a proper cup of coffee in a bar. The buffet breakfasts in some of the mid-range and top hotels can be rather good.

Hotel rates vary wildly for a range of reasons, although the year-on-year tendency is generally upwards. Some hotels have the same prices year-round, while others drop them when things are slow. High season for those hotels that lift their prices starts on 15 April and fizzles out by mid-October (some dip in the hot months of July and August). Some hotels have an intermediate stage that starts on 1 March.

The prices that follow should be regarded as a high season guide. Rooms come with private bathroom (which often means a shower and not a full bathtub) unless otherwise stated. Where prices are mentioned 'with bathroom', the hotel also offers cheaper rooms with communal bathroom facilities.

Check-in & Checkout Times

Hotels do not hold rooms for you indefinitely. Always confirm your arrival, especially if it's going to be late in the afternoon or evening. Generally there is no problem if you have paid a deposit or left a credit card number. While you can check in at any time of the morning, you may not get access to your room until after noon, when it has been vacated and cleaned. Most of the time you will be able to leave your luggage with the reception and go for a wander until the room is ready.

Checkout time is generally noon, although some places can be a little draconian and set a leaving time of 11am, or even 10am (rare)! Technically, if you overstay you can be charged for another night.

Reservations

You are advised to book ahead in summer (from mid-April to October) and for the Easter and Christmas to New Year holiday periods. Frankly, it's not a bad idea at any time. Summer weekends (especially Friday and Saturday nights) are the toughest. The hottest months (especially August) tend to go quieter because the Italian tourist quotient heads for the beaches and hills rather than sweltering in places like Florence – they leave that exercise to the foreigners – making reservations less important.

If you arrive at Stazione di Santa Maria Novella without a hotel booking, the Consorzio ITA (Map pp246–7; ☎ 055 28 28 93; fax 055 247 82 32; ☉ 8.45am-9pm) can book rooms for a small fee.

A cyclist passes the Hotel Botticelli entrance on Via Taddea (p182)

Hotel Associations

The following organisations can book you into member hotels. They usually offer a fair range of possibilities, but rarely drop below two stars.

Associazione Gestori Alloggi Privati (AGAP; ☎ 055 654 08 60; www.agap.it; Via P Mastri 26) This organisation can get you a room in a B&B, an *affittacamere* (room in private house without breakfast) or even a room in some hotels.

Florence Promhotels (☎ 055 55 39 41, 800 86 60 22; www.promhotels.it; Viale Alessandro Volta 72) With this service you can book a wide range of hotels online, customising your choice by checking off special requirements (such as panoramic terrace, disabled access, hairdryer).

Inphonline (☎ 800 00 87 77; www.initalia.it; 9am-7pm Mon-Sat) This phone- and online-booking service operates Italy-wide and is free. You can book hotels, rent cars and organise congresses. They have a fairly limited selection of hotels in all categories in Florence.

Top Quark (☎ 055 33 40 41; www.familyhotels.com; Viale Fratelli Rossi 39/r) This site has about 60 Florentine hotels on the books in all categories. It also has hotels in major centres elsewhere in Italy.

Long-Term Rentals

If you want to rent an apartment in Florence, save your pennies and, if you can, start looking well before you arrive – apartments are difficult to come by and can be very expensive. A one-room studio with kitchenette in the city centre will generally cost around €500 a month. You are unlikely to find a room in a shared student household for less than €250 a month.

Florence & Abroad (Map pp246-7; ☎ 055 48 70 04; www.florenceandabroad.com; Via San Zanobi 58) specialises in short- and medium-term rental accommodation in Florence and the Fiesole area for those with a liberal budget.

If you decide while in Florence that you want to stay, look for rental ads in advert rags such as *La Pulce* (three times per week) and the weekly *Il Mercato della Toscana*. You'll find few ads for shared accommodation, though.

For shared housing, check out the language and other schools frequented by foreigners. You can put up your own ad or hopefully get lucky and find some likely candidates to share with. Other places to look for ads include English bookshops (such as **The Paperback Exchange** (Map pp246-7), Internet cafés, laundrettes and faculty buildings of the **Università degli Studi di Firenze** (Map pp244-5).

Those planning to stay for a week or more either in Florence or the surrounding countryside could consider renting an apartment or villa. Any Italian tourist office abroad can supply you with mountains of brochures for companies brokering such arrangements. The problem is knowing what you are going to get – not always easy to judge, even if you see the photos. Find out exactly what the facilities are and what costs extra (such as heating and use of a swimming pool).

Cuendet & Cie (☎ 0577 57 63 30; www.cuendet.com; Strada di Strove 17, 53035 Monteriggioni, Siena) is a major Italian company with villas in Tuscany. This reliable firm publishes a booklet listing all the villas in its files, many with photos. Prices for an apartment or small villa for four to six people range from around US$500 per week in winter up to US$1300 per week in August. For details, write to Cuendet and ask to be sent a copy of the catalogue or check out the website.

The US-based Web booking service **Rentvillas.Com** (http://rentvillas.com) offers some 800 holiday properties in Tuscany (about 80 in Florence itself).

Cottages & Castles (☎ 03-9853 1142; www.cottagesandcastles.com.au; 11 Laver St, Kew 3101, Victoria, Australia) has a range of holiday villas in Tuscany on its books.

Top Five Hotels with Views

- Albergo La Scaletta (p184)
- Albergo Torre di Bellosguardo (p186)
- Hotel Le Due Fontane (p183)
- Hotel San Giovanni (p179)
- Relais Uffizi (p180)

Sleeping

PIAZZA DEL DUOMO & AROUND

Perhaps surprisingly, the number of hotels in the immediate vicinity of the city's principal monument and symbol is rather low. And of those only a few recommend themselves. Given the proximity of other, more generously served parts of the city, don't waste too much time wandering around looking here if you haven't already booked ahead.

HOTEL BRUNELLESCHI Map pp251–3
☎ 055 2 73 70; www.hotelbrunelleschi.it; Piazza Santa Elisabetta 3; s/d €235/340; **P** ☒ 🖳 ; bus A

Bright, modern (and slightly characterless) rooms have been tacked onto a medieval tower on this quiet square a stone's throw from the Duomo. In Roman times the spot was occupied by baths – you can see vestiges of them in the basement of the tower, otherwise now given over to the hotel bar and conference rooms. The best rooms (on the upper floors) have views of Brunelleschi's nearby cathedral cupola.

HOTEL HELVETIA & BRISTOL
Map pp251–3
☎ 055 2 66 51; www.hotelhelvetiabristolfirenze.it; Via dei Pescioni 2; s/d up to €260/470; **P** ☒ 🖳 ; bus 6 & A

Travel back in time to a moment of plush, self-indulgent luxury. Classic rooms bulge with art, silk drapes, lace and brocade. Antique furnishings, bathrooms of Carrara marble and with Jacuzzi all help you pamper yourself while in Florence. Guests who've savoured the hotel's charm include Bertrand Russell, Pirandello and Stravinsky.

HOTEL SAVOY Map pp251–3
☎ 055 2 73 51; www.roccofortehotels.com; Piazza della Repubblica 7; s/d €300/450; **P** ☒ 🖳 ; bus A

This stylish jewel in the Forte chain offers spacious living in rooms that have a fresh, contemporary feel. Some rooms come with small balconies and big views and all have parquet floors or warm carpet. Bathrooms sparkle with marble and mosaics. You could take a suite as big as an apartment for €1700 plus if you're feeling decadent. If you aren't on your knees after a day of sightseeing, the hotel's fitness centre offers exercise – with yet more heart-stopping views from its windows.

Cheap Sleeps

HOTEL SAN GIOVANNI Map pp251–3
☎ 055 28 83 85; www.hotelsangiovanni.com; Via de' Cerretani 2; s/d/tr without bathroom €46.50/62/82.65, d/tr with bathroom €72.30/87.80; bus 1, 6, 7, 10, 11, 14, 17, 23 & A

Although the stairwell up to the 2nd floor isn't promising, the charming and often spacious rooms in this Italian-Australian–run hotel are worth seeking out. The hotel was once part of the bishop's private residence (see the traces of fresco in several rooms). Eight of the nine rooms have views of the cathedral and Baptistry. Rooms feature polished parquet floors, iron bedheads and marble table tops.

PIAZZA DELLA SIGNORIA & AROUND

Some of the city's most handsome kips are scattered about in the vicinity of Piazza della Signoria. Oddly enough, some of Florence's most challenging innovations in the hotel business are taking place around here. Like the re-opened Hotel Savoy (see above), some newer hotels, such as those run by Ferragamo near the River Arno, have a desire to shed the burden of history and present a fresh, modern concept in hospitality. They might have hit on a formula. After all day pottering about Renaissance Florence, guests probably appreciate a thoroughly modern approach to design and comfort in their rooms.

Those who don't want a modern setting needn't despair, as they are still catered to by the majority, and you'll find wonderful places at varying prices, offering you all the atmosphere and history you can handle.

BERNINI PALACE Map pp251–3
☎ 055 28 86 21; www.baglionihotels.com; Piazza San Firenze 29; s/d €209/319; ☒ 🖳 ; bus 14, 23 & A

This 15th-century mansion has luxury rooms filled with period furniture. The building was used as a temporary parliament from 1865 to 1870, before the latter moved to Rome. Breakfast is served in the splendid, frescoed Sala Corsini, now used as an occasional conference centre.

GALLERY HOTEL ART Map pp251–3
☎ 055 2 72 63; www.lungarnohotels.com; Vicolo dell'Oro 5; d from €315; **P** €29 ☒ ☒ ; bus B

Ferragamo runs this edgy 21st-century designer hotel, a departure from the standard Florentine excursion into antique nostalgia. It caters to a very particular taste, with minimalist décor, a sushi-ish fusion fashion bar and clean-lined rooms. And just to rub in the counter-Renaissance point, you can admire contemporary art along the corridors and in the rooms.

HOTEL CONTINENTALE Map pp251–3
☎ 055 2 72 62; www.lungarnohotels.com/continental_e.shtml; Vicolo dell'Oro 6r; s/d €227/310; 🐾 🖳; bus B

Another in the growing chain of Ferragamo anti-antique hotels, this place right opposite the Gallery Hotel Art shrieks ultranew, a 21st-century pad with its trendy Sky Lounge for drinking in cocktails with sunset views. Modular rooms with CD player (DVD on request), contemporary art and pink chairs are comfortable if cool. Three rooms have private terrace.

HOTEL PORTA ROSSA Map pp251–3
☎ 055 28 75 51; fax 055 28 21 79; Via Porta Rossa 19; s/d from €104/145 with breakfast; ✗ 🐾; bus A

This old workhorse isn't as smart as many in its class but if you enjoy steeping yourself in history, check in. First functioning as an inn back in the 14th century, it exudes nowadays a fading 19th-century charm where rooms are huge and furnished in the antique style. Neither they nor the welcome are as fresh as they might be.

PENDINI Map pp251–3
☎ 055 21 11 70; www.florenceitaly.net; Via Strozzi 2; s/d up to €110/150; 🅿 €24 🐾 🖳; bus A

Pendini's rooms, on the 4th floor, have seen guests come and go since 1879. They are furnished with antiques and in some cases are jumbled with tea tables and other furniture. Reproduction prints add a little gaiety and some rooms look out over Piazza della Repubblica.

RELAIS UFFIZI Map pp251–3
☎ 055 267 62 39; www.relaisuffizi.it; Chiasso del Buco 16; s/d €120/180; 🅿 €30 ✗ 🐾 🖳; bus B

Right in the heart of the action, this stylish kip is hidden away down an alley in a 16th-century building, a hop from Piazza della Signoria. From its breakfast room there are unparalleled views of the square; it's tempting to just sit there and watch life seethe below. Bedrooms are generous, with four-poster beds and tasteful furniture. Most have a bathtub.

Cheap Sleeps
PENSIONE MARIA LUISA DE' MEDICI Map pp251–3
☎ 055 28 00 48; Via del Corso 1; d/tr/q without bathroom €67/93/118, d/tr/q with bathroom €80/113/140; bus 23 & A

Character oozes from the very walls of this eclectic 17th-century mansion. An assortment of rooms, some of them enormous, branches off a long hall cluttered with art and *objects d'art*. Only two rooms have a private bathroom but this place has long been a value *pensione* of choice in Florence.

SANTA MARIA NOVELLA & AROUND

The streets around the train station are lined with cheap hotels and *pensioni*. This is not always a recommendation, but means that you can usually quickly unload your bags and get a kip within a short time of leaving your train. Via della Scala (Map pp251–3), which runs northwest off the piazza, is particularly laden. It is not the most salubrious part of town and some of these places do at least a part-time gig as unofficial brothels. That is by no means always the case, so you need to have a discerning eye.

Via Fiume (Map pp246–7) is equally stacked with hotels but is rather a different story and could be termed the 'upmarket' hotel flank of the train station.

As a whole the area around Piazza Santa Maria Novella is the most probable area in which to hunt down less expensive options.

The area covered in this section is considerably greater, however, stretching east to Via Cavour and along Via de' Tornabuoni to the Arno river, upon which you can spend thousands on lifestyle suites at the city's most exclusive addresses.

GRAND HOTEL Map pp248–50
☎ 055 2 71 61; www.starwood.com; Piazza d'Ognissanti 1; s/d from €635/894; 🅿 🐾 🖳; bus A & B

The most expensive hotels in town (run by the same people) are this and the Excelsior,

Top Five for Luxury

- Bernini Palace (p179)
- Grand Hotel (below)
- Hotel Helvetia & Bristol (p179)
- Hotel Savoy (p179)
- Palazzo Magnani Feroni (p185)

facing each other in self-assured style across Piazza d'Ognissanti. In the Grand Hotel, marble bathrooms, regal furnishings and river views characterise the best rooms. A stroll around the glorious ground floor, with its bars and restaurant, is overwhelming. The **Hotel Excelsior** (☎ 055 2 71 51) is listed on the same website and offers the same prices.

GRAND HOTEL BAGLIONI Map pp251–3

☎ 055 2 35 80; www.hotelbaglioni.it; Piazza dell'Unità Italiana 6; d from €227; P ⊠ 💻; bus 1, 7, 10, 11, 14, 17, 22, 23, 36, 37 & A

Timber beam ceilings, parquet floors and dark wood furnishings lend the rooms here a particular warmth, while the public areas in *pietra serena* (grey 'tranquil stone') have a softly grander tone. Some rooms fall into the 'superior' category and cost an extra €88. The rooftop terrace restaurant and garden have stirring views over the city.

HOTEL DÉSIRÉE Map pp246–7

☎ 055 238 23 82; www.desireehotel.com; Via Fiume 20; s/d €77.50/124; P €20 ⊠ €5; bus 4, 7, 12, 13, 14, 25, 28, 31, 32 & 33

This is a very personable hotel that offers fine rooms, many overlooking a tranquil, leafy courtyard out the back. The spick-and-span, high-ceilinged rooms have mosaic floors, iron or hand-painted timber bedsteads and their own bathrooms. The same people run the Hotel Cellini upstairs, where the rooms have balconies and the views, if anything, are better.

HOTEL LA GIOCONDA Map pp251–3

☎ 055 21 10 23; www.hotellagioconda.it; Via Panzani 2; s without bathroom €70, s/d with bathroom €105/170; P ⊠ ; bus 1, 4, 6, 7, 10, 11, 12, 13, 14, 22, 23, 25, 36 & 37

A cheerful family hotel with a story (see the boxed text below), this place is handily placed between the train station, the Duomo, San Lorenzo and the Basilica di Santa Maria Novella.

HOTEL TORNABUONI BEACCI
Map pp251–3

☎ 055 21 26 45; www.bthotel.it; Via de' Tornabuoni 3; s/d up to €155/240; ⊠ 💻; bus 6, 11, 36, 37 & A

Ignore all the designer frippery around you and head for the 15th-century Palazzo Minerbetti-Strozzi. The Minerbetti were descended from English refugees of the Becket family who wound up in Florence after the assassination of Thomas à Becket in Canterbury Cathedral

Mona Lisa Comes Home

Parisian police were at a loss. On 21 August 1911 Leonardo da Vinci's *La Gioconda* (aka the *Mona Lisa*) disappeared from the Louvre. The theft was shrouded in complete mystery until, some time later, a fellow who signed himself 'Leonard' announced that da Vinci's masterpiece was headed home to Florence, 'where she belongs'. An act thus, not of calculation but of national pride! The announcement did little to calm outraged French spirits and it would be more than two years before the case was resolved, not by the forces of law and order but by a Florentine antiquities dealer, Alfredo Geri, who managed to make contact with 'Leonard'. The thief was actually Vincenzo Peruggia, a housepainter who turned out to be a sandwich short of a picnic (and not even Florentine). Geri finally convinced his man to hand the painting over to him in the hotel that today calls itself the Hotel La Gioconda in December 1913. In the meantime, not a few Florentines had taken up Peruggia's battle cry and demanded that the painting stay in Florence. A little Parisian diplomatic leaning on Rome ensured that *Mona Lisa* returned to her place in the Louvre shortly thereafter.

in 1170. Faded elegance greets you in the period-furnished rooms of various centuries, kept in perfect order by the Bechi family. Enjoy views of central Florence at breakfast from the rooftop terrace (the pigeons are a little pesky though).

PENSIONE LE CASCINE Map pp251–3

☎ 055 21 10 66; www.hotellecascine.it; Largo Alinari 15; s/d up to €120/170 with breakfast; P €12 ⊠ 💻; bus 4, 7, 12, 13, 14, 25, 28, 31, 32 & 33

Near Stazione di Santa Maria Novella, this two-star hotel is one of the better choices in an area with many hotels. Its rooms are attractively furnished and some have balconies. The better rooms are spacious, with divan and generous bathrooms.

Cheap Sleeps
HOTEL ABACO Map pp251–3

☎ 055 238 19 19; www.abaco-hotel.it; Via dei Banchi 1; d without/with bathroom €82/95; ⊠ 💻; bus 1, 4, 6, 7, 10, 11, 12, 13, 14, 22, 23, 25, 36 & 37

This friendly hotel has nine charming baroque rooms with heavy drapes and chunky mirror frames. Antiques rule, and deep-sea blue to rose red colour schemes. There are no singles.

A playful reminder of the city's artistic heritage in a hotel lounge area

HOTEL CESTELLI Map pp251–3
☎ 055 21 42 13; www.hotelcestelli.it; Borgo SS Apostoli 25; s/d without bathroom €52/77, d with bathroom €103; bus B

You enter a bright foyer capped by a grand stained-glass window. Of the eight rooms, all varying in size and quality, the best is the large No 5, with its own divan and window onto the narrow street below. All the rooms are pleasant, although the singles are a tad cramped. You are just around the corner from the Arno here.

HOTEL SCOTI Map pp251–3
☎ 055 29 21 28; www.hotelscoti.com; Via de' Tornabuoni 7; s/d €65/85; bus 6, 11, 22, 36, 37 & A

This hotel on Florence's posh shopping strip is a wonderful haven. Grand rooms sprinkled with antiques form part of a grand apartment in a 15th-century mansion. The frescoed sitting room, complete with chandelier, is conducive to unhurried chats. Renovation in 2003 resulted in only a modest price increase, making this an even more attractive deal than it already was.

SAN LORENZO AREA

Animated by the bustle of the Mercato Centrale, the leather street stalls and the inevitable attraction of the Cappelle Medicee, this area has an in-the-thick-of-things feel about, more animated than the doubtless worthier, more awe-inspiring tourist hot spots of Piazza del Duomo and Piazza della Signoria. Some fine mid-range hotels can be recommended in this busy part of town.

HOTEL ACCADEMIA Map pp251–3
☎ 055 29 34 51; www.accademiahotel.net; Via Faenza 7; s/d €85/150 with breakfast; 🔀 🖳 ; bus 1, 6, 7, 10, 11 & 17

The hotel is within an 18th-century mansion with impressive stained-glass doors, carved wooden ceilings and a cheerful little courtyard. Bedrooms are pleasant and parquet-floored, with bright sparkling bathrooms attached.

HOTEL BELLETTINI Map pp251–3
☎ 055 21 35 61; Via de' Conti 7; s/d/tr €95/130/160; 🔀 🖳 ; bus 1, 6, 7, 10, 11 & 17

This delightful, cosy hotel has around 30 well-furnished rooms – try for one with a view of the Basilica di San Lorenzo. It also has a couple of triples and quads and some slightly cheaper rooms without bathroom. The hotel has a slightly pricier annexe nearby.

HOTEL BOTTICELLI Map pp246–7
☎ 055 29 09 05; www.hotelbotticelli.it; Via Taddea 8; s/d €124/204; 🅿 €21 🔀 ; bus 1, 6, 7, 10, 11 & 17

This charming, bijou hotel near the San Lorenzo market is an attractive deal. The common areas are capped by impressive vaulting and the little rooftop terrace is an enticing place to relax over a drink and enjoy the views. Rooms are elegantly appointed, with timber furnishings and clean, spacious lines. The attic ones with their sloping ceilings are fun.

HOTEL CASCI Map pp251–3
☎ 055 21 16 86; www.hotelcasci.com; Via Cavour 13; s/d/tr/q up to €100/140/180/220; Ⓟ €23-27 ☒ ☒ ☐ ; bus 1, 6, 7, 10, 11 & 17
This friendly family hotel with its attractive olive-green décor offers you the chance to stay in a 15th-century mansion on one of the city's main streets. Look up at the fresco as you scoff down your buffet breakfast, which includes fresh espresso coffee.

HOTEL GLOBUS Map pp251–3
☎ 055 21 10 62; www.hotelglobus.com; Via Sant'Antonino 24; s/d up to €120/170; Ⓟ €18 ☒ ☐ ; bus 1, 6, 7, 10, 11 & 17
Stylishly and sensitively refurbished in 2002, this cosy, welcoming hotel, which once belonged to the composer, Rossini, makes an excellent mid-range choice. The 23 rooms vary greatly and a few have good views over the city. Brand new showers boast hydromassage and the cool-coloured rooms have glass mosaics.

HOTEL IL GUELFO BIANCO Map pp246–7
☎ 055 28 83 30; www.ilguelfobianco.it; Via Cavour 57/r; s €135, d from €180; Ⓟ €18 ☒ ☐ ; bus 1, 6, 7, 10, 11 & 17
Rooms are a curious mix in this central hotel. Bare-brick vaulting and similarly exposed walls set the tone. Juxtaposed with grand old ceramic heating of bygone days are works of contemporary art to lend a modern splash to some rooms. Others have classic ceiling frescoes. A handful of much coveted rooms have a private terrace.

PALAZZO CASTIGLIONI Map pp251–3
☎ 055 21 48 86; pal.cast@flashnet.it; Via del Giglio 8; s/d €180/230; ☒ ☐ ; bus 1, 7, 10, 11, 14, 17 22
A six-room surprise packet on the 2nd floor of a sturdy Renaissance palazzo, this is a lovely option close to the train station. The rooms are decorated with frescoes of a bucolic nature and well appointed.

Cheap Sleeps
HOTEL SAN LORENZO Map pp246–7
☎ 055 28 49 25; www.sanlorenzohotel.it; Via Rosina 4; s/d with shower €65/100; Ⓟ €20 ☐ ; bus 1, 6, 7, 10, 11 & 17

This family *pensione* has eight rooms, including one single with shower (but loo in the corridor). Two of the doubles are likewise without own toilet. The five remaining rooms, some big enough to turn into triples, come with full bathroom. The place is clean and pleasant enough and from some rooms you can espy the bustling Mercato Centrale.

SAN MARCO AREA
A sleepier quarter than most of the rest of central Florence, the San Marco area is not big on accommodation quantity but offers a handful of excellent choices to suit a range of budgets and tastes.

HOTEL LE DUE FONTANE Map pp246–7
☎ 055 21 01 85; www.leduefontane.it; Piazza della SS Annunziata 14; s/d €123/181; Ⓟ ☒ ☐ ; bus 6, 31, 32 & C
This fine old building with well-presented rooms, each of them quite different in terms of size and presentation, is right on one of Florence's finest squares. Doubles overlooking it are spacious, with parquet floors and dark-shaded bedclothes. Such rooms can be a good or bad idea, depending on how early you hope to fall asleep.

HOTEL LOGGIATO DEI SERVITI
Map pp246–7
☎ 055 28 95 92; www.loggiatodeiservitihotel.it; Piazza SS Annunziata 3; s/d €140/205; bus 6, 31, 32 & C
Centuries ago visiting prelates lodged here when in Florence. The building was designed by Antonio da Sangallo to reflect the look of Brunelleschi's Spedale across the square and raised in 1517. It has operated as a hotel since 1924 and now has 29 varied rooms, including several small suites. Rooms are classically furnished and the beds draped in curtains.

HOTEL MONNA LISA Map pp246–7
☎ 055 247 97 51; www.monnalisa.it; Borgo Pinti 27; s/d/tr €201.50/284/413; Ⓟ ☒ ; bus 14 & 23
From the outside, this Renaissance *palazzo* seems to bristle, jealously guarding its Mediterranean garden and centuries-old rooms. Owned by relatives of the 19th-century sculptor Giovanni Dupré, some of whose works are scattered about the place among priceless family heirlooms, the hotel is a gentle haven. Earlier it had belonged to the Neri family and St Philip Neri was born here in 1515. Rooms are smallish but homey. The hotel annexe is not so hot.

HOTEL REGENCY Map pp246–7

☎ 055 24 52 47; www.hotel-regency.it; Piazza Massimo d'Azeglio 3; s/d €363/440; 🖭 🖳 ; bus 6, 31 & 32

Facing a leafy park, this hotel is a quiet, understated place with 49 modern, well-appointed if smallish rooms. It has an almost Anglo-Saxon sobriety about it and the park location just beyond the reach of the hordes is a plus. Rooms are classically decorated without the antique fussiness that dominates in some older hotels. The hotel restaurant is excellent.

Cheap Sleeps

RESIDENZA JOHANNA I Map pp246–7

☎ 055 48 19 86; Via Bonifacio Lupi 14; s/d €57/88; bus 1, 4, 7, 12, 20, 25 & 33

You're unlikely to spend your money much better on a Florentine bed. Set in a 19th century building (also home to the Swedish consulate) fronted by a courtyard in a quiet residential street, this small hotel is run with enthusiasm and care. Rooms are comfortable and furnished as you would expect in a hotel of greater standing. If you have no luck here, ask about its three other places (two nearby).

SANTA CROCE AREA

Better as a hunting ground when your tummy's rumbling, the hotel pickings around here are thin. A few good lower budget options are worth considering though.

ALBERGO BAVARIA Map pp248–50

☎ & fax 055 234 03 13; Borgo degli Albizi 26; s/d €50/70, d/tr/q with shower €85/100/115, d/tr/q with bathroom €98/113/128; bus A

This hotel is housed in the fine Palazzo di Ramirez di Montalvo, built around a peaceful courtyard by Ammannati. Rooms are furnished with fine antique pieces. With its warm ochre colours, low wooden ceilings and flexible pricing, it makes an excellent choice in its category. Reservations, especially between May and July, are imperative.

HOTEL DANTE Map pp248–50

☎ 055 24 17 72; www.hoteldante.it; Via S Cristofano 2; s/d €96/147; 🅿 €10-15 🖭 ; bus C

Tucked away in a quiet street right by the Basilica di Santa Croce, the rooms here are fine without being spectacular. Indeed the decoration is a little chintzy. All have smallish bathrooms but the real distinguishing feature is that three out of the four rooms on each floor have a kitchen, allowing you to eat in.

Cheap Sleeps

HOTEL DALÍ Map pp248–50

☎ 055 234 07 06; www.hoteldali.com; Via dell'Oriuolo 17; s/d without bathroom €40/60, d with bathroom €75; 🅿 ; bus 14 & 23

A friendly, helpful young couple run this spruce, simple and warmly recommended hotel. Try for a room looking over the serene inner courtyard. One room can accommodate up to six so bring the gang. There's free parking, rare as icebergs in Florence.

HOTEL WANDA Map pp248–50

☎ 055 234 44 84; www.hotelwanda.it; Via Ghibellina 51; s/d without own bathroom €70/88, d with shower €119; 🖭 ; bus 14

A somewhat higgledy-piggledy spot close to Piazza di Santa Croce, this hotel has large rooms, many with ceiling frescoes (some people, perhaps with vaguely kinky plans, insist on Room 13, lined with centuries-old mirrors). It is clean and quiet and the same people have an *affittacamere* next door. Most of the rooms are rented out to long-termers but the double looking on to the street is often available.

OLTRARNO

Who needs to be in the thick of things on the north side of the Arno when you could thrive in the atmosphere of the Oltrarno, a mere bridge or two away from the centre? Some hotels on the south bank offer a near country air and several budget hostels also offer their services.

ALBERGO LA SCALETTA Map pp251–3

☎ 055 28 30 28; www.lascaletta.com; Via de' Guicciardini 13 top floor; s/d €93/135; 🖭 ; bus D

Climb to the top floor to reach this charming hotel. Its best point is the breathtaking views over the city from the roof terrace. Rooms are straightforward enough, whitewashed clean with parquet floors and minimal furnishings.

They branch off long, rambling corridors that wind over three levels. Breakfast is included.

CASA GUIDI Map pp248–50
Piazza San Felice 8; 6-person apt per week from €2000; bus 11, 36, 37 & D

Perhaps you have poetic leanings? Why not take up residence where the Brownings did? The place is full of Browning mementos – you'll see they paid up to 25 guineas a week in rent. Contact the **Landmark Trust** (☎ 01628-825925; www.landmarktrust.co.uk; Shottesbrooke, Maidenhead, Berkshire SL6 3SW, UK). Established as a charity in 1965, the trust restores and conserves a host of architectural marvels in the UK, as well as several abroad. Casa Guidi has been restored and is owned by Eton College.

HOTEL SILLA Map pp248–50
☎ 055 234 28 88; www.hotelsilla.it; Via dei Renai 5; s/d €125/170; **P** €15 ⊠ 💻 ; bus 12, 13, 23 & C

Meander into the tranquil Florentine courtyard and you know you are home. The mansion has served as private residence, temporary Allied HQ in late 1944 and convent. It opened as a hotel in 1964 and is set in one of the prettiest corners of the city and a brief walk across Ponte alle Grazie from central Florence. From some of the rooms, furnished in dark timber, you have views across the river to the city centre.

HOTEL VILLA LIBERTY Map pp244–5
☎ 055 681 05 81; www.hotelvillaliberty.com; Viale Michelangelo 40; s/d/tr €139/189/249; **P** ⊠ ; bus 12 & 13

In a leafy location this agreeable Art Nouveau *palazzo* offers spacious, charming rooms with high (in some cases frescoed) ceilings and period furniture. Many look onto the gardens. The place has its own restaurant and bar if a walk into town seems like too much effort. In summer, take the buffet breakfast in the peaceful garden.

PALAZZO MAGNANI FERONI Map p248–9
☎ 055 239 95 44; www.florencepalace.it; Borgo San Frediano 5; ste from €310 with breakfast; **P** ⊠ ; bus 6 & D

You will feel like the guest of some 18th-century Florentine toff. Twelve suites, all the size of decent flats, are richly furnished. The beds are bigger than some peoples' bedrooms and the building retains its salons, billiard room and libraries. Wander up to the rooftop terrace for the views or have a workout in the gym. The staff

bend over backwards. Arriving late at night? No problem, they'll provide you with a welcome meal. Want a shirt made to measure? They'll send someone around. You can even choose the scent you prefer for your soap. Blimey, you may never want to step outside…

PENSIONE BANDINI Map pp248–50
☎ 055 21 53 08; pensionebandini@tiscali.it; Piazza S Spirito 9; d without/with bathroom €108/130; bus D

This rattling old *pensione* overlooks the hippest square in Florence from the 3rd floor. You can hang about the *loggia* overlooking the square or wander around admiring all the trinkets accumulated over the decades. The rooms are not 1st-class in comfort but the position and views from the grand *loggia* running the length of Palazzo Guadagni compensate for any lack in the mod-cons department.

Cheap Sleeps
OSTELLO SANTA MONACA Map pp248–50
☎ 055 26 83 38; www.ostello.it; Via Santa Monaca 6; dm €16; ⊠ 💻 ; bus D

Friendly and run by a cooperative, this hostel doesn't do meals but guests get a special deal at a nearby restaurant. There's a laundrette and also a guests' kitchen. Rental of sheets is included in the price.

Entrance to the Grand Hotel (p180)

NORTH OF THE OLD CITY

Well out of the town centre is an attractive youth hostel option (with a camping ground next door). An assortment of hotels also litters the northern part of the city but as a rule they are inconvenient for the centre.

OSTELLO VILLA CAMERATA Map pp244–5
☎ 055 60 14 51; florenceaighostel@virgilio.net; Viale Augusto Righi 2-4; dm/d/tr €15.50/38/49.50 with breakfast; ⊙ year-round; Ⓟ ☒ ⊡ ; bus 17, 17B & 17C

This HI (Hostels International) hostel, set in a 17th-century villa, is considered one of the most beautiful in Europe. Only members are accepted and the hostel is part of the International Booking Network (IBN), the online booking system for HI (for more details see www.iyhf.org). Dinner costs €8, and there is a bar. You can get the bus from Piazza del Duomo or Stazione di Santa Maria Novella – make sure it's going in the direction of Verga.

SOUTH OF THE OLD CITY

Overlooking the city from a mesmerising hillside position is one of the city's more enticing lodging choices.

ALBERGO TORRE DI BELLOSGUARDO
Map pp244–5
☎ 055 229 81 45; www.torrebellosguardo.com; Via Roti Michelozzi 2; s/d €160/280; Ⓟ ☒ ⊡ ⊠ ; taxi

This is worth considering if only for its position. Long appreciated as a bucolic escape from the simmering heat of summertime Florence, the Bellosguardo hill to the southwest of the city centre offers enchanting views and enticing accommodation in what started life as a small castle in the 14th century. Heavy timber four-poster beds stand in grandiose rooms. Relax in the gardens and admire the grand hall. The strategically placed pool is the best spot to drink in the views.

OUKSIRTS OF FLORENCE

If needing a break from the crowds is required, then head for the hills of Fiesole and around. The fresh air is revitalising.

LE CANNELLE BED & BREAKFAST
Map p254
☎ 055 597 83 36; www.lecannelle.com; Via Gramsci 52-56, Fiesole; s/d €93/114; closed mid-Jan–Feb; ☒ ; bus 7

It's hard to miss the rose-coloured façade of this delightful bed and breakfast, tucked away about 100m east of Piazza Mino da Fiesole, in the heart of the old hill town overlooking Florence. A variety of pleasant, mostly spacious rooms (five in all) with ceramic floors and grand timber beds is on offer. Take breakfast in the cosy dining room, with its timber-beamed ceiling.

VILLA BENCISTÀ Map p254
☎ 055 5 91 63; bencista@uol.it; Via Benedetto da Maiano 4; s/d without bathroom €150/160, s/d with bathroom €160/180; Ⓟ ⊡ ; bus 10

About 1km short of Fiesole proper when coming from central Florence, this is one of the cheaper villa alternatives in the northern hills. The panoramic views alone make it a great place to stay. Rooms are spacious and well equipped.

VILLA POGGIO SAN FELICE Map p254
☎ 055 22 00 16; http://poggiosanfelice.hotel -firenze.net; Via San Matteo in Arcetri 24; s/d €150/200; Ⓟ ☒ ⊠ ; private shuttle

This family escape lies just 5km south of Porta Romana amid the vineyards. Take up residence in one of the five huge guest rooms for your Tuscan country holiday, with Florence just up the road. Can't be bothered with the big city today? Well, flop down by the pool. The rooms are all different, ranging from one with two single four-posters to a romantic double with a huge French bed and lovely views over the terrace. The owners run a twice-daily shuttle to and from central Florence.

VILLA SAN MICHELE Map p254
☎ 055 567 82 00; www.villasanmichele.net; Via Doccia 4, Fiesole; s/d from €646/843; Ⓟ ☒ ⊠ ; private shuttle

A former 15th-century Franciscan monastery, this landmark has become one of the classiest hotel escapes in Florence. Well, around Florence. Sip a cocktail and contemplate the city and the Arno across the cypress tops from this privileged location just outside Fiesole. A grand variety of rooms and suites spreads out across the luxuriant gardens (some junior suites are right by the pool). Even the standard rooms ooze charm, with four-poster beds, timber ceilings and refined country atmosphere. The restaurant has an international reputation. Statuary litters the grounds and public spaces.

Excursions

188

Excursions

Florence lies at the top end of Italy's most publicised region, Tuscany. A rich, roughly triangular area occupying the central-western half of the Italian peninsula, it covers 22,992 sq km. It is bounded to the north by the Apennines, which separate it from northern Italy and the grand Po valley. To the west it faces the Tyrrhenian Sea, while to the east stretch the neighbouring hilly regions of Umbria and Le Marche. To the south stretches Lazio and the capital, Rome.

Florence's rise as the senior medieval city of Tuscany and eventually its capital did not go uncontested. Rivals engaged in a frequently bloody tug-of-war in the competition for local supremacy and in the process became splendid and long-independent centres. None resisted Florence's growing hegemony with greater tenacity than Siena, to the south. Pisa bloomed early as a maritime power but succumbed to Florence in the 15th century. To the north, nearby Lucca managed to remain surprisingly aloof and independent until 1799. This was long after Florence had ceased to be a major player in the European league of nations.

The Tuscan countryside is littered with other lesser-known but often equally striking cities and towns. Each has its own story to tell, from the merchant town of Prato just northwest of Florence to the medieval Manhattan that is San Gimignano. To the south, sandwiched between eternal rivals Florence and Siena, stretches the fabled Chianti wine country.

What we explore in this chapter can be done easily in day trips from Florence. Of course, there is much more to Tuscany. For an extensive survey of its splendours, get Lonely Planet's *Tuscany & Umbria*.

FLORENCE'S MEDIEVAL RIVALS

If Florence is the birthplace of the Renaissance and cradle to its creators, Siena (p190) is its proud Gothic counterpoint. Perched up high like an eagle's eyrie in rugged terrain to the south of Florence, the city's subjugation to its Renaissance rival may not have been a beneficial thing for the Sienese but was possibly a godsend for posterity. Its relegation to a second-tier town put a brake on commercial development in the area and no doubt helped preserve the purity of its Gothic lines while Florence underwent its expansion as Tuscan capital. To the northwest, two other medieval city-states faced vastly different cicumstances. Pisa (p197) had an illustrious but short-lived career as a Mediterranean sea power, and is home to some of the most spectacular Romanesque monuments in Tuscany, not to mention a grand architectural botched job – the Leaning Tower (Torre Pendente). Controlled by Pisa for a while, the nearby walled city of Lucca (p197) is another rich Romanesque treasure chest for both art and architecture.

TUSCAN TOWNS

The extraordinary diversity of Tuscany's towns was born of the fractiousness of the Middle Ages. With the unity imposed by ancient Rome a distant memory, these settlements re-emerged from the nightmarish bog of the Dark Ages with a quite understandably defensive diffidence towards the rest of the world. Feudal warlords ruled them with an iron, and frequently bloody, fist and jealously defended their independence. Inevitably the bigger centres, above all Florence, came to expand their political and economic power, and the lesser towns succumbed one by one. Today, however, they still each stubbornly retain their own charm and character. From the medieval towers of San Gimignano (p196) to the grand cathedral squares of Prato (p200) and Pistoia (p201), these places each have their own signature features. Montelupo (p201) is known for its ceramics, Prato has its wool-production and textile heritage, while the pretty hamlet of Vinci gave its name to one of the greatest figures of the Renaissance.

WINE COUNTRY

The rolling hills of Tuscany's classic-wine **Chianti country** (p194) beckon just to the south of Florence. Walkers and energetic cyclists (those hills certainly work out some previously unperceived muscles) love to frequent here, and with good reason. Picturesque villages like **Greve in Chianti** (p194), **Radda in Chianti** (p194) and **Gaiole in Chianti** (p194) pop out from the hills, each with their own delightful flavour. As you follow the back roads you will inevitably come across castles and country manors in various states of repair. The impressive walls of **Monteriggioni** (p195) will draw you into this now quiet half-abandoned village near Siena, while the tall spindly medieval towers of San Gimignano, beyond the Chianti but justly known for its own wines, is a must on any Tuscan village circuit and too close to Florence not to visit.

SIENA

According to legend Siena was founded by the son of Remus, and the symbol of the wolf feeding the twins Romulus and Remus is as ubiquitous in Siena as in Rome. Probably of Etruscan origin, a proper town only really emerged when, in the 1st century BC, the Romans established a military colony called Sena Julia.

In the 12th century AD Siena's wealth, size and power grew with its involvement in trade (textiles, wine, saffron, spices and wax) and banking. Rivalry with Florence also increased and in 1260 Ghibelline Siena defeated Florence at the Battle of Montaperti. The Florentines later turned the tables and Siena was obliged to join the Tuscan Guelph League.

During this period Siena prospered under the rule of the Consiglio dei Nove (Council of Nine), a group dominated by the upper middle class. Many of the fine buildings in the Sienese Gothic style, which give the city its striking appearance, were constructed under the council's direction, including the cathedral. The Sienese school of painting had its

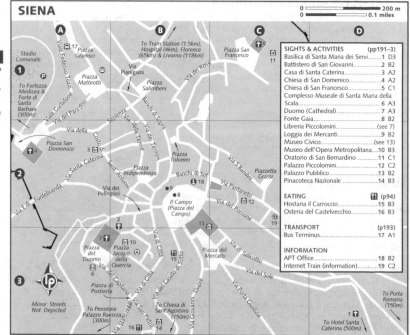

SIENA

SIGHTS & ACTIVITIES	(pp191–3)
Basilica di Santa Maria dei Servi	1 D3
Battistero di San Giovanni	2 B2
Casa di Santa Caterina	3 A2
Chiesa di San Domenico	4 A2
Chiesa di San Francesco	5 C1
Complesso Museale di Santa Maria della Scala	6 A3
Duomo (Cathedral)	7 A3
Fonte Gaia	8 B2
Libreria Piccolomini	(see 7)
Loggia dei Mercanti	9 B2
Museo Civico	(see 13)
Museo dell'Opera Metropolitana	10 B3
Oratorio di San Bernardino	11 C1
Palazzo Piccolomini	12 C2
Palazzo Pubblico	13 B2
Pinacoteca Nazionale	14 B3

EATING	(p94)
Hostaria il Carroccio	15 B3
Osteria del Castelvecchio	16 B3

TRANSPORT	(p193)
Bus Terminus	17 A1

INFORMATION	
APT Office	18 B2
Internet Train (information)	19 C2

Pageantry and sbandieratori (flag-throwers) in Piazza del Campo, Siena

beginnings at this time with Guido da Siena and peaked in the early 14th century with the work of artists like Duccio di Buoninsegna, Simone Martini, and Pietro and Ambrogio Lorenzetti.

Plague in 1348 and foreign rule signalled decline, but the real blow came when Florence's Cosimo I de' Medici, under the banner of Holy Roman Emperor Charles V, conquered Siena in 1555. Florence thus fulfilled a centuries-old dream and proceeded to bar the Sienese from operating banks, thus curtailing Siena's commercial clout for good. The Sienese have never forgotten the horrors of the military campaign or the humiliation of submission to Florence.

Little has changed since medieval times and the compact city centre bristles with architectural jewels.

If you arrive by bus from Florence you will arrive at **Piazza Gramsci**, from where it is a short walk to Piazza San Domenico, which provides a panoramic view of the city. Work on the imposing Gothic **Chiesa di San Domenico** began in the early 13th century, but it has been altered greatly over the centuries. St Catherine of Siena, one of Italy's most revered saints, took her vows in the church's Cappella delle Volte. In the **Cappella di Santa Caterina** the saint's head is contained in a tabernacle on the altar. She died in Rome, where most of her body is preserved, but, in line with the bizarre practice of collecting relics of dead saints, her head was returned to Siena. In a small window box to the right of the chapel are her desiccated thumb and the nasty-looking whip that she flogged herself with for the wellbeing of the souls of the faithful.

Walk east along Via della Sapienza and turn right down Costa di Sant'Antonio. On your right is the **Casa di Santa Caterina**, where the saint was born. The rooms are decorated with frescoes and paintings by Sienese artists, including Sodoma.

Back on Via della Sapienza, continue east and turn right into Banchi di Sopra to reach **Il Campo**. The magnificent, sloping shell-shaped and café-lined square has been the city's civic centre since it was laid out by the Consiglio dei Nove in the mid-14th century. The square's paving is divided into nine sectors, representing the council members. In the upper part is

Il Palio

This spectacular event, held twice yearly on 2 July and 16 August in honour of the Virgin Mary, dates back to the Middle Ages and features a series of colourful pageants, a wild horse race around Il Campo and much eating, drinking and celebrating in the streets.

Ten of Siena's 17 *contrade* (town districts) compete for the coveted *palio* (silk banner). Each of the *contrade* has its own traditions, symbol and colours, and its own church and *palio* museum; rivalry is keen.

On festival days Il Campo becomes a racetrack, with a ring of packed dirt around its perimeter serving as the course. From about 5pm representatives of each *contrada* parade in historical costume, bearing their individual banners.

The race is run at 7.45pm in July and 7pm in August. For not much more than one exhilarating minute, the 10 horses and their bareback riders tear three times around Il Campo with a speed and violence that makes your hair stand on end. Jockeys are as often as not from outside town – Sardinians, known for their horsemanship, frequently saddle up for Il Palio. They can be the target of wild admiration or dark opprobrium, especially if there are suspicions that any have been bribed to throw the race. Unlucky riders have on occasion been the victims of violence from het-up locals. In 2003 an investigation was launched into the deaths of two of the horses as a result of injuries sustained in Il Campo.

Even if a horse loses its rider, it is still eligible to win and since many riders fall each year, it is the horses who are the focus of the event in the end. There is only one rule: riders are not to interfere with the reins of other horses.

Book well in advance if you want to stay in Siena at this time, and join the crowds in the centre of Il Campo at least four hours before the start, or even earlier if you want a place on the barrier lining the track. If you can't find a good vantage point, don't despair – the race is televised live and then repeated throughout the evening on TV (the Sienese extract a mammoth fee from the national network, RAI, to broadcast the event live).

If you happen to be in town in the few days immediately preceding the race, you may get to see the jockeys and horses practising in Il Campo. Between May and October, **Cinema Moderno** (☎ 0577 28 92 01; Piazza Tolomei; admission €5.25; 9.30am-5.30pm) runs a mini-epic 20-minute film of Siena and the Palio that will take your breath away.

the 15th-century **Fonte Gaia** (Gay Fountain), once the city centre's principal public source of water. The fountain's Renaissance panels are reproductions – the originals, by Jacopo della Quercia, are in the impressive Gothic **Palazzo Pubblico** at the piazza's lowest point. Also known as the Palazzo Comunale (town hall), the palace houses the **Museo Civico**, fundamentally a series of rooms with frescoes by artists of the Sienese school. Of particular note is Simone Martini's **Maestà** in the Sala del Mappamondo (Map Room).

The Palazzo Pubblico's graceful 102m *campanile* (bell tower), the **Torre del Mangia**, was completed in 1344. The views from the top are spectacular.

The **Duomo** (Cathedral), begun in 1196 and largely completed by 1215, is one of Italy's great Gothic churches. Giovanni Pisano began the magnificent façade of white, green and red polychrome marble that was completed towards the end of the 14th century. The cathedral's interior is resplendent with artworks. The most precious feature is the inlaid marble floor, decorated with 56 panels depicting historical and biblical subjects.

Through a door from the north aisle is the **Libreria Piccolomini**, which Pope Pius III (pope in 1503) built to house the books of his uncle, Enea Silvio Piccolomini (Pope Pius II). The walls of the small hall are covered by an impressive series of frescoes by Bernardino Pinturicchio. The sculptural group in the centre of the hall, the *Tre Grazie* (Three Graces), is a 3rd-century-AD Roman copy of an earlier Hellenistic work.

The breathtaking art in the **Museo dell'Opera Metropolitana**, adjacent to the cathedral, formerly adorned the latter. The main drawcard is Duccio di Buoninsegna's striking early-14th-century *Maestà*, painted on both sides as a screen for the cathedral's high altar.

Behind the cathedral and down a flight of stairs is the **Battistero di San Giovanni** (Baptistry of St John). The marble font by Jacopo della Quercia is decorated with bronze panels depicting the life of St John the Baptist by artists including Lorenzo Ghiberti and Donatello.

On the southwest side of Piazza del Duomo, the **Complesso Museale di Santa Maria della Scala** (the former pilgrims' hospice) boasts frescoes by Domenico di Bartolo in the main ward and an impressive collection of Roman and Etruscan artefacts.

A short walk south of the cathedral you run into yet more art collections in the 15th-century Palazzo Buonsignori, home to the **Pinacoteca Nazionale** (National Gallery) and masterpieces by Sienese artists. Look for Duccio di Buoninsegna's *Madonna dei Francescani* (Our Lady of the Franciscans), the *Madonna col Bambino* (Our Lady and Christ Child) by Simone Martini and a series of Madonnas by Ambrogio Lorenzetti.

Also worth investigating when they are open are the **Oratorio di San Bernardino**, which is part of the Chiesa di San Francesco complex, and the **Chiesa di Sant'Agostino**. The former houses a modest museum of religious artworks.

From the Loggia dei Mercanti north of Il Campo, take Banchi di Sotto eastwards to the **Palazzo Piccolomini**. Siena's finest Renaissance palace, it houses the city's archives and a small museum. Further east are the 13th-century **Basilica di Santa Maria dei Servi**, with a fresco by Pietro Lorenzetti, and the 14th-century **Porta Romana** city gate.

Sights & Information

APT office (☎ 0577 28 05 51; www.siena.turismo.tosca na.it; Piazza del Campo 56; ☷ 8.30am-7.30pm Mon-Sat Apr-Oct, 8.30am-1pm & 3-7pm Mon-Fri, 8.30am-noon Sat Nov-Mar)

Battistero di San Giovanni (Piazza San Giovanni; admission €2.50, or combined ticket including Centro di Arte Contemporaneo, Museo Civico, Museo dell'Opera Metropolitana, Libreria Piccolomini & Complesso Museale di Santa Maria della Scala €16; ☷ 9am-7.30pm mid-Mar–Sep, 9am-6pm Oct, 10am-1pm & 2-5pm Nov–mid-Mar)

Casa di Santa Caterina (☎ 0577 4 41 77; Costa di Sant'Antonio 6; admission free; ☷ 9am-12.30pm & 3-6pm)

Chiesa di Sant'Agostino (Prato di Sant'Agostino; admission €2; ☷ 10.30am-1.30pm & 3-5.30pm mid-Mar–Oct only)

Chiesa di San Domenico (Piazza San Domenico; admission free; ☷ 7.30am-1pm & 3-6.30pm)

Complesso Museale di Santa Maria della Scala (☎ 0577 22 48 11; www.santamaria.comune.siena.it; Piazza del Duomo 2; adult/child €5.20/3.10, or combined ticket – see Battistero di San Giovanni – €16; ☷ 10am-6pm mid-Mar–Oct, 10.30am-4.30pm Nov–mid-Mar)

Centro di Arte Contemporaneo (☎ 0577 2 20 71; info@papesse.org; Palazzo delle Papesse, Via di Città 126; admission adult/child/child under 7 €5/3.50/free; ☷ noon-7pm Tue-Sun)

Duomo (Cathedral; ☎ 0577 4 73 21; Piazza del Duomo; admission free; ☷ 7.30am-7.30pm Mon-Sat, 2-7.30pm Sun mid-Mar–Oct; 7.30am-5pm Mon-Sat, 2-7.30pm Sun Nov–mid-Mar)

Hospital (☎ 0577 58 51 11; Viale Bracci) Just north of Siena at Le Scotte.

Internet Train (☎ 0577 24 74 60; Via di Pantaneto 54; €4 per hr; ☷ 10am-10pm Mon-Fri, 3-10pm Sun)

Libreria Piccolomini (Piazza del Duomo; admission €1.50, or combined ticket with Battistero di San Giovanni and Museo dell'Opera Metropolitana €7.50, or combined ticket – see Battistero di San Giovanni – €16; ☷ 9am-7.30pm Mon-Sat, 2-7.30pm Sun mid-Mar–Oct; 10am-1pm & 2-5pm Mon-Sat, 2-7.30pm Sun Nov–mid-Mar)

Museo Civico (☎ 0577 29 22 63; Palazzo Pubblico, Il Campo; www.comune.siena.it/museocivico; adult/child €6.50/4, or combined ticket – see Battistero di San Giovanni – €16; ☷ 10am-7pm mid-Mar–Oct, 10am-5.30pm Nov–mid-Mar)

Museo dell'Opera Metropolitana (☎ 0577 28 30 48; Piazza del Duomo 8; www.operaduomo.it; €5.50, or combined ticket – see Battistero di San Giovanni – €16; ☷ 9am-7.30pm mid-Mar–Sep, 9am-6pm Oct, 9am-1.30pm Nov– mid-Mar)

Oratorio di San Bernardino (☎ 0577 28 30 48; Piazza San Francesco; admission €2.50; ☷ 10.30am-1.30pm & 3-5.30pm mid-Mar–Oct only)

Palazzo Piccolomini (Banchi di Sotto; admission free; museum ☷ 9am-1pm Mon-Sat)

Pinacoteca Nazionale (☎ 0577 28 11 61; Via San Pietro 29; adult/child €4/2; ☷ 8.30am-1.30pm Mon, 8.15am-7.15pm Tue-Sat, 8.15am-1.15pm Sun)

Post office (Piazza Matteotti 1; ☷ 8.15am-7pm Mon-Sat)

Questura (police station; ☎ 0577 20 11 11; Via del Castoro)

Torre del Mangia (Palazzo Pubblico; admission €5.50; ☷ 10am-7pm mid-Mar–Oct, 10am-4pm Nov–mid-Mar)

Transport

Distance from Florence 68km
Direction South
Bus Regular SITA and Tra-in buses from Florence (€6.20, 1¼ hours) run at least every hour (direct), arriving in Siena's Piazza Gramsci. More frequent services involve a change of bus at Poggibonsi.
Car Take the SS2, a fast *superstrada* (expressway) connecting Florence and Siena, or the SS222 (Strada Chiantigiana) through the Chianti hills.
Train Siena is not on a major railway line. Services from Florence (€5.40, 1¾ hours) are irregular and involve a change at Empoli *and* a local bus to get you up to the centre of town – take the bus.

Eating

Hostaria Il Carroccio (☎ 0577 4 11 65; Via del Casato di Sotto 32; meal €25-30; ☾ Thu-Mon & Tue lunch) This place, off Il Campo, has excellent pasta. Try the *pici* (a kind of thick spaghetti) followed by the *friselle di pollo ai zucchini* (bite-sized juicy chicken pieces with courgette). The wine list is good.

Osteria del Castelvecchio (☎ 0577 4 95 86, Via Castelvecchio 65; meal €25-30; ☾ Wed-Mon) Highly regarded by locals, this place is delightfully located in an ancient mansion a stone's throw from the cathedral. Vegetables feature in a big way with delicious vegetarian dishes (like *zucchine ripiene* – stuffed courgettes) on the ever-changing menu.

Sleeping

Hotel Santa Caterina (☎ 0577 22 11 05; Via Piccolomini 7; s/d up to €98/144 inc breakfast; P €12; ❄) This elegantly renovated 18th-century villa, just outside the city walls and a stone's throw beyond the Porta Romana, is a tranquil haven. Rooms are tastefully furnished, the breakfast room is light and airy and there's a lovely garden with open views to the surrounding hills.

Pensione Palazzo Ravizza (☎ 0577 28 04 62; www.palazzoravizza.it; Pian dei Mantellini 34; s/d €130/ 160; P ❄ 💻) This delightful Renaissance *palazzo*, which became a guesthouse in the 1920s, boasts rooms with frescoed ceilings and carefully selected antique furniture. The deluxe rooms and suites are costly but enticing.

IL CHIANTI & AROUND

For centuries the medieval communes of Florence and Siena quarrelled nastily over just how much of the hills and valleys that lie between them belonged to each. The final division split the area into Il Chianti Fiorentino and Il Chianti Senese. As you explore this rich wine country, you begin to understand what the fuss was about. Rolling hills and vineyards are interspersed by warm-coloured villages, distinguished country manors and a smattering of *pievi* (Romanesque country churches).

Florence and Siena buried the hatchet long ago (you might not think so to talk to the Florentines and Sienese about one another), leaving the Chianti open to a new invasion. They don't call it Chiantishire for nothing. In some of the small-town tourist offices it is just assumed everyone who wanders in speaks English!

Possibly the country's best-marketed (although not always best-quality) wine comes from here. Who hasn't heard of Chianti? Chianti Classico is the best-known generic label, sold under the Gallo Nero (Black Cockerel) symbol. You can get hold of maps marking wineries if you wish to do a little wine touring. Be aware that many of these places have not adopted the practice of putting out their wares for free tasting as is common in modern wine-producing areas in places like Australia, the USA or South Africa. Many are keen to sell but not so keen to give the stuff away (even by the glass).

About 20km south of Florence on the picturesque Strada Chiantigiana (SS222) that links Florence with Siena is **Greve in Chianti**, the first well-located base for exploring the region. Piazza Matteotti, the unusual triangular square at the centre of the town, is presided over by a statue of Giovanni da Verrazzano. This local hero was the first European explorer who discovered New York harbour. He is commemorated in the New World by the Verrazano Narrows (the good captain lost a 'z' from his name somewhere in mid-Atlantic) bridge, linking Staten Island to Brooklyn.

Montefioralle, only 2km west of Greve, is an ancient castle-village. It's worth the uphill walk, particularly to see its Santo Stefano church, which contains precious medieval paintings.

Castellina in Chianti, 19km south of Greve, was long a frontier town between forever warring Florence and Siena. Wander into this wine town along Via delle Volte, a medieval street crowded in by shops and houses that together form a long vaulted tunnel. The silos at the entrance to town hold vast quantities of Chianti Classico, which you can purchase in more reasonable amounts at **Bottega del Vino** (Via della Roca 11–13).

Just 11km east of Castellina, **Radda in Chianti** has retained much of its traditional charm despite the influx of tourists. The nucleus of the village is Piazza Ferrucci, where the 16th-century **Palazzo del Podestà**, its façade emblazoned with escutcheons of towns and governing podestas, faces the village church, whose *Christ in Majesty* over the main portal is now effaced by the elements. You could push on another 10km east for **Gaiole in Chianti**, a pleasant village surrounded by low hills. Just to the west of the village centre, set in woodland, is the early-12th-century Romanesque *pieve* of Santa Maria a Spaltenna and a small hill fortress.

Two kilometres to the south is the bite-sized **Castello di Metelo**, where you can taste and buy wine. From here you could head south about 20km to Siena along the SS408.

Alternatively, back at Castellina, you could follow a narrow country road to the southwest for 14km to arrive before the walls of the captivating medieval stronghold of **Monteriggioni**, just off the SS2 about 12km short of Siena. The walls date back to the 13th century and, although some of the towers still stand only because of later surgical intervention, the place transports you to another age.

Another route south from Florence could start from the **Certosa di Galluzzo** (p112). You could take the SS2 *superstrada* (motorway) that connects Florence with Siena, or the more tortuous and windy road that runs roughly parallel to it. Follow the latter to Tavernuzze, south of which there is a US WWII cemetery, and on to San Casciano Val di Pesa. An important wine centre, the town came under Florentine control in the 13th century and was later equipped with a defensive wall, parts of which remain intact. The town centre itself is not overly interesting, however, so you could just drink in the views and hit the road again.

Just before Bargino, you could make a detour by taking the side road east for Montefiridolfi. The road winds up onto a high ridge through vineyards and olive groves. Along the way you pass the **Castello di Bibbione**, a ponderous stone manor house. Another 1.5km brings you to a big Etruscan tomb. You can keep going until you hit a crossroads. From there turn west for Tavarnelle Val di Pesa, from where you reach the charming medieval *borgo* (village) of **Barberino Val d'Elsa**, worth a stop for a brief stroll along the main street. You can also reach Barberino by heading directly south from San Casciano.

Just south out of Barberino, a minor road meanders off west for about 15km to reach pretty hill-top **Certaldo**. The upper town (Certaldo Alto) is particularly captivating in the glow of the dying day's sun. It has Etruscan origins, while the lower town in the valley sprang up in the 13th century – by which time both had been absorbed into the Florentine republic.

The **Casa del Boccaccio**, where writer Giovanni Boccaccio (see p35) supposedly died and was buried in 1375, is on the upper town's main drag. It is a largely reconstructed version of his house (severely damaged in WWII). The library has some precious copies of Boccaccio's *Decameron* (p35). Several doors up, the **Chiesa di SS Jacopo e Filippo** houses a cenotaph to the

A village in the Chianti region

writer. The whole walled *borgo* (walled village) of the upper town is dominated by the stout **Palazzo Pretorio** (aka Palazzo del Vicario), whose 14th-century façade is richly decorated with the coats of arms of those who ruled the town down through the centuries. Frescoed halls lead off the charming Renaissance courtyard into an Escher-like construction. One of the main halls now houses a modest collection of Etruscan and Roman artefacts.

From Certaldo it's a pleasant 13km south to **San Gimignano**, surely one of the quinessential symbols of all Tuscany. There is a reason why tourists flock to this medieval 'Manhattan', with its 13 towers (once there were 72) still proudly symbolising the wealth and power of their one-time owners. Such towers, as numerous as the noble families who could afford to build them, bristled all over medieval Tuscan towns and cities. As power in Florence and other major centres was concentrated in the hands of the emerging wealthy merchant class, noble families were increasingly obliged to dismantle these provocative structures. In 1348 the plague decimated San Gimignano's populace. Five years later it submitted to Florence.

Piazza della Cisterna is lined with houses and towers dating from the 13th and 14th centuries. In the adjoining Piazza del Duomo stands the Romanesque cathedral, or **Collegiata**. The frescoes inside are noteworthy and there are beautiful ones by Domenico Ghirlandaio in the **Cappella di Santa Fina**. Across the square, the **Museo d'Arte Sacra** has some fine works of religious art, culled, in the main, from the town's churches.

The **Palazzo del Popolo**, left of the cathedral, still operates as the town hall. From the internal courtyard, climb the stairs to the **Museo Civico**, which features paintings from the Sienese and Florentine schools of the 12th to 15th centuries. Climb the palazzo's **Torre Grossa**.

The **Museo Archeologico** contains a modest archaeological collection and the **Speziera di Santa Fina**, a reconstructed 16th-century pharmacy and herb garden.

Sights & Information

Casa del Boccaccio (☎ 0571 66 42 08; Via Boccaccio, Certaldo; admission €3.10; ☉ 10am-7pm Wed-Mon, 10am-4.30pm Tue, Apr-Sep; 10.30am-4.30pm Wed-Mon Oct-Mar)

Castellina in Chianti tourist office (☎ 0577 74 23 11; Piazza del Comune 1; ☉ 10am-1pm & 3.30-7.30pm Mon-Sat, 10am-1pm Sun)

Certaldo tourist office (☎ 0571 65 27 30; Via Boccaccio 16; ☉ 10am-1pm & 2.30-7pm Tue-Sun, 2.30-7pm Mon Apr-Oct; 10am-12.30pm & 2.30-6.30pm Tue-Sun, 2.30-6.30pm Mon Nov-Mar)

Collegiata(Piazza del Duomo, San Gimignano; adult/child €3.50/1.50, or combined ticket with Museo d'Arte Sacra adult/child €5.50/2.50; ☉ 9.30am-7.30pm Mon-Fri, 9.30am-5.30pm Sat, 1-5pm Sun Apr-Oct; 9.30am-5pm Mon-Sat, 1-5pm Sun Nov–mid-Jan & Mar)

Gaiole in Chianti tourist office (☎ 0577 74 94 11; Via Ricasoli 50; ☉ 9.30am-1pm & 3-6.30pm Mon-Sat Apr-Oct)

Greve in Chianti tourist office (☎ 055 854 62 87; www.chiantichianti.it, Italian only; Via Giuseppe da Verrazzano 59; ☉ 10am-1pm & 2.30-7pm Mon-Fri, 10am-1pm & 2.30-5pm Sat) About 500m short of town when coming in along the SS222 from Florence

Museo Archeologico (☎ 0577 94 03 48; Via Folgore da San Gimignano 11, San Gimignano; adult/child €3.50/2.50, or combined ticket with Museo Civico & Palazzo Pretorio adult/child €7.50/5.50; ☉ 11am-6pm Apr-Oct, 11am-6pm Sat-Thu Nov-Dec)

Museo Civico (☎ 0577 94 00 08; Palazzo del Popolo, San Gimignano; adult/child €5/4, or combined ticket – see Museo Archeologico – adult/child €7.50/5.50; ☉ 9.30am-7.20pm Mar-Oct, 10am-5.50pm Nov-Feb)

Museo d'Arte Sacra (☎ 0577 94 03 16; Piazza Pecori 1, San Gimignano; adult/child €3/1.50, or combined ticket with Collegiata adult/child €5.50/2.50; ☉ 9.30am-7.30pm Apr-Oct, San Gimignano, 9.30am-5pm Nov–mid-Jan & Mar)

Palazzo del Popolo (see Museo Civico)

Palazzo Pretorio (☎ 0571 66 12 19; Certaldo; adult/child €3/1.50, or combined ticket – see Museo Archeologico – adult/child €7.50/5.50; ☉ 9.30am-1pm & 2-7.30pm Apr-Oct, 10.30am-4.30pm Tue-Sun Nov-Mar)

Radda in Chianti tourist office ☎ 0577 73 84 94; Piazza Castello 6; ☉ 10am-12.30pm & 3-6.30pm Mon-Sat Feb-Oct, 10am-noon & 4-6pm Mon-Sat Nov-Jan, 10am-12.30pm Sun May-Sep)

San Gimignano tourist office (☎ 0577 94 00 08; www.sangimignano.com; Piazza del Duomo 1; ☉ 9am-1pm & 3-7pm Mar-Oct, 9am-1pm & 2-6pm Nov-Feb)

Eating

Il Pino (☎ 0577 94 04 15; Via Cellolese 8-10, San Gimignano; meals €35-40; ☉ Fri-Wed) This light airy spot serves truffle-based specialities and home-made desserts.

Mangiango Mangiando (☎ 0558 54 63 72; Piazza Matteotti 80, Greve in Chianti; meals €25; ☉ Mon-Sat) The *pappardelle all'anatra* (ribbon pasta in a duck sauce) is enticing, and one dining room fills with the kitchen aromas.

Trattoria La Mangiatoia (☎ 0577 94 15 28; Via Mainardi 5, San Gimignano; meals €30-40; ☯ Jul-Sep, Wed-Mon Oct-Jun) For a romantic candlelit meal to the gentle accompaniment of classical music in the background, this place is a long-distance favourite with Florentines. Tempting Tuscan cooking is the order of the day.

Sleeping

Albergo del Chianti (☎ 055 85 37 63; www.albergodel chianti.it; Piazza Matteotti 86, Greve in Chianti; s/d €80/98; ☯) Overlooking Greve's central square, this venerable old inn (which dates to the 11th century) offers the luxury of a small pool and gardens.

Castello di Tornano (☎ 0577 74 60 67; www.castellod itornano.it; d €150-420; P ☯ ☲) About 5km south of Gaiole in Chianti, and just left off the winding SS408 road to Siena (along about 1.5km of dirt track), is this medieval Tuscan escape in the heart of wine country. Choose from a selection of lavishly decorated rooms in the mansion or tower. Four-poster beds, heavy drapes and cosy lounge areas characterise this warm stone hideaway. Apartments rented by the week are also available. Taste their wine or go horseriding. Check the website for special offers.

Hotel La Cisterna (☎ 0577 94 03 28; www.hotelcisterna.it; Piazza della Cisterna 24, San Gimignano; s/d €70/120; P €15; ☯ ☲) Spotless rooms with all modern comforts nevertheless exude the charm of a hotel that has been in business for a century. You have a choice of views over the central square or across the valley.

Transport

Distance from Florence Barberino Val d'Elsa 29.5km; Castellina in Chianti 39km; Certaldo 44.5km, Gaiole in Chianti 60km; Greve in Chianti 20km; Montefioralle 22km; Monteriggioni 53km; Radda in Chianti 50km; San Casciano in Val di Pesa 16.5km; San Gimignano 57.5km.

Direction South

Bus Unfortunately buses can be a slow way of getting around. SITA's regular buses run to Greve (€2.90) but take more than an hour! Only two buses run to Radda (€3.50, one hour 40 minutes). Only one leaves at 1.25pm for Gaiole (€4, two hours) via Castellina (€3.50, one hour 40 minutes), which are better linked by bus with Siena (four or five a day). For Monteriggioni the only option is to get a SITA bus from Siena to Poggibonsi and ask to be let off at or near the village en route. Getting back is more hit and miss. Up to 14 buses a day run to San Gimignano from Florence (€5.40, 1¼ hours), but you must change at Poggibonsi.

Car Take the SS222 (Strada Chiantigiana) through the Chianti hills to tour Greve, Castellina, Radda and Gaiole. Otherwise follow the minor road that shadows the SS2 *superstrada* between Florence and Siena. The more ambitious, wanting to reach San Gimignano along one of these routes, will have no choice but to do so by car.

Train Regular trains run from Florence to Certaldo (€3.65, 50 minutes).

PISA & LUCCA

Known today above all for an architectural project gone badly pear-shaped, Pisa of the Leaning Tower was Rome's main naval base during the Punic Wars and a big medieval player in the rough and tumble of Mediterranean trade empire-building. Nearby Lucca, another Roman town that had been founded by the Ligurians, fell under Pisan control in 1314 but later regained independence, which, despite Florence's best efforts, it clung to until 1799.

Pisa's 'Golden Days' began late in the 9th century when it became an independent maritime republic and a rival of Genoa and Venice. The good times rolled on into the 12th and 13th centuries. Some of the city's finest buildings date from this period. Eclipsed by its seafaring rivals, Pisa soon also felt the menace of Florence, which took the city in 1406. The Medicis did at least do the Pisans one favour by re-establishing the city's university. One of its most illustrious lecturers would later be Galileo Galilei, Pisa's favourite son.

The Pisans can justly claim that the Campo dei Miracoli is one of the most beautiful squares in the world. Set astride its immaculate lawns is one of the world's greatest concentrations of Romanesque splendour – the cathedral, the baptistry and the Leaning Tower.

The majesty of Pisa's Duomo (Cathedral) made it a model for Romanesque churches all over Tuscany. Begun in 1064, it is covered inside and out with the alternating bands of dark green and cream marble that were to become characteristic of the Pisan-Romanesque style. Enjoy the depth of detail that Giovanni Pisano imparted to the vibrant early-14th-century marble pulpit in the north aisle, on which he spent 10 years of his life.

The Leaning Tower (Torre Pendente) is one of the world's great cock-ups. The Duomo's *campanile* (bell tower), started in 1173 but built on shaky ground, was always unstable. When it was closed to the public in 1990, it was 4.47m out of plumb and many thought it was going to

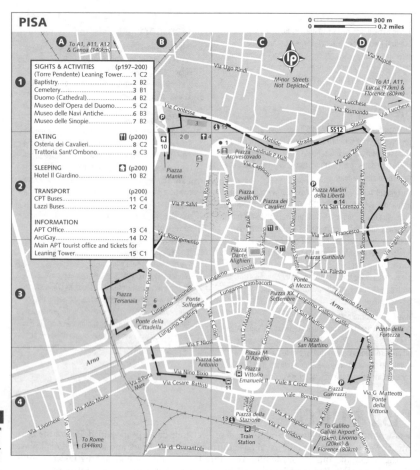

fall. Engineers wrapped cables around the 3rd storey in 1998 and attached them to A-frames. This stabilised the tower while workers removed portions of soil on the north side to create a counter subsidence. The famous lean, now 4.1m off the perpendicular, has been reduced and experts reckon the tower is safe for another 300 years. The slippage that caused the movement in the first place has been arrested.

The unusual round **Battistero** (Baptistry) took centuries to complete, which accounts for the architectural mix. The lower level of arcades is in the Pisan-Romanesque style and the pinnacled upper section and dome are Gothic. The acoustics beneath the dome are remarkable.

Located behind the white wall to the north of the Duomo, the **Campo Santo** (Cemetery) is said to contain soil shipped from Calvary during the Crusades. They say the holy dirt reduces cadavers to skeletons in days! Frescoes saved from Allied bombing of the cloisters in WWII are gathered in a special room.

The **Museo delle Sinopie** houses reddish-brown sketches drawn onto walls as the basis for frescoes, discovered in the cemetery after WWII. The *sinopie* have been restored and provide a fascinating insight into the process of creating a fresco.

The **Museo dell'Opera del Duomo**, near the Leaning Tower, features artworks from the tower, cathedral and baptistery, including an ivory *Madonna col Bambino* (Madonna and Child) by Giovanni Pisano.

The Leaning Tower, Baptistry and Cathedral on the Campo dei Miracoli (Field of Miracles) of Pisa

Take time to walk along the streets of the old city centre, often neglected by high-speed tourists. On the north bank and west of the centre is the **Arsenale**, Pisa's one-time shipyards. They house Le Navi Antiche di Pisa (The Ancient Ships of Pisa), a display of objects (there's even a lion's tooth) recovered from a graveyard of Roman vessels that foundered between the 3rd century BC and the 4th century AD and were discovered in 1998.

The Romanesque **Cattedrale** (Cathedral) of Lucca, 22km north of Pisa, dates from the 11th century and is every bit a rival to its Pisan counterpart. The exquisite façade, in the Lucca-Pisan style, was designed to accommodate the pre-existing bell tower. In the centre of the old town, the **Chiesa di San Michele in Foro** is another dazzling Romanesque church, started in the 11th century. The wedding-cake façade is topped by a figure of the Archangel Michael slaying a dragon. The **Chiesa di San Frediano** is also a must-see with its stunning exterior mosaic.

Lucca's busiest street, **Via Fillungo**, threads its way through the medieval heart of the old city and is lined with fascinating, centuries-old buildings. The **Torre delle Ore** (City Clock Tower) is about halfway along. Just to the east, the houses of **Piazza Anfiteatro** look onto what was the Roman-era amphitheatre.

Take time out from the monuments to amble or cycle (you can rent bicycles at the main tourist office for €10.50 a day) the 3km rim of the city's magnificently intact walls.

Sights & Information

Battistero (Campo dei Miracoli, Pisa; admission €5, or combined ticket including Campo Spirito, Museo dell'Opera del Duomo and Museo delle Sinopie €8.50; admission €6 to two of these monuments, children under 10 visit for free; 8am-7.40pm Jun-Aug, 9am-4.40pm Dec-Feb) For the combined monuments, opening times vary greatly. In some cases there are summer, autumn and winter times, plus weekday and weekend variants. We quote summer and winter 'extremes' here. For the pattern of the day, call ☎ 050 56 05 47, a number covering all monuments and museums.

Campo Santo (Campo dei Miracoli, Pisa; admission €5, or combined ticket – see Battistero – adult/child under

10 €8.50/free; 8am-7.40pm Jun-Aug, 9am-4.40pm Dec-Feb)

Cattedrale (Cathedral; Piazza San Martino, Lucca; admission free; 9.30am-5.45pm Sun-Fri, 9.30am-6.45pm Sat, 1-5.45pm Sun)

Chiesa di San Michele in Foro (Piazza San Michele, Lucca; admission free; 8am-noon & 3-6pm)

Duomo (Campo dei Miracoli, Pisa; admission €2, free Nov-Feb, or combined ticket – see Battistero – adult/child under 10 €8.50/free; 10am-7.40pm Mon-Sat, 1-7.40pm Sun Jun-Aug, 10am-12.45pm & 3-4.45pm Mon-Sat, 3-4.45pm Sun Dec-Feb)

Leaning Tower (Campo dei Miracoli, Pisa; www.opapisa.it; admission €15 (children may not visit for safety reasons); ⏰ 8am-11pm Jun-Aug, 9am-7pm Sep-May) You must book a place, either on the website or in person, to be sure of a visit as numbers allowed up are limited.

Lucca main tourist office (☎ 0583 44 29 44; www.in -lucca.it; Piazzale Verdi; ⏰ 9am-7pm Mar-Oct, 9am-5.30pm Nov-Feb) Along with bags of information, the office also rents out bicycles.

Museo dell'Opera del Duomo (Campo dei Miracoli, Pisa; admission €5, or combined ticket – see Battistero – adult/child under 10 €8.50/free; ⏰ 8am-7.20pm Jun-Aug, 9am-4.20pm Dec-Feb)

Museo delle Sinopie (Piazza Arcivescovado 8, Pisa; admission €5 or combined ticket – see Battistero – adult/child under 10 €8.50/free; ⏰ 8am-7.40pm Jun-Aug, 9am-4.40pm Dec-Feb)

Museo Le Navi Antiche di Pisa (☎ 050 2 14 41; Lungarno Simonelli, Pisa; adult/child €3/free; ⏰ 10am-1pm & 2-6pm Tue-Sun)

Pisa tourist office (☎ 050 56 04 64; www.pisa.turismo .toscana.it; Piazza del Duomo; ⏰ 9am-6pm Mon-Sat, 10.30am-4.30pm Sun)

Pisa train station tourist office (☎ 050 4 22 91; ⏰ 9am-7pm Mon-Sat, 9.30am-3.30pm Sun)

Eating

Osteria dei Cavalieri (☎ 050 58 08 58; Via San Frediano 16, Pisa; meals €30-35; ⏰ Mon-Fri & Sat evening) In what is one of Pisa's most delightful restaurants, you can opt for a single dish (piatto unico) or choose from a mouth-watering menu.

Ristorante Buca di Sant'Antonio (☎ 0583 5 58 81; Via della Cervia 3, Lucca; meals from €35; ⏰ Tue-Sat & Sun lunch) This stylish restaurant is a favourite with discerning

locals, so book ahead. While expensive, it's well worth splashing out for. The menu includes such treats as guinea fowl.

Trattoria Sant'Ombono (☎ 050 54 08 47; Piazza Sant'Ombono 6, Pisa; meals €20-25; ⏰ Mon-Fri & Sat evening) Those traditional red-and-white chequered table clothes, simple cuisine and the location amid old Pisa's produce market makes this a good little lunch stop. Try the vitello tonnato (veal prepared in tuna-based sauce).

Sleeping

Hotel Il Giardino (☎ 050 56 21 01; fax 0558 31 03 92; Piazza Manin 1, Pisa; s/d €70/110; Ⓟ ⌘) You'll find sparkling, well-maintained rooms and friendly staff here. Enjoy breakfast on the tranquil terrace with the city walls and Battistero dome in view.

Piccolo Hotel Puccini (☎ 0583 5 54 21; www.hotelpuccini .com; Via di Poggio 9, Lucca; s/d with bathroom €55/80. Smart, friendly, centrally located and within spitting distance of Piazza San Michele, Hotel Puccini has plenty going for it.

Transport

Distance from Florence Lucca 71km; Pisa 79km
Direction West
Bus Lazzi operates buses to Lucca from Florence (€4.70, 1½ hours) and Pisa (€6.20, two hours). Train is a better bet in both cases.
Car For Pisa take the SS67 superstrada, which is not a toll road. The A11 toll road from Florence skirts around the south of Lucca. The two cities are 22km apart.
Train Regular trains run from Florence to Pisa (€4.85; 1¼ hours) and Lucca (€4.45, 1¼ to 1½ hours). Regular trains also connect Pisa and Lucca (€2, 25 minutes).

PRATO, PISTOIA & AROUND

A 100km western circuit from Florence would see you exploring the industrious towns of Prato and Pistoia, followed by Leonardo da Vinci's birthplace and finally the ceramics centre of Montelupo. It is easily enough done by car but a little more difficult by public transport as the links with Vinci are not so great.

The textile town of **Prato**, 18.5km northwest of Florence, was founded by the Ligurians, taken by the Etruscans and finally absorbed into the Roman federation. By the 11th century Prato was an important centre for wool production and soon fell into Florence's orbit. Today, although capital of a separate province, it is close to being engulfed by Florence's suburban sprawl.

The city's grand Palazzo Duomo is fronted by the 12th-century **Cattedrale di Santo Stefano**. The rather simple Pisan-Romanesque façade features a lunette by Andrea della Robbia, but the most extraordinary element is the **Pulpito della Sacra Cintola** jutting over the piazza on the right-hand side of the main entrance. The pulpit, created by Donatello, was expressly added so that the sacra cintola (sacred girdle) could be displayed to the people five times a year (Easter, 1 May, 15 August, 8 September and 25 December). It is said the Virgin Mary gave the girdle (or belt) to St Thomas, which later found its way to Prato from Jerusalem after the Second Crusade. Mind you, at least one other such girdle has been declared the real thing in the Syrian city of Hom. The original pulpit is housed in the **Museo dell'Opera del Duomo**, accessed through the church's charming cloister.

The small but impressive **Museo di Pittura Murale**, reached through the cloister of the Gothic **Chiesa di San Domenico**, houses a collection of largely Tuscan paintings. Stars include Filippo Lippi, Paolo Uccello and Bernardo Daddi, with his polyptych of the miracle of the Virgin's girdle (it's a bit of a theme here). Enjoy too the 14th- to 17th-century frescoes and graffiti.

Prato's castle, the **Castello dell'Imperatore**, was built in the 13th century by the Holy Roman Emperor Frederick II. It's an interesting example of military architecture but rather bare inside.

Finally, the **Museo del Tessuto** is the only such museum in Italy, dedicated exclusively to textiles, with more than 5000 samples dating from the 5th century to the present day.

Lying at the foot of the Apennines, and barely an energetic spit from Prato, **Pistoia** has grown beyond its well-preserved medieval ramparts and is today a centre for train manufacture. In the 16th century the city's metalworkers also created the pistol, named after the city.

Piazza del Duomo is the focal point of Pistoia's sightseeing wealth. The façade of the **Cattedrale di San Zeno** is Pisan-Romanesque and boasts a lunette by Andrea della Robbia. Inside, in the **Cappella di San Jacopo**, is the remarkable silver Dossale di San Jacopo, or Altarpiece of St James. It was begun in the 13th century, with artisans adding to it over the ensuing two centuries until Brunelleschi contributed the final touch, the two half-figures on the left side.

The venerable building between the cathedral and Via Roma is the **Antico Palazzo dei Vescovi**. Guided tours take place four times a day (on open days) through the wealth of artefacts dating as far back as Etruscan times. Book ahead. Across Via Roma is the **Battistero di San Giovanni** (Baptistry of St John). Elegantly banded in green and white marble, it was started in 1337 to a design by Andrea Pisano.

Dominating the eastern flank of Piazza del Duomo is the Gothic Palazzo del Comune, which houses the **Museo Civico** and its Tuscan art from the 13th to 19th centuries.

The portico of the nearby **Ospedale del Ceppo** will stop even the more monument-weary in their tracks. The unique terracotta frieze by Giovanni della Robbia is a pageant of gay colour and depicts the Seven Works of Mercy, while the five medallions represent the Virtues.

A small country road (SP13) leads south out of Pistoia towards Empoli. After a long series of winding curves through the Monte Albano hills (a beautiful drive) and 1.5km short of Vinci, you come across a sign pointing left (east) to the bare **Casa di Leonardo** in a place called **Anchiano**. Here it is believed Leonardo da Vinci was born, the bastard child of a Florentine solicitor, Piero.

Back down on the SP13, you are just short of Vinci itself. The town is dominated by the **Castello dei Guidi**, named after the feudal family that lorded it over this town and surrounds until Florence took control in the 13th century. Inside the castle nowadays is the **Museo Leonardiano**, which contains an intriguing set of over 50 models based on Leonardo's far-sighted designs.

From Vinci head south to Empoli, where you can pick up a train for Florence. En route you could call into **Montelupo**, a market town on the confluence of the Arno and Pesa, and celebrated centre of Tuscan ceramics production since medieval times. There is no shortage of shops here to browse or bequeath money to. In the third week of every month a pottery market is held, while in the last week of June the town hosts an international ceramics fair.

Sights & Information

Antico Palazzo dei Vescovi (☎ 0573 36 92 72; Piazza del Duomo 4, Pistoia; admission €3.60; 🕒 10am-1pm & 3-5pm Tue, Thu & Fri)

Battistero di San Giovanni (Piazza del Duomo, Pistoia; admission free; 🕒 10am-6pm Jun-Aug, 7am-12.30pm & 3.30-7pm Tue-Sun Sep-May)

Cappella di San Jacopo (Piazza del Duomo, Pistoia; adult/child €2/0.50; 🕒 10am-noon & 4-7.30pm)

Casa di Leonardo (☎ 0571 5 60 55, Anchiano; admission free; 🕒 9.30am-7pm Apr-Sep, 9.30am-6pm Oct-Mar)

Castello dell'Imperatore (☎ 0574 3 82 07; Piazza Santa Maria delle Carceri, Prato; admission €2, or combined ticket including Museo dell'Opera del Duomo & Museo di Pittura Murale €5; 🕒 9am-1pm)

Cattedrale di Santo Stefano (Piazza del Duomo, Prato; 🕒 7am-noon & 3.30-7pm Mon-Sat, 7am-noon & 3.30-8pm Sun)

Cattedrale di San Zeno (Piazza del Duomo, Pistoia; 🕒 7am-12.30pm & 3.30-7pm)

Museo Civico (☎ 0573 37 12 96; Piazza del Duomo 1, Pistoia; adult/child €3.10/1.55; 🕒 10am-7pm Tue-Sat, 9am-12.30pm Sun & public holidays)

Detour: Bathing in Montecatini

Those in need of a long, healthy spa bath could clip along to Montecatini, 15km down the A11 from Pistoia on the way to Lucca. Known to the Romans (who had a penchant for hot baths) and for a while owned by the all-grasping Medici, the hot springs of Montecatini Terme only came into their own in the mid-18th century under the watchful eye of the Hapsburg Grand Duke of Tuscany Pietro Leopoldo. Under his reign the present town began to take shape and the first baths were developed. They became particularly popular in the late 19th and early 20th centuries, fuelling a construction boom in elegant hotels.

Today nine separate thermal bath installations operate, mostly from May to October (only the Hotel Excelsior's facilities open year-round). Water bubbles up from a depth of 80m, collecting minerals and salts along the way. This water is used for treatments, medical and aesthetic, ranging from hydrotherapy to cleansing douches, as well as mud therapy and massages. An afternoon at the baths costs €5.50. An all-out body and facial with mud followed by bath costs around €100.

When you've had enough, take the funicular up to pretty Montecatini Alto, whose charming central square is graced with cafés that have long attracted lovers of the water in search of an energising post-relaxation drink. For more details, contact the **APT office** (☎ 0572 77 22 44; Viale Verdi 66; ⏱ 9am-12.30pm & 3-6pm Mon-Sat, 9am-noon Sun) or the **Terme di Montecatini information office** (☎ 0572 77 81; www.termemontecatini.it; Viale Verdi 41; ⏱ 8am-1pm & 3.30-6.30pm Mon-Fri, 8am-1pm Sat & Sun).

Museo dell'Opera del Duomo (☎ 0574 2 93 39; Piazza del Duomo 49, Prato; adult/child €5/3, or combined ticket – see Castello dell'Imperatore – €5; ⏱ 9.30am-12.30pm & 3-6.30pm Mon & Wed-Sat, 9.30am-12.30pm Sun)

Museo del Tessuto (☎ 0574 61 15 03; Via Santa Chiara 24, Prato; adult/child €4/3; ⏱ 10am-6pm Wed-Mon)

Museo di Pittura Murale (☎ 0574 44 05 01; Piazza San Domenico, Prato; admission adult/child €5/3, or combined ticket – see Castello dell'Imperatore – €5; ⏱ 10am-6pm Mon & Wed-Sat, 10am-1pm Sun)

Museo Leonardiano (☎ 0571 5 60 55; Via della Torre, Vinci; adult/child/student €5/2/3.50; ⏱ 9.30am-7pm Apr-Sep, 9.30am-6pm Oct-Mar)

Ospedale del Ceppo (Piazza Giovanni XXIII, Pistoia)

Pistoia tourist office (☎ 0573 2 16 22; www.pistoia.turis mo.toscana.it; Piazza del Duomo 4; ⏱ 9am-1pm & 3-6pm Jun-Aug, Mon-Sat Sep-May)

Prato tourist office (☎ 0574 2 41 12; www.prato.turis mo.toscana.it; Piazza Santa Maria delle Carceri; ⏱ 9am-1.30pm & 2-7pm Mon-Sat Apr-Oct, 9am-1.30pm & 2-7pm Mon-Sat Nov-Mar)

Eating

Osteria Cibbé (☎ 0574 60 75 09; Piazza Mercatale 49, Prato; meals €25; ⏱ Mon-Sat) This *osteria* shelters beneath ancient vaults and offers traditional local cuisine. The *sedani ripieni* (celery stuffed with meat) is a Prato speciality. Or try *minestra di riso e lampredotto* (broth with rice and veal tripe).

Ristorante San Jacopo (☎ 0573 2 77 86; Via Crispi 15, Pistoia; meals €25-30; ⏱ Wed-Sun & Tue dinner) House specialities here include Tuscan greats like *pappardelle alle lepre* (wide flat pasta ribbons with stewed hare, red wine and tomato sauce).

Sleeping

Hotel Flora (☎ 0574 3 35 21; fax 0574 40 02 89; Via B Cairoli 31, Prato; s/d €90/140 inc breakfast; P €10; ☒ 🖳) This attractive three-star is in the town centre. Most of the bedrooms, with parquet floors, have been recently renovated.

Hotel Leon Bianco (☎ 0573 2 66 75; Via Panciatichi 2, Pistoia; www.hotelleonbianco.it; s/d €65/95; P €5; ☒ 🖳) A friendly, family-owned hotel, and by far the most venerable in town, it has operated as an inn since the 15th century.

Transport

Distance from Florence Montelupo 23.5km; Pistoia 37km; Prato 18.5km; Vinci 61km (via Pistoia).
Direction West
Bus Regular Copit buses connect Vinci with Empoli (€1.90, 25 minutes), itself served by trains from Florence via Montelupo.
Car The best way to do this circuit, especially if you want to complete it in a day, is by car. Otherwise all the destinations except Vinci are easily reached by train. Take the A11 west out of Florence for both Prato and Pistoia. From Pistoia the minor SP13 route winds up into the Monte Albano hill country on its way south to Vinci (24km) – car is the only way to do this stretch. From there you can drop south to Empoli and turn east on the SS67 for Florence via Montelupo.
Train Regular trains run from Florence to Prato (€1.55, 25 minutes), Pistoia (€2.60, 40 minutes) and Montelupo (€2.05, 25 minutes).

Directory

Directory

TRANSPORT

AIR

Flying into Florence for most people actually means flying into Pisa's Galileo Galilei airport, 80 minutes away by direct train. Pisa is an important central Italian hub and flights arrive from most main European centres (for travel details see Airports below). A handful of European and domestic flights serve Florence's smaller Amerigo Vespucci airport. To broaden your options, you could also fly into Bologna. For most intercontinental air travel you will have to change flights at least once, either in Rome or Milan or at another major European hub.

Flights

Look out for budget airline deals. Of the several low-budget airlines now operating out of the UK, only the Irish airline Ryanair serves Pisa and none fly to Florence. EasyJet flies to Bologna, which is a feasible option. The airport is 6km north of Bologna and connected by regular buses and taxi to the city centre. From there Florence is one hour away by train. In all, it is only marginally more complicated than approaching Florence from Pisa. These airlines work on a first-come, first-serve basis: the earlier you book on a flight, the less you pay. As flights fill the price of a ticket also rises. These no-frills airlines skip extras such as inflight meals (although you can buy snacks).

Within Italy, air travel is expensive. In the northern half of the country (eg from Rome, Milan and Venice) it makes more sense to go by train, as the time saving by air is rarely that great and the economic savings by train are considerable. Alitalia and Meridiana are the main airlines serving Florence and Pisa.

Most airlines, especially budget ones, prefer website bookings. Useful sites to search for competitive fares are www.planesimple.co.uk, www.opodo.co.uk, www.expedia.co.uk and www.cheapflights.com.

Airlines

Most airlines don't have shopfront offices in Florence, so you'll need to go online, call the following numbers or try a travel agent. Most airlines also have desks at the airports they serve.

Air Dolomiti (☎ 01803 869 900 in Germany, 800 013 366 in Italy; www.airdolomiti.it) Flights to Pisa from Munich.

Air Littoral (☎ 0825 834 834 in France, 035 23 30 04 in Italy; www.airlittoral.com) Flights from Nice (and other French cities via Nice) to Florence.

Air One (☎ 199 20 70 80; www.flyairone.it) Flights between Florence and Nice (the carrier's partner airline Lufthansa).

Alitalia (☎ 848 865 641/2/3, 055 2 78 81; Vicolo dell'Oro 1; www.alitalia.it)

British Airways (☎ 0870 850 9850 in the UK, 199 712 266 in Italy; www.britishairways.com)

EasyJet (☎ 08706 000 000 in the UK, 848 887 766 in Italy; www.easyjet.com) The nearest this company flies to Florence is Bologna (from London Stansted), an hour away by train.

Meridiana (☎ 199 111 333 or ☎ 055 230 23 14; Lungarno Soderini 1; www.meridiana.it) Flights from Amsterdam, Barcelona, Sardinia and Sicily to Florence; flights between Pisa and Sardinia. It also offers flights to Bologna from Naples, Sardinia and Sicily.

Qantas Airways (☎ 131 313 in Australia; ☎ 06 52 48 27 25, 800 78 53 61 in Italy; www.qantas.com.au) Flights from Australia.

Ryanair (☎ 0871 2460 000 in the UK, 899 289 993 in Italy; www.ryanair.com) Flights from London Stansted, Brussels (Charleroi), Frankfurt (Hahn) and Lübeck to Pisa.

Airports

Florence's **Amerigo Vespucci airport** (☎ 055 306 17 00/2; www.safnet.it) is 5km northwest of the city centre at Via del Termine 11. The main building serves as the departures (partenze) hall, while arrivals (arrivi) is in a smaller building just to the rear of the building. In the latter you'll find a tourist office (which is also where to get information on lost luggage – bagagli smarriti), car rental outlets and an ATM (automated teller machine). There's a bank in the departures lounge. There is no left-luggage service at this airport.

ATAF (☎ 800 42 45 00; www.ataf.net), Florence's local transport company, and **SITA** (☎ 800 37 37 60; www.sita-on-line.it), a regional bus company, together operate the **Vola in Bus** shuttle service between Florence's airport and the SITA terminal in Via Santa Caterina da Siena, near the main train station. It costs €4, takes about 25 minutes and runs every half-hour from 5.30am to 11pm.

Trains for the airport from Florence depart from platform No 5 at Stazione di Santa Maria Novella. Check in your luggage at the station (halfway along platform No 5) 15 minutes before the train departs.

Trains run roughly hourly from 10.26am to 6.45pm (fewer trains operate on Sunday and holidays) from the airport. From Florence, trains leave roughly every hour from 6.46am to 4pm, with a final service leaving at 10.25pm (Via Pistoia). Tickets cost €5.25 and the trip takes about 80 minutes (but check, because some trains take longer and some require a change at Pisa Centrale). The railways run a bus instead of the train from the airport at 12.49am for late arrivals. It goes to the Stazione di Santa Maria Novella in Florence after a stop in Empoli.

A handful of trains take a long route via Lucca, Pistoia and Prato and take about two hours to reach Florence.

A taxi from Florence's Amerigo Vespucci airport will cost around €15 and take about 20 minutes, depending on traffic, to reach the city centre.

Pisa's **Galileo Galilei airport** (☎ 050 50 07 07, ☎ 050 84 93 00 or ☎ 055 21 60 73 for flight information in Florence; www.pisa -airport.com) is the main gateway for passengers bound for Florence. The long, low terminal building is divided into arrivals on the left and departures on the right. There is a tourist office in the arrivals section at the end of the hall. It handles left luggage and you can buy bus and train tickets too. There is a bank with an ATM roughly where the arrivals and departures sections intersect. Car rental agencies, including Avis, Europcar, Maggiore, Thrifty and others, are all represented in the terminal building.

From Pisa airport your only option for Florence is a train (80 minutes). Turn left out of the departures hall and walk onto the railway platform. The local bus No 3 runs from the airport into central Pisa every 20 minutes (€0.77). Buy tickets at tobacconists.

From Pisa a taxi to Florence would cost a fortune – in excess of €200. A taxi from Pisa airport into the centre of town is about €8.

Bologna's **Guglielmo Marconi airport** (☎ 051 314 04 99; www.bologna-airport.it) has check-in desks on both the ground and 1st floors (departure gates are on the 1st floor). You'll find a general information desk on the ground floor, and several ATMs and bureaux de change scattered about across the two floors. There is no left-luggage service but a lost-luggage service operates on the ground floor. You'll find shops and cafés on both floors. There is also a panoramic terrace on the top floor where you can watch flights come and go.

An **Aerobus** (Trasporti Pubblica Bologna; ☎ 199 111 101) service runs every half-hour between Bologna's airport and central city train station (€4.05, 6km away).

Masses of trains run between Florence and Bologna, taking from one to 1½ hours. The first from Bologna leaves at 5.13am and the last at 10.48pm. Tickets cost up to €10.75 depending on the type and speed of service.

From Bologna it would be prohibitively expensive to catch a taxi to Florence. From Bologna airport into the city centre is approximately €16.

BICYCLE

Cycling is a good way to get around central Florence. Some rental options include:

Alinari (Map pp246–7; ☎ 055 21 12 92; Via Guelfa 81/r; road bikes €2.50/7/12/45 per hr/5 hr/day/week; mountain bikes €3/13/18/80 per hr/5 hr/day/week; ⊙ daily Mar-Oct, Mon-Sat Nov-Feb) Alinari also opens rental outlets at several camping grounds in summer – check at the APT office for details (see p220).

Florence by Bike (Map pp246–7; ☎ 055 48 89 92; www .florencebybike.it; Via San Zanobi 120-122/r; standard bicycles €12 per day; scooters from €30 per day; ⊙ 9am-7.30pm)

BUS
Florence

ATAF (Azienda Trasporti Area Fiorentina; Map pp246–7; ☎ 800 42 45 00; www.ataf.net) buses serve the city centre, Fiesole and other areas in the city's outskirts. ATAF is planning to have a hyper-modern 8km tramway built between the Stazione di Santa Maria Novella and the southwest satellite suburb of Scandicci by mid-2006.

USEFUL BUS ROUTES

Several main bus stops for most routes are around Stazione di Santa Maria Novella. Many routes stop operating by 9pm or so. Some of the most useful routes operate from a stop just outside the southeast exit of the station below Piazza Adua (Map pp246–7), including the following:

No 7 For Fiesole.

No 13 Circular route to Piazzale Michelangelo via Ponte alle Grazie (on the way there) and Porta al Prato (on the way back).

No 70 Night bus on a circular route for Campo Marte train station via the Duomo (on the way there) and Piazza dell'Indipendenza (on the way back).

A network of dinky little ecological (three of them electric) minibuses *(bussini)* operates around the centre of town. They can be handy for those getting tired of walking or needing to backtrack right across town. Only Linea D (which runs on a special diesel formula) operates from 7am to 9.20pm (every eight to 10 minutes). The others run from about 8am to 8.20pm Monday to Saturday. You can get a map of the routes published by ATAF from tourist offices.

Linea A This route runs from the Stazione di Santa Maria Novella to Piazza della Repubblica via Via del Parione, Piazza d'Ognisanti and Piazza Santa Trinita, before going along Via Ghibellina and Piazza dei Ciompi to Piazza Beccaria. From there it returns to the train station via Borgo degli Albizi, Via della Vigna Nuova and Piazza dell'Unità.

Linea B From Piazza Piave, this route runs to the Uffizi via Via dei Neri, on to Ponte Santa Trinita and then to Ponte alla Carraia, which it crosses before following the river west to Ponte alla Vittoria. This it crosses and then turns east along Lungarno Vespucci and heads back to Piazza Piave along the riverside.

Linea C Starting at Piazza San Marco, this route passes along Via degli Alfani, Piazza Sant'Ambrogio, Via de' Pepi, Piazza Santa Croce and across Ponte alle Grazie to Piazza di Santa Maria Soprarno. It then recrosses Ponte alle Grazie and returns to Piazza San Marco via Borgo Allegri, Piazza dei Ciompi, Piazza Sant'Ambrogio and Via Colonna.

Linea D This route starts at the Stazione di Santa Maria Novella and weaves down to Ponte di Vespucci, from where it passes on along Borgo San Frediano, Lungarno Guicciardini, past Ponte Vecchio, down Via de' Bardi, and along the *lungarni* to Piazza Ferrucci. It then returns to Ponte Vecchio, turns down past Palazzo Pitti, up Via Sant'Agostino, through Piazza del Carmine and back across Ponte di Vespucci to the train station.

NIGHT BUSES
Of the four so-called night-bus routes, three operate only between 9pm and 1am. The only true night bus *(autobus notturno)* is No

70, which is a circle route starting at Stazione di Santa Maria Novella and passing through Piazza San Marco, Piazza del Duomo, Campo di Marte, Ponte Rosso, Piazza dell'Indipendenza and back to the train station. It operates about every 30 minutes from 12.30am to 6am.

TICKETS
Bus tickets should be bought at tobacconists or automated vending machines at major bus stops before you get on the bus and must be validated in the machine as you enter. You can buy tickets and pick up a useful routes brochure at the **ATAF information office** (Map pp246–7) on Largo Alinari, just outside the southeast exit of Stazione di Santa Maria Novella.

Tickets cost €1 for one hour and €1.80 for three hours. A 24-hour ticket costs €4.50. A four-ticket set *(biglietto multiplo)* costs €3.90 (each ride valid for an hour). You are supposed to stamp these in the machine when you get on your first bus. There are tickets for any number of days up to one week (€16). If you are hanging around Florence longer, you might want to invest in a monthly ticket *(mensile)* at €31 (€20.70 for students).

There is a special 30-day ticket for using the *bussini* (lines A to D) only. It costs €14.

The fine for being caught without a ticket on public transport is €40 – in addition to the price of the ticket, of course, so it's better to be safe than sorry.

Tuscany
Lazzi and SITA run buses to various destinations in Tuscany. Other companies cover this region, including the following:

CAP (Map pp246–7; ☎ 055 21 46 37; www.capautolinee.it; Largo Fratelli Alinari 9)

COPIT (Map pp246–7; ☎ 055 21 46 37; www.copitspa.it, Italian only; Largo Fratelli Alinari 11) Also operates from near the train station to Tuscan destinations.

Long-Distance Buses
Buses leave from a variety of terminals scattered about Stazione di Santa Maria Novella. **Eurolines** (www.eurolines.com), in conjunction with local bus companies across Europe, is the main international carrier. Eurolines' website provides links to the sites of all the national operators. In Florence, Eurolines tickets can be bought at the **Lazzi bus office** (Map pp246–7; ☎ 055 21 55 55; www.lazzi.it; Piazza Stazione 3), on the corner of Piazza Adua. Buses run

several times a week from London, Paris, Barcelona and other European centres.

Lazzi is responsible for long-haul bus services to other parts of Italy, mostly on routes south where train services are either nonexistent or painfully slow. Destinations include Potenza and Matera (Basilicata), and some in Apulia as well as Calabria. **SITA** (Map pp246–7; ☎ 800 37 37 60; www.sita-on-line.it, Italian only; Via Santa Caterina da Siena 15) is just to the west of Stazione di Santa Maria Novella and also offers a handful of long-distance services, most to southern Italy.

Lazzi operates a couple of services to the Abruzzo and Le Marche regions via Perugia.

CAR & MOTORCYCLE
Driving to Florence

Florence is 1235km from Berlin, 1555km from London, 1138km from Paris, 1665km from Madrid, 605km from Geneva, 296km from Milan and 267km from Rome.

The main points of entry to Italy are the Mont Blanc tunnel from France at Chamonix, which connects with the A5 for Turin and Milan; the Grand St Bernard tunnel from Switzerland, which also connects with the A5; and the Brenner Pass from Austria, which connects with the A22 to Bologna. Mountain passes in the Alps are often closed in winter, making the tunnels a more reliable option.

Florence is connected by the A1 to Bologna and Milan in the north, and Rome and Naples in the south. The Autostrada del Mare (A11) connects Florence with Prato, Lucca, Pisa and the coast, and a *superstrada* (expressway) joins the city to Siena. Exits from the autostrade (four- to six-lane motorways) into Florence are well signposted, and there are tourist offices on the A1 both north and south of the city. From the north on the A1, exit at Firenze Nord and follow the bull's-eye *centro* signs; if approaching from Rome, exit at Firenze Sud.

Many of Italy's autostrade are toll roads and the tolls tend to be expensive. You sometimes have the choice of the toll road and a busy *strada statale* (main road; represented on maps as 'S' or 'SS'). These tend to pass through towns and can double your travel time. Smaller roads are known as *strade provinciali* (represented on maps as 'P' or 'SP').

Vehicles must be roadworthy, registered and insured (third party at least). Also ask your insurer for a European Accident Statement form, which can simplify matters in the event of an accident. A European breakdown assistance policy, such as the AA Five Star Service or the RAC Eurocover Motoring Assistance in the UK, is a good investment.

You can pay for petrol with most credit cards at most service stations. Those on the autostrade are open 24 hours per day. Otherwise, opening hours are generally around 7am to 12.30pm and 3.30pm to 7.30pm (7pm in winter). Most are closed on Sunday and public holidays; others close on Monday. Don't assume you can't get petrol if you pass a station that is closed. Quite a few have self-service pumps that accept banknotes.

Driving & Parking in Florence

During 2004 a series of automatic barriers around the historic centre of Florence will make it impossible for all but electronic passholders to enter the old city centre. It probably doesn't matter as the best advice is to leave the car alone while in Florence anyway. Finding parking space is part of the headache. Apart from sometimes very expensive car parks, there are two kinds of parking in Florence. Those areas delineated by white lines are for residents only. The rest are blue (with a red dot) and are metered. Nonresidents must pay to park round the clock, so that feeding the parking meter for 24 hours would cost a total of €31 (it costs €3 for the first hour, €2 each hour thereafter from 8am to 8pm, and €0.50 an hour from 8pm to 8am). There is an alternative. You can request from your hotel the authorisation to obtain a €8 24-hour parking permit for the blue areas.

You can risk parking in the residents' parking zones (white lines). Foreign-registered cars are less likely to attract a fine, and even if they do, you can't really be obliged to pay unless the parking cops actually see you.

If you intend to take your risks and park for days on end, keep an eye out for signs displaying a street-sweeping vehicle. The signs indicate the day of the week and time that cars must be moved to allow street sweepers through. This is usually between midnight and 6am; thus 'Sabato 0 a 6' indicates that from midnight on Friday until 6am on Saturday the street needs to be clear. Your car will be towed if left in such a zone. In areas where they don't do this so regularly, temporary signs announcing the next day it will be done are posted a few days before the street sweepers appear.

If your car is towed away, call the **Depositaria Comunale** (Car Pound; ☎ 055 78 38 82; Ponte a Greve, Lotto Zero).

Rental

Car rental agencies are found in the Borgo Ognissanti area, including the following:

Alinari (see p205) Mopeds and scooters are available from €30 to €33 for five hours, or from €47 to €55 per day.

Avis (Map pp246–7; ☎ 055 21 36 29; Borgo Ognissanti 128/r)

Europcar (Map p248–9; ☎ 055 29 04 37; Borgo Ognissanti 53/r)

Happy Rent (Map pp246–7; ☎ 055 239 96 96; Borgo Ognissanti 153/r)

Hertz (Map pp246–7; ☎ 055 239 82 05; Via Maso Finiguerra 33/r)

Thrifty (Map pp246–7; ☎ 055 28 71 61; Borgo Ognissanti 134/r)

TAXI

Taxis (☎ 055 42 42, 055 47 98, 055 44 99, 055 43 90) can be found outside Stazione di Santa Maria Novella and at other ranks around town. Flagfall is €2.45, on top of which you pay €0.79 per kilometre within the city limits (€1.43 per kilometre beyond).

TRAIN

Train is the most convenient overland option for reaching Florence from other Italian cities or abroad. For information on travelling from the UK, contact the **Rail Europe Travel Centre** (☎ 0870 5848848; www.raileurope.co.uk; 178 Piccadilly, London W1V 0BA). For travel within Italy, you can get information at your nearest train station or travel agent. Alternatively, contact **Trenitalia** (☎ 892021; www.trenitalia.it).

A wide variety of trains run on the Italian rail network. They start with all-stops *locali*, which generally don't travel much beyond their main city of origin or province. Next come the *regionali*, which also tend to be slow, but cover greater distances. *Interregionali* cover greater distances still and don't necessarily stop at every station.

On InterCity (IC) trains, fast services that operate between major cities, you generally have to pay a supplement on top of the normal cost of a ticket. EuroCity (EC) trains are the international version.

High-speed *pendolini* and other top-of-the-range services, which on high-speed track can zip along at more than 300km/h, are collectively known as Eurostar Italia (ES).

Apart from the standard division between 1st and 2nd class (*prima classe* and *seconda classe*) on the faster trains (generally you can get 2nd-class seats only on *locali* and *regionali* services), you usually have to pay a supplement for being on a fast train, which can be paid separately from the ticket (you might decide to avoid the supplement one way and take a slower train) *before* boarding the train.

You can buy railway tickets (for major destinations on fast trains at least) at the station (often crowded) and from most travel agents. There are automatic machines at the station that accept credit cards and cash.

Validate your ticket in the orange machines on station platforms or you could get a hefty on-the-spot fine when the ticket inspector comes around.

Florence Train Station

Florence is an important railway hub, and from the city's main train station, **Stazione di Santa Maria Novella** (Firenze SMN for short; Map pp246–7), you can get direct trains heading in most directions. Its line connects with Milan, Bologna and Rome. Trains also fan out to various parts of Tuscany, although buses can be more convenient for exploring the region around Florence.

The rail travel information office at the western end of the main vestibule of the Stazione di Santa Maria Novella opens from 7am to 9pm. You will also find a tourist office **Consorzio ITA** (which can book hotels; see p220), currency exchange bureaux, a bank (with ATM), phones and **left-luggage** (*deposito*; Map pp246–7; €3 per item for first 12hr, €2 for each 12hr block thereafter; ☼ 6am-midnight).

TRAVEL AGENTS

Florence is not awash with good-value travel agents but you could try the following:

Centro Turistico Studentesco e Giovanile (CTS; Map pp251–3; ☎ 055 28 95 70; www.cts.it; Via dei Ginori 25/r) The main Italian student and youth travel organisation.

CTS (Map pp244–5; ☎ 055 33 41 64; www.cts.it; Via Maragliano 86/i) A second branch of this student travel organisation.

PRACTICALITIES

ACCOMMODATION

Sleeping options range from a series of youth hostels through to some grand old hotels, with prices to match. See the Sleeping chapter earlier for recommendations. The options are presented by district and in alphabetical order. The emphasis is on mid-range accommodation but we have slipped in some of the city's great top-range hotels too. Each section ends with a Cheap Sleeps list for those travelling on a tighter budget.

High season is most of the year for most hotels, which means that you should be prepared to pay their top rates. Many hotels do not alter their rates significantly during the year. The depths of winter (late November to December, except Christmas, and mid-January to March) are quieter in Florence, when hoteliers sometimes chop more than half off their top asking price. The same is also true of the sweltering month of August.

For more information on prices, reservations and accommodation websites and so on, turn to the beginning of the Sleeping chapter (pp176–8).

BUSINESS
Opening Hours
In general, shops are open 9am to 1pm and 3.30pm to 7.30pm (or 4pm to 8pm) Monday to Saturday. They may remain closed on Monday morning, or Wednesday afternoon or Saturday afternoon or both afternoons. Laws on opening hours are fairly flexible so shopkeepers have a large degree of discretion.

Big department stores, such as Coin and La Rinascente, and most supermarkets are open around 9am to 7.30pm Monday to Saturday.

Banks open from 8.30am to 1.30pm and 3.30pm to 4.30pm Monday to Friday, but hours often vary. A few may open on Saturday morning.

Bars (the Italian way, ie coffee-and-sandwich places) and cafés generally open 7.30am to 8pm, although some stay open after 8pm and turn into pub-style drinking and meeting places. Pubs and bars mostly shut by 1am, except on Friday and Saturday nights, when quite a few will kick on until 2am or 3am.

For lunch (pranzo), restaurants usually open from 12.30pm to 3pm, but many prefer taking orders after 2pm. At nights, opening hours for dinner (cena) vary, but people start sitting down to dine at around 8.30pm. It's difficult to find a place still serving after 10.30pm.

Doing Business in Florence
People wishing to make the first moves towards expanding their business into Italy

should contact their own country's trade department (such as the DTI in the UK). The commercial department of the Italian embassy in your own country should also have information – at least on red tape.

In Italy, the trade office of your embassy can provide tips and contacts.

A GSM mobile phone and a good laptop computer will probably be all you need to do business in Florence. However, some of the better hotels have secretarial assistance for guests. Other companies that might be of help are listed in the Yellow Pages (Pagine Gialle) under *Uffici Arredati e Servizi*. Translators/interpreters are listed under *Traduzioni Servizio* or *Traduttori ed Interpreti*. You'll also find a couple of dozen listed in the *English Yellow Pages in Italy*.

Florence has several conference centres. The **Firenze Convention Bureau** (☎ 055 497 32 01; www.firenzeconventionbureau.it; Guardiola del Pratello Orsini 1, 50123 Florence) has many events organisers and support services (such as interpreters) listed on its website. Connected with it is **Firenze Expo & Congress** (☎ 055 497 21; www.firenze-expo.it; Piazza Adua 150123 Florence), which can organise big events in such historic sites as the Fortezza da Basso and the city's main conference centre, the **Palazzo degli Affari** (Map pp246–7; Piazza Adua 1, 50123 Florence), which has conference halls, seating for almost 2000 people, interpreting and translation services and a buffet area. Various trade fairs are held here throughout the year.

CHILDREN
Children may well weary of traipsing around worthy art galleries and grand churches. A few books could help you get the kids involved in the sightseeing, such as *Bambini alla Scoperta di Firenze* (translated as *Florence for Kids*). It uses an entertaining approach, with quizzes and other learning prompts. *Florence for Teens* has lots of bite-sized history lessons and pictures. *Florence: A Young Traveller's Guide* has many detailed illustrations of monuments and breezy text.

For more information on how to amuse the kids, see Lonely Planet's *Travel with Children*. See the boxed text for activities with children, p62.

Baby-sitting
Most of the medium- and upper-range hotels in Florence can offer or organise a baby-sitting service.

CLIMATE

Florence's position in a river basin, walled in by hills to the south and the foothills of the Apennines to the north, largely determines its climate. In summer the city is a like a pressure cooker as heat and humidity soar. July is the worst month (closely followed by August) and there are days when there is not a whisper of air. The average highs hover around 31°C. Occasionally you can enjoy the temporary relief of a cracking good thunderstorm.

Winter, on the other hand, is cool and often wet, although mercifully it doesn't last too long. Average temperatures in January range between 1°C and 10°C and snow is rare.

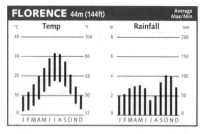

COURSES

Florence has more than 30 schools offering courses in Italian language and culture. Many other schools offer courses in art, including painting, drawing, sculpture and art history, and several offer cooking courses, although they are more expensive than schools in places like Siena, Perugia and Urbino.

Florence's APT office also has lists of schools and courses, which it will mail on request.

Non-EU citizens who want to study at a university or language school in Italy must have a study visa – obtained from your nearest Italian embassy or consulate. You will normally require confirmation of your enrolment, payment of fees and proof of adequate funds to support yourself before a visa is issued.

The cost of language courses in Florence depends on the school, the length of the course (one month is usually the minimum duration) and its intensity. Local authorities sometimes run courses (not at regular intervals) generally for free and aimed at impecunious migrants, for a couple of hours a week.

Centro Lingua Italiana Calvino (Map pp246–7; ☎ 055 28 80 81; www.clicschool.it; Viale Fratelli Rosselli 74) You have the option of standard and intensive courses here, the latter totalling 30 hours per week (€225) but this place is in an unattractive location around the back end of Stazione di Santa Maria Novella.

Centro Lorenzo de' Medici (Map pp246–7; ☎ 055 28 73 60; www.lorenzodemedici.it; Via Faenza 43) This school is popular with American students. Four hours per day for a month costs €590. It offers many levels and a variety of courses in art, cooking, history and the like. You can also arrange individual tuition.

Istituto Europeo (Map pp251–3; ☎ 055 238 10 71; www.istitutoeuropeo.it; Piazzale delle Pallottole 1) One-week/four-week course costs €202/460. It offers discount scholarships for students.

Istituto di Lingua e Cultura Italiana per Stranieri Michelangelo (Map pp248–50; ☎ 055 24 09 75; Via Ghibellina 88) Four-week course (80 hours) costs €510. The school will organise private one-on-one courses, starting at €728 a week (four hours a day).

Scuola Leonardo da Vinci (Map pp246–7; ☎ 055 26 11 81; www.scuolaleonardo.com; Via Bufalini 3) Four-week course costs €500. Courses offered range from two to 24 weeks, usually averaging four hours of class per day. A heavily intensive course (120 hours in four weeks) costs €780.

Scuola Toscana (Map pp248–50; ☎ 055 24 45 83; http: inter-med.net/scuolatoscana; Via de' Benci 23) This school focuses on business customers, with a variety of courses. Two-week course (four hours a day in class and one hour of one-on-one teaching) costs €866 including accommodation.

Società Dante Alighieri (Map pp246–7; ☎ 055 247 89 81; www.dantealighieri.it; Via Gino Capponi 4) The national cultural association, with branches across the country and worldwide, offers a broad range of courses. One month (80 hours) costs €455. The society is housed in the 16th-century former Oratorio di San Pierino, whose courtyard retains many frescoes from that time.

Many of the schools already listed also offer a programme of courses on art history, cooking, art, music and the like.

Art courses range from one-month summer workshops to longer-term professional diploma courses. Schools will organise accommodation for students, on request and at added cost, either in private apartments or with Italian families. The APT office in Via Cavour has exhaustive lists on courses offered in subjects such as theatre, fashion, ceramics and leather. Here are some of them:

Accademia Italiana (Map pp248–50; ☎ 055 28 46 16; www.accademiaitaliana.com; Piazza de' Pitti 15) This school offers a wide range of design programmes, including one-month courses and more rigorous semester courses in painting, graphic arts, fashion design and related fields.

Istituto per l'Arte e il Restauro (Map pp248–50; ☎ 055 24 60 01; www.spinelli.it; Palazzo Spinelli, Borgo Santa Croce 10) Here you can learn to restore anything from paintings to ceramics, interior and graphic design, gilding and marquetry. It has short courses and full academic programmes. For the latter, you are looking at €8800 a year.

Cordon Bleu (Map pp248–50; ☎ 055 234 54 68; www.cordonbleu-it.com; Via di Mezzo 55/r) This is the place to go to learn some stylish cooking methods. Classes have from eight to 15 students. A basic eight-lesson cooking course costs €415.

Florence Dance Centre (Map pp248–50; ☎ 055 28 92 76; www.florencedance.org; Borgo della Stella 23/r) This centre offers a range of courses in classical, jazz and modern dance. The school was founded and is still run by the ballerina Marga Nativo.

Università Internazionale dell'Arte (Map pp244–5; ☎ 055 57 02 16; www.uiafirenze.com; Villa Il Ventaglio, Via delle Forbici 24-26) Those contemplating serious art studies could look into courses offered by this institution. They range from museum studies through restoration to specialist courses in such areas as African art history.

CUSTOMS

People entering Italy from outside the EU are allowed to bring in duty-free one bottle of spirits, one bottle of wine, 50mL of perfume and 200 cigarettes.

Duty-free allowances for travel between EU countries were abolished in 1999. For duty-paid items bought at normal shops in one EU country and taken into another, the allowances are 90L of wine, 10L of spirits, unlimited quantities of perfume and 800 cigarettes. VAT-free (value-added tax) shopping is available in the duty-free shops at airports for people travelling between EU countries.

DISABLED TRAVELLERS

The **Comune di Firenze** (City Council; www.co munefirenze.it) publishes a booklet, *Guida alle Strutture e ai Servizi della Città*, which lists hundreds of places, including churches, museums, banks, hotels and restaurants, with an accessibility rating and description. The booklet comes with a map of central Florence outlining accessible footpaths and crossings for those in wheelchairs. It is sometimes available at the tourist offices.

About half of Florence's ATAF buses are equipped for wheelchair access, and ATAF expects its fleet of some 500 buses to be fully modified by about 2005 (depending on finances). The problem is that uneven bus stops sometimes provide obstacles about which ATAF can do little. ATAF and the tourist offices sometimes have a map showing bus routes with specially equipped buses.

Organisations

Accessible Travel & Leisure (☎ 01452-729739; www.ac cessibletravel.co.uk; Avionics House, Naas Lane, Gloucester GL2 4SN). Claims to be the biggest UK travel agent dealing with travel for the disabled. The company encourages the disabled to travel independently.

Holiday Care (☎ 0845 124 9971; www.holidaycare .org.uk; 2nd flr, Imperial Bldgs, Victoria Rd, Horley, Surrey RH6 7PZ). Information on hotels with disabled access, where to hire equipment and tour operators dealing with the disabled.

Royal Association for Disability & Rehabilitation (RADAR; ☎ 020-7250 3222; www.radar.org.uk; Unit 12, City Forum, 250 City Rd, London EC1V 8AS) Publishes *European Holidays & Travel Abroad: A Guide for Disabled People*, which provides a good overview of facilities available to disabled travellers throughout Europe.

DISCOUNT CARDS

The ISIC (International Student Identity Card) seems to be of limited use in Italy, as the staff at most sights want proof that you are under 26. Those who qualify should get the Euro<26 card, available from most national student organisations or check out their website: www.euro26.org. ISIC information is located at www.isic.org.

ELECTRICITY

The electric current in Florence is 220V, 50Hz, as in the rest of continental Europe. Some countries outside Europe (such as the USA and Canada) use 110V, 60Hz power, which means that certain appliances from those countries may perform poorly. It is safest to use a transformer. Plugs have two round pins, as in the rest of continental Europe.

EMBASSIES & CONSULATES

Most countries have an embassy in Rome. Look them up under 'Ambasciate' in that city's Yellow Pages (Pagine Gialle). Various countries maintain consulates in Florence, including the following:

Germany (Map pp246–7; ☎ 055 29 47 22; Lungarno Amerigo Vespucci 30)

Netherlands (Map pp246–7; ☎ 055 47 52 49; Via Cavour 81)

Switzerland (Map pp244–5; ☎ 055 22 24 31; Piazzale Galileo 5)

UK (Map pp251–3; ☎ 055 28 41 33; Lungarno Corsini 2)

USA (Map pp246–7; ☎ 055 26 69 51; Lungarno Amerigo Vespucci 38)

EMERGENCIES

Tourists who want to report thefts or obtain a residence permit will need to go to the *questura*, or **main police station** (Map pp246–7; ☎ 055 4 97 71; Via Zara 2). The rather self-important building is a late-18th-century curio originally been built to be a hospital. The police also operate a special unit to assist tourists, the **Polizia Assistenza Turistica** (Map pp248–50; ☎ 055 20 39 11; Via Pietrapiana 50/r; ⏲ 8.30am-7.30pm Mon-Fri, 8.30am-1.30pm Sat).

Military Police *(carabinieri)*	☎ 112
Police *(polizia)*	☎ 113
Fire Brigade *(vigili del fuoco)*	☎ 115
Highway Rescue *(soccorso stradale)*	☎ 116
Ambulance *(ambulanza)*	☎ 118

GAY & LESBIAN TRAVELLERS

Homosexuality is legal in Italy and reasonably well tolerated in Florence, although open displays of gay affection are not always well received – a little discretion is advisable.

The city offers a handful of gay bars and clubs, but Florentine gays agree the options are limited (they blame tourist lit and guidebooks for creating an unduly positive image of Florentine gay life!). If you're looking to do some night-time cruising, head for Le Cascine park, especially in the area around the Rio Grande disco. Be aware that the activity comes with a degree of risk attached. As the local gay association strenuates, attacks do take place and too few victims do not come forward.

ArciGay (www.arcigay.it), the national gay organisation, has general information on the gay and lesbian scene in Italy, while the companion **Gay.It** website (http://it.gay.com, Italian only) provides listings information for everything from bars and discos to gay beaches and beauty centres across the country. The Tuscan branch of **ArciGay** (Map p198; ☎ 050

55 56 18; www.gaytoscana.it, Italian only; Via San Lorenzo 38) is based in Pisa. In paper, your best bet is the *Chiquito Italian Gay Travel Guide* (€8), available in good bookshops in Florence.

In Florence, **Azione Gay e Lesbica Finisterrae** (Map pp244–5; ☎ 055 67 12 98; www.azionegayelesbica.it, Italian only; Via Manara 12) welcomes newcomers to town and keeps tabs on what's going on in local gay circles.

Ireos (Map pp251–3; ☎ 055 21 69 07; www.ireos.org, Italian only; Via de' Serragli 3/5) is a gay-lesbian association that organises cultural events and runs a medical and psychological counselling service. It is possible to organise HIV tests here.

At the **Libreria delle Donne** (☎ 055 234 78 10; www.women.it/libreriafirenze/fili.htm, Italian only; Via Fiesolana 2b) women's bookshop and attached women's cooperative you can obtain information on the lesbian scene in Florence.

HOLIDAYS

For Florentines, the main holiday periods remain summer (July and especially August), the Christmas–New Year period and Easter. August is a peculiar time as all Italy grinds to a halt, especially around Ferragosto (15 August), when just about everything closes. Travelling to and around Florence in this busy holiday period is far from ideal (for information on the city's colourful festivals and other events, see p9). Here follows a list of national public holidays.

New Year's Day (Anno Nuovo) 1 January

Epiphany (Befana) 6 January

Good Friday (Venerdì Santo) March/April

Easter Monday (Pasquetta/Giorno dopo Pasqua) March/April

Liberation Day (Giorno della Liberazione) April 25 – marks the Allied Victory in Italy and the end of the German presence and Mussolini in 1945.

Labour Day (Giorno del Lavoro) 1 May

Feast of the Assumption (Ferragosto) 15 August

All Saints' Day (Ognissanti) 1 November

Feast of the Immaculate Conception (Concezione Immaculata) 8 December

Christmas Day (Natale) 25 December

Boxing Day (Festa di Santo Stefano) 26 December

INTERNET ACCESS

Travelling with a portable computer is a great way to stay in touch with life back home, but unless you know what you're doing it's fraught with potential problems. Make sure you have a universal AC adaptor, a two-pin plug adaptor for Europe and a reputable 'global' modem. Italian telephone sockets are mostly the US RJ-11 type (if you find yourself confronted with the old-style Italian three-prong socket, most electrical stores can sell you an adaptor). Some of the better hotels are set up with internet connections and sometimes just plugging into the hotel room's phone socket will be sufficient (although frequently this will not work as you have to go through a switchboard). If you need more detailed information on travelling with a portable computer, contact www.teleadapt.com.

Major Internet Service Providers (ISPs) like **CompuServe** (www.compuserve.com) have dial-in nodes in Italy; download a list of the dial-in numbers before you leave home.

Some Italian servers can provide short-term accounts for local Internet access. **Agora** (☎ 800 30 49 99; www.agoratelematica.it) is one of them. Several Italian ISPs offer free Internet connections: contact **Tiscalinet** (www.tiscali.it), **kataweb** (www.kataweb.it) and **Libero** (www.libero.it).

If you intend to rely on Internet cafés, you'll need to carry three pieces of information: your incoming (POP or IMAP) mail server name, your account name and your password.

Internet Cafés

Florence is awash with Internet centres. Some offer student rates and also have deals on cards for several hours' use at much reduced rates. A handful of options follow:

CyberOffice (Map pp246–7; ☎ 055 21 11 03; Via San Gallo 4/r; €3.50 per hr; ☼ 9am-8pm Mon-Fri & 11am-6pm Sat)

Il Cairo Phone Center (Map pp248–50; ☎ 055 263 83 36; Via de' Macci 90/r; from as little as €1.80 per hr; ☼ 9.30am-9pm)

Internet Train (www.internettrain.it; Italian only) Has 14 branches around town. Services include mobile-phone rental, Fedex express courier, fax, scanning, printing, film processing and CD writing. One hour online costs €4 (or €20 for six hours). Branches include Via dell'Oriuolo 40/r (Map pp248–50; ☎ 055 234 53 22; ☼ 10am-10.30pm Mon-Thu, 10am-8pm Fri-Sat, 3-7pm Sun), Via Guelfa 54-56/r (Map pp246–7; ☎ 055 264 51 46; ☼ 9am-11pm Mon-Fri, 10am-8pm Sat, noon-9pm Sun), Via de' Benci 36/r (Map pp248–50; ☎ 055 263 85 55; ☼ 9.30am-1am Mon-Fri, 10am-1am Sat, noon-1am Sun), Borgo San Jacopo

30/r (Map pp251–3; ☎ 055 265 79 35; ☼ 11am-11pm Mon-Fri, noon-8pm Sat-Sun), Via Porta Rossa 38/r (Map pp251–3; ☎ 055 274 10 37) and Borgo de la Croce 33/r (Map pp251–3; ☎ 055 234 78 52; ☼ 10am-midnight) A handy one is in the subterranean pedestrian passage beneath Stazione di Santa Maria Novella (☎ 055 239 97 20; ☼ 9am-8.30pm Mon-Fri, 11am-8pm Sat-Sun).

The Netgate (Map pp248–50; ☎ 055 234 79 67; www.thenetgate.it; Via Sant'Egidio 14/r; €4 per hr, €32 per 10 hrs; ☼ 10am-8.30pm Mon-Fri, 2-8.30pm Sat) Has four other branches, including one in the underground shopping passage below Stazione di Santa Maria Novella, and terminals set up in a long list of shops, hotels and cafés around town.

Webpuccino (Map pp251–3; ☎ 055 277 64 69; www.webpuccino.it; Via de' Conti 22/r; €4 per hr; ☼ 10am-10pm Mon-Sat, 11am-9pm Sun) It offers Campus mobile phone rental too, as well as digital photo printing and CD burning.

Your Virtual Office (Map pp251–3; faenza@caironet.it; Via Faenza 49r; €4.50 per hr, €2.60 per hr 9.30am-12.30pm & 5.30-8.30pm; ☼ 8.30am-midnight) Burns data, photos etc onto CDs. Equipment is not top of the range.

LOST PROPERTY

Lost property (oggetti smarriti) can be collected (on the assumption it has been found and handed in!) from an office operated by the city council and the **vigili urbani** (local police; Map pp244–5; ☎ 055 328 39 42/43; Via Circondaria 19), located northwest of the city centre.

MAPS

The free map of Florence distributed by the tourist office is not helpful at all, and a sensible investment would be Lonely Planet's fold-out Florence City Map. It is plastic-coated, virtually indestructible and indicates all the major landmarks, museums and shops, as well as containing a comprehensive street index. Another worthwhile purchase is Florence, which is produced by the Touring Club Italiano (TCI), which also publishes a paper map of the city centre.

MEDICAL SERVICES
Medical Cover

All foreigners have the same right as Italians to free emergency medical treatment in a public hospital. EU citizens are entitled to the full range of health care services in public hospitals free of charge, but you will need to present your E111 form (inquire at your national health service before leaving home). Australia has a reciprocal arrangement with Italy that entitles Australian citizens to free public health care – carry your Medicare card.

Citizens of New Zealand, the USA and Canada and other countries have to pay for anything other than emergency treatment. Most travel insurance policies include medical cover.

The Italian public health system is administered by local centres generally known as Unità Sanitaria Locale (USL) or Unità Socio Sanitaria Locale (USSL). These are usually listed under 'U' in the telephone book (or sometimes under 'A' for Azienda USL). Under these headings you'll find long lists of offices – look for Poliambulatorio (Polyclinic) and the telephone number for medical appointments *(accetazione sanitaria)*. You are required to call this number to make an appointment – there is no point in just rolling up. Clinic opening hours vary widely, with the minimum generally being about 8am to 12.30pm Monday to Friday. Some clinics also open for a couple of hours in the afternoon and/or on Saturday morning. In the case of an emergency, head for the *pronto soccorso* unit of any hospital.

For minor health problems, you can try your local pharmacy *(farmacia)*, where pharmaceuticals tend to be sold more freely without prescription than in places such as the USA, Australia or the UK (see p215).

If your country has a consulate in Florence, staff there should be able to refer you to doctors who speak your language. The APT has lists of doctors and dentists of various nationalities. If you have a specific health complaint, obtain the necessary information and referrals for treatment before leaving home.

The following medical services may be of use to travellers.

Centro MTS (Malattie a Trasmissione Sessuale; Map pp246–7; ☎ 055 275 86 94; Piazza Brunelleschi 4; ☙ 8am-noon Mon-Fri) Anonymous walk-in service where you can get AIDS tests at the rear end of the Ospedale di Santa Maria Nuova.

Guardia Medica (☎ 055 47 78 91; ☙ 8pm-8am Mon-Fri, 10am on Sat to 8am Mon) Night-time call-out doctors (locums) service.

Misericordia di Firenze (Map pp251–3; ☎ 055 21 22 22; Vicolo degli Adimari 1; medical attention centre for tourists ☙ 1.30-5pm Mon-Fri) Also runs an ambulance service.

Ospedali Riuniti di Careggi (Map p254; ☎ 055 427 71 11; Viale Morgagni 85) The city's main hospital but a long way from the centre.

Ospedale di Santa Maria Nuova (Map pp246–7; ☎ 055 2 75 81; Piazza di Santa Maria Nuova 1) Just east of the Duomo. In an emergency go to the *pronto soccorso*.

Tourist Medical Service (Map pp246–7; ☎ 055 47 54 11; Via Lorenzo Il Magnifico 59; ☙ Open 24 hrs) No appointment is required. Doctors speak English, French and German.

METRIC SYSTEM

Italy uses the metric system. Basic terms for weight include *un etto* (100g) and *un chilo* (1kg). Like other continental Europeans, the Italians indicate decimals with commas and thousands with points.

MONEY

As in 11 other EU nations (Austria, Belgium, Finland, France, Germany, Greece, Ireland, Luxembourg, the Netherlands, Portugal and Spain), the euro has been Italy's currency since 2002. During 2003 it rose to record levels against other major currencies like the US dollar and UK pound.

See p15 for a discussion of the economy and costs.

Changing Money

You can exchange money in banks, at post offices or in currency exchange booths (bureaux de change). Banks are the most reliable option and tend to offer the best rates. You should look around and ask about commissions, which can fluctuate considerably. There are plenty of banks throughout the city centre.

Check commissions at bureaux de change. Change (branches all over town) charges up to a staggering 11.9% on foreign-currency travellers cheques! Travelex (which has absorbed the grand old name of travel, Thomas Cook) charges 4.5% for cash or travellers cheques (except Travelex cheques, which are commission-free).

American Express (Map pp251–3; ☎ 055 5 09 81; Via Dante Alighieri 22/r; ☙ 9am-5.30pm Mon-Fri, 9am-12.30pm Sat)

Travelex (Map pp251–3; ☎ 055 28 97 81; Lungarno degli Acciaioli 6/r; ☙ 8.45am-8pm Mon-Sat, 9am-6pm Sun)

Credit/Debit Cards

Major cards, such as Visa, MasterCard, Maestro and Cirrus cards, are accepted throughout

Italy. They can be used in many hotels, restaurants and shops. Credit cards can also be
used in ATMs displaying the appropriate sign,
or (if you have no PIN) you can obtain cash
advances over the counter in many banks –
MasterCard and Visa cards are among the most
widely recognised for such transactions. Check
charges with your bank.

It is not uncommon for ATMs in Italy to re-
ject foreign cards. Don't despair or start wasting
money on international calls to your bank. Try
a few more ATMs displaying your credit card's
logo before assuming the problem lies with
your card rather than with the local system.

If your card is lost, stolen or swallowed by
an ATM, you can telephone toll-free to have an
immediate stop put on its use. For MasterCard,
the number in Italy is ☎ 800 87 08 66; for Visa
it's ☎ 800 81 90 14; and for Diners Club ☎ 800
86 40 64.

Amex is also widely accepted (although not
as commonly as Visa or MasterCard). If you lose
your Amex card, call ☎ 800 87 43 33.

Exchange Rates

See the inside front cover for exchange rates
at the time of going to press. For the latest
rates, check out www.oanda.com.

Travellers Cheques

These are a safe way of carrying your money
because they can be replaced if lost or stolen.
Most banks and exchange bureaux will cash
them. Travelex, Amex and Visa are widely accepted brands. If you lose your Amex cheques,
call a 24-hour toll-free phone number (☎ 800
87 20 00). For Visa cheques, call ☎ 800 87 41
55; for MasterCard or Travelex cheques, call
☎ 800 87 20 50.

It's vital to keep your initial receipt, along
with a record of your cheque numbers and
the ones you have used, separate from the
cheques themselves.

Take your passport when you go to cash
travellers cheques.

NEWSPAPERS & MAGAZINES

A wide selection of national daily newspapers
from around Europe (including the UK) is available at newsstands all over central Florence
and at strategic locations like the train and bus
stations. The *International Herald Tribune*, *Time*,
the *Economist*, *Der Spiegel* and a host of other
international magazines are also available.

Italian Press

There is no 'national' paper as such, but rather
several important dailies published out of major
cities. These include Milan's *Corriere della Sera*,
Turin's right-wing *La Stampa* and Rome's centre-
left *La Repubblica*. This trio forms what could
be considered the nucleus of a national press,
publishing local editions throughout Italy.

The main local paper is *La Nazione*. Compared with the likes of the *Corriere della Sera*,
it is pretty poor on both national and foreign
news, but if you are more interested in what's
happening in Florence and around the region,
it's the paper of choice. You will find a fairly
decent cinema and theatre listings section in
it too. Competition comes from the slightly
racier *Il Corriere di Firenze*. You can also get a
Florence edition of *Il Giornale della Toscana*.

Useful Publications

In amid the landslide of printed information
and disinformation available from the tourist
offices is a handy booklet called *Florence –
Concierge Information*. It is an advertising vehicle for local enterprises (shops, restaurants,
shipping services and the like) aimed at visitors
to Florence. The bimonthly magazine, in Italian
and English, is loaded with all sorts of useful
and less useful information on most aspects
of the city. *Firenze Spettacolo*, the city's definitive entertainment publication, is available
monthly at newsstands.

PHARMACIES

Some pharmacies open extended hours (8am-
9pm). Tourist offices can provide lists. Twenty-
four-hour pharmacies include the following:

All'Insegna del Moro (Map pp251–3; ☎ 055 21 13 43;
Piazza di San Giovanni 28)

Farmacia Comunale (Map pp246–7; ☎ 055 21 67 61;
Stazione di Santa Maria Novella)

Molteni (Map pp251–3; ☎ 055 28 94 90; Via de' Calzaiuoli 7/r)

POST

Le Poste (☎ 160; www.poste.it), Italy's postal
service, is notoriously slow but has improved
over the past few years.

Stamps *(francobolli)* are available from post
offices and authorised tobacconists (look for
the official *tabacchi* sign: a big 'T', often white
on black).

One of the delightfully detailed signs over a handmade paper shop in Florence (p165)

The **central post office** (Map pp251–3; Via Pellicceria; 8.15am-7pm Mon-Fri; 8.15am-12.30pm Sat) is off Piazza della Repubblica. Another big one is on the corner of Via Giuseppe Verdi and Via Pietrapiana (Map pp248–50).

Postal Rates

The cost of sending a letter airmail *(via aerea)* depends on its weight and where it is being sent. For regular post, letters up to 20g cost €0.41 within Europe and €0.52 to Africa, Asia, the Americas, Australia and New Zealand. Postcards cost the same.

Few people use the regular post, preferring the slightly more expensive priority mail service *(posta prioritaria)*, guaranteed to deliver letters sent to Europe within three days and to the rest of the world within four to eight days. Letters up to 20g sent priority post cost €0.62 within Europe, and €0.77 to the Americas, Africa, Asia, Australia and New Zealand. Letters weighing 21g to 100g (standard/priority) €0.77/1.24 within Europe, and €1.03/1.55 to Africa, Asia, the Americas, Australia and New Zealand.

Sending Mail

Officially, letters sent priority post within Italy should arrive the following working day, those posted to destinations in Europe and the Mediterranean basin within three days, and those to the rest of the world in four to eight days. The post office claims an 85% success rate in meeting these targets.

Parcels *(pacchetti)* can be sent from any post office. You can purchase posting boxes or padded envelopes from most post offices. Padded envelopes are also available from stationery shops *(cartolerie)* and some tobacconists. Parcels usually take longer to be delivered than letters. A different set of postal rates applies.

Receiving Mail

Poste restante is known as *fermoposta* in Italy. Letters marked thus will be held at the Fermo Posta counter in the main post office in the relevant town. You need to pick up your letters in person and present your passport as ID. The counter at Florence's central post office is through the first door on the left as you enter the post office from Via Pellicceria. Poste restante mail should be addressed as follows:

John SMITH,
Fermo Posta,
Posta Centrale,
50100 Florence,
Italy

Amex card or travellers cheque holders can use the free client mail-holding service at the Florence office (see Money, p214).

RADIO

There are three state-owned stations: RAI-1 (1332kHz AM or 89.7MHz FM), RAI-2 (846kHz AM or 91.7MHz FM) and RAI-3 (93.7MHz FM). They offer a combination of classical and light music with news broadcasts and discussion programmes.

Many of the local stations are a little bland. For a good mix of contemporary music you could try Controradio on 93.6 AM or Nova Radio on 101.5 FM.

You can pick up the BBC World Service on medium wave at 648kHz, on short wave at 6.195MHz, 9.410MHz, 12.095MHz and 15.575MHz, and on long wave at 198kHz, depending on where you are and the time of day. Voice of America (VOA) can usually be found on short wave at 15.205MHz.

RECEIPTS

Laws aimed at tightening controls on the payment of taxes in Italy mean that the onus is on the buyer to ask for and retain receipts for all goods and services. This applies to everything from a litre of milk to a haircut. Although it rarely happens, you could be asked by an officer of the *guardia di finanza* (fiscal police) to produce the receipt immediately after you leave a shop. If you don't have it, the officer may levy a fine of €50 to €1000.

SAFETY

All in all Florence is a fairly secure city, although petty crime (in particular theft) is a problem and its unwitting victims are often strangers in town.

You need to keep an eye out for pickpockets and bagsnatchers in the most heavily touristed parts of town, especially around the Duomo and the train station.

Prevention is better than cure. Only walk around with the amount of cash you intend to spend that day or evening. Hidden moneybelts or pouches are a good idea. The popular 'bum bags' and external belt pouches people wear around their tummies are like a shining beacon to potential thieves.

Never leave anything visible in your car and preferably leave nothing at all. Foreign and hire cars are especially vulnerable.

If anything does get lost or stolen, report it to the police and get a written statement from them if you intend to claim on insurance.

Drug abuse is a visible problem in some parts of town. You may never even realise it is an issue, but a couple of squares become hangouts for junkies into the evening. One such spot is Piazza SS Annunziata. Keep alert in the area around the train station, especially at night, and around Piazza San Pier Maggiore too. It is not a major problem and the people concerned are unlikely to be a direct nuisance to you, but it is worth being aware of the issue.

TAXES

A value-added tax (known as Imposta di Valore Aggiunto, or IVA) of around 20% is slapped on to just about everything in Italy.

Tourists who are resident outside the EU may claim a refund on this tax if they spend more than a certain amount (€155) in the same shop on the same day. The refund applies only to items purchased at retail outlets affiliated to the system – these shops display a 'Tax-free for Tourists' sign. If you don't see this sign, ask the shopkeeper. You must fill out a form at the point of purchase and have it stamped and checked by Italian customs when you leave the country (you will need to show the receipt and possibly your purchases). At major airports and some border crossings, you can then get an immediate cash refund at specially marked booths; alternatively, return the form by mail to the vendor, who will make the refund, either by cheque or to your credit card.

For information, consult the rules brochure available in affiliated stores.

TELEPHONE

The public pay phones liberally scattered about come in four types. Most accept only *carte/schede telefoniche* (phonecards). Some also accept coins and others accept special credit cards produced by Telecom – the formerly state-owned telecommunications company – and even commercial credit cards. A few send faxes.

You can buy phonecards (€2.50 or €5) at post offices, tobacconists, newspaper stands and from vending machines in Telecom offices. Remember to snap off the perforated corner before using them. Beware of a phone scam. On some phones you may notice stickers advertising cheap international call rates with your credit card. You dial a toll-free number and make the call and hey presto! Your 'cheap' international call could cost as much as €50 a minute!

You will find Telecom phones in unstaffed offices near the ATAF information booth in Largo Alinari, just outside the southeast exit of Stazione di Santa Maria Novella (Map pp246–7; ☉ 7am-10pm) and Via Cavour 21/r (Map pp251–3; ☉ 7am-11pm).

Calling Florence from Abroad

Dial the international access code (☎ 00 in most countries), followed by the code for Italy (☎ 39) and the full number, including the initial 0. To call the number ☎ 055 234 77 77 in Florence, you need to dial the international access code, followed by ☎ 39 055 234 77 77.

Costs

Call rates have been simplified in Italy. A local call (comunicazione urbana) from a public phone costs €0.10 every minute and 21 seconds. For a long-distance call within Italy (comunicazione interurbana) you pay €0.10 when the call is answered and the same for every 57 seconds.

The cost of calling abroad has fallen. A three-minute phone call from a pay phone to most of Europe and North America will cost about €1.90. For Australasia, three minutes cost €4.10, although calling from a private phone is less. Calling foreign mobile phones is more costly to Europe and North America, but the same to Australia and New Zealand.

Domestic Calls

Area codes are an integral part of Italian telephone numbers. The codes all begin with 0 and consist of up to four digits. You must dial this whole number, even if calling from next door. Thus, any number you call in the Florence area will begin with 055.

Mobile phone numbers begin with a three-digit prefix such as ☎ 330, 335, 347, 368 etc. Free-phone or toll-free numbers are known as numeri verdi (green numbers) and start with ☎ 800. National rate phone numbers start with ☎ 848 and 199. Some new six-digit national rate numbers are also coming into use (such as that now used by Trenitalia for national rail information).

For national directory enquiries, call ☎ 12.

Fax

You can send faxes from post offices and some tobacconists, copy centres and stationers. Faxes can also be sent from some Telecom public phones. To send a fax within Italy, expect to pay €1.30 per page. International faxes vary. To the UK, for instance, you pay €2.46 for the first page and €2.15 per page thereafter.

There is a fax poste restante service at the main post office – have faxes sent to you at Fax Fermo Posta (window 15), ☎ 055 21 49 53. To retrieve the fax you will need photo ID.

International Calls

Direct international calls can be made from public telephones by using a phonecard. Dial ☎ 00 to get out of Italy, then the relevant country and city codes, followed by the telephone number.

Useful country codes are: Australia ☎ 61, Canada and the USA ☎ 1, France ☎ 33, Germany ☎ 49, Ireland ☎ 353, New Zealand ☎ 64, and the UK ☎ 44. For international directory inquiries, call ☎ 176.

Reverse-charge (collect) international calls can be made from a public telephone, by dialling ☎ 170 (for European countries, dial ☎ 15). It is easier and often cheaper to use the Country Direct service. You dial the number and request a reverse-charge call through the operator in your country. Numbers for this service include the following:

Australia (Telstra)	☎ 172 10 61
Australia (Optus)	☎ 172 11 61
Canada	☎ 172 10 01
France	☎ 172 00 33
New Zealand	☎ 172 10 64
UK (BT)	☎ 172 00 44
UK (BT Chargecard Operator)	☎ 172 01 44
USA (AT&T)	☎ 172 10 11
USA (IDB)	☎ 172 17 77
USA (MCI)	☎ 172 10 22
USA (Sprint)	☎ 172 18 77

International Phonecards & Call Centres

Some private companies distribute international phonecards offering cheaper rates on long-distance calls. Some are better than others but few are available in Florence. Keep an eye out at newspaper kiosks, tobacconists and the like. Another option are call centres like **Il Cairo Phone Center** (Map pp248–50; ☎ 055 263 83 36; Via de' Macci 90/r; ☉ 9.30am-9pm).

Mobile Phones

You can buy SIM cards in Italy for your own national mobile phone (provided what you own is a GSM dual- or tri-band cellular phone) and buy prepaid time. This only works if your national phone hasn't been code blocked, something you might want to find out before leaving home. If you buy a SIM card and find your phone *is* blocked you won't be able to take it back. You need your passport to open any kind of mobile phone account, prepaid or otherwise.

Both TIM (Telecom Italia Mobile) and Vodaphone-Omnitel offer *prepagato* (prepaid) accounts for GSM phones (frequency 900 MHz). The card can cost €50 to €60, which includes some prepaid phone time. You can then top up in their shops or by buying cards in outlets like tobacconists and newsstands.

TIM and Vodaphone-Omnitel retail outlets operate in virtually every Italian town. Call rates vary according to an infinite variety of call plans.

Wind and Blu are two smaller mobile phone operators with consequently fewer outlets around the country.

US mobile phones generally work on a frequency of 1900 MHz, so for use in Italy, your US handset will have to be tri-band.

You can rent mobile phones at Webpuccino (see Internet Cafés, p213). The total cost (including €35 of prepaid calls) to set up the deal is €80.

TELEVISION

The three state-run stations, RAI-1, RAI-2 and RAI-3, are run by Radio e Televisione Italiane. Historically, each has been in the hands of one of the main political groupings in the country, although in the past few years these affiliations have become less clear-cut. It remains a fact that the appointment of station directors and senior staff is highly politicised.

Of the three, RAI-3 tends to have some of the more interesting programmes. Generally, however, these stations and the private Canale 5, Italia 1, Rete 4 and La 7 tend to serve up a diet of indifferent news, tacky variety hours (with lots of near-naked tits and bums, appalling crooning and vaudeville humour) and game shows. Talk shows, some interesting but many nauseating,

also abound. Several minor local stations also operate but are generally of minimal interest.

TIME

Italy (and hence Florence) is one hour ahead of GMT/UTC during winter, and two hours during the daylight-saving period from the last Sunday in March to the last Sunday in October. Most other Western European countries are on the same time as Italy year-round, the major exceptions being the UK, Ireland and Portugal, which are one hour behind.

When it's noon in Florence, it's 3am in San Francisco, 6am in New York and Toronto, 11am in London, 9pm in Sydney and 11pm in Auckland. Note that in North America and Australasia, the changeover to/from daylight saving usually differs from the European date by a couple of weeks.

TIPPING

You are not expected to tip on top of restaurant service charges, but it is common to leave a small amount, say €1 a person. If there is no service charge, the customer might consider leaving a 10% tip, but this is by no means obligatory. In bars, Italians often leave any small change as a tip, often only €0.05 or €0.10. Tipping taxi drivers is not common practice, but you should tip the porter at higher-class hotels.

Bargaining is common in flea markets but not in shops, although you might find that the proprietor is disposed to giving a discount if you are spending a reasonable amount of money. It's quite acceptable to ask if there is a special price for a room in a *pensione* or hotel if you plan to stay for more than a few days. Indeed, there is no harm in trying to bargain down room prices.

TOILETS

Stopping at a bar or café for a quick coffee and then a trip to the toilet is the common solution to those sudden urges at awkward times. Make sure your chosen bar actually has a toilet before committing yourself!

TOURIST INFORMATION
Tourist Offices Abroad

Information on Florence is available from the following branches of the Ente Nazionale Italiano per il Turismo (ENIT), the Italian State Tourism Board:

Australia (☎ 02 9262 1666; enitour@ihug.com.au; Level 26, 44 Market St, Sydney 2000)

Canada (☎ 416 925 4882; enit.canada@on.aibn.com; Suite 907, South Tower, 175 Bloor St East, Toronto, Ontario M4W 3R8)

France (☎ 01 42 66 03 96; enit.parigi@wanadoo.fr; 23 rue de la Paix, 75002 Paris)

Germany (☎ 030 247 83 97; enit-berlin@t-online.de; Kontorhaus Mitte, Friedrichstrasse 187, D-10117 Berlin)

Germany (☎ 089 531 317; enit-muenchen@t-online.de; Goethestrasse 20, 80336 Munich)

Germany (☎ 069 259 126; enit.ffm@t-online.de; Kaiserstrasse 65, 60329 Frankfurt)

Netherlands (☎ 020 616 82 44; enitams@wirehub.nl; Stadhouderskade 2, Amsterdam 1054 ES)

Switzerland (☎ 01 211 79 17; enit@bluewin.ch; Urania-strasse 32, 8001 Zürich)

UK (☎ 020 73551557; italy@italiantouristboard.co.uk; 1 Princess St, London W1R 9AY)

USA (☎ 312 644 0996; enitch@italiantourism.com; 500 North Michigan Ave, Suite 2240, Chicago, IL 60611)

USA (☎ 310 820 1898; enitla@earthlink.net; Suite 550, 12400 Wilshire Blvd, Los Angeles, CA 90025)

USA (☎ 212 245 4822; enitny@italiantourism.com; Suite 1565, 630 Fifth Ave, New York, NY 10111)

Tourist Offices in Florence

Azienda di Promozione Turistica (APT; Map pp251–3; ☎ 055 29 08 32; www.firenzeturismo.it; Via Cavour 1/r; 🕓 8.30am-6.30pm Mon-Sat, 8.30am-1.30pm Sun)

APT (Map p254; ☎ 055 31 58 74; Amerigo Vespucci airport, Via del Termine II; 🕓 7.30am-11.30pm)

Comune di Firenze tourist office (Map pp251–3; ☎ 055 21 22 45; Piazza della Stazione 4; 🕓 8.30am-7pm Mon-Sat & 8.30am-2pm Sun) Florence's city council operates this tourist office.

Comune di Firenze tourist office (Map pp251–3; ☎ 055 234 04 44; Borgo Santa Croce 29/r; 🕓 8.30am-7pm Mon-Sat & 8.30am-2pm Sun) A branch of the city council's tourist office.

Consorzio ITA (Informazioni Turistiche e Alberghiere; Map pp246–7; Stazione di Santa Maria Novella; ☎ 055 28 28 93; 🕓 8.45am-9pm) You can pick up basic information here, although its main role is to book hotels (see also the Sleeping chapter, p179).

Tourist Help (Map pp251–3; 🕓 8.30am-7pm) The police and tourist office combine to operate these help points for the disoriented at the Ponte Vecchio and Piazza della Repubblica.

Tourist Helpline

The APT office located at Via Cavour 1/r also offers a special summer service known as **Florence SOS Turista** (☎ 055 276 03 82; 🕓 10am-1pm & 3-6pm Mon-Sat, Apr-Oct) for tourists needing guidance on matters such as disputes over hotel bills.

Useful Websites

A plethora of websites is dedicated to all things Florentine. Some of the more useful sites include the following:

ATAF (www.ataf.net) All you ever wanted to know about Florence's public transport system.

Comune di Firenze (www.comune.firenze.it) Florence's town council's official website, in Italian and English, with some interesting background information on the city and events announcements. You can find useful items such as the day's late-opening pharmacies.

Ente Nazionale Italiano per il Turismo (www.enit.it) The Italian national tourist body's website has information on everything from local tourist office addresses to town-by-town museum details and general introductions to food, art and history. Look for upcoming cultural events too.

Fionline (www.fionline.it) This provides general information, with news and views, information for businesspeople and some tourism content.

Firenze.net (www.firenze.net) This site is full of useful listings information, ranging from monuments to the latest events, from bars to B&Bs. The nightlife section has some good tips but tends to be a little out of date.

Florence 2000 (www.florence2000.it) An online hotel reservation site for Florence in English.

Go Tuscany (www.firenze.net/events, English only) This site is aimed at the expat community and English-speaking visitors to the region. It contains tips on places to stay and eat both in and outside Florence, itineraries in Tuscany, classified ads and an events calendar.

Michelangelo Buonarroti (www.michelangelo.com/buonarroti.html) For information on the life and works of one of the greatest figures of the Florentine Renaissance.

Niccolo Machiavelli (www.the-prince-by-machiavelli.com) Could be useful for budding tyrants. Here you can read the English translation of Machiavelli's controversial treatise on how to rule, *The Prince*, and commentaries on its interpretation.

Trenitalia (www.trenitalia.it) Plan rail journeys, check timetables and prices and book tickets on Italy's national railways site.

Welcome to Florence (www.firenzeturismo.it) The Florence APT tourist office site.

Directory – Practicalities

VISAS

Italy is one of 15 member countries of the Schengen Convention, under which all EU member countries (except the UK and Ireland) plus Iceland and Norway have abolished checks at common borders. The other EU countries are Austria, Belgium, Denmark, Finland, France, Germany, Greece, Luxembourg, the Netherlands, Portugal, Spain and Sweden. Legal residents of one Schengen country do not require a visa for another Schengen country. Citizens of the UK and Ireland are also exempt, and nationals of some other countries, including Canada, Japan, New Zealand and Switzerland, do not require visas for tourist visits of up to 90 days to any Schengen country.

Various other nationals not covered by the Schengen exemption can also spend up to 90 days in Italy without a visa. These include Australian, Israeli and US citizens.

All non-EU nationals entering Italy for any reason other than tourism (such as study or work) should contact an Italian consulate, as they may need a specific visa. They should also insist on having their passport stamped on entry as, without a stamp, they could encounter problems when trying to obtain a residence permit (permesso di soggiorno).

If you are a citizen of a country not mentioned in this section, check with an Italian consulate whether you need a visa. The standard tourist visa issued by Italian consulates is the Schengen visa, valid for up to 90 days. A Schengen visa issued by one Schengen country is generally valid for travel in all other Schengen countries. However, individual member countries may impose additional restrictions on certain nationalities. You should check visa regulations with the consulate of each Schengen country you plan to visit. These visas are not renewable inside Italy.

Permits

EU citizens do not need permits to live, work or start a business in Italy. They are, however, advised to register with a questura if they take up residence and apply for a residence permit (permesso di soggiorno). That is the first step to acquiring an ID card (carta d'identità). While you're at it, you'll need a codice fiscale (tax-file number) if you wish to be paid for most work in Italy. Go to the questura (Map pp246–7; ☎ 055 4 97 71; Via Zara 2) to obtain precise information on what is required. Study

and work visas (all non-EU citizens require them) must be applied for in your country of residence.

WOMEN TRAVELLERS

Florence is not a dangerous city but women travelling alone may find that they are plagued by unwanted male attention. In bars and discos especially the attention can be more intense than you'd like. If you do get talking but would rather you hadn't, reference to your husband (marito), boyfriend (fidanzato) or even children (figli) may put a brake on your interlocutor's ardour.

Artemisia (Map pp244–5; ☎ 055 60 13 75; Via del Mezzetta 1 Interno) A help organisation for women and minors who have been the victims of physical and/or sexual assault. It can provide legal advice and counselling.

Libreria delle Donne (☎ 055 234 78 10; www.women.it /libreriafirenze/fili.htm; Via Fiesolana 2/b) Drop into this women's bookshop for information on local women's groups and lesbian issues.

WORK

It is illegal for non-EU citizens to work in Italy without a permesso di lavoro (work permit), but trying to obtain one through your Italian consulate can be a pain. EU citizens are allowed to work in Italy, but they still need to obtain a permesso di soggiorno (residence permit) from a questura. Immigration laws require foreign workers to be 'legalised' through their employers. This applies even to cleaners and babysitters. The employers then pay pension and health insurance contributions. This doesn't mean that illegal work can't still be found.

Employment Options

The best options are trying to find work in some bars, restaurants and shops (such as leather outlets). Non-EU citizens, even if they have no kitchen experience and little Italian, can sometimes get 'cooking' work, which can be little more than assembling preprepared pizzas. Even qualified cooks could earn as little as €5 to €10 per hour for long hours. We are talking about the tourist-trap restaurants that are quite happy to serve up deep-frozen, precooked stuff. What's worse? Eating it or preparing it?

Another option is au pair work organised before you come to Italy. A useful guide is The Au Pair and Nanny's Guide to Working Abroad by Susan Griffith & Sharon Legg. Susan Griffith's

Work Your Way Around the World is also worth looking at.

The easiest source of work for foreigners is teaching English (or another foreign language), but even with full qualifications, a non-EU citizen will find it difficult to secure a permanent position. Most of the larger, more reputable schools will hire only people with work or residence permits or both, but their attitude can become more flexible if demand for teachers is high and they come across someone with good qualifications.

The **British Institute** (Map pp251–3; Piazza degli Strozzi 2; ☎ 055 26 77 81) is the main UK centre for English teaching in Florence (you can also take Italian classes). The institute has a library at Lungarno Guicciardini 9 (Map pp248–50).

Translating and interpreting could be an option if you are fluent in Italian and a language in demand.

University students or recent graduates might be able to arrange an internship with companies located in Florence. The **Association of International Students for Economics and Commerce** (www.aiesec.org), with branches throughout the world, helps member students find internships in related fields. For information on membership, check out the website.

Language

Language

It's true – anyone can speak another language. Don't worry if you haven't studied languages before or that you studied a language at school for years and can't remember any of it. It doesn't even matter if you failed English grammar. After all, that's never affected your ability to speak English! And this is the key to picking up a language in another country. You just need to start speaking.

Learn a few key phrases before you go. Write them on pieces of paper and stick them on the fridge, by the bed or even on the computer – anywhere that you'll see them often.

You'll find that locals appreciate travellers trying their language, no matter how muddled you may think you sound. So don't just stand there, say something! If you want to learn more Italian than we've included here, pick up a copy of Lonely Planet's comprehensive but user-friendly *Italian phrasebook*.

SOCIAL
Meeting People
Hello.
Buon giorno.
Goodbye.
Arrivederci.
Please.
Per favore.
Thank you (very much).
(Mille) Grazie.
Yes/No.
Sì/No.
Do you speak English?
Parla inglese?
Do you understand (me)?
(Mi) capisce?
Yes, I understand.
Sì, capisco.
No, I don't understand.
No, non capisco.

Could you please ...?
Potrebbe ...?
repeat that	ripeterlo
speak more slowly	parlare più lentamente
write it down	scriverlo

Going Out
What's on ...?
Che c'è in programma ...?
locally	in zona
this weekend	questo fine settimana
today	oggi
tonight	stasera

Where are the ...?
Dove sono ...?
clubs	dei clubs
gay venues	dei locali gay
places to eat	posti dove mangiare
pubs	dei pub

Is there a local entertainment guide?
C'è una guida agli spettacoli in questa città?

PRACTICAL
Question Words
Who?	Chi?
What?	Che?
When?	Quando?
Where?	Dove?
How?	Come?

Numbers & Amounts
1	uno
2	due
3	tre
4	quattro
5	cinque
6	sei
7	sette
8	otto
9	nove
10	dieci
11	undici
12	dodici
13	tredici
14	quattordici
15	quindici
16	sedici

17	diciasette
18	diciotto
19	dicianove
20	venti
21	ventuno
22	ventidue
30	trenta
40	quaranta
50	cinquanta
60	sessanta
70	settanta
80	ottanta
90	novanta
100	cento
1000	mille
2000	duemila

Days

Monday	lunedì
Tuesday	martedì
Wednesday	mercoledì
Thursday	giovedì
Friday	venerdì
Saturday	sabato
Sunday	domenica

Banking

I'd like to ...
Vorrei ...

cash a cheque	riscuotere un assegno
change money	cambiare denaro
change some travellers cheques	cambiare degli assegni di viaggio

Where's the nearest ...?
Dov'è il ... più vicino?

automatic teller machine	bancomat
foreign exchange office	cambio

Post

Where is the post office?
Dov'è la posta?

I want to send a ...
Voglio spedire ...

fax	un fax
parcel	un pachetto
postcard	una cartolina

I want to buy ...
Voglio comprare ...

an aerogram	un aerogramma
an envelope	una busta
a stamp	un francobollo

Phone & Mobile Phones

I want to buy a phone card.
Voglio comprare una scheda telefonica.
I want to make ...
Voglio fare ...

a call (to ...)	una chiamata (a ...)
reverse-charge/ collect call	una chiamata a carico del destinatario

Where can I find a/an ...?
Dove si trova ...
I'd like a/an ...
Vorrei ...

adaptor plug	un addattatore
charger for my phone	un caricabatterie
mobile/cell phone for hire	un cellulare da noleggiare
prepaid mobile/ cell phone	un cellulare prepagato
SIM card for your network	un SIM card per vostra rete telefonica

Internet

Where's the local Internet café?
Dove si trova l'Internet point?

I'd like to ...
Vorrei ...

check my email	controllare le mie email
get online	collegarmi a Internet

Transport

What time does the ... leave?
A che ora parte ...?

bus	l'autobus
plane	l'aereo
train	il treno

What time's the ... bus/vaporetto?
A che ora passa ... autobus/batello?

first	il primo
last	l'ultimo
next	il prossimo

Are you free? (taxi)
È libero questo taxi?
Please put the meter on.
Usa il tassametro, per favore.
How much is it to ...?
Quant'è per ...?
Please take me to (this address).
Mi porti a (questo indirizzo), per favore.

FOOD

breakfast	prima colazione
lunch	pranzo
dinner	cena
snack	spuntino/merenda
eat	mangiare
drink	bere

Can you recommend a ...
Potrebbe consigliare un ...?

bar/pub	bar/pub
café	bar
restaurant	ristorante

Is service/cover charge included in the bill?
Il servizio/coperto è compreso nel conto?

For more detailed information on food and dining out, see the Eating chapter, pp125–140.

EMERGENCIES

It's an emergency!
È un'emergenza!
Could you please help me/us?
Mi/Ci può aiutare, per favore?

Call the police/a doctor/an ambulance!
Chiami la polizia/un medico/
un'ambulanza!
Where's the police station?
Dov'è la questura?

HEALTH

Where's the nearest ...?
Dov'è ...più vicino?

chemist (night)	la farmacia (di turno)
dentist	il dentista
doctor	il medico
hospital	l'ospedale

I need a doctor (who speaks English).
Ho bisogno di un medico (che parli inglese).

Symptoms

I have (a) ...
Ho ...

diarrhoea	la diarrea
fever	la febbre
headache	mal di testa
pain	un dolore

Glossary

abbonamento mensile – monthly pass for public transport
ACI – Automobile Club Italiano (Italian Automobile Association)
affitacamere – rooms for rent in private houses
albergo, alberghi (pl) – hotel (up to five stars)
alimentari – grocery shop
amaro – Italian liqueur (literally: 'bitter')
ambasciata – embassy
APT – Azienda di Promozione Turistica (provincial tourist office)
autostazione – bus station/terminal
autostrada, autostrade (pl) – motorway, highway

bacaro – old-style bar
baggagli smarriti – lost luggage
baldacchino – canopy of fabric or stone over an altar, shrine or throne in a Christian church
benzina – petrol
biblioteca, biblioteche (pl) – library
biglietteria – box or ticket office
biglietto – ticket
birreria – brewery or pub
borgo, borghi (pl) – walled village
bottega – shop
bussino – electric minibus network that operates around the centre of Florence

calcio – football (soccer)
campanile – a bell tower, usually free standing
cappella – chapel
carabinieri – police with military and civil duties
carnevale – carnival period between Epiphany and Lent
carta d'identità – identity card
cartoleria – stationery shop
casa – house, home
castello – castle
cattedrale – cathedral
cenacolo – refectory
centro – city centre
centro storico – historic centre, old city
chiesa, chiese (pl) – church
chilo – kilogram
chiostro – cloister; covered walkway, usually enclosed by columns, around a quadrangle
ciborio – goblet-shaped lidded vessel used to hold consecrated hosts for Holy Communion
cimitero – cemetery
CIT – Compagnia Italiana di Turismo (Italy's national travel agency)
collina – hill (*colle* in place names)
colonna – column
comune – equivalent to a municipality or county; town or city council; historically, a commune (self-governing town or city)
corso – main street

CTS – Centro Turistico Studentesco e Giovanile (Centre for Student and Youth Tourists)
cupola – dome

deposito bagagli – left luggage
digestivo – after-dinner liqueur

enoteca – specialist wine shop/bar
(un) etto – 100 grams

fermoposta – poste restante
ferragosto – Feast of the Assumption; more often refers to the major August (summer) holiday period
ferrovia – train station
festa – feast day; holiday
fiaschetteria – snack bar, serving alcohol
fiume – river
fornaio – bakery
fortezza – fort
francobolli – stamps
FS – Ferrovie dello Stato; Italian State Railway

gabinetto – toilet, WC
gelateria – ice-cream parlour
guardia di finanza – fiscal/finance police

IAT – Informazioni e Assistenza ai Turisti (local tourist office)
insula – multistorey apartment block
IVA – Imposta di Valore Aggiunto (value-added tax)

largo – (small) square
lavanderia – laundrette
libreria – bookshop
locanda – inn, small hotel
loggia – covered area on the side of a building, porch
lungarni – roads that follow the course of the river Arno

marche da bollo – tax stamps for official payments
mercato – market
merceria – haberdashery shop
mescita di vini – wine outlet
mezzo porzione – half or child's portion
motorino – moped
municipio – town hall
(le) mura – city wall
musei statali – state museums

numeri verdi – toll-free numbers

oggetti smarriti – lost property
orto botanico – botanical gardens
ospedale – hospital
ostello – hostel
osteria – cheap restaurant

palazzo, palazzi (pl) – mansion, palace, large building of any type (including an apartment block)
panetteria – bakery

passeggiata – traditional evening stroll
pasticceria – cake/pastry shop
pellicola – roll of film
pensione – small hotel
permesso di lavoro – work permit
permesso di soggiorno – permit to stay in Italy for a nominated period
piazza, piazze (pl) – square
piazzale – (large) open square
pietà – literally pity or compassion; sculpture, drawing or painting of the dead Christ supported by the Madonna
pinacoteca – art gallery
piscina – pool
ponte – bridge
porta – city gate
posta – post office
posta prioritaria – priority mail
prepagato – prepaid phone account
pronto soccorso – first aid; *(riparto di) pronto soccorso* is a casualty/emergency ward

questura – police station

regioni – administrative regions in Italy, such as Tuscany
ricevuta – receipt
Risorgimento – late-19th-century movement led by Garibaldi and others to create a united, independent Italian state
robbiane – terracotta medallions; architectural feature

sala – room in a museum or a gallery
salumeria – delicatessen
scala – staircase
sedia a rotelle – wheelchair
seggiolone – child's high chair
senza piombo – unleaded (petrol)
servizio – service charge in restaurants
sindaco – mayor
stazione – station
stazione di servizio – petrol or service station
supplemento – supplement, payable on a fast train

tabaccheria – tobacconist's shop
tavola calda – (literally 'hot table') self-serve buffet
teatro – theatre
terme – baths, hot springs
torre – tower

ufficio postale – post office

via – street, road
via aerea – air mail
vicolo – alley, alleyway
vigili urbani – municipal police
vinaio – wine bar or shop

Behind the Scenes

THE LONELY PLANET STORY

The story begins with a classic travel adventure: Tony and Maureen Wheeler's 1972 journey across Europe and Asia to Australia. There was no useful information about the overland trail then, so Tony and Maureen published the first Lonely Planet guidebook to meet a growing need.

From a kitchen table, Lonely Planet has grown to become the largest independent travel publisher in the world, with offices in Melbourne (Australia), Oakland (USA), London (UK) and Paris (France).

Today Lonely Planet guidebooks cover the globe. There is an ever-growing list of books and information in a variety of media. Some things haven't changed. The main aim is still to make it possible for adventurous travellers to get out there – to explore and better understand the world.

At Lonely Planet we believe travellers can make a positive contribution to the countries they visit – if they respect their host communities and spend their money wisely.

THIS BOOK

This third edition of *Florence* was written by Damien Simonis, as were the previous two. The guide was commissioned in Lonely Planet's London office and produced by:

Commissioning Editor Fiona Christie

Coordinating Editor Melissa Faulkner

Coordinating Cartographer Marion Byass

Layout Designer David Kemp

Editors & Proofreaders Emily Coles, John Hinman

Cover Designer Nic Lehman

Series Designer Nic Lehman

Series Design Concept Nic Lehman & Andrew Weatherill

Layout Manager Adriana Mammarella

Managing Cartographer Mark Griffiths

Managing Editor Martin Heng

Mapping Development Paul Piaia

Project Manager Rachel Imeson

Language Editor Quentin Frayne

Regional Publishing Manager Katrina Browning

Series Publishing Manager Gabrielle Green

Series Development Team Jenny Blake, Anna Bolger, Fiona Christie, Kate Cody, Erin Corrigan, Janine Eberle, Simone Egger, James Ellis, Nadine Fogale, Roz Hopkins, Dave McClymont, Leonie Mugavin, Rachel Peart, Ed Pickard, Michele Posner, Howard Ralley & Dani Valent

Thanks to Bruce Evans, Michala Green, Kate McDonald & Katrina Webb

Cover Michelangelo's *David*, Galleria dell'Accademia, Hannah Levy/Lonely Planet Images (top); Ponte Vecchio at dusk, Jon Davison/Lonely Planet Images (bottom); football game by the Arno, Martin Hughes/Lonely Planet Images (back)

Internal photographs by Juliet Coombe/Lonely Planet Images except for the following:

p17, p20, p25, p30, p42, p54, p59, p70 (#2, 3, 4), p71 (#1, 2, 3), p72 (#2), p73 (#4), p74 (#2, 3), p122, p136, p150, p153, p155 (#1, 3, 4), p159 (#1, 4), p160 (#1, 2, 4), p162 (#2, 3, 4), p165, p173, p191, p195, p199 Martin Hughes/Lonely Planet Images; p2 (#1) Dallas Stribley/Lonely Planet Images; p2 (#2) Greg Elms/Lonely Planet Images; p2 (#3) Oliver Strewe/Lonely Planet Images; p2 (#5) and p155 (#2) Damien Simonis/Lonely Planet Images; p162 (#1) Jon Davison/Lonely Planet Images.

All images are the copyright of the photographers unless otherwise indicated. Many of the images in this guide are available for licensing from Lonely Planet Images: www.lonelyplanetimages.com.

SEND US YOUR FEEDBACK

We love to hear from travellers – your comments keep us on our toes and help make our books better. Our well-travelled team reads every word on what you loved or loathed about this book. Although we cannot reply individually to postal submissions, we always guarantee that your feedback goes straight to the appropriate authors, in time for the next edition. Each person who sends us information is thanked in the next edition – and the most useful submissions are rewarded with a free book.

To send us your updates – and find out about LP events, newsletters and travel news – visit our award-winning website: www.lonelyplanet.com.

Note: We may edit, reproduce and incorporate your comments in Lonely Planet products such as guidebooks, websites and digital products, so let us know if you don't want your comments reproduced or your name acknowledged. For a copy of our privacy policy visit www.lonelyplanet.com/privacy.

THANKS

DAMIEN SIMONIS

Grazie tante a Monica Fontani for welcoming me back so warmly to the Arno, and to her humorous band of friends. Also to Julie Boyer, who has chosen to make her home here after much commuting between Florence and California (what a choice!).

Thanks also to the staff of the APT office in Florence for their time-saving help. A big grazie mille goes to Miles Roddis, valiant walker, trusted midshipman and colleague. He tramped the Tuscan trails ahead of me this time and generously lent me the fruit of his research. Also to Martin Hughes for his work on *Florence Condensed*.

Finally, thanks and more to Janique, who was never far away as I trailed the broiling streets of midsummer Florence (not something I recommend to readers), wondering how I could be so silly as to choose August for this kind of caper.

OUR READERS

Many thanks to the travellers who used the last edition and contacted us with helpful hints, useful advice and interesting anecdotes: Steve Bailey, Stephen Boyd, Jennifer Burns, Rochelle Byles, Justin Carter, Russ Crum, Anthony T. Di Lullo, Kate Dix, Mike Hudson, Joel Janco, Amy Lahti, Dr Andrew Levison, Greg Middleton, Craig Miesse, Megan Murphy, Jiun Hao Neoh, Lizzie Nicholls, Jelena Popovic, Alexander Rahlis, Norman Rosen, Karl Ruppenthal, Emily Sachs, Jennifer Slepin, Betsy Thayer, Ian Ward-Brown, David & Myra Zoll

Notes

Notes

Notes

Index

See also separate indexes for Eating (p241), Shopping (p241) and Sleeping (p242).

Index

241

MAP LEGEND

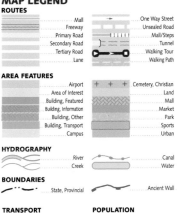

ROUTES

Mall
Freeway
Primary Road
Secondary Road
Tertiary Road
Lane
One Way Street
Unsealed Road
Mall/Steps
Tunnel
Walking Tour
Walking Path

AREA FEATURES

Airport
Area of Interest
Building, Featured
Building, Information
Building, Other
Building, Transport
Campus
Cemetery, Christian
Land
Mall
Market
Park
Sports
Urban

HYDROGRAPHY

River
Creek
Canal
Water

BOUNDARIES

State, Provincial
Ancient Wall

TRANSPORT

Ferry
Rail
Rail Bridge

POPULATION

◉ CAPITAL (STATE)
● Medium City
● Town, Village

SYMBOLS

SIGHTS/ACTIVITIES
🛕 Christian
✡ Jewish
🏛 Monument
🖼 Museum, Gallery
🏊 Pool
● Point of Interest

EATING
🍴 Eating

DRINKING
🍺 Drinking

ENTERTAINMENT
🎭 Entertainment

SHOPPING
🛍 Shopping

SLEEPING
🛏 Sleeping
⛺ Camping

TRANSPORT
✈ Airport, Airfield
🚌 Bus Station
🚉 General Transport

INFORMATION
💲 Bank, ATM
🛂 Embassy/Consulate
➕ Hospital, Medical
ℹ Information
@ Internet Facilities
🅿 Parking Area
⛽ Petrol Station
🚓 Police Station
✉ Post Office, GPO
☎ Telephone

Map Section

CENTRAL FLORENCE

SIGHTS & ACTIVITIES (pp61–114)
Campo Sportivi ASSI 1 F6
Cenacolo di San Salvi...............................2 G4
Le Pavoniere Swimming Pool.....................3 A3
Museo Stibbert...4 D1
Nannini Swimming Pool.............................5 H5
Tchaikovsky's Villa...................................6 D6
Torre del Gallo...7 E6

EATING 🍴 (pp125–40)
Ashoka...8 C4
Baroncini...9 C1

DRINKING 🍸 (pp142–7)
Central Park..10 C3
Pinocchio Club..11 G5
Porto di Mare...12 B4
Rio Grande...13 B4
Universale..14 B4

ENTERTAINMENT 🎭 (pp141–54)
Auditorium Flog......................................15 D1
Arena Chiardiluna (Cinema)....................16 B4
Arena di Marte (Cinema, Palasport).......17 G3
Stadio Comunale Artemio Franchi..........18 G3
Teatro Comunale....................................19 C4

SHOPPING 🛍 (pp163–74)
Mercato delle Cascine............................20 B3

SLEEPING 🛏 (pp175–86)
Albergo Torre di Bellosguardo..........21 B5
Hotel Villa Liberty.................................22 F6
Ostello Villa Camerata...........................23 H2

INFORMATION
CTS...24 B2
Swiss Consulate.....................................25 D6

OTHER
Artemisia...26 H4
Azione Gay e Lesbica Finisterrae...........27 G4
Oggetti Smarriti (Lost Property)............28 C2
Società Canottieri Comunali...................29 G5
Università Internazionale dell'Arte.........30 G2

244

E   F   G   H

LP

1

Via Bolognese

Via Faentina

Torrente Mugnone

23

2

Via Vittorio Emanuele II

Piazza
delle Cure

Viale Alessandro Volta

30

Via San Domenico

Viale Augusto Righi

Ponte
Rosso

Viale Don G Minzoni

Viale del Mille

Viale Alessandro Volta

Via Cairoli

Via A Baldesi

Via Lorenzo il Magnifico

Piazza
della
Libertà

Via G Marconi

Viale Spartaco
Lavagnini

Viale Giacomo Matteotti

Piazza
Savonarola

18

3

Giardino

Campo
di Marte

Viale Pasquale Paoli

17

Via Giuseppe La Farina

Piazza
San Marco

Giardino

Stazione Campo
di Marte

Via Lungo l'Affrico

Via Mannelli

Via Gabriele d'Annunzio

Viale Antonio

Piazza M
d'Azeglio

Via del Mezzetta

26

Viale Edmondo de Amicis

27

2

Via Andrea del Sarto

4

uomo

Gramsci

Via Vincenzo Gioberti

Via Cimabue

Via G Amendola

Via Aretina

Chianti

Piazza di
Santa Croce

Via Arnolfo

Via Piagentina – Via Campofiore

Madonnone
Bellariva

5

Lungarno Aldo Moro

Ponte
alle
Grazie

ARNO

Lungarno del Tempio

Lungarno Cristoforo Colombo

San Niccolò

Piazza
Giuseppe
Poggi

Ponte
San Niccolò

Ponte G
Da Verrazzano

5

Via dell'Erta Canina

Piazzale
Michelangelo

Lungarno Francesco Ferrucci

29

Via di Villamagna

Via Coluccio Salutati

11

Viale Michelangelo

22

Via Donato Giannotti

Cimitero
delle
Porte Sante

Viale Galileo
Galilei

Monte Alle Croci

1

6

7

SAN MARCO & NEARBY QUARTERS

SIGHTS & ACTIVITIES	(pp61–114)
Cappellone degli Spagnoli	1 C6
Cenacolo di Foligno	2 C5
Cenacolo di Sant'Apollonia	3 E4
Chiesa di San Marco	(see 11)
Chiesa di SS Annunziata	4 F5
Chiesa e Convento di Santa Maria Maddalena de' Pazzi	5 G6
Chiesa Russa Ortodossa	6 D2
Florence By Bike	7 E4
Galleria dell'Accademia	8 E5
Loggia di San Paolo	9 C6
Museo Archeologico	10 F5
Museo di San Marco	11 E4
Opificio delle Pietre Dure	12 E5
Rotonda del Brunelleschi	13 F5

EATING	(pp125–40)
Caffellatte	14 F6
Da Nerbone	15 D5
Dioniso	16 E5
EDI House	17 G3
Il Vegetariano	18 E4
I' Tozzo Di Pane	19 D5
La Bottega del Gelato	20 F2
Mario	21 D5
Ostaria dei Cento Poveri	22 B6
Ristorante Lobs	23 C5
Ristorante ZàZà	24 D5
Trattoria il Contadino	25 B6

DRINKING	(pp142–7)
Bebop	26 E6
Jazz Club	27 F6
La Rotonda	28 A6
Soulciety Club	29 E4
The Chequers Pub	30 C6
The Joshua Tree	31 F5
Zona 15	32 F5

ENTERTAINMENT	(pp141–54)
Box Office Ticket Outlet	33 B4
Cinema Fulgor	34 B6
Parterre	35 F2
Teatro della Pergola	36 F6

SHOPPING	(pp163–74)
Officina Profumo Farmaceutica di Santa Maria Novella (Pharmacy)	37 B6

Stefano Alinari	38 D4
Stockhouse Il Giglio	39 B6
The Paperback Exchange	40 G6

SLEEPING	(pp175–86)
Hotel Accademia	41 C4
Hotel Botticelli	42 D5
Hotel Cellini	(see 43)
Hotel Désirée	43 C5
Hotel Il Guelfo Bianco	44 E5
Hotel Le Due Fontane	45 F5
Hotel Loggiato dei Serviti	46 F5
Hotel Monna Lisa	47 F6
Hotel Regency	48 H5
Hotel San Lorenzo	49 D5
Residenza Johanna I	50 E3

TRANSPORT	(pp203–8)
Alinari Bike Rentals	51 D4
ATAF Bus Stop for Nos 7, 13, & 70	52 C5
ATAF Local Bus Stop	53 B5
Avis Car Rental	54 A6
CAP & COPIT Bus Station	55 C5
City Sightseeing Bus	56 C5
Happy Rent	57 A6
Hertz Car Rental	58 B6
Lazzi Bus Station & Ticket Office	59 C5
SITA Bus Station	60 B5
Thrifty	61 A6
Ticket Windows	62 B5

INFORMATION	
ATAF Ticket & Information Office	63 C5
Consorzio ITA Office	64 C5
CyberOffice	65 E5
Dutch Consulate	66 F4
German Consulate	67 A6
Internet Train	68 D5
Telecom Phones	69 C5
Train Information	70 B5
US Consulate	71 A6

246 See Oltrarno & Nearby Quarters Map (pp248–9)

A B C D

1

See San Marco & Nearby
Quarters Map (pp246-7)

Ponte
Amerigo
Vespucci

Via degli Agli

Via degli Adimari

Piazza del
Adimari

Via Roma

Via del Campidoglio

Via dei Pescioni

Via delle Belle Donne

Via del Sole

144

156

136

147

91

96

88

6

150

Via del Porcellana

Borgo Ognissanti

Piazza di
San Paolino

Piazza degli
Ottaviani

Via Palazzuolo

51

Lungarno
Amerigo Vespucci

Piazza
d'Ognissanti

Ospedale di
San Giovanni
di Dio

133

75

Via de' Fossi

Via de' Moro

Piazza San
Pancrazio

Via della Vigna Nuova

Via degli Strozzi

Piazza della
Repubblica

Via Spezie

Via Anselmi

98

Piazza Carlo
Goldoni

Via del Parione

Lungarno Corsini

Piazza
Santa
Trinita

Via de' Tornabuoni

Via de'
Lamberti

Via della

Piazza
de' Davanzati

Via de' Calimaru

Via de' Porta Rossa

ARNO

Via L. Bartolini

Via Sant'
Onofrio

Via del
Tiratoio

Piazza
del Tiratoio

Via del
Piaggione

50

125

141

Borgo San Frediano

Piazza
de' Nerli

Via del Drago d'Oro

Via del Leone

Lungarno Soderini

Piazza di
Cestello

Ponte alla
Carraia

10

177

San Frediano

76

157

154

68

N Sauro

135

163

Piazza Lungarno Guicciardini

Via di Santo Spirito

Santo
Spirito

86

166

40

Ponte
Santa Trinita

Lungarno degli Acciaiuoli

Ponte
Vecchio

Borgo SS Apostoli

Via Por Santa Maria

Piazza
Santo
Stefano

Piazza
Saltarelli

Piazza
Signo

Via delle Terme

65

70

Piazza del
Carmine

Borgo della Stella

109

168

3

153

Via Santa Monaca

Via Maffia

Piazza
Piattellina

95

Via dell'Ardiglione

Via S. Agostino

Via S. Serragli

Piazza
Torquato
Tasso

49

97

Via della Chiesa

82

7

Piazza
Santo Spirito

53

56

55

88

Piazza
de' Frescobaldi

4

Via di Coverelli

37

43

42

44

Via de' Velluti

Via de' Michelozzi

94

Via Toscanella

Via de' Ramaglianti

Borgo San Jacopo

Via de' Guicciardini

Piazza
de' Rossi

Piazza di
Santa Maria
Sopramo

Via de' Bardi

Piazza Santa
Maria Sopra

See Piazza Del Duomo & Nea
Quarters Map (pp252-3)

35

165

16

39

24

21

Corridoio
Vasariano

Costa di San Giorgio

Mercato
dell'Antiquariato

155

34

Via Mazzetta

Via Maggio

So. de' Pitti

59

175

Via del Campuccio

Giardino
Torrigiani

146

Via S. Tegolaio

Piazza
San Felice

Piazza
de' Pitti

Palazzo
Pitti

20

1

19

29

Via Santa Maria

Via delle Caldaie

Borgo Tegolaio

Via del Ronco

Via della Meridiana

Viale Francesco Petrarca

Via de' Serragli

Via Romana

69

17

Via Forte di
San Giorgio

Forte di
Belvedere

Porta S
Giorg

Via di San Leonardo

Vic della Cava

Giardino di Boboli
(Boboli Gardens)

Fontana del
Forcone

Viale dei Cipressi

Isolotto

26

Piazza
della Calza

Porta
Romana

Piazzale
di Porta
Romana

Istituto
d'Arte

Via Madonna

Via della Pace

Via del Mascherino

Via del
Baluardo

Bobolino

Chiesa di San
Leonardo

Viale del Poggio Imperiale

Via Senese

Via Cantagalli

Viale Nicolò Machiavelli

Via Michele di Lando

Map labels (streets, piazzas, and landmarks):

Via G Leopardi
Via A Manzoni
Piazza di S Benedetto
Via dell'Oche
Via del Procconsolo
Via Sant'Egidio
Via dell'Oriuolo
Borgo Pinti
Via Fiesolana
Via de' Pilastri
Sinagoga
Via de Giosuè Carducci
Via della Mattonaia
Via del Corso
Piazza di Donati
Borgo degli Albizi
Piazza G Salvemini
Via de' Pepi
Via di Mezzo
Piazza Sant'Ambrogio
Borgo della Croce
Piazza C Beccaria
Via Dante Alighieri
Piazza San Pier Maggiore
Borgo degli Albizi
Via Pietrapiana
Piazza de' Cerchi
Via de' Pandolfini
Via Martiri del Popolo
Piazza dei Ciompi
Piazza Ghiberti
ondotta
Via Ghibellina
Via dell'Ulivo
Buonarotti
Mercato di Sant'Ambrogio
Via de' Magazzini
Via della Vigna Vecchia
Teatro Verdi
Via Giuseppe Verdi
Via delle Stinche
Via G da Verrazzano
Via del Fico
Via dell'Agnolo
Via Mino
Via de' Gondi
Palazzo Vecchio
Borgo de' Greci
Via Isola delle Stinche
Via delle Pinzochere
Borgo Allegri
Via de' Macci
Via Ghibellina
Via Vinegia
Via de' Rustici
Piazza de' Peruzzi
Via Torta
Via Bentaccordi
Via dell'Anguillara
Piazza di S Simone
Via Cristofani
Via Michelangelo Buonarroti
Via dei Neri
Via dei Benci
Via de' Bentaccordi
Piazza di Santa Croce
Via delle Conce
Via dei Conciatori
Via Pietro Thouar
Via Osteria del Guanto
Via de' Castellani
Via delle Casine
Via de' Malcontenti
Piazza de' Giudici
Lungarno Generale Diaz
Via Magliabechi
Borgo Santa Croce
Via di San Giuseppe
Biblioteca Nazionale
Corso dei Tintori
Via Vincenzo Malenchini
Piazza dei Cavalleggeri
Via Tripoli
Viale della Giovine Italia
Piazza Piave
Lungarno delle Grazie
Lungarno della Zecca Vecchia
Lungarno Torrigiani
Ponte alle Grazie
ARNO
Lungarno G Pecori Giraldi
Via de' Bardi Costa Scarpuccia
Piazza Demidoff
Lungarno Serristori
Via dei Renai
Palazzo Serristori
Lungarno Benvenuto Cellini
Via della Fornace
Via dei Bastioni
Piazza de' Mozzi
Via del Giardino Serristori
Via di San Niccolò
Piazza Giuseppe Poggi
San Niccolò
Via di San Niccolò
Viale Giuseppe Poggi
Via di Belvedere
Via del Bastioni
Via dell'Erta Canina
Viale Giuseppe Poggi
Piazzale Michelangelo
Via di San Salvatore al Monte
Viale Michelangelo
Viale Michelangelo
Via di San Miniato al Monte
Viale Galileo Galilei
Via Monte alle Croci
Via del Monte alle Croci
Monte alle Croci
Cimitero delle Porte Sante
Via delle Porte Sante
Via Giramonte

Scale: 0 – 200 m / 0 – 0.1 miles

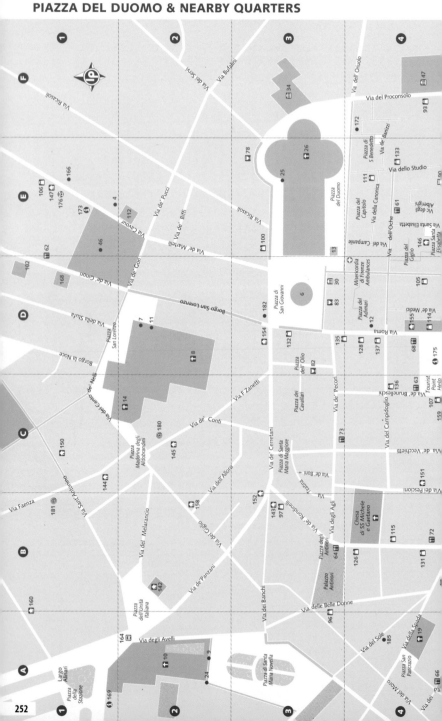

GREATER FLORENCE

0 — 2 km
0 — 1 mile

To Arezzo (49km)

Settignano

Fiesole

Via Gabriele D'Annunzio

Via della Cave di Maiano

V D Pelagaccio

Via Giuseppe Mantellini

Via Faentina

Via Bolognese

Via San Domenico

Via del Salviatino

Via Aretina

Stazione Campo di Marte

FLORENCE (FIRENZE)

Arno

Giardino di Boboli (Boboli Gardens)

Stazione di Santa Maria Novella

Stazione Porta al Prato

Via Della Panche

See Central Florence Map (pp244–5)

Via Reginaldo Giuliani

Stazione di Rifredi

Via Unità d'Asiatio

Cascine

Via Francesco Baracca

Stazione delle Cascine

Amerigo Vespucci Airport

Via di Rimaggio

Via Pistoiese

Via de' Cattani

Via Prasaese

Via Canova

Viale Etruria

Bellosguardo

Via Senese

Galluzzo

To Rome (240km)

Matteo di Arcetri

A1

Scandicci

Casellina

L'Olmo

A1

Autostrada del Sole

To Pisa (35km)

Autostrada Firenze-Mare

To Pistoia (25km)

254